THE

MEDAL NEWS

YEARBOOK

1995

Edited by
James Mackay, MA, DLitt
John W. Mussell
and
the Editorial Team of MEDAL NEWS

ISBN 1 870192 05 2

Published by
TOKEN PUBLISHING LIMITED
105 High Street, Honiton, Devon EX14 8PE

© Token Publishing Ltd.

Printed in Great Britain by Pensord Press Ltd., Tram Road, Blackwood, Gwent.

1

CONTENTS

INDEX TO ADVERTISERS

ACKNOWLEDGEMENTS

The Publishers would like to thank the many people whose support and assistance has made this publication possible. A large number of people—both private individuals and members of the trade—have given generously of their time to ensure that this first edition of the MEDAL NEWS YEARBOOK is a success. It would be invidious to pick out any one person by name but we are particularly indebted to the people who checked the proofs and who burned the midnight oil checking the many hundreds of prices.

Special thanks are due to John Hayward for providing the illustrations and to Jo Jenvey for producing the artwork for the medal ribbon charts.

Front cover design by Visionary Ideas.

PREFACE

We are proud to present this first edition of the MEDAL NEWS YEARBOOK and we feel confident that it will prove itself to be a valuable publication and a worthy companion to our monthly magazine MEDAL NEWS. The Yearbook has been produced to be of useful interest to the professional or serious numismatist as well as an invaluable guide to the beginner. It is not intended that this book should be regarded as the standard work: this task is admirably filled by the enormous number of specialist publications that are already available to the collector—most of which are listed in the appropriate section of these pages—but as a quick ready-reference guide we hope that the YEARBOOK will become a useful tool.

The prices quoted in this publication are intended to be a true reflection of the current market and have been arrived at by specialists who constantly study the auction prices realised and dealers' lists. The prices in the YEARBOOK show the average figure range that a dealer would expect to sell a medal for. As most collectors realise, the dealer has to make a living from buying and selling, therefore the price a dealer can pay for an item must of necessity be considerably less than his selling price! It is important to remember that each medal is an individual item and the recipient's history can make the world of difference between a medal realising the top figure or the lower one. Nevertheless, the prices quoted are the opinion of our experts and ultimately any item is only really worth what a buyer will pay.

An enormous number of hours have been spent compiling the directory sections of the YEARBOOK but inevitably these may contain out-of-date or incorrect information. We would appreciate any comments or corrections on any section of the book which will enable us to up-date our data-base in time for the next edition. Any important up-dating will be featured regularly in MEDAL NEWS which is published ten times a year and together with the YEARBOOK will continue to cater for the needs of the collector.

An important feature of the 1995 MEDAL NEWS YEARBOOK is the incorporation of a complete subject index for MEDAL NEWS—printed on coloured stock for easy identification. It is intended to include an annual index each year in the YEARBOOK but if required these are also available as separate publications.

DECEMBER

31

THAT WAS THE YEAR THAT WAS!

An at-a-glance résumé of the main events and occurrences that affected the medal hobby during the past months, as reported in MEDAL NEWS . . .

January 1993
Sotheby's announced that, henceforward, sales of medals would be confined to their Sussex salerooms at Billingshurst.

Christie's announced an increase in their Buyer's Premium, from 10 to 15 per cent, in line with the increase already adopted by Sotheby's.

The Victorian Military Fair, staged by the Victorian Military Society at the Victory Services Club, London (January 30), broke all previous attendance records, with over 1000 visitors.

The Second World War medal group, including the Military Cross, awarded to the late Robert Maxwell, sold for £14,000 at Sotheby's. The purchaser was not a medal collector, but an ex-serviceman who announced that he hoped to re-sell the group and give the profit to the fund on behalf of the Mirror Group's pensioners who were cheated by the frauds of Maxwell.

February 1993
First Medal and Militaria Fair at the Princes' Hall, Aldershot (February 28). Its central location and excellent facilities attracted record attendances and plenty of interest in the "home of the British Army".

Exhibition of water colours and drawings by Western Desert veteran Eric Dawson at the National Army Museum commemorated the 50th anniversary of the Battle of El Alamein.

March 1993
The Kuwaiti Government announced the award of the Liberation Medal to all Allied personnel (including British servicemen and civilians) involved in Operation Desert Storm for the liberation of the sheikhdom from Iraq in 1991. The medal consists of five classes, based on the rank of the recipient. Regrettably, the British Government stated that while British personnel might accept the medals they were not permitted to wear them.

The Crimean War Society staged a combined Annual General Meeting and Open Day at the National Army Museum (March 16). The programme included a lecture on the British cavalry at Balaklava, a Crimean Wargame, a painting competition and displays of medals, insignia and militaria associated with the campaign.

At the Glendining's sale (March 24) a First World War memorial plaque named to Violet Porter fetched £1000. Although more than 1.3 million plaques were issued in respect of those killed in action, fewer than 600 were named to women, hence the exceptional interest and value. The orders and medals of General Sir Reginald Wingate sold for £22,000 in the same sale.

Spink & Son auctioned (March 31) the collection of medals formed by Surgeon H. Mitchell, late of the Army Medical Staff, who died in 1917. The collection, ranging from the Armada of 1588 to the First World War, included two George III American Indian Chiefs' medals which fetched £2400 and £2300 respectively. The top price was £2700, realised by the Kelat-i-Ghilzie Medal awarded to Artillery Gunner John Napier.

April 1993
First medal sale to be held at Sotheby's auction rooms in Billingshurst, West Sussex (April 5).

The Secretary of State for Defence announced battle honours for the Gulf War: *Kuwait 1991* (Royal Navy), *Gulf 1991* (RAF) and *Gulf 1991, Wadi Al Batin* and *Western Iraq* (Army).

Christie's International PLC acquired Spink & Son Ltd for £7.1 million. The sale included the orders and medals production side of Spink's business.

Fierce debate in the House of Lords over the Government's controversial decision to allow British subjects to accept the Russian Arctic Convoy Medal but not to wear it in public. The medal was instituted by the USSR in 1985 and some 12,000 British ex-servicemen were entitled to the award. Britons serving with the European Community monitoring mission in the former Yugoslavia had been advised not to accept the EC Medal, although Her Majesty the Queen had agreed that Britons could accept the UN Medal for services in Bosnia.

The Imperial War Museum launched its education outreach project "This is the Blitz". The scheme offered exciting teaching sessions for primary and secondary groups studying National Curriculum, Standard Grade and GCSE history. The project, which continued till December 3, was sponsored by BP.

May 1993

Two-day Irish International Coin, Stamps and Collectables Fair, in the Royal Hospital, Kilmainham, Dublin, the largest event of its kind ever staged in Ireland, with medals and militaria well to the fore.

The 50th anniversary of the epic raid of the RAF on the Eder and Mohne dams of the Ruhr Valley was marked by an exhibition which ran to the end of October at the RAF Museum, Hendon. The exhibition, entitled "On Target", traced the history of bombing from the early days of metal darts dropped from aircraft to today's highly sophisticated laser-guided "smart" bombs used in the Gulf War. As well as a wide range of bomber aircraft, from the Halifax and Lancaster of the Second World War to the Vulcan and the Tornado, the exhibition included a reconstruction of the office used by Sir Barnes Wallis, inventor of the bouncing bomb.

The VC group awarded to Wing Commander Guy Gibson, leader of the Dambusters raid, on permanent display in the Bomber Command Hall at the Royal Air Force Museum, Hendon, the bequest of his widow who died recently.

Lady Sue Ryder, widow of Lord Leonard Cheshire, presented his VC group to the Imperial War Museum in the presence of Her Majesty Queen Elizabeth the Queen Mother, at a ceremony marking the 50th anniversary of 617 Squadron RAF. The group will eventually be permanently displayed in the VC/GC Hall.

June 1993

Bonham's staged their first medal sale (June 10), organised by Daniel Fearon, previously a director of Glendining's.

July 1993

Her Majesty the Queen agrees for Britons serving in the EC monitoring mission in Yugoslavia to accept the relevant UN medal. but they have been advised not to accept the medal awarded by the EC.

August 1993

The first Victoria Cross medal group awarded to an Australian serving in the Vietnam War sold for A$165,000 (£69,915) at Sotheby's in Melbourne (August 9). The group was purchased by Brigadier Alf Garland on behalf of the Returned Services League, partly with donations received from the public and partly from money raised by members of the Australian Defence Force. The VC, sold with seven other gallantry and campaign medals, was to be presented to the Australian War Memorial in Canberra. One of only four VCs awarded to Australians in Vietnam, the group was awarded posthumously to Warrant Officer Class II Kevin Arthur "Dasher" Wheatley of the Australian Army Training Team in December 1966.

September 1993

The first auction held by Spink & Son under the new Christie's management (September 23). Richard Bishop of Christie's became Auction Administrator for the Coin and Medal Departments, John Hayward was appointed Senior Executive Consultant to the Medal Auctions and Medal Collectors Departments, and Andrew Litherland continued in his role as Departmental Director. An unexpected highlight of the sale was the Dickin Medal awarded to Simon, the ship's cat aboard HMS *Amethyst*, which sold for £21,000 (pre-sale estimate £3000–£5000). The purchaser was a film company, makers of an animated film about a cat called Simon, while the underbidder was rumoured to be a pet-food company.

Orders and Medals Research Society Convention successfully held at a prestigious new venue in the New Connaught Rooms, Holborn, London (September 25).

October 1993

Malcolm Rifkind, Secretary of State for Defence, announced the long-awaited changes in British gallantry awards for the armed forces. While the Victoria Cross remains as the first-level decoration, the CGM, DCM and DSO for gallantry are to be replaced by a new decoration awarded regardless of rank. At the third level, however, each service will retain the DSC, MC and DFC respectively, but the corresponding other ranks' awards (DSM, MM and DFM) are to be abolished. The oak leaf signifying a mention in despatches is to continue, and a new award, the Queen's Commendation for Valuable Services, is to be used to recognise other acts such as outstanding service in technical and administrative posts.

The unique Sea Gallantry Medal, awarded to Chief Officer James Whitely for his heroic action on the SS Colorado when it was torpedoed on October 20, 1917, with a second action clasp for gallantry aboard the SS Urbino on February 6, 1921, was sold for £2100 at Bonham's (October 19).

The RAF Apprentices Exhibition was opened at the Royal Air Force Museum, Hendon by Air Chief Marshal Sir Michael Armitage, KCB, CBE, a former RAF apprentice (October 27).

The Natal Rebellion Medal 1906 awarded to Sergeant-Major M. K. Gandhi was stolen from the home of the Gandhi family in Durban. Gandhi, later to become leader of the movement for Indian independence, served as a stretcher bearer during the rebellion, tending sick and dying Zulus who were denied medical treatment by white nurses and doctors.

November 1993

A new permanent gallery devoted to the British Army from 1816 to 1914 was inaugurated at the National Army Museum, thus continuing the story of the British soldier told in the *Road to Waterloo* gallery and taking the narrative down to the outbreak of the First World War.

Sotheby's disposed of one of the most remarkable assemblies of medals and decorations ever awarded to the members of one family, spanning the period from the Crimea to the First World War and including one VC, two GCBs, one CB, one KCVO, five DSOs, three CMGs, one CBE, two OBEs and one MBE. The Hart Family medals, comprising twelve lots, realised £36,500, the highlight being the VC group of General Sir Reginald Hart which alone fetched £20,000 (November 30).

December 1993

To mark the RAF Museum, Hendon's 21st anniversary as Britain's national museum of aviation, a photographic display traced the history of the Museum from the days when it was an airfield.

The National Army Museum acquired the George Cross awarded to Bombardier M. M. Reed, 2nd Marine AA Battery, RA, for bravery on board SS Cormount whilst on convoy duty, June 20–21, 1941.

January 1994

A civilian employed at the House of Commons was charged under the Army, Navy and Air Force Act for wearing medals to which he was not entitled, an offence which carries a maximum penalty of £50. He was observed during the annual Remembrance Day parade at the Cenotaph in Whitehall wearing the General Service Medal, South Atlantic Medal and UN Medal.

February 1994

The first Napoleonic Fair was held at the Royal National Hotel, Bedford Way, London (February 6), devoted to the medals, badges, militaria and literature of the French Revolutionary and Napoleonic Wars.

Her Majesty's Government announced the introduction of a new award, to be entitled the Accumulated Service Medal, providing a means of recognition for service personnel who had served more than one tour of duty in an area where a clasp to the Campaign Service Medal had been awarded.

Her Majesty the Queen granted permission for recipients of the Russian Convoy 40th Anniversary of Victory Medal to wear it. The medal was struck at Moscow in 1985 and was awarded to veterans of the Arctic Russian convoys of the Second World War. The London Gazette stated that Her Majesty was "graciously pleased" to approve the medal and added that Her Majesty "had in mind the changing circumstances in Russia since the medal was first issued and the improvement of relations". It was not envisaged, however, that such permission would be forthcoming for other commemorative medals issued more than five years after the event, in keeping with the rule applied by King George VI in 1951, and because of the general rule against the wearing of foreign medals.

March 1994

A new "Memorial Archive" for personal diaries, letters and unpublished memoirs of service personnel and civilians involved in this century's wars launched by the Imperial War Museum. The archive will eventually be available for public study and selected items will be published in a special newsletter.

The section of foreign orders at Spink's auction (March 29) astounded the cataloguers by achieving very high prices.

April 1994

Nancy Wake, the famous French Resistance heroine of the Second World War, known to the Gestapo as "The White Mouse", sells her George Cross and other medals at Sotheby's in Melbourne for A$156,500 (£75,283).

First awards made under the new "egalitarian" awards system, showing no distiction between ranks, made to an Army Corporal (Military Cross for Yugoslavia) and a Staff Sergeant (DFC for Northern Ireland).

May 1994

Joint meeting of the Orders and Medals Research Society and the Birmingham Medal Society to celebrate the latter's 30th anniversary (May 14).

June 1994

The VC group to Pte H. May, 1st Bn Cameronians (Scottish Rifles), was purchased at Wallis & Wallis on behalf of the Cameronians Regimental Museum for £18,250. The VC was awarded for conspicuous bravery in rescuing a wounded man under fire on October 22, 1914.

To mark the 50th anniversary of D-Day, numerous events took place throughout the country and on the beaches and battle sites in France, involving thousands of serving servicemen as well as veterans.

Read MEDAL NEWS every month for the latest medal news!

MARKET TRENDS

Although the United Kingdom was in the depths of one of the worst recessions in living memory for much of the period under review, from late 1992 to the end of 1993, there was precious little evidence of this in the salerooms. It was a period characterised by a plethora of good material and if it perhaps lacked the absolutely superlative items which made 1988-89, for example, so memorable, it could boast a wealth of medals and groups of the first rank, both in terms of their quality and condition, and in regard to their social and historical interest, always potent factors in a collecting field where the human factors are paramount.

One interesting trend emerged in the period under review and that was the development of sales with a specific theme. Sotheby's pioneered this concept, and held reasonably successful sales with medals pertaining to the Army and Royal Air Force respectively. The Army sale had less than 10 per cent unsold, but regrettably this included several of the star items, such as a Zulu War VC and the fine medal group of Field Marshal Sir Richard Hull. This was compensated for, however, in the lots of more modest importance which sold well in excess of their pre-sale estimates.

This sale demonstrated quite forcibly that the added dimension in medal-collecting of personal interest can make a world of difference to the price realised. Because medals are named to their recipient, much of the value—so difficult for auction describers to quantify at times—lies in the personal interest not only inherent in the name of the recipient but, from a subjective viewpoint, in the particular interests of the bidder. Thus a MC group, estimated at £600–£800, sold eventually for £2600 not just because the recipient had fought with Wingate's Chindits in Burma but also because of the almost indefinable appeal of this group to at least two of the bidders. The RAF sale which followed likewise experienced some mixed results. It would be very tempting to suppose that, from their failure to attract the prices looked for, the Air Force Cross groups (including an AFC and bar to a member of the Schneider Trophy team) are currently over-rated, but their time will come again. Certainly interest in the other lots was very brisk and prices were well up to estimate on the whole. The somewhat mixed results of these two sales has led a few people to question the value of thematic sales. It would appear, however, that the age-old rules relating to

supply and demand are prevalent, and RAF medals do not sell as well as Army groups merely for the simple reason that there are far fewer RAF medal collectors competing for the material. And it must be borne in mind that when something truly spectacular comes on the scene, such as the Nicholson Battle of Britain VC, the sky is the limit (no pun intended).

There was a time, not so long ago, when collector-interest in medals was largely confined to military campaign medals and gallantry awards. True, there were a dedicated few hardy independent spirits who struck out in other directions; but the days when the collector of Boer War tributes or Boys Brigade medals was derided by the mainstream majority are over. One area which suffered comparative neglect but which has come to the fore in recent years is life-saving medals. There was consequently keen interest when the collection formed by Captain James Hartford came under the hammer at Glendining's in October 1992 and produced some highly gratifying results. These medals sold well right across the board, the star item being the first Lloyd's gold medal, awarded to Sir Raymond Beck in 1919, which sold for £3700 against a pre-sale estimate of £1000–£1500. Bonham's sale of 19 October 1993 contained the unique Sea Gallantry Medal with second award clasp which sold for £2100 against an estimate of £800–£1000.

So, too, non-military awards for bravery have come into their own. At Buckland, Dix & Wood in October 1993 an interesting George Medal group awarded to a British Railways lampman, A. J. A. Rivers, fetched £2000 (estimate £1500–£1800), enhanced no doubt by the inclusion of the Boy Scouts gilt cross for gallantry, the *Daily Herald* Order of Industrial Heroism and the Carnegie Hero Fund Medal. The Scout medal, incidentally, had been won by Mr Rivers when he only 12 years of age.

One of the more exotic lots in the Glendining's sale of October 1992 comprised the Chinese Imperial awards to John Penniall, Chief Instructor at Nanking Naval College, which made £2500 against an estimate of £1000–£1500. Similarly, Spink's sale around the same time produced good results overall, but proportionately those which performed best were those consisting of medals that would formerly have been regarded as in the byways or backwaters of the hobby. In this instance, the medals and groups to volunteers, yeomanry and militia stole the show, and although the sums realised were not in the same league as the more glamorous gallantry awards, they were in percentage terms much more satisfying, and indicate that the trend nowadays is towards the hitherto unconsidered areas.

During the period under review there have been several big named collections formed over very many years. These prestigious collections deservedly get the limelight and attract a correspondingly large number of dedicated specialist collectors and dealers, with satisfying results all round. Christie's scored something of a double whammy in November 1992 with a sale which began with some choice material from the collection of the late and legendary Alec Purves, one of the doyens of medal scholarship. Alec wrote widely and extensively on the subject of medals and his catholicity was reflected in the diverse nature of the 126 lots on offer. This material attracted fierce bidding with spectacular results. A scarce Shannon Navy group of four brought £850 (estimate £450–£500), a most unusual Chinese Order of the Crystal Button fetched £1150 (£400–£500), a unique London Scottish George Medal went to £1200 (£700–£800) and an Afghanistan Medal and Kandahar Star to a piper in the 92nd Highlanders soared to £880 (£200–£250). One might reflect that the estimates in

this section had erred on the cautious side, but in fairness to the estimators a figure adjacent to the upper pre-sale estimate would not have been far out under normal circumstances. One must make allowance for the choice condition and the high level of interest, not only in the medals *per se* but on account of their having come from the Purves Collection.

This proved to be a fine curtain-raiser for the main part of the sale, devoted to the collection formed by Hal Giblin. Here was, indeed, a feast for the connoisseur of fine medals, although there was a certain amount of trepidation concerning the release of such a vast quantity of First World War material on to the market at one time. This is a danger inherent in the dispersal of any assemblage of this nature. The activities of the truly dedicated collector (especially if he has the wherewithal to indulge himself) may be likened to the energetic beaver building his dam. His efforts have the effect of stemming the normal flow, reducing the available material to a trickle to be fought over by competitors and thereby tending to raise market values appreciably. Conversely the disposal of such a vast collection in a single sale, or even phased over a period of months or years, however, can be like the deluge resulting when the dam bursts. Those who have previously scrambled for the crumbs are now deluged with an *embarras de richesse*, and there is naturally a tendency for the market to sag for some time, until the slack can be taken up again as a result of the influx of new collectors and new money.

It has to be said that, in this instance, the gloomy prognostications of some pundits were confounded. All but two items found a buyer, and while there were a few bargains to be had, the majority of lots sold on or above estimate, sometimes handsomely in excess at that.

There is, of course, the converse argument that good material which has lain dormant for many

DSO and bar group from the Hart family medals sold by Sotheby's in November 1993—the group realised £3450, whilst a superb VC, GCB, KCVO group from the same family sold for £23,000.

years will always excite the keen interest of collectors when it is eventually returned to the market. This was certainly true in the case of the St Aubrey collection of campaign medals which was dispersed at Sotheby's at the end of November 1993. This was a solid, honest-to-goodness sale which, while it may have lacked the truly spectacular material that hits the headlines, nevertheless provided collectors with a field-day. The prices were generally very good, reflecting the buoyant demand for campaign material right across the board. The few items which failed to come up to expectation were flawed in some respect, so there were perfectly obvious reasons for their failure. There is no doubt that collectors are now much more knowledgeable within their chosen fields, and also was the case 20 or 30 years ago.

The spectacular named sales are only the highlights of the year at auction. For every VC or large gallantry and campaign group there must be hundreds of single medals or common First War groups, the unspectacular collection fodder that provides the auctioneers with their bread and butter and keeps the hobby ticking over. At this end of the spectrum it is that extra factor, the human interest angle, which can make all the difference, much depending on the circumstances surrounding the persons to whom the medals were awarded. This is a factor capable of an infinite variety of permutations and combinations that it is not always possible to assess the likely value in advance of the sale.

The appeal of "odd men" medals is obvious, but the capricious performance of medals which, on the face of it, have little to commend them, can be baffling at times. But one has to realise that there are now not only those looking for medals awarded to particular county regiments, but also those seeking medals to recipients with their own surnames, and doubtless there are other reasons, even more obscure and quixotic, which enhance the desirability of a medal which might, to most of us, seem not to rise above the ordinary.

The thematic element is becoming increasingly important. Thus medals with a medical interest invariably fetch good prices, and the Meeanee Medal of 1843 to Surgeon Alexander Campbell was no exception when it sold for £1900 at Spink's in March 1993 after some spirited bidding (estimate £500–£600).

One trend which has emerged lately is the demand for medals awarded to women. This has led to some spectacular results. Some of these are predictable; when one considers how few of the 1.3 million next of kin bronze memorial plaques of the First World War were issued in respect of women (a mere 600), it is understandable that these should command relatively high prices. Several have passed through the salerooms in the past year, and one at least has broken through the magic four-figure barrier.

The appearance of the Royal Red Cross group to Sister M. E. Powell, attached to the West African Frontier Force, was expected to attract fierce competition when it came under the hammer at Spink's on 28 April. In the end, a very determined purchaser had to go to £5200 (estimate £2000). One of only 35 Egypt Medals 1882–89 awarded to nurses was sold by Buckland, Dix and Wood on 12 May for £720 (estimate £400–£500) and a rare Egypt Royal Red Cross group of four to Matron M. C. Gerrard sold for £5600, no doubt the medical and feminine interests clashed to add spice to the bidding.

Glendining's sale on 25 November 1992 included a Hong Kong Defence Corps Medal with reverse to HKVDC Nursing Detachment, and this understandably fetched £600, almost three times its lower pre-sale estimate. Significantly, it was knocked down to a Hong Kong Chinese collector.

This reflects another trend that has become more noticeable of late, the repatriation of fine and rare material to its country of origin. At one time colonial awards were a very recherche aspect of medal-collecting, exciting little interest among mainstream collectors. At best they were of little account in the country whence they had come; at worst they were probably regarded as symbols of an outmoded Empire and colonial exploitation. With the passage of time, however, they have first become respectable and latterly eminently desirable, seen in their true perspective as an aspect of many an emergent nation's infancy, and now they are being enthusiastically (and sometimes at great price) returned to that part of the world in which they were earned.

Among the more offbeat groups to come under the hammer was that awarded to Sergeant Murgu, a Rumanian diplomat who served in the British Pioneer Corps in the Second World War. This group, with various collateral material, sold for £900 at Wallis & Wallis. Two George III medals awarded to North American Indian Chiefs sold for £2400 and £2300 (£1500–£2000 and £1200–£1500 respectively) at Spink's on 31 March.

Incidentally American interest in British medals is understandable when the medals in question have a North American slant. Thus a Military GSM with campaign clasp Chateauguay sold for £2000—twice estimate—in the Spink's sale.

Medals from the Napoleonic period continue to sell strongly. This is one of the undoubted blue chips of the medallic world. Army Gold Medals and Gold Crosses are now of such rarity that they inevitably command five-figure sums when they make their fleeting appearance in the salerooms. At the other end of the spectrum even the once humble Waterloo Medal regularly commands a good four-figure sum when the recipient served in one of the more actively engaged regiments. A fine Military GSM and Waterloo pair awarded to a colour sergeant in the 92nd Highlanders fetched £1600 at Glendining's on 23 June (estimate £600–£800). Another Waterloo Medal made £3400 at Glendining's in September, but the recipient was Captain Edward Payne of the 2nd Dragoons, one of six officers to command a troop in the celebrated charge of the Union Brigade, hence the comparatively high price paid.

After a fairly quiet summer the 1993–94 season got off to a flying start with a number of excellent sales around the time of the Orders & Medals Research Society's Convention at the end of September. Glendining's kicked off on 22 September with a fine general sale in which only 7 per cent of the 500 lots failed to find a buyer. It may be significant that the unsold lots contained a high proportion of RAF medals and groups, pointing to continuing sluggishness in this sector of the market. It should be pointed out, however, that many lots which apparently fail to reach a satisfactory figure at auction are subsequently disposed of privately to the satisfaction of the vendor.

The first Spink sale under Christie's aegis also took place late in September 1993 and was well supported by both dealers and private collectors. The surprise result was the £21,000 paid for the Dickin Medal awarded to Simon the ship's cat aboard HMS *Amethyst* during the Yangtze Incident of 1949. Estimated at £3000–£5000 but enormously hyped up in the national media before the sale, it was contested by a film company and the makers of a well-known brand of pet food. It seems ironic that a greater price can be placed on the actions of an animal merely doing what it does best (killing mice, regardless of the external circumstances) than on those of human beings who, knowing full well the dangers inherent in their actions, still go ahead and perform acts of matchless heroism. This is the sort of price we have come to expect for the better class of VC; but there's no accounting for taste, nor the purchasing powers of the animal lobby when it rises to the occasion.

Single campaign medals continue to be extremely popular, especially those with more than one campaign clasp. A Naval GSM 1793–1840 with six clasps was regarded as somewhat speculative because only four of the clasps could actually be confirmed from the medal rolls. For this reason it was estimated conservatively at £1800–£2200 by Spink's, but the eventual purchaser was happy to part with £6600. In this instance, further research may well have tipped the balance.

Foreign medals and decorations, generally unnamed, are more of a pig in a poke. In this instance aesthetics often play a major part, with the more spectacular looking pieces in great demand.

There is strong evidence, however, that interest in this area is hardening of late, and not just from informed overseas collectors either. Of course, it may only be yet another case of collectors, finding their previously chosen field priced beyond their reach, turning to one of the less fancied areas and developing their interests therein.

Another area which is now proving lucrative is miniatures. In this instance, however, good provenance is essential, and supporting collateral or documentary evidence can make all the difference. There were several remarkable lots of miniatures at auction in the past year, one of the outstanding being a Military GSM with 15 clasps which made £680 at Bonham's sale on 19 October against a pre-sale estimate of £300–£500. A miniature group attributed to Surgeon Joseph Lee of the 78th Highlanders who won the VC at Lucknow, was sold by Buckland, Dix & Wood for £800.

If any sector of the market may be said to be sluggish at the present time it is that dealing with medals for the more recent campaigns. This is understandably a rather problematical area because relatively little material has percolated on to the market as yet. Doubtless many collectors are holding back from paying over the top, reasoning that with a little patience they will be able to purchase medals from the Falklands and Gulf Wars at a fraction of the prices now being asked. The comparative reticence with regard to some not so recent campaigns—the Korean War springs to mind—is more difficult to understand. When we discussed this phenomenon with one collector he summed it up succinctly: "The glamour and romance of warfare vanishes proportionately the closer you get to the present time."

The "Dickin" medal as awarded to Ship's Cat Simon for his role during the Yangtse Incident.

Some Notable Results

Victoria Cross Groups

Captain Frederick T. Peters, Oran, 1942	£30,000	(£30,000)
Percy Dean, RNVR, Zeebrugge 1918	£24,000	(£20,000)
Private Lewis, Welch Regiment	£23,000	(£10-12,000)
General Sir Reginald Hart	£20,000	(£20,000+)
Lieut. White MGC, France 1918	£18,000	(£14-16,000)

Outstanding Groups

General Sir Reginald Wingate	£22,000	(£15-20,000)
Dambusters raid DFC group	£12,000	(£8-10,000)
Duffadar Yakute, Afghan War IOM	£5200	(£2000-2500)

ENTERING
A NEW ERA

During the past year the armed forces of the UK have borne the brunt of government cuts and the numbers of men and women serving continues to decrease. Nevertheless UK personnel can still be found at the forefront of any conflict thoughout the world, offering firepower where it is needed as well as training, support and vital back-up for the troops in the front line in any trouble-spot when they are called on. To recognise this continual devotion, the government has taken a serious look at the medallic rewards and a number of changes have taken place recently which reflect the changing attitudes of a modern society.

THE ACCUMULATED CAMPAIGN SERVICE MEDAL

The conditions of awards of a new medal—the *"Accumulated Campaign Service Medal"*—are framed carefully to recognise mainly those members of the Armed Forces who have constantly served in Northern Ireland on emergency tours of six months duration.

The Medal is to be awarded to holders of the General Service Medal 1962 on completion of 36 months accumulated campaign service since August 14, 1969.

This limitation excludes service in the many campaigns since the Second World War, in Kenya, Cyprus, Borneo, Radfan and South Arabia. It could cause some heartburn in those who retired in the early 1970s after one or two emergency tours in Northern Ireland following distinguished service in some of the excluded campaigns! As both the Falklands war and the Gulf have their own campaign medals, service in these two conflicts is also excluded. Service in the more recent campaigns which qualify for the General Service Medal 1962 does count. These include Dhofar (October 1, 1969 to September 30, 1976) and the Lebanon (February 7, 1983 to March 9, 1984).

Recognition is progressive. Any holder of the Accumulated Campaign Service Medal shall be awarded a Clasp for each further period of 36 months accumulated campaign service. A Rose Emblem denoting the award of a Clasp shall be worn on the ribbon when the ribbon only is worn. Silver Emblems will be worn for the first three Clasps, a silver gilt Emblem will denote the fourth Clasp and a silver gilt and two silver Emblems for any further Clasp.

Part-time members of the Forces based in Northern Ireland posed a problem for the drafters of the conditions. For these the Medal is to be awarded on completion of 1,000 days of qualifying service, and the Clasps to the Medal shall be awarded for each further period of 1,000 days.

The Royal Warrant was presented to Parliament by the Prime Minister by Command of Her Majesty in January 1994. A copy may be obtained from HMSO, price £1.10. According to the Royal Warrant: "the Medal shall be circular in form and in silver, that it shall bear on the obverse the Crowned Effigy of the Sovereign and on the reverse the inscription *For Accumulated Campaign Service* set within a four part ribbon surrounded by a branch of oakleaves with laurel and olive leaves woven through the motto ribbon. The Medal shall be worn by recipients on the left breast on a ribbon 1¼ inches in width in purple and green with a stripe of gold to denote excellence".

Some readers may be surprised that the Medal has been inserted in the official Order of Precedence after the Medal for Meritorious Service and before the Long Service and Good Conduct Medal. It seems odd not to position it at the end of Campaign Medals, particularly as all qualifying service takes place in a campaign environment. Perhaps the reason is to emphasise the role of the Medal in recognising long service in a campaign already acknowledged by the award of the General Service Medal 1962.

The discovery of those entitled to the new medal, both serving and retired, will not be completed overnight. Whilst over 250,000 members of the Service have earned the General Service Medal 1962 since its introduction, it is estimated that only about 20,000 will qualify for the Accumulated Campaign Service Medal.

For the first time those members of the Armed Forces who have spent most of their service going to Northern Ireland on six month emergency tours, followed by a short rest and then returning for a further tour will have full recognition for their involvement over many years. It must be fairer than having just one medal, with one clasp, to show for such a long stint.

The medal is without precedent—perhaps that is why it took so long to introduce it. It has long been high on the list of medal priorities within the Ministry of Defence. It is to be hoped it satisfies the aspirations of those who earn the new medal. Indications are that they are well pleased.

The Accumulated Campaign Service Medal.

OPERATIONAL GALLANTRY AWARDS

In October 1993, Malcolm Rifkind, Secretary of State/Defence, announced a number of far-reaching changes to the system of recognising gallantry in the armed forces. The most fundamental change being the abandonment of rank-related awards.

For ease of reference the following chart will help correlate the new system with the old. Under the new system the Distinguished Service Order is awarded for "Leadership" only, but cannot be awarded posthumously.

LEVEL OF GALLANTRY	ARMED FORCES OPERATIONAL GALLANTRY AWARDS	
	OLD SYSTEM	NEW SYSTEM
1st	VC (all ranks)	**VC** (all ranks)
2nd	Distinguished Service Order (Officer)	
	Conspicuous Gallantry Medal) Other ranks Distinguished Conduct Medal) depending Conspicuous Gallantry Medal (Flying)) on service	**Conspicuous Gallantry Cross** (all ranks)
3rd	Distinguished Service Cross) Officers Military Cross) depending Distinguished Flying Cross) on service	**Distinguished Service Cross** **Military Cross**
	Distinguished Service Medal) Other ranks Military Medal) depending Distinguished Flying Medals) on service	**Distinguished Flying Cross** (all ranks—depending on service)
4th	MID (all ranks)	**MID** (all ranks)

STORAGE OF MEDALS

The vexing question of storing medals is one which crops up regularly. Just what are the problems ... and what are the solutions? This article, by *L. R. Green, Higher Scientific Officer at the Department of Conservation, The British Museum,* helps to provide the final answer

Metals can corrode in the presence of certain volatile materials. These substances are present in the atmosphere, but generally at low concentrations. However, materials such as wood, fabric and adhesives, used in a storage system, may emit these substances causing higher concentrations which can cause deterioration of objects in the storage area.

Silver is tarnished by reducible sulphides, commonly hydrogen sulphide and carbonyl sulphide, which can be emitted by fabrics, especially those made of wool, and by some adhesives.

Copper and its alloys are corroded by chlorides, sulphides and organic acids. The source of these may again be fabrics, but also certain plastics. For example, polyvinyl chloride (PVC) can give off chlorine containing gases.

Acidic papers and boards, wood, wood composites and some adhesives can give off organic acids. The corrosion of lead is initiated by acetic acid and basic lead carbonate is formed. Formaldehyde, which is given off by wood composites can also corrode lead by the formation of lead formate.

The following recommendations for the storage of coins and medals are based on tests carried out in the Conservation Research Section of the Department of Conservation in The British Museum to evaluate the suitability of materials for use with metals.

Materials recommended for use

Wood and wood-composite cabinets and trays

These are usually suitable for the storage of silver artefacts. However, in our tests, lead almost always corroded, and copper occasionally corroded in the presence of wood, especially oak. In general, when any wood is to be used, it should be well seasoned and dried. Tropical hardwood, e.g. mahogany, are the least harmful.

Wood-composites, such as plywood, fibreboard and blockboard, are generally unsuitable for use with lead, and often unsuitable for use with copper. This is due to harmful, volatile materials emitted by both the wood component and the adhesive or binder component. Manufacturers are becoming aware of problems associated with volatile gases, and some types of fibreboards, e.g. Medite, are designed to have low level emissions of formaldehyde. These low emission fibreboards are often suitable for use, though testing of each type is recommended.

Plastic cabinets and trays

Plastic cabinets and trays are an alternative to using wood and specialist ranges are available from a number of manufacturers and have been found to be suitable for use with all metals.

Metal cabinets

Stove-enamelled metal cabinets may be used for storage of all types of materials. A wide variety of these are available, but they are not designed specifically for the storage of medals.

Adhesives

Cascamite (a powdered urea formaldehyde adhesive) is a general woodwork glue which may be used for construction of cabinets and inserts. Glues base on polyvinyl acetate emulsions should be avoided.

Lining materials

Drawers or trays within the cabinets are often lined. Plastazote, a polyethylene foam, available in a variety of colours, may be used as an insert with suitably sized profiles cut out to accommodate the coins. The foam will afford protection to the coins, as it will prevent them moving around and suffering mechanical damage when the drawers or trays are opened and closed.

Textiles may be used to line drawers and trays. The use of felt should be avoided since it causes silver to tarnish. Other fabrics can also cause problems. The Conservation Research Section has a large collection of fabrics which have been tested and will undertake tests on any sample on a commercial basis.

Paper envelopes

Many envelopes are made of poor quality paper, which will become acidic and unsuitable for use in storage. Therefore envelopes should be made from archival quality paper on board.

Plastic envelopes and boxes

Some plastics may degrade and produce harmful vapours or droplets of plasticiser. Therefore, archival quality plastic envelopes should be used. These are made of polyester or high quality polythene. The medals can be stored individually in plastic boxes such as clear, colourless polystyrene boxes. These may be lined with plastazoate foam to avoid mechanical damage.

Fabric and paper discs

Woollen felt discs should not be used in proximity with silver, as they emit sulphide gases which will cause rapid tarnishing. A loop nylon fabric may be a suitable alternative, as it has similar quantities of felt. It will not fray when cut, acts as a "cushion", and is available in a variety of colours.

Paper discs should be made of archival quality paper or board.

Inks

Inks used for annotating paper discs should have a permanent colour, and be tested for acidity prior to use. Several pens have been tested by scientists in Glasgow. The following were found to be suitable for archival purposes: Artline Calligraphy Pen black EK 243; Edding Profipen 0.1 1800; Pentel Document pens permanent MR 205 (black or blue); GPO standard ballpoint pen PO SP15.

Other Considerations

Absorbents

Should an artefact be particularly prone to corrosion, an absorbent material may be incorporated into its storage container. Charcoal cloth, a fabric made of activated carbon may be used to absorb all types of gases. Zinc oxide pellets, which react with hydrogen sulphide and hence reduce the rate at which silver tarnishes, can also be used.

Light

On occasions, whilst on display, silver items have acquired a white "bloom". This has been shown to be a result of photochemical degradation of the original silver chloride patina forming powdery metallic silver.

It is unlikely that medals would be continually exposed to bright light whilst in storage, but this potential hazard should be borne in mind.

Conclusions

Care must be taken when selecting material for use in the storage of medals, as corrosive gases can be emitted by a variety of substances. As an extra precaution, an absorbent material may be incorporated into the storage system.

In addition to the information given in this article, advice on the selection of materials can be obtained from the author at the Conservation Research Section of the Department of Conservation, The British Museum, London WC1B 3DG.

The original version of this article first appeared in Spink's *Numismatic Circular,* May 1991, and subsequently in MEDAL NEWS, February 1992.

IS THAT MEDAL RENAMED?

Trying to determine whether a medal is correctly named is a problem that every collector has to face at some time or another. R. J. Scarlett offers advice and a few simple guidelines for the inexperienced collector. This advice can only be a general guide, but such guidelines can be helpful provided that readers remember that there are always exceptions to the rule.

When checking for evidence of renaming always examine the medal with the aid of a magnifying glass. It is useful to bear in mind the following points:

1. Generally speaking, it is easier to re-name engraved medals than those that bear impressed namings. An engraved medal is relatively quick and easy to rename as it is necessary to remove less metal to erase the original naming.

    To rename a medal with an impressed naming requires special tools which are not easy to obtain.

    This having been said, it should be pointed out that many of the most notorious cases of renaming (especially with more expensive medals), done with the intention to deceive, have involved impressed medals.
2. Always consider whether the style of naming is correct for the particular medal under consideration, also for the particular clasp(s) concerned and for the regiment, etc. Sometimes medals issued for the same campaign are named in different styles depending on the unit involved and the clasp(s). A good example of this is the India General Service medal 1854–95. Such information can be acquired in part from books and articles, but these can be inaccurate or not sufficently specialised. The best way to acquire knowledge is by examining as many medals as possible. Always take full advantage of medal fairs, auction viewings, visits to dealers' premises and chances to look at friends' medal collections to enhance your knowledge.
3. Before a medal can be renamed, the original naming must be removed and one can usually see some evidence of this, such as in the form of file marks. Figure 1 shows the results of an attempt to remove a

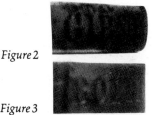

Figure 2

Figure 3

recipient's name from a medal—notice the many scratch marks caused by the file.

Unless the removal of the original naming has been done extremely carefully the edge of the medal may have a "rounded" appearance, instead of being square and flat. Figure 2 shows a renamed medal with edge view silhouette. See how "rounded" the edge is when compared with the flat edge of a correctly named medal in *Figure 3*.

4. If the suspender on the medal is assumed to be the 12 o'clock position, the naming on most medals appears on the edge between 9 o'clock and 3 o'clock. When the original naming is removed this thins down the rim between these two points. This is well illustrated in Figures 4 and 5. The former (4) shows a renamed medal with a thin rim while the naming has been removed and the latter (5) shows a correct medal with an even rim all round. The removal of the original naming will also reduce the size of the medal and this can be checked by using either a micrometer or a vernier calliper. The diameter of the medal should be measured across the 9 o'clock to 3 o'clock position and then across the 1 o'clock to 7 o'clock position. If the medal is not renamed, the two measurements should be the same. A "suspect" medal can also be checked for size against a known genuine medal, although it should be noted that a random check of say 10 similar medals will show variations in size.
5. Traces of an original naming may be visible under the new naming. Figures 6, 7 and 8 show examples of this. In Figure 6, traces are seen under the new naming and also beyond the end of it. Figure 7 shows

Figure 1

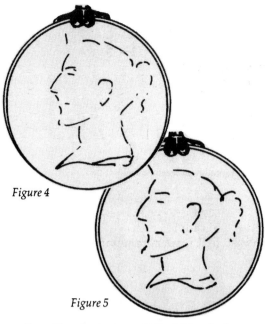

Figure 4

Figure 5

These kinds of corrections to namings were necessary because of human error and hence cannot really be classified as renamings.

Why do renamed medals exist on the market? The majority were not produced to deceive medal collectors, but are the result of officers and men losing their own medals and having to find replacements. The obvious and easiest remedy was to buy someone else's medals and have them renamed. Servicemen out to impress their friends and family were not above adding an extra medal to their rows and what better proof of entitlement than to see that the medal had their name on it. Many such medals were renamed by local jewellers.

Most collectors shun renamed medals and they are not usually offered for sale. An "official" correction unfortunately mars the appeal of a medal and hence affects the price. However some medals are very skillfully renamed with the sole intention of deceiving the unwary collector and dealer. This is especially so with rare and, therefore more expensive medals. The best advice is to use the check list given in this article and then, if still in doubt, consult a competent authority.

the outline of an impressed letter "A" under the new "S" and also shows traces of file marks. Figure 8 has a small impressed "T" appearing between the "L" and "A" of the new naming.

To recap, always check a medal for the following points

a. Is it named in the correct style.
b. Does the edge show file marks?
c. Is the edge flat?
d. Is the rim thinned at any point?
e. Is the diameter the same all round?
f. Are there traces of the original naming?
g. Has the medal been checked in all respects with a known correct medal?

A term which often appears in auction house and dealers' lists is "officially corrected" and "corrrected". Normally these expressions refer to instances where a single letter in the naming has been corrected by the issuing authority or by the recipient in order to rectify spelling mistakes, etc. Figures 9 and 10 show examples of "official" corrections. In both cases, traces of file marks can be seen and the corrected letter is impressed more heavily than the other letters.

Examples of privately corrected errors can be seen in Figures 11 and 12, here the new letters have been engraved rather than impressed and so do not match the rest of the naming. Traces of file marks are also visible. Figure 13 shows an example of where the correction is an "addition" due to the recipient's naming being incorrectly spelt. It is corrected by the addition of the letter "E", which is engraved and hence does not match the rest of the impressed naming. The engraved full-stop after the "K" can just be seen beneath the new "E". Figure 14 shows a Naval General Service medal 1793–1840, where the recipient has had his original rank removed and his later rank of "Lieut" added. Again this is engraved and does not match the rest of the naming, which is correctly impressed. Once more, notice the traces of file marks and the original impressed full-stop some way beyond the "Lieut".

S. BORDERERS.

Figure 6

74. SGT: R

Figure 7

GULAR

Figure 8

W. MᶜMINN. DE

Figure 9

STR: 2 CL H S

Figure 10

. A MITCHELL. B. W

Figure 11

74 PTE W. MAKISON

Figure 12

P. COOKE.

Figure 13

RD, LIEUᵀ

Figure 14

Glendining's
LONDON

THE MEDAL AUCTIONEERS

*The Waterloo medal to Captain Edward Payne, Scots Greys,
sold for £3,400, September 21, 1993.*

For further information contact
Pierce Noonan
Consultant Michael Naxton

Glendining's, 101 New Bond Street, London W1Y 9LG.
Telephone: 071-493 2445. Fax: 071-491 9181

Glendining's — a division of Phillips the International Fine Art Auctioneers

ORDERS OF CHIVALRY

The most colourful and romantic of all awards are those connected with the orders of chivalry. Many of them have their origins in the Middle Ages, when knights in armour formed the elite fighting force in every European country. This was the period when knights jousted in tournaments as a pastime, between going off to the Holy Land on the wars of Christendom known as the Crusades. This was the era of such popular heroes as Richard the Lionheart, William the Lion, Robert the Bruce, the Black Prince, Pepin of Herstal and John the Blind King of Bohemia. Their exploits have passed into the folklore of Europe, together with the legends of Roland and his Paladins or King Arthur and the Knights of the Round Table.

From the idea of a select band of knights, pledged to the support of a king or an ideal (usually religious), sprang the orders of chivalry. Many of these existed in the Middle Ages but most of them died out as feudalism went into decline. In some cases they survived; in others they disappeared for centuries, only to be resurrected at a later date. Still others were devised and instituted in relatively modern times, and indeed, continue to evolve. For example, Canada instituted the Order of Canada in 1967 and both Australia and New Zealand introduced their own orders in 1975.

In their original form membership of the orders of chivalry were just as highly coveted as they are today, but the insignia was usually simple or even non-existent. The complicated system of insignia which now surrounds these orders is fairly modern, dating from the 16th century or later. Nowadays most orders also exist in several classes, with the insignia becoming increasingly elaborate with each higher class.

Britain's senior order is the Garter, and although it consists of one class only it provides a good example of the pomp and ceremony which often surrounds these awards. It was founded by King Edward III and is said to derive its name from the fact that the King was attending a dance one day, when a lady's garter slipped from her leg and fell to the floor. To save her the embarrassment of retrieving her garter—and thus letting everyone know it was hers—the King himself picked it up and tied it round his own leg. Lest anyone should doubt that it was his garter he said, in court French, "Let evil be to him who evil thinks". From this curious incident came the idea of a very exclusive order of knighthood, consisting of the sovereign and 26 knights.

The insignia of this order consists of a Garter, a mantle of blue velvet lined with taffeta with the star of the Order embroidered on the left breast, a hood of crimson velvet, a surcoat of crimson velvet lined with white taffeta, a hat of black velvet lined with white taffeta, with a plume of white ostrich and black heron feathers fastened by a band of diamonds, a collar of gold composed of buckled garters and lovers' knots with red roses, the George (an enamelled figure of St George slaying the dragon) suspended from the collar, the Lesser George or badge, worn from a broad blue sash passing over the left shoulder to the right hip, and the star, a silver eight-pointed decoration bearing the red cross of St George surrounded by the garter and motto.

The insignia is exceptionally elaborate, the other orders of chivalry varying considerably in their complexity according to the class of the order. The full insignia is only worn on special occasions. In the case of the Garter usually the Lesser George and the breast star are worn on their own.

On the death of a Knight of the Garter the insignia must be returned to the Central Chancery of Orders of Knighthood, and therefore few examples of the Garter ever come on to the market. Those that do are usually examples from the 17th and 18th centuries when regulations regarding the return of insignia were not so strict. In the case of the lesser orders, insignia is returnable on promotion to a higher class. All collar chains are returnable, although that of the Order of St Michael and St George could be retained prior to 1948.

British orders are manufactured by firms holding contracts from the Central Chancery of Orders of Knighthood, and the values quoted in this Yearbook are for the official issues. It should be noted, however, that holders of orders frequently have replicas of breast stars made for use on different uniforms and it is sometimes difficult to tell these replicas from the originals as in many cases the replicas were made by the court jewellers responsible for making the originals. In addition, many jewellers in such European capitals as Vienna, Berlin and Paris have a long tradition of manufacturing insignia of orders for sale to collectors.

The badges and breast stars of orders of chivalry are very seldom named to the recipient and therefore lack the personal interest of campaign medals and many gallantry awards. For this reason they do not command the same interest or respect of collectors. Nevertheless, in cases where the insignia of orders can be definitely proved to have belonged to some famous person, the interest and value are enhanced. In any case, these orders are invariably very attractive examples of the jeweller's art, and they often possess titles and stories as colourful and romantic as their appearance.

1. THE MOST NOBLE ORDER OF THE GARTER

KG Star

Lesser George

Instituted: 1348.

Ribbon: 100mm plain dark blue. Not worn in undress uniform.

Garter: Dark blue velvet. Two versions may be encountered, with embroidered lettering and other details, or with gold lettering, buckle and tab. Worn on the left leg by gentlemen and on the left forearm by laides.

Collar Chain: Gold composed of alternate buckled garters, each encircling a red enamelled rose, and lovers' knots in gold although sometimes enamelled white.

Collar badge: An enamelled figure of St George fighting the dragon.

Star: Originally always embroidered in metal thread, a style which continues in the mantle to this day. Prior to 1858 knights often purchased metal stars in addition and since that date metal stars have been officially issued. These consist of a silver eight-pointed radiate star bearing in its centre and red cross of St George on a white ground, surrounded by the garter and motto HONI SOIT QUI MAL Y PENSE.

Sash Badge: The Lesser George, similar to the collar badge but encircled by an oval garter bearing the motto.

Comments: *Membership of the Order of the Garter is confined to the reigning sovereign, the Prince of Wales and 25 other Knights, and is the personal gift of the monarch. In addition to the 25 Knights there have, from time to time, been extra Knights, invariably non-Christians such as the Sultans of Turkey or the Emperor of Japan. The Emperor Hirohito, incidentally had the dubious distinction of being the only person awarded the Garter twice: in 1922 and again in 1971, having forfieted the original award as a result of the Japanese entry into the Second World War in 1941. Sir Winston Churchill was invested with the insignia originally presented in 1702 to his illustrious ancestor, the Duke of Marlborough. All official insignia is returnable to the Central Chancery of Knighthood on the death of the holder.*

VALUE:

Collar chain	Rare
Collar badge (the George)	£50,000–100,000
Star (in metal)	£1500–5000
Star (embroidered)	£400–1000
Sash badge (Lesser George)	£3000–40,000
Garter (embroidered)	£300–500
Garter (gold lettering and buckle)	£1200–2500

*Prices are for privately made examples many of which are jewelled and enamelled.

2. THE MOST ANCIENT AND MOST NOBLE ORDER OF THE THISTLE

KT Star

Instituted: 1687.

Ribbon: 100mm plain dark green. Not worn in undress uniform.

Collar Chain: Gold of alternate thistles and sprigs of rue enamelled in proper colours.

Collar Badge: A gold and enamelled figure of St Andrew in a green gown and purple surcoat, bearing before him a white saltire cross, the whole surrounded by rays of gold.

Star: Silver, consisting of a St Andrew's cross, with other rays issuing between the points of the cross and, in the centre, on a gold background, a thistle enamelled in proper colours surrounded by a green circle bearing the Latin motto NEMO ME IMPUNE LACESSIT (no one assails me with impunity).

Sash Badge: A gold figure of St Andrew bearing before him a white enamelled saltire cross, surrounded by an oval collar enamelled green bearing the motto, surmounted by a gold cord fitted with a ring for suspension.

Comments: *This order is said to have been founded in AD 787, alluding to barefoot enemy soldiers who cried out when they trod on thistles and thus alerted the Scots of an imminent attack. The order had long been defunct when it was revived by King James VII and II and re-established in December 1703 by Queen Anne. It now consists of the sovereign and 16 Knights, making it the most exclusive of the orders of chivalry. At death, the official insignia is returned to the Central Chancery.*

VALUE:

Collar chain	Rare
Collar badge	Rare
Star (metal)	£1500–4000
Star (embroidered)	£400–600
Sash badge	£5000–8000

Sash Badges

3. THE MOST ILLUSTRIOUS ORDER OF ST PATRICK

KP Star

Sash Badge

Instituted: February 5, 1783.

Ribbon: 100 mm sky-blue. Not worn in undress uniform.

Collar Chain: Gold, composed of five roses and six harps alternating, each tied together with a gold knot. The roses are enamelled alternately white petals within red and red within white.

Collar Badge: An imperial crown enamelled in proper colours from which is suspended by two rings a gold harp and from this a circular badge with a white enamelled centre embellished with the red saltire cross on which is surmounted a green three-petalled shamrock its leaves decorated with gold crowns, the whole surrounded by a gold collar bearing the Latin motto QUIS SEPARABIT (who shall separate us?) with the date of foundation in roman numerals round the foot MDCCLXXXII.

Star: A silver eight-pointed star, having in its centre, on a white field, the saltire cross of St Parick in red enamel charged with a green trefoil bearing a gold crown on each leaf.

Sash Badge: The saltire cross in red enamel surmounted by a green shamrock with gold crowns as above, surrounded by an oval collar of pale blue with the Latin motto round the top and the date of foundation round the foot, the whole enclosed by a gold and white enamel surround charged with 32 shamrocks.

Comments: *Founded by King George III to reward the loyalty of Irish peers during the American War of Independence, it originally comprised the monarch and 15 Knights. In 1833 it was extended to include the Lord-Lieutenant of Ireland and 22 Knights, with certain extra and honorary knights. Appointments of non-royal Knights to the Order ceased with the partition of Ireland in 1922,although three of the sons of King George V were appointed after that date—the Prince of Wales (1927), the Duke of York (1936) and the Duke of Gloucester (1934). It became obsolete in 1974 with the death of the last holder. All items of official insignia were returned at death. Unlike the other two great orders, the sash for this Order is worn in the manner of the lesser orders, over the right shoulder.*

VALUE:

Collar chain	Rare
Collar badge	£8000–12,000
Star (metal)	£1500–3000
Star (embroidered)	£400–600
Sash badge	£5000–7000

4. THE MOST HONOURABLE ORDER OF THE BATH

GCB Star (Military)

Instituted: 1725.

Ribbon: 38mm.

Collar Chain: Gold composed of nine crowns and eight devices, each consisting of a rose, a thistle and a shamrock issuing from a sceptre all enamelled in their proper colours. The crowns and devices are joined by gold, white-enamelled knots.

Collar Badge: A skeletal gold badge with an oval collar inscribed TRIA JUNCTA IN UNO (three joined in one) in white enamelled letters, enclosing a thistle, rose and shamrock issuing from a sceptre, with a crown above the sceptre and two crowns below, at the sides.

Star: A silver flaming star surmounted by a circular gold band enamelled red bearing the motto round the top and having a laurel spray round the foot, enclosing three gold crowns enamelled in red.

Sash Badge: As the Collar Badge but smaller and without white enamelling.

Comments: *Established by King George I, this was a single-class Order comprising the monarch, a prince of the blood royal, a Great Master and 35 Knights of Companions (KB). It was re-organised at the conclusion of the Napoleonic Wars (see below).*

VALUE:

Collar chain	£18,000–25,000
Collar badge	Rare
Star (metal)	£2000–3500
Star (embroidered)	£400–800
Sash badge	£2000–3000

KNIGHT GRAND CROSS

The Order was re-organised in 1815 in two divisions, Military and Civil. The Military Division had three classes: Knight Grand Cross (GCB), Knight Commander (KCB) and Companion (CB), while the Civil Division continued with the single class of Knight Grand Cross. In 1847 the Civil Division came into line with the Military, and divided into three classes.

Metal: Gold (1815–87): silver-gilt (since 1887).

Collar Badge: The Military Badge is a gold Maltese cross of eight points, each point tipped with a small gold ball, and in each angle between the arms of the cross is a gold lion. In the centre of the cross is a device comprising a rose, thistle and shamrock issuing from a sceptre, and three imperial crowns . This device is surrounded by a red enamelled circle on which appears the Latin motto TRIA JUNCTA IN UNO (three joined in one) in gold lettering. The circle is surrounded by two branches of laurel, enamelled green, and below is a blue enamelled scroll with the German motto ICH DIEN (I serve) in gold.

The Civil Badge is of gold filigree work, and oval in shape. It consists of a bandlet bearing the motto, and in the centre is the usual device of the rose, thistle and shamrock issuing from a sceptre, together with the three crowns.

Star: A gold Maltese cross of the same pattern as the Military Badge, mounted on a silver flaming star (Military); or a silver eight-pointed star with a central device of three crowns on a silver ground, encircled by the motto on a red enamelled ribbon (Civil).

Sash Badges: Similar to the Collar Badges, they were originally made in gold but since 1887 silver-gilt has been substituted.

VALUE:	Military	Civil
Collar chain (gold)	£18,000–25,000	£18,000–25,000
Collar chain (silver gilt)	£8000–10,000	£8000–10,000
Collar badge (gold)	£2000–3500	£800–1000
Star (metal)	£500–1000	£300–400
Star (embroidered)	£300–500	£200–300
Sash badge (gold)	£1800–3000	£800–1000
Sash badge (gilt)	£800–1000	£400–600

4. THE MOST HONOURABLE ORDER OF THE BATH *continued*

KCB Star (Civil)

GCB Sash Badge (Civil)   *KCB Neck Badge (Military)*

KNIGHTS COMMANDERS (KCB) AND COMPANIONS (CB)

Holders of the KCB wear a neck badge suspended by a ribbon as well as a breast star. Prior to 1917 Companions wore a breast badge, the same way as a medal: but in that year it was converted into a neck badge.

Star: (KCB): (Military) a star with the gold Maltese cross omitted, and in the shape of a cross pattée, the three crowns and motto in the centre surrounded by a green enamelled laurel wreath. (Civil) similar but omitting the laurel wreath.

Breast Badge (CB): Similar to the Star but smaller.

Neck Badge (KCB): Similar to the Collar badges of the GCB but smaller, in Military and Civil versions as above.

Neck Badge (CB): Similar to the above, but smaller.

VALUE:

	Military	Civil
Knight Commander		
Star (metal)	£300–500	£200–400
Star (embroidered)	£150–400	£100–250
Neck badge (gold)	£700–1200	£400–500
Neck badge (gilt)	£350–450	£200–250
Companion		
Breast badge (gold)	£600–1200	£350–400
Breast badge (gilt)	£350–450	£180–220
Neck badge (gilt)	£300–400	£140–180

5. THE ROYAL GUELPHIC ORDER

Instituted: 1815.
Ribbon: 44mm light blue watered silk.

KNIGHTS GRAND CROSS (GCH)

KCH Star (Military)

Collar Chain: Gold, with lions and crowns alternating, linked by scrolled royal cyphers.

Collar Badge: An eight-pointed Maltese cross with balls on each point and a lion passant gardant in each angle. (Obverse) in the centre, on a ground of red enamel, is a white horse of Hanover surrounded by a circle of light blue enamel with the motto in gold lettering NEC ASPERA TERRENT (difficulties do not terrify). Surrounding this circle is a green enamelled laurel wreath. (Reverse) the monogram GR in gold letters on a red ground, surmounted by the British crown and surrounded by a gold circle with the date of the institution MDCCCXV. In the Military version two crossed swords are mounted above the cross and below a Hanoverian crown. In the Civil version the swords are omited, and the wreath is of oak-leaves instead of laurel.

Star: A radiate star with rays grouped into eight points, the centre being similar to the Collar Badge. Behind the laurel wreathed centre are two crossed swords (Military); in the Civil version the swords are omitted and the wreath is of oak leaves.

Sash Badge: Similar to the Collar Badge but smaller.

Comments: *Founded by HRH the Prince Regent (later King George IV), it took its name from the family surname of the British sovereigns from George I onwards and was awarded by the crown of Hanover to both British and Hanverian subjects for distinguished services to Hanover. Under Salic Law, a woman could not succeed to the Hanoverian throne, so on the death of King William IV in 1837 Hanover passed to Prince Augustus, Duke of Cumberland, and thereafter the Guelphic Order became a purely Hanoverian award.*

VALUE:

	Military	Civil
Collar chain (gold)	£7000–9000	£7000–9000
Collar chain (silver gilt)	£4000–5000	£4000–5000
Collar Chain (copper gilt)	£2000–5000	£2000–3000
Collar badge	£5000–6000	£2500–3500
Star	£1000–2000	£500–1000
Sash badge	£6000–8000	£3000–4000

KNIGHTS COMMANDERS (KCH) AND KNIGHTS (KH)

Knights Commanders wore a neck badge suspended by a ribbon, and a breast star, while Knights wore a breast badge only.
Star: As above, but smaller.
Neck Badge: Similar to the Collar Badge but smaller.
Breast Badge: Two versions, in gold and enamel or silver and enamel.

VALUE:

	Military	Civil
Star	£600–1000	£400–600
Neck badge	£1500–2000	£800–1200
Breast badge (gold)	£800–1200	£500–700

KH Breast Badge (Military)

29

6. THE MOST DISTINGUISHED ORDER OF ST MICHAEL AND ST GEORGE

Instituted: 1818.
Ribbon: 38mm three equal bands of Saxon blue, scarlet and Saxon blue.

KNIGHTS GRAND CROSS (GCMG)

Knights Grand Cross wear a mantle of Saxon blue lined with scarlet silk tied with cords of blue and scarlet silk and gold, and having on the left side the star of the Order. The chapeau or hat is of blue satin, lined with scarlet and surmounted by black and white ostrich feathers. The collar, mantle and chapeau are only worn on special occasions or when commanded by the sovereign, but in ordinary full dress the badge is worn on the left hip from a broad ribbon passing over the right shoulder and the star on the left breast.

Collar Chain: Silver gilt formed alternately on lions of England, Maltese crosses enamelled in white, and the cyphers SM and SG with, in the centre, two winged lions of St Mark each holding a book and seven arrows.

Star: A silver star of seven groups of rays, with a gold ray between each group, surmounted overall by the cross of St George in red enamel. In the centre is a representation of St Michael encountering Satan within a blue circular riband bearing the motto AUSPICIUM MELIORIS AEVI (A token of a better age).

Sash Badge: A gold seven-pointed star with V-shaped extremities, enamelled white and edged with gold, surmounted by an imperial crown. In the centre on one side is a representation in enamel of St Michael encountering Satan and on the other St George on horseback fighting the dragon. This device is surrounded by a circle of blue enamel bearing the Latin motto in gold lettering. Silver-gilt was substituted for gold in 1887.

Comments: *Founded by HRH the Prince Regent and awarded originally to citizens of Malta and the Ionian Islands in the Adriatic Sea, both of which had been ceded to Britain during the Napoleonic Wars. The Ionian Islands were transferred to Greece in 1859. Towards the end of the 19th century, however, the Order was awarded to those who had performed distinguished service in the colonies and protectorates of the British Empire and in more recent times it has been widely used as an award to ambassadors and senior diplomats as well as colonial governors.*

VALUE:	
Collar chain	£1200–1400
Star	£500–600
Sash badge (gold)	£3000–4000
Sash badge (gilt)	£600–800

GCMG Star

6. THE MOST DISTINGUISHED ORDER OF ST MICHAEL AND ST GEORGE *continued*

KCMG Star

KNIGHTS COMMANDERS (KCMG) AND COMPANIONS (CMG)

Knights Commanders wear the badge suspended round the neck from a narrower ribbon of the same colours, and a breast star; Companions wear a neck badge. In undress uniform Knights Grand Cross and Knights Commanders wear the ribbon of Companions of the Order. Prior to 1917 Companions wore a breast badge, worn the same way as a medal, but this was then changed to a neck badge.

Star: A silver eight-pointed star charged with the red St George's cross and having the same central device as the GCMG Star. This was introduced in 1859.

Neck Badge: Similar to the sash badge of the GCMG but smaller. Those worn by KCMG were of gold and enamel until 1887 but silver-gilt and enamel thereafter. The CMG neck badges are invariably of enamel and silver-gilt.

Breast Badge: Similar to the star of the KCMG but smaller and made of gold and enamel till 1887, and silver gilt and enamel from then till 1917.

VALUE:
Knight Commander	
Star	£300–400
Neck badge (gold)	£800–900
Neck badge (gilt)	£350–450
Companion	
Breast badge (gold)	£500–600
Breast badge (gilt)	£350–400
Neck badge (gilt)	£250–350

7. THE MOST EXALTED ORDER OF THE STAR OF INDIA

Instituted: 1861.
Ribbon: Broad light blue with white edges (GCSI); 50mm plain white (KCSI); 38mm plain white (CSI).

KNIGHTS GRAND COMMANDERS (GCSI)

KCSI Neck Badge

The insignia of consisted of a gold collar and badge, a mantle of light blue satin with a representation of the star on the left side and tied with a white silk cord with blue and silver tassels. The collar and mantle were only worn on special occasions and in ordinary full dress uniform a GCSI wore the star on the left breast and the badge on the left hip from a broad sash of light blue edged in white.

Collar Chain: Gold formed of lotus flowers, palm branches and united red and white roses.

Badge: An onyx cameo bearing the left-facing bust of Queen Victoria wearing an imperial crown, set in a gold ornamental oval containing the motto of the Order HEAVEN'S LIGHT OUR GUIDE in diamonds, on a pale blue ground surmounted by a five-pointed star in chased silver.

Star: A five-pointed star in diamonds resting on a circular riband of light blue enamel bearing the motto in diamonds, the whole set on a circular star of golden rays.

Comments: *Founded by Queen Victoria a few years after the British Crown took over the administration of India from the Honourable East India Company, it was intended primarily as an award to loyal Indian princes. The highest class was designated Knight Grand Commander, rather than Cross, because the majority of recipient were not Christians (either Hindus or Muslims). The Order at first consisted of the sovereign, a Grand Master (the Viceroy of India), 36 Knights Grand Commanders (18 British and 18 Indian), 85 Knights Commanders and 170 Companions. The GCSI was the most lavish of all British orders. It lapsed in 1947 when the sub-continent attained independence. Until then all insignia of this Order was returnable on the death of recipients. After 1947, however, recipients or their heirs were allowed in certain cases to purchase the star and badges of any of the three applicable classes, but not the collar chain of the Knight Grand Commander.*

VALUE:

Collar chain	Rare
Star and badge	£26,000–32,000

KNIGHTS COMMANDERS (KCSI) AND COMPANIONS (CSI)

Knights Commanders wore a badge round the neck and a star on the left breast, while Companions originally had a breast badge which was transmuted into a neck badge from 1917 onwards.

Star: Similar to that of the GCSI but in silver.

Neck Badge: Similar to the collar badge of the GCSI but smaller and less ornate.

Breast Badge: Similar to the above but smaller and less ornate and fitted with a straight bar suspender. Subtle differences in the ornament at the foot of the blue border and the external ornament at the sides and foot of the oval.

Comments: *The second and third classes of the Order were awarded to Indian and British subjects of the armed forces and Indian Civil Service for distinguished service of not less than 30 years' duration.*

VALUE:

Star and Neck badge (KCSI)	£4000–6000
Breast badge (CSI)	£2500–3000
Neck badge (CSI)	£1400–1600

8. THE MOST EMINENT ORDER OF THE INDIAN EMPIRE

Instituted: 1878.
Ribbon: Broad of imperial purple (GCIE); 50mm imperial purple (KCIE); 38mm imperial purple (CIE).

KNIGHTS GRAND COMMANDERS (GCIE)

KCIE Neck Badge

The insignia consisted of a collar, badge and mantle of imperial purple or dark blue satin lined with white silk and fastened with a white silk cord with gold tassels, and having on the left side a representation of the Star of the Order. On ordinary full-dress occasions, however, Knights Grand Commanders wore the badge on the left hip from a broad sash, and a star on the left breast.

Collar Chain: Silver-gilt, composed of elephants, lotus flowers, peacocks in their pride and Indian roses with, in the centre, the imperial crown, the whole linked together by chains.

Badge: A gold five-petalled rose, enamelled crimson and with a green barb between each petal. In the centre is an effigy of Queen Victoria on a gold ground, surrounded by a purple riband originally inscribed VICTORIA IMPERATRIX but from 1901 onwards inscribed IMPERATRICIS AUSPICIIS (under the auspices of the Empress).

Star: Composed of fine silver rays with smaller gold rays between them, the whole alternately plain and scaled. In the centre, within a purple circle bearing the motto and surmounted by the imperial crown in gold, is the effigy of Queen Victoria on a gold ground.

Comments: *Founded by Queen Victoria after assuming the title of Empress of India, it was originally confined to Companions only, together with the Sovereign and Grand Master. Members of the Council of the Governor-General were admitted ex officio as Companions. It was intended for award in respect of meritorious services in India but from the outset it was regarded as a junior alternative to the Star of India. In 1886 the Order was expanded to two classes by the addition of Knights Commanders up to a maximum of 50 in number. In 1887, however, it was again re-organised into three classes: up to 25 Knights Grand Commanders (GCIE), up to 50 Knights Commanders (KCIE) and an unlimited number of Companions (CIE). The Order has been in abeyance since 1947.*

VALUE:

Collar chain	Rare
Star and badge	£4000–5000

KNIGHTS COMMANDERS (KCIE) AND COMPANIONS (CIE)

The insignia of Knights Commanders consisted of a neck badge and a breast star, while that of Companions was originally a breast badge, converted to a neck badge in 1917.

Star: Similar to that of the GCIE but fashioned entirely in silver.

Neck badge: Similar to the collar or sash badge of the GCIE but in correspondingly smaller sizes and differing in minor details.

Breast badge: Similar to the sash badge of the GCIE but differing in minor details, notably the spacing ornament at the foot of the blue circle. Two versions exist, with or without INDIA on the petals of the lotus flower.

VALUE:

Knights Commanders	
Star and Neck badge	£1400–2000
Companions	
Breast badge (INDIA)	£800–1000
Breast badge (smaller, without INDIA)	£400–450
Neck badge	£300–350

9. THE ROYAL FAMILY ORDER

Instituted: 1820.

Ribbon: 50mm sky blue moire (1820); 38mm dark blue bordered by narrow stripes of yellow and broader stripes of crimson with narrow black edges (1902); 50mm pale blue moire (1911); 50mm pink moire (1937); 50mm pale yellow silk moire (1953). These ribbons are tied in a bow and worn on the left shoulder.

Descriptions: An upright oval heavily bordered by diamonds and surmounted by a crown, also embellished in diamonds. The oval contains a miniature portrait of the sovereign in enamels.

Comments: *Awarded to the Queen and female relatives of the reigning monarch. It was instituted by King George IV who conferred such orders on his sister, Princess Charlotte Augusta, wife of Frederick William, King of Wurttemberg, and his niece Princess Augusta Caroline, who married the Grand Duke of Mecklenburg-Strelitz. Queen Victoria instituted a separate Order (see next entry), but this Order was revived by King Edward VII in 1902 and continued by successive sovereigns ever since. Special badges are given to ladies-in-waiting. The insignia of these Family Orders very seldom appear on the market and on account of their immense rarity they are unpriced here.*

VALUE:	
George IV	Rare
Edward VIII	Rare
George V	Rare
George VI	Rare
Elizabeth II	Rare
Ladies-in-waiting badges	From £1000

10. THE ROYAL ORDER OF VICTORIA AND ALBERT

Instituted: 1862.

Ribbon: 38mm white moire, in the form of a bow worn on the left shoulder.

Description: An upright oval onyx cameo bearing conjoined profiles of HRH Prince Albert, the Prince Consort and Queen Victoria. The badges of the First and Second Classes are set in diamonds and surmounted by an imperial crown similarly embellished, the badge of the Second Class being rather smaller. The badge of the Third Class is set in pearls, while that of the Fourth Class takes the form of a monogram "V & A" set with pearls and surmounted by an imperial crown.

VALUE:	
First Class	£24,000–26,000
Second Class	£16,000–18,000
Third Class	£10,000–12,000
Fourth Class	£ 4000–5000

11. THE IMPERIAL ORDER OF THE CROWN OF INDIA

Instituted: January 1, 1878.

Ribbon: 38mm light blue watered silk with narrow white stripes towards the edges, formed in a bow worn on the left shoulder.

Description: A badge consisting of the royal and imperial monogram VRI in diamonds, turquoises and pearls, surrounded by an oval frame and surmounted by a jewelled imperial crown.

Comments: *Awarded by Queen Victoria to the princesses of the royal and imperial house, the wives or other female relatives of Indian princes and other Indian ladies, and of the wives or other female relatives of any of the persons who had held or were holding the offices of Viceroy and Governor-General of India, Governors of Madras or Bombay, or of Principal Secretary of State for India, as the sovereign might think fit to appoint. This order, conferred on females only, became obsolete in 1947.*

VALUE:	
Breast badge	£6000–10,000

12. THE ROYAL VICTORIAN ORDER

Instituted: April 1896.
Ribbon: Dark blue with borders of narrow red, white and red stripes on either side.

KNIGHTS GRAND CROSS AND DAMES GRAND CROSS (GCVO)

The insignia consists of a mantle of dark blue silk, edged with red satin, lined with white silk, and fastened by a cordon of dark blue silk and gold; a gold collar and a badge, worn only on special occasions. Knights wear the badge on the left hip from a broad ribbon worn over the right shoulder, with a star on the left breast, while Dames wear a somewhat narrower ribbon over the right shoulder with the badge, and a star similar to that of the Knights. Dames' insignia are smaller than those of the Knights.

Collar: Silver gilt composed of octagonal pieces and oblong perforated and ornamental frames alternately linked together with gold. The pieces are edged and ornamented with gold, and each contains on a blue-enamelled ground a gold rose jewellerd with a carbuncle. The frames are gold and each contains a portion of inscription VICTORIA BRITT. DEF. FID. IND. IMP. in letters of white enamel. In the centre of the collar, within a perforated and ornamental frame of gold, is an octagonal piece enamelled blue, edged with red, and charged with a white saltire, superimposed by a gold medallion of Queen Victoria's effigy from which is suspended the badge.

Badge: A white-enamelled Maltese cross of eight points, in the centre of which is an oval of crimson enamel bearing the cypher VRI in gold letters. Encircling this is a blue enamel riband with the name VICTORIA in gold letters, and above this is the imperial crown enamelled in proper colours.

Star: Of chipped silver of eight points on which is mounted a white-enamelled Maltese cross with VRI in an oval at the centre.

Comments: *Awarded for extraordinary, important or personal services to the sovereign of the Royal Family. Ladies became eligible for the Order in 1936. Most of the badges of the Royal Victorian Order are numbered on the reverse and are returnable on promotion. Honourary awards are unnumbered.*

VALUE:

	Knights	Dames
Collar	£5000–6000	£6000–7000
Star and Badge	£900–1200	£1000–1200

GCVO star

KNIGHTS COMMANDERS (KCVO), DAMES COMMANDERS (DCVO), COMMANDERS (CVO), LIEUTENANTS (LVO) AND MEMBERS (MVO)

The insignia of the Second, Third, Fourth and Fifth Classes follows the usual pattern. Knights wear a neck badge and a breast star, Dames a breast star and a badge on the left shoulder from a ribbon tied in a bow, Commanders the same neck badge (men) or shoulder badge (women), Lieutenants a somewhat smaller breast badge worn in line with other medals and decorations (men) or a shoulder badge (women) and Members breast or shoulder badges in frosted silver instead of white enamel. The two lowest classes of the Order were originally designated member Fourth Class or member Fifth Class (MVO), but in 1988 the Fourth Class was renamed Lieutenant (LVO) and the Fifth Class simply Member (MVO).

VALUE:

	Gentlemen	Ladies
Neck badge and brest star	£400–600	£500–600
Neck badge (CVO)	£300–350	£400–450
Breast or shoulder badge (LVO)	£200–250	£250–300
Breast or shoulder badge (MVO)	£180–220	£220–250

13. ROYAL VICTORIAN MEDAL

Instituted: April 1896.

Ribbon: As for the Royal Victorian Order (above); foreign Associates, however, wear a ribbon with a central white stripe added.

Metal: Silver-gilt, silver or bronze.

Size: 36mm.

Description: (Obverse) the effigy of the reigning sovereign; (reverse) the royal cypher on an ornamental shield within a laurel wreath.

Comments: *Awarded to those below the rank of officers who perform personal services to the sovereign or to members of the Royal Family. Originally awarded in silver or bronze, a higher class, in silver-gilt, was instituted by King George V. Only two medals (both silver) were issued in the brief reign of King Edward VIII (1936) and only four bronze medals were issued in the reign of King George VI. Any person in possession of the bronze medal to whom a silver medal is awarded, can wear both, and the silver-gilt medal in addition if such be conferred upon him or her. Clasps are awarded for further services to each class of the medal, while the medals may be worn in addition to the insignia of the Order if the latter is subsequently conferred. To distinguish between British and foreign recipients, King George VI decreed in 1951 that the ribbon worn by the latter should have an additional stripe, these recipients to be designated Associates. In 1983 the order for wearing this medal was altered, and it was no longer to be worn after campaign medals but took precedence over them.*

VALUE:

	Silver-gilt	Silver	Bronze
Victoria	—	£100–120	£60–80
Edward VII	£250–300	£120–150	£80–100
George V	—	£80–90	£250–300
Edward VIII	—	Rare	—
George VI	£100–120	£80–120	Rare
Elizabeth II	£120–140	£100–120	£60–80

14. THE ROYAL VICTORIAN CHAIN

Instituted: 1902.

Ribbon: None.

Metal: Silver gilt

Description: A chain consisting of three Tudor roses, two thistles, two shamrocks and two lotus flowers (the heraldic flowers of England, Scotland, Ireland and India respectively), connected by a slender double trace of gold chain. At the bottom of the front loop is a centre piece consisting of the royal cypher in enamel surrounded by a wreath and surmounted by a crown. From this centrepiece hangs a replica of the badge of a Knight Grand Cross of the Royal Victorian order. Ladies were the insignia in the form of a shoulder badge suspended from a miniature chain with links leading to a rose, thistle, shamrock and lotus. An even more elaborate collar, with diamonds encrusting the crown and cypher, was adopted in 1921 and there is a ladies' version of this as well.

Comments: *Sometimes regarded as the highest grade of the Royal Victorian Order, it is actually a quite separate Order and was introduced by King Edward VII for conferment as a special mark of the sovereign's favour, and then only very rarely, upon Royalty, or other especially distinguished personages, both foreign and British.*

VALUE

	Gentlemen	Ladies
Chain (1902–21)	Rare	Rare
Chain with diamonds	Rare	Rare

15. ORDER OF MERIT

Instituted: 1902.

Ribbon: 50mm half blue, half crimson.

Metal: Gold.

Size: Height 50mm; max. width 35mm.

Description: A pattee convexed cross, enamelled red, edged blue. (Obverse) FOR MERIT in the centre surrounded by a white band and a laurel wreath enamelled in proper colours. (Reverse) the royal cypher in gold on a blue ground with a white surround and a laurel wreath as above. The cross is surmounted by a Tudor crown to which is attached a ring for suspension. Naval and military recipients have crossed swords in the angles of the cross.

Comments: *This highly prestigious Order consists of the sovereign and a maximum of 24 members in one class only. There is, however, no limit on the number of foreign honorary members, although only ten have so far been admitted to the Order. It was intended for award to those whose achievements in the fields of art, music and literature were outstanding, but it was later extended to naval and military leaders in wartime. To date, fewer than 160 awards have been made, including a mere five ladies, from Florence Nightingale (1907) to Baroness Thatcher. The insignia of those appointed since 1991 have to be returned on the death of the recipient. The insignia of members appointed prior to that date is retained, but understandably few items have come on to the market.*

VALUE:

	Military	Civil
Edward VII	£5000–6000	£3500–4500
George V	£5000–6000	£3000–4000
George VI	Rare	£4000–5000
Elizabeth II	Rare	£3500–4500

16. THE MOST EXCELLENT ORDER OF THE BRITISH EMPIRE

GBE Star (2nd type)

CBE Badge (2nd type)

Instituted: June 1917.

Ribbon: 38mm originally purple, with a narrow central scarlet stripe for the Military Division; rose-pink edged with pearl grey, with a narrow central stripe of pearl-grey for the Military Division (since 1936).

Comments: *Founded by King George V during the First World War for services to the Empire at home, in India and in the overseas dominions and colonies, other than those rendered by the Navy and Army, although it could be conferred upon officers of the armed forces for services of a non-combatant character. A Military Division was created in December 1918 and awards made to commissioned officers and warrant officers in respect of distinguished service in action. The insignia of the Civil and Military Divisions is identical, distinguished only by the respective ribbons.*

KNIGHTS AND DAMES GRAND CROSS (GBE)

The insignia includes a mantle of rose-pink satin lined with pearl-grey silk, tied by a cord of pearl-grey silk, with two rose-pink and silver tassels attached. On the left side of the mantle is a representation of the star of the First Class of the Order. The mantle, collar and collar badge are only worn on special occasions. In dress uniform, however, the badge is worn over the left hip from a broad (96mm) riband passing over the right shoulder, while Dames wear the badge from a narrower (57mm) ribbon in a bow on the left shoulder; both with the breast star of the Order.

Collar: Silver-gilt with medallions of the royal arms and of the royal and imperial cypher of King George V alternately linked together with cables. In the centre is the imperial crown between two sea lions. The collar for Dames is somewhat narrower than that for Knights.

Badge: A cross patonce in silver-gilt the arms enamelled pearl-grey. In the centre, within a circle enamelled crimson, the figure of Britannia, replaced since 1936 by the conjoined left-facing crowned busts of King George V and Queen Mary, surrounded by a circle inscribed FOR GOD AND THE EMPIRE.

Star: An eight-pointed star of silver chips on which is superimposed the enamelled medallion as for the badge (Britannia or George V and Queen Mary). The star worn by Dames is smaller.

VALUE:

	Britannia	King and Queen
Knights Brand Cross		
Collar	£5000–6000	£5000–6000
Badge and star	£900–1000	£1000–1200
Dames Grand Cross		
Collar	£6000–7000	£6000–7000
Badge and star	£1000–1200	£1200–1400

16. THE MOST EXCELLENT ORDER OF THE BRITISH EMPIRE *continued*

KBE Star

KNIGHTS COMMANDERS (KBE), DAMES COMMANDERS (DBE), COMMANDERS (CBE) AND MEMBERS (MBE)

The insignia of these four Classes follows the same pattern as other Orders. Both Britannia and King and Queen medallion types have been issued.

Star: A star of four large points and four minor points in chipped silver, with the enamelled medallion superimposed. The star worn by Dames is smaller.

Neck Badge: Similar to the badge of the GBE but smaller and worn from a 44mm ribbon round the neck (men) or from a shoulder bow (ladies). Worn by KBE, DBE and CBE.

Breast Badge: As above, but in silver-gilt (OBE) or frosted silver (MBE), with shoulder versions for ladies, worn with a 38mm ribbon.

VALUE:	Britannia	King and Queen
Badge and Star (KBE,)	£250–300	£350–400
Badge and Star (DBE)	£350–400	£450_550
Neck badge (CBE)	£100–120	£120–150
Shoulder badge (CBE)	£140–160	£180–220
Breast badge (OBE)	£30–40	£50–60
Shoulder badge (OBE)	£35–45	£55–65
Breast badge (MBE)	£30–40	£50–60
Shoulder badge (MBE)	£35–45	£55–65

OBE badge (silver-gilt) and reverse of the MBE badge (frosted silver)

17. MEDAL OF THE ORDER OF THE BRITISH EMPIRE

Instituted: June 1917.

Ribbon: 32mm plain purple (Civil), with a narrow scarlet central stripe (Military).

Medal: Silver.

Size: 30mm.

Description: (Obverse) a seated figure of Britannia facing right, her left arm extended and her right holding a trident, with the inscription FOR GOD AND THE EMPIRE round the upper part of the circumference; (reverse) the royal and imperial cypher CRI surmounted by a Tudor crown, the whole enclosed in a cable circle. Fitted with a plain ring for suspension.

Comments: *Instituted as a lower award connected with the Order, it consisted originally of a Civil Division, but a Military Division, distinguishable solely by the ribbon, was added in December 1918. This medal was issued unnamed but many were subsequently engraved or impressed on the rim privately. Fewer than 2000 medals were awarded before they were discontinued in 1922.*

VALUE:

Medal unnamed as issued	£70–80
Military award with named medal group	£140–180
Civil award with supporting documents	£100–120

18. EMPIRE GALLANTRY MEDAL

Instituted: December 29, 1922.

Ribbon: Originally plain purple (Civil), with a thin scarlet central stripe (Military; from July 1937 rose-pink with pearl-grey edges (Civil) and a central pearl-grey stripe (Military). A silver laurel branch was added to the ribbon (1933), with a smaller version for wear on the ribbon alone.

Metal: Silver.

Size: 36mm.

Description: (Obverse) the seated figure of Britannia, her left hand resting on a shield and her right holding a trident, with a blazing sun upper right. The words FOR GOD AND THE EMPIRE inscribed round the upper part of the circumference, with FOR in the wave lower left above the exergue which bears the word GALLANTRY. (Reverse) four lions passant gardant, two on each side, with the cypher of the reigning sovereign in the centre surmounted by an imperial crown. Round the foot, in two concentric arcs, are the words INSTITUTED BY KING GEORGE V. It is suspended from a straight bar ornamented with laurel leaves. Named in seriffed capitals engraved round the rim.

Comments: *This medal replaced the Medal of the Order of the British Empire and was awarded for specific acts of gallantry. It was abolished on the institution of the George Cross in September 1940, while it was announced in the London Gazette of April 22, 1941 that a recipient still living on September 24, 1940 should return it to the Central Chancery of the Orders of Knighthood and become a holder of the George Cross instead. Not all EGMs, however, were exchanged or returned. A total of 130 medals was issued, 64 being civil, 62 military and 4 honorary.*

VALUE:

George V	£3000–3500
George VI	£3000–3500

19. BRITISH EMPIRE MEDAL

Instituted: December 1922.
Ribbon: As above, but without the silver laurel branch.
Metal: Silver.
Size: 36mm.
Description: As above, but with the words MERITORIOUS SERVICE in the exergue. Suspended from a straight bar ornamented with oak leaves. A silver bar decorated with oak leaves was introduced in March 1941 for further acts, and is denoted by a silver rosette on the ribbon worn on its own. An emblem of crossed silver oak leaves was introduced in December 1957 to denote a gallantry award, a smaller version being worn on the ribbon alone. Named in engraved capitals round the rim.
Comments: *Formally entitled the Medal of the Order of the British Empire for Meritorious Service, it is generally known simply as the British Empire Medal. It is awarded for meritorious service by both civil and military personnel. The medal may be worn even if the recipient is promoted to a higher grade of the Order. The gallantry awards, instituted in December 1957, ceased in 1974 on the introduction of the Queen's Gallantry Medal.*

VALUE

	Military	Civil
George V	£140–160	£100–120
George VI GRI cypher	£80–150	£40–80
George VI GVIR cypher	£80–150	£40–80
Elizabeth II	£100–150	£40–80
Elizabeth II with gallantry emblem	£300–600	£200–300

20. THE ORDER OF THE COMPANION OF HONOUR

Instituted: June 1917
Ribbon: 38mm carmine with borders of gold thread.
Metal: Silver gilt.
Size: Height 48mm; max. width 29mm.
Description: An oval badge consisting of a medallion with an oak tree, a shield bearing the royal arms hanging from one branch, and on the left a knight armed and in armour, mounted on a horse. The badge has a blue border with the motto IN ACTION FAITHFUL AND IN HONOUR CLEAR in gold letters. The oval is surmounted by an imperial crown. Gentlemen wear the badge round their necks, while ladies wear it from a bow at the left shoulder.
Comments: Instituted at the same time as the Order of the British Empire, it carries no title or precedence although the post-nominal letters CH are used. The Order consists of the sovereign and one class of members. Not more than 50 men or women who have rendered conspicuous service of national importance were admitted, but in 1943 this was increased to 65. The Order is awarded in Britain and the Commonwealth on a quota basis: UK (45), Australia (7), New Zealand (2), other countries (11). It is awarded for outstanding achievements in the arts, literature, music, science, politics, industry and religion.

VALUE

Gentlemen	£1400–2000
Ladies	£1400–2000

21. THE BARONET'S BADGE

Instituted: 1629

Ribbon: 30mm orange watered silk (Nova Scotia); 44mm orange bordered with narrow blue edges (other Baronets).

Metal: Gold or silver-gilt.

Size: Height 55mm; max. width 41mm(Nova Scotia) or 44mm (later badges).

Description: An upright oval badge with a plain ring suspension. The badge of the Baronets of Nova Scotia was originally skeletal, with a shield bearing the lion rempant of Scotland, decorated with pearls and enamels, surmounted by a Scottish crown and surrounded by a blue border inscribed in gold FAX MENTIS HONESTAE GLORIA. The remaining badges (authorised in 1929) have a solid ground and a central shield with the red hand of Ulster surmounted by a crown and a border of gold and blue enamel decorated with roses (England), shamrocks (Ireland), roses and thistles combined (Great Britain) or roses, thistles and shamrocks combined (United Kingdom). Engraved on the reverse with the recipient's title and date of creation.

Comments: *In an ingenious attempt to raise money without recourse to Parliament, King James I sold grants of land in Nova Scotia. Five years later King Charles I conferred on holders of this land the dignity and rank of Baronets of Nava Scotia, with the title Sir, and decreed that such baronets should wear round their necks "an orange tawny ribbon whereon shall be pendent an escutcheon". After the Union of 1707 Baronets of Scotland properly charged their arms with the badge of Ulster, the red hand, being created Baronets of the United Kingdom. No Baronets of Scotland have been created since 1707, or of Irleand since 1801. Later baronets are of Great Britain, or of the United Kingdom. Badges for the latter were not introduced until 1929, the tercentenary year of the original institution.*

Baronet's badge—United Kingdom

VALUE:	Gold	Silver-gilt
Nova Scotia, 18th–early		
19th centuries	£1500–3000	£500–800
Nova Scotia, late 19th and		
20th centuries	£1400–1600	£400–600
England (rose surround)	£800–1000	£400–600
Ireland (shamrock surround)	£800–1000	£400–600
Great Britain (roses and thistles)	£800–1000	£400–600
United Kingdom (roses, thistles and		
shamrocks)	£800–1000	£400–600

22. THE KNIGHT BACHELOR'S BADGE

Instituted: 1929.

Ribbon: 38mm scarlet with broad yellow borders.

Metal: Silver-gilt and enamels.

Size: Height 81mm; max. width 60mm. Reduced in 1933 and 1974.

Description: An upright oval medallion enclosed by a scroll, bearing a cross-hilted sword, belted and sheathed, pommel upwards, between two spurs, rowels upwards, the whole set about with the sword-belt.

Comments: *The title Knight Bachelor (KB) was introduced by King Henry III to signify that the title would die with the holder, and not be transmited to the holder's heir. The badge was authorised by King George V at the same time as the Baronet's Badge, in response to a request from the Imperial Society of Knights Bachelors who wished to have a distinctive badge denoting their rank. The original badge was of the dimensions given above and affixed to the breast by means of a pin on the reverse. This badge was reduced in size in 1933 and again in 1974 when it was fitted with a ring for suspension by a ribbon round the neck.*

Knight Bachelor's badge

VALUE:	
First type (1929)	£160–200
Smaller type (1933)	£140–180
Neck badge (1974)	£180–220

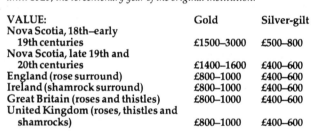

23. THE ORDER OF ST JOHN OF JERUSALEM

Instituted: May 14, 1888.
Ribbon: Plain black watered silk.
Metal: Gold, silver-gilt and silver, or base metal.
Sash Badge: An eight-pointed Maltese cross in white enamel with two lions and two unicorns in the angles in gold (Grand Cross), silver-gilt (Knights of Justice) or silver (Knights of Grace).
Neck Badge: Worn by Commanders (Brothers) are somewhat smaller than the above, and those worn by Commanders (Sisters) are smaller still.
Star: The eight-pointed Maltese cross in white enamel without the lions and unicorns (Grand Cross and Justice) or with lions and unicorns (Grace).
Breast Badge: Worn by Officers (Brothers) from a ribbon and ring suspension, it was originally an eight-pointed Maltese cross of plain silver (1926–39). Those worn from the shoulder bow by Officers (Sisters) are invariably enamelled. Those worn by Serving Brothers and sisters were later (1939–47) circular skeletal badges with a ring suspension and the eight-pointed cross set in a silver rim. Since 1947 the circular badge has the cross in white enamel on a black-enamelled background set in a silver rim.
Donats' Medals: Gold, silver or medal, consisting of the badge of the Order with the upper arm of the cross replaced by an ornamental piece of metal for suspension.
Comments: *The Most Venerable Order of St John of Jerusalem is of great antiquity, dating from the eleventh century and originally the Knights Hospitallers of Jerusalem who subsequently moved to Rhodes, then Malta and are now based, as the Sovereign Order, in Rome with branches in many countries. The British branch was incorporated by Queen Victoria under Royal Charter in 1888 and granted the epithet Venerable in 1926, at which time it was reorganised into five Classes like certain other Orders. Both men and women are eligible for membership. Her Majesty the Queen is the Sovereign Head of the Order. Next in authority is the Grand Prior. Apart from the mantle of black velvet worn on special occasions, the Grand Prior wears the cross as a neck badge. Bailiffs Grand Cross and Dames Grand Cross wear the badge from a riband over the right shoulder, together with a breast star. Knights and Dames of Justice and Knights and Dames of Grace wear neck or shoulder badges and breast stars of various sizes and qualities, Commanders (Brothers) wear a neck badge and Commanders (Sisters) a shoulder badge, Officers wear a breast or shoulder badge, and Serving Brothers and sisters wear a circular medal. Associates are non-British subjects or non-Christians who have rendered conspicuous service to the Order and may be attached to any grade of the Order. They wear the insignia of that grade, originally distinguished only by a central narrow white stripe on the ribbon, but now all ribbons are identical. Donats are people who have made generous contributions to the funds of the Order. They are not enrolled as members of the Order but receive medals in gold, silver or bronze.*

VALUE:

	Gold	Silver/Gilt	Bronze
Bailiff badge and star	£1500–2200	£800–1000	—
Dame Grand Cross	£1500–2000	£500–600	—
Knight of Justice			
neck badge and star	£800–900	£250–350	£150–250
Dame of Justice			
shoulder badge and star	£800–900	£250–350	£200–300
Knight of Grace			
neck badge and star	—	£250–350	£150–250
Dame of Grace			
shoulder badge and star	—	£250–350	£150–250
Commander (Brother) neck badge	—	£150–200	£80–100
Commander (Sister) shoulder badge	—	£40–60	£30–50
Officer breast badge, plain silver	—	£40–40	—
Office breast badge, enamelled	—	£40–60	£30–50
Officer (Sister) enamelled badge	—	£40–60	£30–50
Serving Brother/Sister 1926–39	—	£50–60	£30-50
Serving Brother/Sister 1939–47	—	£40–50	£40–60
Serving Brother/Sister 1947–	—	—	£30–50
Donat's medals	£80–100	£40–50	£30–40

DECORATIONS

The award of decorations for distinguished military service is an ancient institution. In his *Antiquities of the Jews*, the historian Josephus relates that, in the third century BC, King Alexander was so pleased with Jonathan the High Priest that he sent him a gold button as a mark of favour for his skill in leading the Jews in battle. Subsequently Jonathan was presented with a second gold button for his gallant conduct in the field, making these incidents among the earliest recorded for which specific military awards were granted. The award of jewels, gold buttons and badges for valour was carried on in most European countries on a sporadic basis but the present system of decorations is essentially a modern one dating back no farther than the middle of the seventeenth century. Earlier medals were quasi-commemorative and include the famous Armada Medal of 1588. A few medals in silver or gold were awarded to officers for distinguished service during the English Civil War, although the first "official" rewards in Britain were probably those issued by Parliament to naval officers following their victories over the Dutch fleet in 1653.

Decorations may be divided into those awarded for individual acts of heroism and those conferred in recognition of distinguished military, political or social service. In general terms collectors prefer a decoration awarded for bravery in the field rather than a political honour given automatically to a civil servant, just because he happens to have been in a particular grade for a certain number of years. The debasement of civil awards, such as the OBE and MBE, is reflected in the relative lack of interest shown by collectors.

It is generally true to say that military decorations are more desirable, but it is important to note that one decoration may be more highly prized than another, while the same decoration may well be more valuable to collectors when issued in one period rather than in another. At one extreme is the greatly coveted Victoria Cross, only 1354 of which (including three bars) have been awarded since its inception. VCs won during the Crimean War (111 awarded) are usuallyless highly regarded than Crosses awarded during the First World War, where, although numerically greater (633) they were far more dearly won. Second World War Crosses are correspondingly more expensive as only 182 were awarded and even now comparatively few of them have ever come on to the market. Today, while pre-1914 Crosses would rate at least £10,000 and those from the First World War slightly more, Second World War Crosses start around £20,000 but have been known to fetch several times as much, depending on the precise circumstances and the branch of the services.

At the other extreme is the Military Medal, of which no fewer than 115,589 were awarded during the First World War alone. For this reason a MM from this period can still be picked up for under £100, whereas one from the Second World War would usually fetch about four times as much, and awards made during the minor campaigns of the 1930s or the Korean War often rate at least ten times as much.

The value of a decoration, where its provenance can be unquestionably established, depends largely on the decoration itself, whether awarded to an officer or an enlisted man, the individual circumstances of the award, the campaign or action concerned, the regiment, unit or ship involved, and the often very personal details of the act or acts of bravery. These factors are extraordinarily difficult to quantify, hence the frequent large discrepancies in the prices fetched by decorations at auction.

The addition of even relatively common decorations, such as the Military Cross or the Military Medal to the average First World War campaign medal group, invariably enhances its value very considerably while the addition of bars for subsequent awards likewise rates a good premium. Decorations awarded to officers tend to fetch more than those awarded to other ranks, mainly because they are proportionately rarer but also because it is usually easier to trace the career details of an officer.

Sometimes the rank of the recipient may have a bearing on the demand for a particular decoration: e.g. Military Crosses awarded to warrant officers are scarcer than those awarded to subalterns and captains. The branch of the armed services may also have some bearing. Thus a Military Medal awarded to a member of the RAF rates far higher than one awarded to a soldier, while a medal awarded to a seaman in one of the naval battalions which fought on the Western Front is also equally desirable.

Initially the Distinguished Service Order could be won by commissioned officers of any rank but after 1914, when the Military Cross was instituted, it was usually restricted to officers of field rank. DSOs awarded to lieutenants and captains in the Army in both World Wars are therefore comparatively rare and invariably expensive, usually as they were awarded for acts of heroism which in earlier campaigns might have merited the VC.

The opportunity for individual acts of bravery varied from service to service, and in different conflicts. Thus sailors in the Second World War generally had less scope than air crew. Consequently specifically naval awards, such as the Conspicuous Gallantry Medal and the Distinguished Service Cross, are much more scarce than the corresponding RAF awards for Conspicuous Gallantry and the Distinguished Flying Cross.

The addition of bars to gallantry decorations greatly enhances the scarcity and value of such medals. The VC, for example, has been won by only three men on two occasions; none of these VC and bar combinations has ever come on the market, but should one come up for sale, it is certain that the price would be spectacular. The average First World War MM is today worth around £60, but with a bar for second award its value immediately jumps to about three times as much, while MMs with two or more bars are very much more expensive.

It is important to note that in some cases (the DSO for example) decorations were issued unnamed; for this reason the citation or any other supporting documents relevant to the award should be kept with the decoration wherever possible to confirm its attribution.

Condition

The same terms are applied to describe the condition of medals and decorations as apply to coins, although the wear to which they are put is caused by other factors. In modern times, when the number of occasions on which medals are worn are relatively few and far between, the condition of most items will be found to be Very Fine (VF) to Extremely Fine (EF). Indeed, in many cases, the medals may never have been worn at all. A good proportion of Second World War medals and decorations are found in almost mint condition as they were not issued till long after the war, by which time their recipients had been demobilised. In some cases they even turn up still in the original cardboard box in which they were posted to the recipients or their next-of-kin.

Before the First World War, however, the wearing of medals was customary on all but the most informal occasions and when actually serving on active duty. Thus medals could be, and often were, subject to a great deal of wear. Medals worn by cavalrymen are often found in poor condition, with scratches and edge knocks occasioned by the constant jangling of one medal against another while on horseback. Often the medals in a group have an abrasive effect on each other. For this reason the Queen's Medal for Egypt (1882) is comparatively rare in excellent condition, as it was usually worn in juxtaposition to the bronze Khedive's Star whose points were capable of doing considerable damage to its silver companion. Apart from these factors it should also be remembered that part of the ritual of 'spit and polish' involved cleaning one's medals and they were therefore submitted to vigorous cleaning with metal polish over long periods of service.

For these reasons medals are often sold by dealers "as worn"—a euphemism which conceals a lifetime of hardy service on the chest of some grizzled veteran. Because of the strong personal element involved in medal-collecting, however, genuine wear does not affect the value of a medal to the same degree that it would in other branches of numismatics. There is a school of thought which considers that such signs enhance the interest and value of a medal or group.

This line of thinking also explains the controversy over medal ribbons. Some military outfitters still carry extensive stocks of medal ribbons covering every campaign from Waterloo onwards, so that it is a very easy matter to obtain a fresh length of ribbon for any medal requiring it, and there is no doubt that the appearance of a piece is greatly improved by a clean, bright new ribbon. On the other hand, that ribbon was not the one actually worn by Corporal Bloggs on parade and, to the purist, it would spoil the total effect of the medal. Some collectors therefore retain the original ribbon, even though it may be faded and frayed. As ribbons are things which one cannot authenticate, however, there seems to be little material benefit to be gained from clinging rigidly to a tattered strip of silk when an identical piece can be obtained relatively cheaply. In reality, most collectors compromise by obtaining new ribbons while preserving the old lengths out of sentiment.

Pricing

The prices quoted are *average* figures for medals and decorations as individual items. Combinations with other decorations and campaign medals will produce a value usually well in excess of the aggregate of the individual items. Value will depend to a large extent on the personal factors and circumstances of the award, but where general factors are involved (e.g. the design of the medal, the period of issue or the campaign concerned, or in some cases the branch of the services) these are itemised separately. "—" indicates that no examples have come onto the market. The figure in brackets (where available) is the *approximate* number awarded.

In the lists which follow, it should be assumed that decorations were instituted by Royal Warrant, unless otherwise stated.

24. VICTORIA CROSS

DRIVER F.LUKE
37ᵀᴴ BATTERY R.F.A

Instituted: January 1856.
Ribbon: Crimson. Originally naval crosses used a blue ribbon, but since 1918 the crimson (Army) ribbon has been used for all awards. A miniature cross emblem is worn on the ribbon alone in undress uniform.
Metal: Bronze, originally from Russian guns captured in the Crimea. Modern research, however, reveals that guns captured in other conflicts, e.g. China, have also been used at various periods.
Size: Height 41mm; max. width 36mm.
Description: A cross pattée. (Obverse) a lion statant gardant on the royal crown, with the words FOR VALOUR on a semi-circular scroll. (Reverse) a circular panel on which is engraved the date of the act for which the decoration was awarded. The Cross is suspended by a ring from a seriffed "V" attached to a suspension bar decorated with laurel leaves. The reverse of the suspension bar is engraved with the name, rank and ship, regiment or squadron of the recipient.
Comments: *Introduced as the premier award for gallantry, available for all ranks, to cover all actions since the outbreak of the Crimean War in 1854, it was allegedly created on the suggestion of Prince Albert, the Prince Consort. Of the 1354 awards since 1856, 832 have gone to the Army, 107 to the Navy, 31 to the RAF, ten to the Royal Marines and four to civilians. Second award bars have been awarded three times. The facility for posthumous awards, made retrospective to 1856, began in 1902 and was confirmed in 1907, while the early practice of forfeitures (eight between 1863 and 1908) was discontinued after the First World War.*

VALUE:

	Royal Navy	Army	RFC/RAF
1856–1914 (522)	£15,000–20,000	£10,000–15,000	—
1914–18 (633)	£15,000–25,000	£10,000–20,000	£80,000–120,000
1920–45 (187)	£30,000–40,000	£20,000–30,000	£40,000–60,000
post-1945 (12)	—	From £50,000	—

NB These prices can only be construed as a general guide. Quite a few awards would exceed these price ranges, particularly Commonwealth examples or those appertaining to well known actions.

25. NEW ZEALAND CROSS

Instituted: 10 March 1869 (by an Order in Council, Wellington).
Ribbon: 38mm crimson.
Metal: Silver with gold appliqué.
Size: Height 52mm; max. width 32mm.
Description: A silver cross pattée with a six-pointed gold star on each limb. In the centre are the words NEW ZEALAND within a gold laurel wreath. The cross is surmounted by a gold Tudor crown which is attached by a ring and a seriffed "V" to a silver bar ornamented with gold laurel leaves, through which the ribbon passes. The recipient's name and details are engraved on the reverse.
Comments: *The rarest of all gallantry awards, it was conferred for bravery during the second series of Maori Wars (1860-72). Only 23 Crosses were awarded, the last being authorised in 1910. This medal was called into being solely because local volunteer forces were not eligible for the VC. Replicas of the Cross have been authorised by the New Zealand government.*

VALUE: £15,000–20,000

26. GEORGE CROSS

Instituted: 24 September 1940.

Ribbon: 38mm dark blue. A silver miniature cross emblem is worn on the ribbon alone.

Metal: Silver.

Size: Height 48mm; max. width 45mm.

Description: A plain bordered cross with a circular medallion in the centre depicting the effigy of St George and the Dragon after Benedetto Pistrucci, surrounded by the words FOR GALLANTRY. In the angle of each limb is the Royal cypher GVI. The plain reverse bears in the centre the name of the recipient and date of the award. The Cross hangs by a ring from a silver bar adorned with laurel leaves.

Comments: *The highest gallantry award for civilians, as well as for members of the armed forces in actions for which purely military honours would not normally be granted. It superseded the Empire Gallantry Medal whose holders were then required to return it and receive the GC in exchange. By Warrant of December 1971 suviving recipients of the Albert and Edward Medals were also invited to exchange their awards for the GC—a move which created a controversy which is still continuing, particularly among those who received the Albert Medal. Perhaps the most famous Cross was that conferred on the island of Malta in recognition of its gallantry during the Second World War. Apart from exchange awards, between 1940 and 1947 the GC was awarded to 102 men and four women; since 1947 a further 40 awards have been made. To date no second award bars have been awarded.*

VALUE:

Service awards 1940 to date	£4000–6000
Civilian awards 1940 to date	£2500–3500
Service exchange pre-1940	£2500–3000
Civilian exchange pre-1940	£1500–2000

27. DISTINGUISHED SERVICE ORDER

Instituted: 1886.

Ribbon: 29mm crimson with dark blue edges.

Metal: Originally gold; silver-gilt (since 1889).

Size: Height 44mm; max. width 41.5mm.

Description: A cross with curved ends, overlaid with white enamel. (Obverse) a green enamel laurel wreath enclosing an imperial crown; (reverse) the royal monogram within a similar wreath. It is suspended from its ribbon by a swivel ring and a straight laureated bar. Additional awards are denoted by bars ornamented by a crown. Silver rosettes on the ribbon alone are worn in undress uniform. Since its inception, the DSO has been issued unnamed, but since 1938 the year of award has been engraved on the reverse of the lower suspension bar as well as the reverse of the bars for second or subsequent awards.

Comments: *Intended to reward commissioned officers below field rank for distinguished service in time of war, and for which the VC would not be appropriate. Previously the CB had sometimes been awarded to junior officers, although intended mainly for those of field rank. It was also available to officers in both the other armed services. In September 1942 the regulations were relaxed to permit award of the DSO to officers of the Merchant Navy who performed acts of gallantry in the presence of the enemy. As a result of the recent changes to the operational gallantry award system (see page 16), the DSO will now be awarded for "Leadership" only (it will not be awarded posthumously). It has been replaced by the Conspicuous Gallantry Cross as the reward for gallantry—full details of this new award are still awaited.*

VALUE:

	Unnamed single	Attributable group
Victoria, gold (153)	£1200–1500	£2000–3000
Victoria, silver-gilt (1170)	£500–700	£800–1500
Edward VII (78)	£700–900	£1800–2200
George V (9900)	£350–400	£500–700
George VI 1st type 1938–48 (4880)	£450–550	£800–1200
George VI 2nd type 1948–52 (63)	£800–1200	£2500–3000
Elizabeth II (110)	£600º800	£2500–4000

28. IMPERIAL SERVICE ORDER

Instituted: August 1902.

Ribbon: 38mm three equal sections of blue, crimson and blue.

Metal: Silver with gold overlay.

Size: Height 61mm; max. width 55mm.

Description: The badge consists of a circular gold plaque bearing the royal cypher and surrounded by the words FOR FAITHFUL SERVICE. This plaque is then superimposed on a seven-pointed silver star surmounted by a crown and ring for suspension. The badge of the ISO awarded to women is similar but has a laurel wreath instead of the star-shaped base.

Comments: *Instituted by King Edward VII as a means of rewarding long and faithful service in the lower echelons of the Civil Service at home and overseas. Women were admitted to the order in 1908. The order was generally awarded automatically after 25 years service at home, 20 years and 6 months (India) and 16 years in the tropics, but in exceptional cases awards were made for "eminently meritorious service" irrespective of qualifiying period.*

VALUE:			
	Edward VII	Gentleman	£100–120
		Lady	£200–300
	George V	Gentleman	£90–110
		Lady	£180–220
	George VI	Gentleman	£100–120
		Lady	£180–220
	Elizabeth II	Gentleman	£120–150
		Lady	£150–180

29. IMPERIAL SERVICE MEDAL

Instituted: August 1902.

Ribbon: Same as above.

Metal: Silver and bronze.

Description: Originally similar to the ISO but with a silver plaque and bronze star or wreath. In 1920 the ISM was transformed into a circular medal of silver with the sovereign's effigy on the obverse and a reverse depicting a naked man resting from his labours, with FOR FAITHFUL SERVICE in the exergue.

Comments: *Instituted at the same time as the ISO but intended for junior grades of the Civil Service.*

VALUE:		
	Edward VII Gentleman	£40–50
	Lady	£110–130
	George V Star (Gentlemen)	£30–40
	George V Wreath (Ladies)	£80–120
	George V Circular type	£8–12
	George VI	£8–12
	Elizabeth II	£8–12

30. INDIAN ORDER OF MERIT

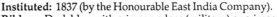

Instituted: 1837 (by the Honourable East India Company).

Ribbon: Dark blue with crimson edges (military) or crimson with dark blue edges (civil).

Metal: Silver and gold.

Size: Height 41mm; max. width 40mm.

Description: An eight-pointed star with a circular centre surrounded by a laurel wreath and containing crossed sabres and the relevant inscription. The star is suspended by a curvilinear suspension bar. The different classes were denoted by the composition of the star, noted below.

Comments: *The oldest gallantry award of the British Empire, it was founded in 1837 by the Honourable East India Company. Twenty years later it became an official British award when the administration of India passed to the Crown after the Sepoy Mutiny. Originally known simply as the Order of Merit, it was renamed in 1902 following the introduction of the prestigious British order of that name. There were three classes of the order, promotion from one class to the next being the reward for further acts of bravery. A civil division (also in three classes) was introduced in 1902. Ten years later the military division was reduced to two classes, when troops of the Indian Army became eligible for the VC. The civil division became a single class in 1939 and the military in 1945. Both divisions came to an end with the British Raj in 1947.*

VALUE:

Military Division

1837-1912 Reward of Valor	
1st class in gold (42)	£1400–1600
2nd class in silver and gold (130)	£400–500
3rd class in silver (2740)	£100–150
1912-1939 Reward of Valor	
1st class in silver and gold (26)	£400–500
2nd class in silver (1215)	£100–150
1939-1944 Reward for Gallantry	
1st class in silver and gold (2)	Rare
2nd class in silver (332)	£180–220
1945-1947 Reward for Gallantry (44mm diameter)	Rare

Civil Division

1902-1939 For Bravery (35mm diameter)	
1st class in gold (0)	—
2nd class in silver and gold (0)	—
3rd class in silver (39)	£600–800
1939-1947 For Bravery (26mm diameter)	
Single class (10)	Rare

NB These prices represent unattributable pieces. Values can climb rapidly when in company with related campaign medals, particularly for the Victorian era.

31. ROYAL RED CROSS

Instituted: 27 April 1883.
Ribbon: 25mm dark blue edged with crimson, in a bow.
Metal: Gold (later silver-gilt) and silver.
Size: Height 41mm; max. width 35mm.
Description: (Obverse) The *1st class* badge was originally a gold cross pattée, enamelled red with gold edges, but from 1889 silver-gilt was substituted for gold. At the centre was a crowned and veiled portrait, with the words FAITH, HOPE and CHARITY inscribed on three arms, and the date 1883 on the lower arm. Subsequently the effigy of the reigning monarch was substituted for the allegorical profile; (reverse) crowned royal cypher. *2nd Class:* in silver, design as the 1st class but the inscriptions on the arms appear on the reverse. Awards from 1938 have the year of issue engraved on the reverse of the lower arm.
Comments: *This decoration had the distinction of being confined to females until 1976. It is conferred on members of the nursing services regardless of rank. A second class award was introduced in November 1915. Bars for the first class were introduced in 1917. Holders of the second class are promoted to the first class on second awards. Holders of the first class decoration are known as Members (RRC) while recipients of the second class are Associates (ARRC).*

VALUE:

	First class (RRC)	Second class (ARRC)
Victoria, gold	£800–1000	—
Victoria, silver-gilt	£400–500	—
Edward VII	£500–550	—
George V	£100–150	£40–50
George V, with bar	£300–350	—
George VI GRI	£150–200	£80–100
George VI GVIR	£200–300	£150–180
Elizabeth II	£200–250	£100–150

32. DISTINGUISHED SERVICE CROSS

Instituted: June 1901.
Ribbon: 36mm three equal parts of dark blue, white and dark blue.
Metal: Silver.
Size: Height 43mm; max. width 43mm.
Description: A plain cross with rounded ends. (Obverse) crowned royal cypher in the centre, suspended by a ring; (reverse) plain apart from the hallmark. From 1940 onwards the year of issue was engraved on the reverse of the lower limb.
Comments: *Known as the Conspicuous Service Cross when instituted, it was awarded to warrant and subordinate officers of the Royal Navy who were ineligible for the DSO. In October 1914 it was renamed the Distinguished Service Cross and thrown open to all naval officers below the rank of lieutenant-commander. Bars for second awards were authorised in 1916 and in 1931 eligibility for the award was enlarged to include officers of the Merchant Navy. In 1940 Army and RAF officers serving aboard naval vessels also became eligible for the award. Since 1945 fewer than 100 DSCs have been awarded. As a result of the recent changes to the operational gallantry award system (see page 16), this award is now available to both officers and other ranks, the DSM having been discontinued.*

VALUE:

	Unnamed single	Attributable group
Edward VII	Rare	£5000–7000
George V	£250–300	£400–500
George VI GRI	£300–350	£400–600
George VI GVIR	Rare	£2000–2500
Elizabeth II	Rare	£2000–3000

33. MILITARY CROSS

Instituted: 31 December 1914.
Ribbon: 38mm three equal bars of white, deep purple and white.
Metal: Silver.
Size: Height 46mm; max. width 44mm.
Description: An ornamental cross with straight arms terminating in broad finals decorated with imperial crowns. The royal cypher appears at the centre and the cross is suspended from a plain silver suspension bar.
Comments: *There was no gallantry award, lesser than the VC and DSO, for junior Army officers and warrant officers until shortly after the outbreak of the First World War when the MC was instituted. Originally awarded to captains, lieutenants and warrant officers of the Army (including RFC), it was subsequently extended to include equivalent ranks of the RAF when performing acts of bravery on the ground and there was even provision for the Royal Naval Division and the Royal Marines during the First World War. Awards were extended to majors by an amending warrant of 1931. Bars for second and subsequent awards have a crown at the centre. The MC is always issued unnamed, although since about 1938 the reverse of the cross or bar is officially dated with the year of issue. As a result of the recent changes to the operational gallantry award system (see page 16), this award is now available to both officers and other ranks, the Military Medal having been discontinued.*

VALUE:	Unnamed single	Attributable group
George V 1914-1920 (37,000)	£150–180	£250–300
George V 1914-1920 one bar (3000)	£200–220	£400–600
George V 1914-1920 two bars (170)	£250–300	£1800–2000
George V 1914-1920 three bars (4)	—	—
George V 1921-1936 (350)	—	£400–800
George V 1921-1936 one bar (31)	—	£800–1200
George VI GRI 1939-1945 (11,000)	£220–250	£400–500
George VI GRI one bar (500)	£350–400	£600–800
George VI GVIR (158)	Rare	£1500–2000
Elizabeth II	Rare	£2000–3000
Elizabeth II one bar	Rare	Rare

34. DISTINGUISHED FLYING CROSS

Instituted: June 1918.
Ribbon: 30mm diagonal alternate stripes of white and deep purple.
Metal: Silver.
Size: Height 60mm; max. width 54mm.
Description: (Obverse) a cross flory terminating with a rose, surmounted by another cross made of propeller blades charged in the centre with a roundel within a laurel wreath. The horizontal arms bear wings and the crowned RAF monogram at the centre; (reverse) the royal cypher above the date 1918. The cross is suspended from a bar decorated with a sprig of laurel.
Comments: *Established for officers and warrant officers of the RAF in respect of acts of valour while flying in active operations against the enemy. The DFC is issued unnamed, but Second World War crosses usually have the year of issue engraved on the reverse of the lower limb. As a result of the recent changes to the operational gallantry award system (see page 16), this award is now available to both officers and other ranks, the Distinguished Flying Medal having been discontinued.*

VALUE:	Unnamed single	Attributable group
George V 1918-20 (1100)	£400–500	£700–900
George V 1918-20 one bar (70)	£500–600	£1000–1500
George V 1918-20 two bars (3)	—	Rare
George V 1920-36 (130)	—	£800–1000
George V 1920-36 one bar (20)	—	£1400–1800
George V 1920-36 two bars (4)	—	Rare
George VI GRI 1939-45 (20,000)	£350–420	£500–2500
George VI 1939-45 one bar (1550)	£450–520	£650–3500
George VI 1939-45 two bars (42)	—	£1600–5000
George VI GVIR 1948-52 (401)	Rare	£800–2000
Elizabeth II (260)	Rare	£1200–3000

35. AIR FORCE CROSS

Instituted: June 1918.

Ribbon: 30mm originally horizontal but since June 1919 diagonal alternate stripes of white and crimson.

Metal: Silver.

Size: eight 60mm; max. width 54mm.

Description: (Obverse) the cross consists of a thunderbolt, the arms conjoined by wings, base bar terminating in a bomb, surmounted by another cross of aeroplane propellers, the finials inscribed with the royal cypher. A central roundel depicts Hermes mounted on a hawk bestowing a wreath; (reverse) the royal cypher and the date 1918.

Comments: *This decoration, for officers and warrant officers of the RAF performing acts of valour while flying, though not on active operations against the enemy, was instituted in June 1918.*

VALUE:

	Unnamed single	Attributable group
George V 1918-20 (680)	£400–450	£600–700
George V 1918-20 one bar (12)	—	£1000–1200
George V 1918-20 two bars (3)	—	Rare
George V 1920-36 (160)	—	£700–800
George VI GRI (2000)	£350–400	£500–600
George VI one bar (26)	£450–500	£1000–1200
George VI two bars (1)	—	—
George VI GVIR (980)	£500–600	£800–1000
Elizabeth II	£500–600	£800–1000

36. ORDER OF BRITISH INDIA

Instituted: 1837 by the Honourable East India Company.

Ribbon: Worn around the neck, the base colour of the ribbon was originally sky blue but this was altered to crimson in 1838, allegedly because the hair oil favoured by Indians of all classes would soon have soiled a light ribbon. From 1939 onwards the first class ribbon had two thin vertical lines of light blue at the centre, while the second class ribbon had a single vertical line. Originally these distinctive ribbons were only worn in undress uniform (without the insignia itself), but from 1945 they replaced the plain crimson ribbons when worn with the decoration.

Metal: Gold.

Size: Height 42mm; max. width 38mm.

Description: The first class badge consists of a gold star with a crown between the upper two points and a blue enamelled centre bearing a lion surrounded by the words ORDER OF BRITISH INDIA enclosed in a laurel wreath. The second class badge is smaller, with dark blue enamel in the centre and with no crown.

Comments: *Intended for long and faithful service by native officers of the Indian Army, it was thrown open in 1939 to officers of the armed forces, frontier guards, military police and officers of the Indian native states. There were two classes, promotion to the first being made from the second. Recipients of both classes were entitled to the letters OBI after their names, but holders of the first class had the rank of Sardar Bahadur, while those of the second were merely Bahadur. A few awards were made by Pakistan to British officers seconded to the Pakistani forces at the time of independence.*

VALUE:

1st class, light blue centre and dark blue surround	£400–500
1st class, dark blue centre and light surround (1939)	£400–450
2nd class	£300–350

NB The prices quoted are for unattributable awards.

37. ORDER OF BURMA

Instituted 1940.
Ribbon: 38mm dark green with light blue edges.
Metal: Gold.
Size: Height 52mm; max. width 38mm.
Description: The badge consists of a gold-rayed circle with a central roundel charged with a peacock in his pride azure, surmounted by an imperial crown.
Comments: *Instituted by King George VI, three years after Burma became independent of British India. Only 24 awards were made, to Governor's Commissioned Officers for long, faithful and honourable service in the army, frontier force and military police of Burma. By an amendment of 1945 the order could also be awarded for individual acts of heroism or particularly meritorious service. It was abolished in 1947.*

VALUE: Rare

38. KAISAR-I-HIND MEDAL

Instituted: May 1900.
Ribbon: 37mm bluish green.
Metal: Gold, silver or bronze.
Size: Height 61mm; max. width 34mm.
Description: An oval badge surmounted by the imperial crown. (Obverse) the royal cypher set within a wreath; (reverse) FOR PUBLIC SERVICE IN INDIA round the edge and KAISAR-I-HIND (Emperor of India) on a scroll across the centre against a floral background.
Comments: *Queen Victoria founded this medal for award to those, regardless of colour, creed or sex, who had performed public service in India. Originally in two classes George V introduced a 3rd Class in bronze. The medals were originally large and hollow but were changed to smaller in diameter and solid during the reign of George V.*

VALUE:

	1st class (gold)	2nd class (silver)	3rd class (bronze)
Victoria	£600–700	£200–250	–
Edward VII	£600–650	£180–220	–
George V 1st	£500–600	£150–180	–
George V 2nd	£450–500	£100–120	£80–100
George VI	£500–600	£100–120	£80–100

39. ALBERT MEDAL

Instituted: 7 March 1866.

Ribbons: Originally 16mm blue with two white stripes (gold 1st class), changed on introduction of the 2nd class to 35mm blue with four white stripes. The 2nd class remained 16mm blue with two white stripes until 1904 when it was changed to 35mm blue with two white stripes. For the gold 1st class medal the ribbon was 35mm crimson with four white stripes, that for the 2nd class originally 16mm crimson with two white stripes, changing in 1904 to a 35mm ribbon.

Metal: Gold (early issues gold and bronze); bronze.

Size: Height 57mm; max. width 30mm.

Description: The badge consists of an oval enclosing the entwined initials V and A. The sea medals have, in addition, an anchor. The oval is enclosed by a bronze garter with the words FOR GALLANTRY IN SAVING LIFE, with AT SEA or ON LAND as appropriate, and enamelled in blue or crimson respectively. The whole is surmounted by a crown pierced by a ring for suspension. The first class medal was originally worked in gold and bronze and later in gold alone, the second class in bronze alone.

Comments: *Named in memory of the Prince Consort who died in 1861, this series of medals was instituted for gallantry in saving life at sea. An amendment of 1867 created two classes of medal and ten years later awards were extended to gallantry in saving life on land. In 1917 the title of the awards was altered, the first class becoming the Albert Medal in Gold and the second class merely the Albert Medal. In 1949 the Medal in Gold was abolished and replaced by the George Cross and henceforward the Albert Medal (second class) was only awarded posthumously. In 1971 the award of the medal ceased and holders were invited to exchange their medals for the George Cross.*

VALUE:

	Civilian	Service
Gold Sea (25)	£3500–4500	£4500–5500
Bronze Sea (216)	£2200–2500	£2500–3000
Gold Land (45)	£2500–3000	£3000–4000
Bronze Land (282)	£1600–2000	£2000–2500

40. UNION OF SOUTH AFRICA QUEEN'S MEDAL FOR BRAVERY (WOLTEMADE MEDAL)

Instituted: 1939 by the Government of the Union of South Africa.

Ribbon: Royal blue with narrow orange edges.

Metal: Gold or silver.

Size: 37mm.

Description: (Obverse) an effigy of the reigning sovereign; (reverse) a celebrated act of heroism by Wolraad Woltemade who rescued sailors from the wreck of the East Indiaman *De Jong Thomas* which ran aground in Table Bay on 17 June 1773. Seven times Woltemade rode into the raging surf to save fourteen seamen from drowning, but on the eighth attempt both rider and horse perished.

Comments: *This medal was awarded to citizens of the Union of South Africa and dependent territories who endangered their lives in saving the lives of others. It was awarded very sparingly, in gold or silver.*

VALUE:

George VI Gold (1)	—
George VI Silver (34)	Rare
Elizabeth II Silver (1)	—

41. DISTINGUISHED CONDUCT MEDAL

Instituted: 1854.

Ribbon: 32mm crimson with a dark blue central stripe.

Metal: Silver.

Size: 36mm.

Description: (Obverse) originally a trophy of arms but, since 1902, the effigy of the reigning sovereign; (reverse) a four-line inscription across the field FOR DISTINGUISHED CONDUCT IN THE FIELD.

Comments: *The need for a gallantry medal for other ranks was first recognised during the Crimean War, although previously the Meritorious Service Medal (qv) had very occasionally been awarded for gallantry in the field. The medals have always been issued named, and carry the number, rank and name of the recipient on the rim, together with the date of the act of gallantry from 1881 until about 1901. Bars are given for subsequent awards and these too were dated from the first issued in 1881 until 1916 when the more usual laurelled bars were adopted. Since 1916 it has ranked as a superior decoration to the Military Medal. As a result of the recent changes to the operational gallantry award system (see page 16), the decoration has been replaced by the Conspicuous Gallantry Cross—full details of this new award are still awaited.*

VALUE:

Crimea (800)	£600–4000
Indian Mutiny (17)	£5500–7000
India general service 1854-95	£1500–3000
Abyssinia 1867-8 (7)	£2000–3000
Ashantee 1873-4 (33)	£1800–2000
Zulu War 1877-9 (16)	£3000–5000
Afghanistan 1878-80 (61)	£1800–2500
First Boer War 1880-1 (20)	£2500–3000
Egypt & Sudan 1882-9 (134)	£2500–3000
India 1895-1901	£1500–2200
Sudan 1896-7	£1500–4000
Second Boer War 1899-1902 (2090)	£450–750
Boxer Rebellion 1900	£3000–7000
Edward VII	Many rarities
George V 1st type (25,000)	£280–1000
George V 2nd type 1930-7 (14)	£800–2000
George VI, IND IMP 1937-47	£800–2000
George VI, 2nd type 1948-52 (25)	£1500–3000
Elizabeth II, BR: OMN:	£2500–4000
Elizabeth II, DEI GRATIA	£2500–6000

42. DISTINGUISHED CONDUCT MEDAL (DOMINION & COLONIAL)

Instituted: 31 May 1895.

Ribbon: 32mm crimson with a dark blue central stripe.

Metal: Silver.

Size: 36mm.

Description: As above, but the reverse bears the name of the issuing country or colony round the top.

Comments: *A separate DCM for warrant officers, NCOs and men of the colonial forces. Medals were struck for the Cape of Good Hope, New Zealand, New South Wales, Queensland, Tasmania, Natal and Canada, but only the last two actually issued them and the others are known only as specimens.*

VALUE:

Victoria Canada (1)	Rare
Victoria Natal (1)	Rare
Edward VII Natal (9)	Rare

43. DISTINGUISHED CONDUCT MEDAL (KAR & WAFF)

Instituted: early 1900s.
Ribbon: As above.
Metal: Silver.
Size: 3mm
Description: As no. 40, with either King's African Rifles or West Africa Frontier Force around the top of the reverse.
Comments: *Separate awards for gallantry were instituted in respect of the King's African Rifles (East Africa) and the West Africa Frontier Force (Nigeria, Sierra Leone, Gambia and the Gold Coast). These were issued until 1942 when they were superseded by the British DCM.*

VALUE:	Attributable groups
Edward VII KAR (2)	—
Edward VII WAFF (55)	Rare
George V KAR (190)	£300–450
George V WAFF (165)	£400–500

44. CONSPICUOUS GALLANTRY MEDAL

Instituted: 1855.
Ribbon: 31mm white (Royal Navy) or sky blue (RAF) with dark blue edges.
Metal: Silver.
Size: 36mm.
Description: (Obverse) the effigy of the reigning monarch; (reverse) the words FOR CONSPICUOUS GALLANTRY in three lines within a crowned laurel wreath.
Comments: *Conceived as the naval counterpart to the DCM, it was instituted for award to petty officers and seamen of the Royal Navy and to NCOs and other ranks of the Royal Marines. Originally awarded only for gallantry during the Crimean War, it was revived in 1874 to recognise heroism during the Ashantee War and has since been awarded, albeit sparingly, for other wars and campaigns. The Crimean issue utilised the dies of the Meritorious Service Medal which had the date 1848 below the truncation of the Queen's neck on the obverse. The raised relief inscription MERITORIOUS SERVICE on the reverse was erased and the words CONSPICUOUS GALLANTRY engraved in their place. When the decoration was revived in 1874 a new obverse was designed without a date while a new die, with the entire inscription in raised relief, was employed for the reverse. In 1943 the CGM was extended to NCOs and other ranks of the RAF. Both naval and RAF medals are identical, but the naval medal has a white ribbon with dark blue edges, whereas the RAF award has a pale blue ribbon with dark blue edges. It ranks as one of the rarest decorations: the only two medals issued in the present reign were awarded to an airman in the RAAF for gallantry in Vietnam (1968) and to a seaman during the South Atlantic War (1982). As a result of the recent changes to the operational gallantry award system (see page 16), the decoration has been replaced by the Conspicuous Gallantry Cross—full details of this new award are still awaited.*

VALUE:	Attributable groups
Victoria 1st type (11)	£2500–3000
Victoria 2nd type (51)	£2000–5000
Edward VII (2)	£8000–9000
George V (110)	£1800–2500
George VI Navy (72)	£3000–10,000
George VI RAF (111)	£2500–4500
Elizabeth II Navy (1)	—
Elizabeth II RAF (1)	—

45. GEORGE MEDAL

Instituted: 1940.

Ribbon: 32mm crimson with five narrow blue stripes.

Metal: Silver.

Size: 36mm.

Description: (Obverse) the effigy of the reigning monarch; (reverse) St George and the Dragon, modelled by George Kruger Gray, after the bookplate by Stephen Gooden for the Royal Library, Windsor.

Comments: *Awarded for acts of bravery where the services were not so outstanding as to merit the George Cross. Though primarily a civilian award, it has also been given to service personnel for heroism not in the face of the enemy. Of the approximately 2000 medals awarded, 1030 have been to civilians.*

VALUE:

	Civilian	Service
George VI 1st type 1940-47	£400–500	£600–800
George VI 2nd type 1948-52	£400–500	£700–800
Elizabeth II 1st type 1953	£600–800	£1000–1500
Elizabeth II 2nd type	£800–900	£1200–1600

46. KING'S POLICE MEDAL

Instituted: 7 July 1909.

Ribbons: 36mm Originally deep blue with silver edges, but in 1916 a central silver stripe was added. Gallantry awards have thin crimson stripes superimposed on the silver stripes.

Metal: Silver.

Size: 36mm.

Description: (Obverse) the monarch's effigy; (reverse) a standing figure with sword and shield inscribed TO GUARD MY PEOPLE. The first issue had a laurel spray in the exergue, but in 1933 two separate reverses were introduced and the words FOR GALLANTRY or FOR DISTINGUISHED SERVICE were placed in the exergue.

Comments: *Instituted to reward "courage and devotion to duty" in the police and fire services of the UK and overseas dominions. Recognising the bravery of the firemen during the Blitz, the medal was retitled the King's Police and Fire Services Medal in 1940, but no change was made in the design of the medal itself. From 1950, the gallantry medals were only awarded posthumously and all medals were discontinued in 1954 when seperate awards were established for the two services (see numbers 46 and 47).*

VALUE:

Edward VII (100)	£400–500
George V 1st type coinage head (1900)	£150–300
George V 2nd type crowned head	£200–300
George V for Gallantry (350)	£350–450
George V for Distinguished Service	£180–220
George VI 1st type for Gallantry (440)	£450–550
George VI 2nd type for Gallantry (50)	£500–700
George VI 1st type for Distinguished Service	£180–220
George VI 2nd type for Distinguished Service	£180–220

47. QUEEN'S POLICE MEDAL

Instituted: 19 May 1954.

Ribbon: Three silver stripes and two broad dark blue stripes.

Metal: Silver.

Size: 36mm.

Description: (Obverse) effigy of the reigning sovereign; (reverse) a standing figure (as on the KPM) but the laurel spray has been restored to the exergue and the words FOR GALLANTRY or FOR DISTINGUISHED POLICE SERVICE are inscribed round the circumference.

VALUE:

Elizabeth II for Gallantry (23)	£500–600
Elizabeth II for Distinguished Service (1100)	£250–350

48. QUEEN'S FIRE SERVICE MEDAL

Instituted: 19 May 1954.

Ribbon: Red with three yellow stripes (distinguished service) or similar, with thin dark blue stripes bisecting the yellow stripes (gallantry).

Metal: Silver.

Size: 36mm

Description: (Obverse) effigy of the reigning monarch; (reverse) standing figure with sword and shield (as on KPM), laurel spray in the exergue, and inscription round the circumference FOR GALLANTRY or FOR DISTINGUISHED FIRE SERVICE.

VALUE:

Elizabeth II for Gallantry	Rare
Elizabeth II for Distinguished Service	£250–300

49. KING'S POLICE MEDAL (SOUTH AFRICA)

Instituted: 24 September 1937.

Ribbon: Silver with two broad dark blue stripes.

Metal: Silver.

Size: 36mm.

Description: (Obverse) effigy of George VI and title including the words ET IMPERATOR (1937-49), George VI minus IMPERATOR (1950-52) and Queen Elizabeth II (1953-60). (Reverse) as UK but inscribed in English and Afrikaans. Inscribed FOR BRAVERY VIR DAPPERHEID or FOR DISTINGUISHED SERVICE VIR VOORTREFLIKE DIENS.

Comments: *Awarded to members of the South Africa Police for courage and devotion to duty. In 1938 it was extended to cover the constabulary of South West Africa.*

VALUE:

George VI 1st type 1937-49	
for Gallantry (10)	Rare
for Distinguished Service (13)	Rare
George VI 2nd type 1950-52	
for Distinguished Service (13)	Rare
Elizabeth II 1953-60	
for Gallantry (20)	Rare
Elizabeth II 1953-69	
for Distinguished Service (3)	Rare

50. EDWARD MEDAL (MINES)

Instituted: July 1907.
Ribbon: Dark blue edged with yellow.
Metal: Silver or bronze.
Size: 33mm.
Description: (Obverse) the monarch's effigy; (reverse) a miner rescuing a stricken comrade, with the caption FOR COURAGE across the top (designed by W. Reynolds-Stephens).
Comments: *Awarded for life-saving in mines and quarries, in two grades: first class (silver) and second class (bronze). Interestingly, the cost of these medals was borne not by the State but from a fund created by a group of philanthropic individuals led by A. Hewlett, a leading mine-owner. Medals were engraved with the names of the recipient from the outset, but since the 1930s the date and sometimes the place of the action have also been inscribed. The medal is now only granted posthumously, living recipients having been invited to exchange their medals for the GC, under Royal Warrant of 1971. This is one of the rarest gallantry awards, only 77 silver and 318 bronze medals having been granted since its inception.*

VALUE:

	Silver	Bronze
Edward VII	£600–800	£400–500
George V 1st type	£600–800	£400–500
George V 2nd type	£1200–1500	£600–800
George VI 1st type	£1500–1800	£1200–1400
George VI 2nd type	—	Rare
Elizabeth II	Not issued	From £1800

51. EDWARD MEDAL (INDUSTRY)

Instituted: December 1909.
Ribbon: As above.
Metal: Silver or bronze.
Size: 33mm.
Description: (Obverse) effigy of the reigning monarch; (reverse) originally a worker helping an injured workmate with a factory in the background and the words FOR COURAGE inscribed diagonally across the top. A second reverse, depicting a standing female figure with a laurel branch and a factory skyline in the background, was introduced in 1912.
Comments: *Awarded for acts of bravery in factory accidents and disasters. Like the Mines medal it was also available in two classes, but no first class medals have been awarded since 1948. This medal is now only awarded posthumously, living recipients having been invited to exchange their medals for the GC, under Royal Warrant of 1971. A total of 25 silver and 163 bronze awards have been issued.*

VALUE:

	Silver	Bronze
Edward VII	Rare	Rare
George V 1st Obv, 1st Rev	—	£1500–1800
George V 1st Obv, 2nd Rev	£1400–1500	£400–500
George V 2nd Obv, 2nd Rev	Rare	£1200–1400
George VI 1st type	—	£1000–1200
George VI 2nd type	Not issued	Rare
Elizabeth II 1st type	Not issued	Rare
Elizabeth II 2nd type	Not issued	Rare

52. INDIAN DISTINGUISHED SERVICE MEDAL

Instituted: 25 June 1907.
Ribbon: Crimson with broad dark blue edges.
Metal: Silver.
Size: 36mm.
Description: (Obverse) the sovereign's effigy; (reverse) the words FOR DISTINGUISHED SERVICE in a laurel wreath.
Comments: *Awarded for distinguished service in the field by Indian commissioned and non-commissioned officers and men of the Indian Army, the reserve forces, border militia and levies, military police and troops employed by the Indian Government. An amendment of 1917 extended the award to Indian non-combatants engaged on field service, bars for subsequent awards being authorised at the same time. It was formally extended to the Royal Indian Marine in 1929 and members of the Indian Air Force in 1940. Finally it was extended in 1944 to include non-European personnel of the Hong Kong and Singapore Royal Artillery although it became obsolete in 1947.*

VALUE:
Edward VII (140)	£450–500
George V KAISAR-I-HIND (3800)	£150–250
George V 2nd type (140)	£300–400
George VI (1190)	£150–250

53. BURMA GALLANTRY MEDAL

Instituted: 10 May 1940.
Ribbon: Jungle green with a broad crimson stripe in the centre.
Metal: Silver.
Size: 36mm.
Description: (Obverse) the effigy of King George VI; (reverse) the words BURMA at the top and FOR GALLANTRY in a laurel wreath.
Comments: *As Burma ceased to be part of the Indian Empire in April 1937 a separate gallantry award was required for its armed services. The Burma Gallantry Medal was awarded by the Governor to officers and men of the Burma Army, frontier forces, military police, Burma RNVR and Burma AAF, although by an amendment of 1945 subsequent awards were restricted to NCOs and men. The medal became obsolete in 1947 when Burma became an independent republic and left the Commonwealth. Just over 200 medals and three bars were awarded, mainly for heroism in operations behind the Japanese lines.*

VALUE:
£1500–2000

54. DISTINGUISHED SERVICE MEDAL

Instituted: 14 October 1914.
Ribbon: Dark blue with two white stripes towards the centre.
Metal: Silver.
Size: 36mm.
Description: (Obverse) the sovereign's effigy; (reverse) a crowned wreath inscribed FOR DISTINGUISHED SERVICE.
Comments: *Awarded to petty officers and ratings of the Royal Navy, NCOs and other ranks of the Royal Marines and all other persons holding corresponding ranks or positions in the naval forces, for acts of bravery in face of the enemy not sufficiently meritorious to make them eligible for the CGM. It was later extended to cover the Merchant Navy and Army, the WRNS and RAF personnel serving aboard ships in the Second World War. Of particular interest and desirability are medals awarded for outstanding actions, e.g. Jutland, Q-Ships, the Murmansk convoys, the Yangtze incident and the Falklands War. First World War bars for subsequent awards are dated on the reverse, but Second World War bars are undated. As a result of the recent changes to the operational gallantry award system (see page 16), this award has been replaced by the DSC which is now available both to officers and other ranks.*

VALUE:

George V uncrowned head 1914-30 (4100)	£150–1000
George VI IND IMP 1938-49 (7100)	£200–500
George VI 2nd type 1949-53	£800–2000
Elizabeth II BR OMN 1953-7	£2000–3000
Elizabeth II 2nd type	£2000–4000

55. MILITARY MEDAL

Instituted: 25 March 1916.
Ribbon: Broad dark blue edges flanking a central section of three narrow white and two narrow crimson stripes.
Metal: Silver.
Size: 36mm.
Description: (Obverse) the sovereign's effigy—six types to date; (reverse) the crowned royal cypher above the inscription FOR BRAVERY IN THE FIELD, enclosed in a wreath.
Comments: *Awarded to NCOs and men of the Army (including RFC and RND) for individual or associated acts of bravery not of sufficient heroism as to merit the DCM. In June 1916 it was extended to women, two of the earliest awards being to civilian ladies for their conduct during the Easter Rising in Dublin that year. Some 115,600 medals were awarded during the First World War alone, together with 5796 first bars, 180 second bars and 1 third bar. Over 15,000 medals were conferred during the Second World War, with 177 first bars and 1 second bar. About 300 medals and 4 first bars were awarded for bravery in minor campaigns between the two world wars, while some 932 medals and 8 first bars have been conferred since 1947. As a result of the recent changes to the operational gallantry award system (see page 16), this award has been replaced by the MC which is now available both to officers and other ranks.*

VALUE:

George V uncrowned head 1916-30	£100–180*
women	£800–1500
George V crowned head 1930-38	£1600–2000
George VI IND IMP 1938-48	£300–1000
George VI 2nd type 1948-53	£800–2000
Elizabeth II BR: OMN 1953-8	£1800–3000
Elizabeth II 2nd type	£1800–4000

Groups to RFC and RND will be considerably higher.

56. DISTINGUISHED FLYING MEDAL

Instituted: 1918.

Ribbon: Originally purple and white horizontal stripes but since 1919 thirteen narrow diagonal stripes alternationg white and purple.

Metal: Silver.

Size: 42mm tall; 34mm wide.

Description: An oval medal, (obverse) the sovereign's effigy; (reverse) Athena Nike seated on an aeroplane, with a hawk rising from her hand. Originally undated, but the date 1918 was added to the reverse with the advent of the George VI obverse. The medal is suspended by a pair of wings from a straight bar.

Comments: *Introduced at the same time as the DFC, it was awarded to NCOs and men of the RAF for courage or devotion to duty while flying on active operations against the enemy. During the Second World War it was extended to the equivalent ranks of the Army and Fleet Air Arm personnel engaged in similar operations. First World War medals have the names of recipients impressed in large seriffed lettering, whereas Second World War medals are rather coarsely engraved. Approximately 150 medals have been awarded since 1945. As a result of the recent changes to the operational gallantry award system (see page 16), this award has been replaced by the DFC which is now available both to officers and other ranks.*

VALUE:

George V uncrowned head 1918-30 (105)	£700–2000
George V crowned head 1930-38	£2000–3500
George VI IND IMP 1938-49 (6500)	£400–2000
George VI 2nd type 1949-53	£1000–2000
Elizabeth II	£1200–2000

57. AIR FORCE MEDAL

Instituted: 1918.

Ribbon: Originally horizontal narrow stripes of white and crimson but since July 1919 diagonal narrow stripes of the same colours.

Metal: Silver.

Size: 42mm tall; 32mm wide.

Description: An oval medal with a laurel border. (Obverse) the sovereign's effigy; (reverse) Hermes mounted on a hawk bestowing a laurel wreath. The medal is suspended by a pair of wings from a straight bar, like the DFM.

Comments: *Instituted at the same time as the AFC, it is awarded to NCOs and men of the RAF for courage or devotion to duty while flying, but not on active operations against the enemy. About 100 medals and 2 first bars were awarded during the First World War, 106 medals and 3 bars between the wars and 259 medals during the Second World War.*

VALUE:

George V uncrowned head 1918-30	£600–1000
George V crowned head 1930-38	£2000–3000
George VI IND IMP 1939-49	£500–800
George VI 2nd type 1949-53	£500–800
Elizabeth II	£500–800

58. CONSTABULARY MEDAL (IRELAND)

Instituted: 1842.
Ribbon: Originally light blue, but changed to green in 1872.
Metal: Silver.
Size: 36mm.
Description: (Obverse) a crowned harp within a wreath of oak leaves and shamrocks, with REWARD OF MERIT round the top and IRISH CONSTABULARY round the foot. In the first version the front of the harp took the form of a female figure but later variants had a plain harp and the shape of the crown and details of the wreath were also altered. These changes theoretically came in 1867 when the Constabulary acquired the epithet Royal, which was then added to the inscription round the top, although some medals issued as late as 1921 had the pre-1867 title. (Reverse) a wreath of laurel and shamrock, within which are engraved the recipient's name, rank, number, date and sometimes the location of the action.
Comments: *Originally awarded for gallantry and meritorious service by members of the Irish Constabulary. From 1872, however, it was awarded only for gallantry. It was first conferred in 1848 and became obsolete in 1922 when the Irish Free State was established. Bars for second awards were authorised in 1920. About 315 medals and 7 bars were awarded (or, in some cases, second medals—the records are inconclusive), mostly for actions in connection with the Easter Rising of 1916 (23) or the subsequent Anglo-Irish War of 1920 (180) and 1921 (55).*

VALUE:

First type	Rare
Second type	£800–1200

59. INDIAN POLICE MEDAL

Instituted: 23 February 1932.
Ribbon: Crimson flanked by bands of dark blue and silver grey. From 1942 onwards an additional silver stripe appeared in the centre of the ribbon intended for the gallantry medal.
Metal: Bronze.
Size: 36mm.
Description: (Obverse) the King Emperor; (reverse) a crowned wreath inscribed INDIAN POLICE, with the words FOR DISTINGUISHED CONDUCT across the centre. In December 1944 the reverse was re-designed in two types, with the words FOR GALLANTRY or FOR MERITORIOUS SERVICE in place of the previous legend.
Comments: *Intended for members of the Indian police forces and fire brigades as a reward for gallantry or meritorious service. The medal became obsolete in 1950 when India became a republic.*

VALUE:

George V	£200–300
George VI Distinguished Conduct	£250–300
George VI for Gallantry	£300–400
George VI for Meritorious Service	£200–300

60. BURMA POLICE MEDAL

Instituted: 14 December 1937.

Ribbon: A wide central blue stripe flanked by broad black stripes and white edges.

Metal: Bronze.

Size: 36mm.

Description: (Obverse) the effigy of George VI; (reverse) similar to the Indian medal (first type) and inscribed FOR DISTINGUISHED CONDUCT, irrespective of whether awarded for gallantry or distinguished service.

Comments: *Introduced following the separation of Burma from India, it was abolished in 1948. All ranks of the police, frontier force and fire brigades, both European and Burmese, were eligible.*

VALUE:

For Gallantry (53)	£700–800
For Meritorious Service (80)	£400–500

61. COLONIAL POLICE MEDAL

Instituted: 10 May 1938.

Ribbon: Blue with green edges and a thin silver stripe separating the colours, but the gallantry award had an additional thin red line through the centre of each green edge stripe.

Metal: Silver.

Size: 36mm.

Description: (Obverse) the sovereign's effigy; (reverse) a policeman's truncheon superimposed on a laurel wreath. The left side of the circumference is inscribed COLONIAL POLICE FORCES and the right either FOR GALLANTRY or FOR MERITORIOUS SERVICE.

Comments: *Intended to reward all ranks of the police throughout the Empire for acts of conspicuous bravery or for meritorious service. The number to be issued was limited to 150 in any one year. Only 450 were awarded for gallantry, whilst almost 3000 were issued for meritorious service.*

VALUE:

George VI GRI for Gallantry	£250–400
George VI GRI for Meritorious Service	£130–160
George VI GVIR for Gallantry	£300–500
George VI GVIR for Meritorious Service	£130–160
Elizabeth II 1st type for Gallantry	£400–500
Elizabeth II 1st type for Meritorious Service	£150–180
Elizabeth II 2nd type for Gallantry	£400–500
Elizabeth II 2nd type for Meritorious Service	£150–180

62. COLONIAL FIRE BRIGADE MEDAL

Instituted: 10 May 1938.

Ribbon: As above.

Metal: Silver.

Size: 36mm.

Description: (Obverse) the effigy of the reigning sovereign; (reverse) a fireman's helmet and axe, with the inscription COLONIAL FIRE BRIGADES FOR GALLANTRY or FOR MERITORIOUS SERVICE.

Comments: *As No. 59 this medal was intended to reward all ranks of the Colonial fire brigades but very few were awarded for gallantry.*

VALUE:

George VI GRI for Gallantry	Rare
George VI GRI for Meritorious Service	Rare
George VI GVIR for Gallantry	Rare
George VI GVIR for Meritorious Service	£130–160
Elizabeth II 1st type for Gallantry	From £750
Elizabeth II 1st type for Meritorious Service	£150–180
Elizabeth II 2nd type for Gallantry	£300–400
Elizabeth II 2nd type for Meritorious Service	£90–110

63. QUEEN'S GALLANTRY MEDAL

Instituted: 20 June 1974.

Ribbon: Dark blue with a central pearl-grey stripe bisected by a narrow rose-pink stripe.

Metal: Silver.

Size: 36mm.

Description: (Obverse) the Queen's effigy; (reverse) an imperial crown above THE QUEEN'S GALLANTRY MEDAL flanked by laurel sprigs.

Comments: *Awarded for exemplary acts of bravery. Although intended primarily for civilians, it is also awarded to members of the armed forces for actions which would not be deemed suitable for a military decoration. With the introduction of the QGM the gallantry awards of the MBE and BEM came to an end. A bar is added for a second award. Fewer than 400 medals have been awarded.*

VALUE:

Service award	£1400–2000
Civilian award	£600–800

64. ALLIED SUBJECTS' MEDAL

Instituted: November 1920.

Ribbon: Bright red with a light blue centre, flanked by narrow stripes of yellow, black and white (thus incorporating the Belgian and French national colours).

Metal: Silver or bronze.

Size: 36mm.

Description: (Obverse) the effigy of King George V; (reverse) designed by Edmund Dulac, the female allegory of Humanity offering a cup to a British soldier resting on the ground, with ruined buildings in the background.

Comment: *Shortly after the cessation of the First World War it was proposed that services rendered to the Allied cause, specifically by those who had helped British prisoners of war to escape, should be rewarded by a medal. The decision to go ahead was delayed on account of disagreement between the War Office and the Foreign Office, but eventually the first awards were announced in November 1920, with supplementary lists in 1921 and 1922. Medals were issued unnamed and almost half of the total issue, namely 56 silver and 247 bronze medals, were issued to women.*

VALUE:

Silver (134)	£500–700
Bronze (574)	£300–400

NB These prices are for unattributable awards.

65. KING'S MEDAL FOR COURAGE IN THE CAUSE OF FREEDOM

Instituted: 23 August 1945
Ribbon: White with two narrow dark blue stripes in the centre and broad red stripes at the edges.
Metal: Silver.
Size: 36mm.
Description: (Obverse) the crowned profile of King George VI; (reverse) inscribed, within a chain link, THE KING'S MEDAL FOR COURAGE IN THE CAUSE OF FREEDOM.
Comments: *Introduced to acknowledge acts of courage by foreign civilians or members of the armed services "in the furtherance of the British Commonwealth in the Allied cause" during the Second World War. Like its First World War counterpart, it was intended mainly to reward those who had assisted British escapees in enemy-occupied territories. About 3200 medals were issued, commencing in 1947.*

VALUE: £250–300 (unattributable)

66. KING'S MEDAL FOR SERVICE IN THE CAUSE OF FREEDOM

Instituted: 23 August 1945.
Ribbon: White with a central red bar flanked by dark blue stripes.
Metal: Silver.
Size: 36mm.
Description: (Obverse) effigy of King George VI; (reverse) a medieval warrior in armour carrying a broken lance, receiving nourishment from a female.
Comments: *Introduced at the same time as the foregoing, it was intended for foreign civilians who had helped the Allied cause in other less dangerous ways, such as fund-raising and organising ambulance services. 2490 medals were issued.*

VALUE: £150–200 (unattributable)

67. SEA GALLANTRY MEDAL

Instituted: 1855, under the Merchant Shipping Acts of 1854 and 1894.
Ribbon: Bright red with narrow white stripes towards the edges.
Metal: Silver or bronze.
Size: 58mm or 33mm.
Description: (Obverse) Profile of Queen Victoria; (reverse) a family on a storm-tossed shore reviving a drowning sailor. Both obverse and reverse were sculpted by Bernard Wyon.
Comments: *Exceptionally, this group of medals was authorised not by Royal Warrant but by Parliamentary legislation, under the terms of the Merchant Shipping Acts of 1854 and 1894. The 1854 Act made provision for monetary rewards for life saving at sea, but in 1855 this was transmuted into medals, in gold, silver or bronze, in two categories, for gallantry (where the rescuer placed his own life at risk) and for humanity (where the risks were minimal). The gold medal, if ever awarded, must have been of the greatest rarity. These medals, issued by the Board of Trade, were 58mm in diameter and not intended for wearing. The only difference between the medals lay in the wording of the inscription round the circumference of the obverse. Later medals were issued by the Ministry of Transport. In 1903*

Edward VII ordered that the medal be reduced to 1.27 inches (33mm) in diameter and fitted with a suspension bar and ribbon for wearing. Both large and small medals were always issued with the recipient's name round the rim.

VALUE:

	Silver	Bronze
Victoria Gallantry	£350–400	£150–250
Victoria Humanity	Rare	Rare
Edward VII Gallantry (large)	Rare	Rare
Edward VII Gallantry (small)	£450–500	£400–450
Edward VII Humanity (small)	£450–500	£400–450
George V	£300–400	£200–300
George VI 1st type	Rare	Rare
George VI 2nd type	—	Rare
Elizabeth II	Rare	Rare

68. SEA GALLANTRY MEDAL (FOREIGN SERVICES)

Instituted: 1841.

Ribbon: Plain crimson till 1922; thereafter the same ribbon as the SGM above.

Metal: Gold, silver or bronze.

Size: 36mm or 33mm.

Description: The large medal had Victoria's effigy (young head) on the obverse, but there were five reverse types showing a crowned wreath with PRESENTED BY (or FROM) THE BRITISH GOVERNMENT inside the wreath. Outside the wreath were the following variants:
1. Individually struck inscriptions (1841-49 but sometimes later).
2. FOR SAVING THE LIFE OF A BRITISH SUBJECT (1849-54)
3. FOR ASSISTING A BRITISH VESSEL IN DISTRESS (1849-54)
4. FOR SAVING THE LIVES OF BRITISH SUBJECTS (1850-54)
There are also unissued specimens or patterns with a Latin inscription within the wreath VICTORIA REGINA CUDI JUSSIT MDCCCXLI.
The small medal, intended for wear, has five obverse types combined with four reverse types: as 2 above (1854-1906), as 3 above (1854-1896), as 4 above (1854-1926), or FOR GALLANTRY AND HUMANITY (1858 to the present day).

Comments: *Although intended to reward foreigners who rendered assistance to British subjects in distress some early awards were actually made for rescues on dry land. Originally a special reverse was struck for each incident, but this was found to be unnecessarily expensive, so a standard reverse was devised in 1849. Medals before 1854 had a diameter of 45mm and were not fitted with suspension. After 1854 the diameter was reduced to 33mm and scrolled suspension bars were fitted. Of the large medals about 100 gold, 120 silver and 14 bronze were issued, while some 10 gold and 24 bronze specimens have been recorded.*

VALUE:

	Gold	Silver	Bronze
Victoria large	£1400–1800	£400–500	£400–500
Victoria small	£1000–1200	£250–350	—
Edward VII	£1000–1500	£400–500	—
George V	£1000–1200	£250–350	—
George VI	—	Rare	—
Elizabeth II	Rare	Rare	—`

69. BRITISH NORTH BORNEO COMPANY'S BRAVERY CROSS

Instituted: 1890 by the British North Borneo Company.
Ribbon: Yellow watered silk.
Metal: Silver or bronze.
Size: 36mm.
Description: The cross pattée has a central medallion bearing a lion passant gardant with the Company motto PREGO ET PERAGO (I pray and accomplish) within a garter. The arms of the cross are inscribed BRITISH NORTH BORNEO with FOR BRAVERY in the lower limb.
Comments: *Both silver and bronze crosses were manufactured by Joseph Moore of Birmingham.*

VALUE:

Silver	£300–350
Bronze	£150–200

70. NATIVE CHIEFS' MEDAL

Instituted: 1920.
Ribbon: Yellow with two white central stripes (silver-gilt) or a single white stripe (silver).
Metal: Silver or silver-gilt.
Size: 40mm x 34mm (oval) or 36mm (circular).
Description: Originally an oval badge with collar. (Obverse) the crowned effigy of the monarch; (reverse) a warship, symbolic of imperial power. The Queen's Medal for Chiefs is circular with a beaded frame and has a crowned effigy of Elizabeth II entitled QUEEN ELIZABETH THE SECOND. It is fitted with a plain ring for suspension.
Comments: *Various large silver medals were struck for award to native chiefs in various parts of the world, from the eighteenth century onwards, and of these the awards to American Indian chiefs are probably the best known. In 1920, however, a standard King's Medal for Chiefs was instituted. It was awarded exceptionally in silver-gilt (first class), and usually in silver (second class). The oval medal was worn round the neck from a silver collar. The more modern issues, however, are intended for wear with a ribbon from the breast.*

VALUE:

	Silver-gilt	Silver
George V	£800–1000	£700–800
George VI	£800–1000	£500–600
Elizabeth II	£800–1000	£600–700

Examples of MINIMUM Prices paid for Gallantry Medals

by

ROMSEY MEDALS

Distinguished Conduct Medals

World War I accompanied by campaign medals:

Corps	£180.00
Infantry	£230.00
Cavalry & Tanks	£300.00

World War II & post war, singles or in groups:

Corps	£800.00
Infantry	£1,000.00
Cavalry & Tanks	£1,250.00
Para & SAS by negotiation	

Distinguished Flying Medals

World War I accompanied by campaign medals   £1,100.00

World War II & post war, singles or in groups   £500.00

Other Gallantry & Campaign Medals urgently required

Medals must be in good condition and correctly named

*Medals can be sent by registered post
for an immediate valuation and offer.*

5 Bell Street, Romsey, Hants S051 8GY
Tel: (0794) 512069   Fax: (0794) 830332

CAMPAIGN MEDALS

The evolution of medals struck to commemorate, and later to reward participants in, a battle or campaign was a very gradual process. The forerunner of the modern campaign medal was the Armada Medal, cast in gold or silver, which appears to have been awarded to naval officers and distinguished persons after the abortive Spanish invasion of 1588. The obverse bears a flattering portrait of Queen Elizabeth (thought to have been designed by Nicholas Hilliard, the celebrated miniaturist) with a Latin inscription signifying "enclosing the most precious treasure in the world" (i.e. the Queen herself). On the reverse, the safety of the kingdom is represented by a bay tree growing on a little island, immune from the flashes of lightning which seem to strike it. This medal, and a similar type depicting the Ark floating calmly on a stormy sea, bore loops at the top so that a chain or cord could be passed through it for suspension from the neck of the recipient.

The Civil War produced a number of gallantry medals, mentioned in the previous section; but in 1650 Parliament authorised a medal which was struck in silver, bronze or lead to celebrate Cromwell's miraculous victory over the Scots at Dunbar. This was the first medal granted to all the participants on the Parliamentary side, and not restricted to high-ranking officers, or given for individual acts of heroism.

The Dunbar Medal thus established several useful precedents, which were eventually to form the criteria of the campaign medal as we know it today. After this promising start, however, the pattern of medals and their issue were much more restrictive. Naval medals were struck in gold for award to admirals and captains during the First Dutch War (1650–53), while the battle of Culloden (1746) was marked by a medal portraying the "Butcher" Duke of Cumberland, and granted to officers who took part in the defeat of the Jacobites.

In the second half of the eighteenth century there were a number of medals, but these were of a private or semi-official nature. The Honourable East India Company took the lead in awarding medals to its troops. These medals were often struck in two sizes and in gold as well as silver, for award to different ranks. The siege of Gibraltar (1779–83) was marked by an issue of medals to the defenders, but this was made on the initiative (and at the expense) of the garrison commanders, Generals Eliott and Picton, themselves.

During the French Revolutionary and Napoleonic Wars several medals were produced by private individuals for issue to combatants. Alexander Davison and Matthew Boulton were responsible for the medals granted to the officers and men who fought the battles of the Nile (1798) and Trafalgar (1805). Davison also produced a Trafalgar medal in pewter surrounded by a copper rim; it is recorded that the seamen who received it were so disgusted at the base metal that they threw it into the sea! At the same time, however, Government

recognition was given to senior officers who had distinguished themselves in certain battles and engagements and a number of gold medals were awarded. The events thus marked included the capture of Ceylon (1795–96) and the battles of Maida, Bagur and Palamos.

Towards the end of the Napoleonic Wars an Army Gold Medal was instituted in two sizes—large (generals) and small (field officers). Clasps for second and third battles and campaigns were added to the medal, but when an officer became eligible for a third clasp the medal was exchanged for a Gold Cross with the names of the four battles engraved on its arms. Clasps for subsequent campaigns were then added to the cross (the Duke of Wellington receiving the Gold Cross with nine clasps). A total of 163 crosses, 85 large and 599 small medals was awarded, so that, apart from their intrinsic value, these decorations command very high prices when they appear in the saleroom.

The first medal awarded to all ranks of the Army was the Waterloo Medal, issued in 1816 shortly after the battle which brought the Napoleonic Wars to an end. No action was taken to grant medals for the other campaigns in the Napoleonic Wars until 1847 when Military and Naval General Service Medals were awarded retrospectively to veterans who were then still alive. As applications were made, in some cases, in respect of campaigns more than fifty years earlier, it is hardly surprising that the number of medals awarded was comparatively small, while the number of clasps awarded for certain engagements was quite minute. The Military General Service Medal was restricted to land campaigns during the Peninsular War (1808–13), the American War (1812–14) and isolated actions in the West Indies, Egypt and Java, whereas the Naval GSM covered a far longer period, ranging from the capture of the French frigate *La Cleopatra* by HMS *Nymphe* in June 1793, to the naval blockade of the Syrian coast in 1840, during the British operations against Mehemet Ali. Thus Naval Medals with the clasp for Syria are relatively plentiful (7057 awarded) while in several cases clasps were awarded to one man alone, and in seven cases there were no claimants for clasps at all. It is worth bearing in mind that applications for the medals and clasps resulted mainly from the publicity given by printed advertisements and notices posted up all over the country. With the poor general standard of literacy prevalent at the time, many people who were entitled to the medals would have been quite unaware of their existence.

The Naming of Medals

The Military and Naval GSMs, with their multitudinous combinations of clasps, have long been popular with collectors, but the other campaign medals of the past century and a half have a strong following as well. With the exception of the stars and medals awarded during the Second World War, all British campaign medals have usually borne the name of the recipient and usually his (or her) number, rank and regiment, unit or ship as well. This brings a personal element into the study of medals which is lacking in most other branches of numismatics. The name on a medal is very important for two reasons. It is a means of testing the genuineness, not only of the medal itself, but its bar combination, and secondly it enables the collector to link the medal not only with the man who earned it, but with his unit or formation, and thus plays a vital part in the development of naval or military history, if only a small part in most cases.

Much of the potential value of a medal depends on the man who won it, or the unit to which he belonged. As it would be impossible to collect medals in a general fashion, the collector must specialise in some aspect of the subject, restricting his interests perhaps to one medal (the Naval GSM) or a single group (British campaigns in India), or to medals awarded to the men of a particular regiment. The information given on the rim or back of a medal is therefore important in helping to identify it and assign it to its correct place. Even this has to be qualified to some extent. Some regiments are more popular than others with collectors and much depends on the part, active or passive, played by a unit in a particular battle or campaign for which the medal was awarded. Then again, the combination of event with the corps or regiment of the recipient must also be considered.

At one extreme we find the Royal Regiment of Artillery living up to its motto *Ubique* (everywhere) by being represented in virtually every land action (and not a few naval actions, as witness the Atlantic Star worn by former Maritime Gunners), so that a comprehensive collection of medals awarded to the RA would be a formidable feat.

At the other extreme one finds odd detachments, sometimes consisting of one or two men only, seconded from a regiment for service with another unit. The Indian GSM, with bar for Hazara (1891), is usually found named to personnel of the 11th Bengal Lancers and various battalions of the Bengal Infantry, but according to the medal rolls it was also given to six men of the 2nd Manchester Regiment, two men of the Queen's Regiment and one each to troopers of the 2nd and 7th

Dragoon Guards. Whereas a specimen of the IGS medal with this bar is not hard to find named to a soldier in one of the Bengal units, it constitutes a major rarity when awarded to one of the "odd men" and its value is correspondingly high.

As the personal details given on a medal regarding the recipient are so important, it is necessary for the collector to verify two facts—that the person whose name is on the medal was actually present at the action for which either the medal or its bars were awarded, and secondly, that the naming of the bar and the attachment of the bars is correct and not tampered with in any way. As regards the first, the Public Record Office at Kew, London is a goldmine of information for all naval and military campaigns. Apart from despatches, reports and muster rolls covering the actions, there are the medal rolls compiled from the applications for medals and bars. Transcriptions of the medal rolls are held by regimental museums and also by such bodies as the Military Historical Association and the Orders and Medals Research Society. Details of these and other clubs and societies devoted to medal collecting are given on page 237.

The presence of a name on the roll does not mean that a medal or clasp was inevitably awarded; conversely authenticated medals are known to exist named to persons not listed on the medal roll. There are often divergences between the muster and medal rolls. Moreover, discrepancies in the spelling of recipients' names are not uncommon and bars are sometimes found listed for regiments which were not even in existence when the battle was fought! This is explained, however, by the fact that a man may have been serving with one unit which took part in the campaign and subsequently transferred to another regiment. When claiming his medal he probably gave his *present* unit, rather than the one in which he was serving at the time of the action.

Unfortunately cases of medals having been tampered with are by no means rare, so it is necessary to be able to recognise evidence of fakery. A favourite device of the faker is to alter the name and personal details of the recipient and to substitute another name in order to enhance the medal's value. This is done simply by filing the inscription off the rim and adding a new one. In order to check for such alterations a similar medal of proven genuineness should be compared with a pair of fine callipers. Take the measurements at several points round the rim so that any unevenness should soon be apparent (see pages 20–21).

We cannot stress too much the importance of being closely familiar with the various styles of naming medals. Over the past 150 years an incredible variety of lettering—roman, italic, script, sans-serif, seriffed in all shapes and sizes—has been used at one time or another. In some cases the inscription was applied by impressing in raised relief; in others the inscription was punched in or engraved by hand. If a medal is normally impressed and you come across an engraved example you should immediately be on your guard. This is not an infallible test, however, as medals have been known with more than one style of naming, particularly if duplicates were issued at a much later date to replace medals lost or destroyed.

A rather more subtle approach was adopted by some fakers in respect of the Naval GSM. The three commonest clasps—*Algiers* (1362), *Navarino* (1137) and *Syria* (7057)—were awarded to many recipients possessing common names such as Jones or Smith which can be matched with recipients of some very rare clasps. In the case of the Naval GSM the ship on which the recipient served is not given, thus aiding the fraudulent substitution of clasps. It is necessary, therefore, to check the condition of clasps, even if the naming appears to be correct. Points to watch for are file or solder marks on the rivets which secure the clasps to each other and to the suspender of the medal. This test is not infallible as clasps *do* occasionally work loose if subject to constant wear (particularly if the recipient was a cavalryman, for obvious reasons). But clasps whose rivets appear to have been hammered should automatically be suspect, until a check of the medal rolls pass them as authentic. Examples of the earlier medals, particularly those awarded to officers, may be found with unorthodox coupling. Major L. L. Gordon, in his definitive work *British Battles and Medals*, mentions a Naval GSM awarded to one of his ancestors, with clasps for *Guadaloupe* and *Anse la Barque* in a large rectangular style which must have been unofficial. The medal is quite authentic, so it must be presumed that officers were allowed a certain degree of latitude in the manner in which they altered their medals.

Medals with clasps awarded for participation in subsequent engagements are invariably worth much more than the basic medal. In general, the greater number of clasps, the more valuable the medal, although, conversely, there are a few instances in which single-clasp medals are scarcer than twin-clasp medals. There is no short answer to this and individual rare clasps can enhance the value of an otherwise common medal out of all proportion. Thus the Naval GSM with clasp for *Syria* currently rates £150–175, but one of the two medals known to have been issued with the *Acheron* clasp of 1805 would easily rate twelve times as much. Again, relative value can only be determined by reference to all the circumstances of the award.

The person to whom a medal was issued has considerable bearing on its value. If the recipient belonged to a regiment which played a spectacular part in a battle, this generally rates a premium. The rank of the recipient also has some bearing; in general the higher the rank, the more valuable the medal. Medals to commissioned officers rate more than those awarded to NCOs and other ranks, and the medals of British servicemen rate more as a rule than those awarded to native troops. Medals granted to women usually command a relatively good premium. Another grim aspect is that medals issued to personnel who were wounded or killed in the campaign also rate more highly than those issued to servicemen who came through unscathed.

With the collector of British campaign medals the person to whom the medal was awarded becomes almost as important as the medal itself. It is not sufficient to collect the medal and leave it at that. The collector must investigate it and delve into the archives to find out all

that he can about the recipient. The Public Record Office and regimental museums have already been mentioned, but do not overlook the usefulness of such reference tools as the monumental Mormon International Genealogical Index (now on microfiche and available in good public libraries and county record offices). All of these should help you to flesh out the bare bones of the details given in the muster and medal rolls.

Medal Groups

Apart from the combination of clasps on a medal and the significance of the recipient, there is a third factor to be considered in assessing the value of medals, namely the relationship of one medal to another in a group awarded to one person. Just as the number of clasps on a medal is not in itself a significant factor, so also the number of medals in a group is not necessarily important *per se*. Groups of five or more medals, whose recipient can be identified, are by no means uncommon. For example, a fairly common five medal group would consist of 1914–15 Medal, War Medal and Victory Medal (for the First World War) and the Defence Medal and War Medal (for the Second World War). Thousands of men served throughout the first war to do duty, in a less active role, during a part at least of the second, long enough to qualify for the latter pair of medals.

It should be noted that none of the medals awarded for service in the Second World War was named to the recipient, so that groups comprising such medals alone cannot be readily identified and are thus lacking in the interest possessed by those containing named medals. Six-medal groups for service in the Second World War are not uncommon, particularly the combination of 1939–45 Star, Africa Star, Italy Star, France and Germany Star, Defence Medal and War Medal which was awarded to Army personnel who served from any time up to late 1942 and took part in the campaigns of North Africa and Europe.

Conversely it would be possible for troops to have served over a longer period and seen more action, and only been awarded the 1939–45 Star, Burma Star (with Pacific bar) and the War Medal. Naval groups consisting of the 1939–45 Star, Atlantic Star (with bar for France and Germany), Italy Star and War Medal are less common and therefore more desirable (with, of course, the rider that it must be possible to identify the recipient), while the most desirable of all is the three-medal group of 1939–45 Star (with Battle of Britain bar), Air Crew Europe Star (with bar for France and Germany) and the War Medal. Such a group, together with a Distinguished Flying Cross awarded to one of The Few, is a highly coveted set indeed, providing, as always, that one can prove its authenticity. In any event, the addition of a named medal to a Second World War group (e.g. a long service award, a gallantry medal, or some other category of medal named to the recipient), together with supporting collateral material (citations, log-books, pay-books, service records, newspaper cuttings, etc), should help to establish the provenance of the group.

71. LOUISBURG MEDAL

Date: 1758.
Campaign: Canada (Seven Years War).
Branch of Service: British Army and Navy.
Ribbon: 32mm half yellow, half black.
Metals: Gold, silver or bronze.
Size: 42mm.
Description: The medal shows the globe surrounded by allegorical figures of victory and flanked by servicemen.
Comments: *More in the nature of a decoration, this medal was only given to certain recipients for acts of bravery or distinguished service in the capture in July 1758 of Louisburg in Canada during the Seven Years War. James Wolfe and Jeffrey Amherst commanded the land forces and Edward Boscawen the fleet.*

VALUE:

Gold	Rare
Silver	£2000–4000
Bronze	£600–800

72. CARIB WAR MEDAL

Date: 1773.
Campaign: Carib rebellion, St Vincent.
Branch of Service: Local militia or volunteers.
Ribbon: None.
Metal: Silver.
Size: 52mm.
Description: (Obverse) bust of George III in armour; (reverse) Britannia offering an olive branch to a defeated Carib, the date MDCCLXXIII in the exergue.
Comments: *The Legislative Assembly of St Vincent in the West Indies instituted this award to members of the militia and volunteers who served in the campaign of 1773 which put down a native rebellion that had been fomented by the French.*

VALUE:

Silver	£700–800

73. DECCAN MEDAL

Date: 1784.
Campaign: Western India and Gujerat 1778-84.
Branch of Service: HEIC forces.
Ribbon: Yellow cord.
Metals: Gold or silver.
Size: 40.5mm or 32mm.
Description: (Obverse) a rather languid Britannia with a trophy of arms, thrusting a laurel wreath towards a distant fort. (Reverse) an inscription in Farsi signifying "As coins are current in the world, so shall be the bravery and exploits of these heroes by whom the name of the victorious English nation was carried from Bengal to the Deccan. Presented in AH 1199 [1784] by the East India Company's Calcutta Government".
Comments: *The first medals struck by order of the Honourable East India Company were conferred on Indian troops for service in western India and Gujerat under the command of Warren Hastings. They were struck at Calcutta in two sizes; both gold and silver exist in the larger size but only silver medals in the smaller diameter.*

VALUE:

40.5mm gold	£4000–6000
40.5mm silver	£600–800
32mm silver	£350–450

74. DEFENCE OF GIBRALTAR

Eliott's medal   *Picton's medal*

Date: 1783.
Campaign: Siege of Gibraltar 1779-83.
Branch of Service: British and Hanoverian forces.
Ribbon: None.
Metal: Silver.
Size: 59mm (Picton) and 49mm (Eliott).
Description: Eliott's medal was confined to the Hanoverian troops, hence the reverse inscribed
    BRÜDERSCHAFT (German for "brotherhood") above a wreath containing the names of the three
    Hanoverian commanders and General Eliott. The obverse, by Lewis Pingo, shows a view of the Rock and
    the naval attack of 13 September 1782 which was the climax of the siege. Picton's medal, awarded to the
    British forces, has a larger than usual diameter, with a map of the Rock on the obverse and a 22-line text—the
    most verbose British medal—above a recumbent lion clutching a shield bearing the castle and key emblem of
    Gibraltar on the reverse.
Comments: *Several medals of a private nature were struck to commemorate the defence of Gibraltar during the Franco-*
    Spanish siege of 1779–83, but those most commonly encountered are the silver medals which were provided by George
    Augustus Eliott and Sir Thomas Picton, the military commanders.

VALUE:

Picton medal	£350–500
Eliott medal	£300–400

75. MYSORE MEDAL

Date: 1792.
Campaign: Mysore 1790-92.
Branch of Service: HEIC forces.
Ribbon: Yellow cord.
Metal: Gold or silver.
Size: 43mm or 38mm.
Description: (Obverse) a sepoy of the HEIC Army holding British and Company flags over a trophy of arms with the fortress of Seringapatam in the background; (reverse) a bilingual inscription (in English and Farsi). The medal has a ring for suspension round the neck by a cord.
Comments: *Indian officers and men who served under Marquis Cornwallis and Generals Abercromby and Meadows received this medal for service in the campaign which brought about the downfall of Tippoo Sultan of Mysore.*

VALUE:

43mm gold (subadars)	£4000–6000
43mm silver (jemadars)	£600–800
38mm silver (other ranks)	£350–450

76. ST VINCENT'S BLACK CORPS MEDAL

Date: 1795.
Campaign: Carib rebellion 1795.
Branch of Service: Local militia volunteers.
Ribbon: None.
Metal: Bronze.
Size: 48.5mm.
Description: (Obverse) the winged figure of Victory brandishing a sword over a fallen foe who has abandoned his musket; (reverse) native holding musket and bayonet, BOLD LOYAL OBEDIENT around and H.G.FEC. in exergue.
Comments: *Awarded to the officers and NCOs of the Corps of Natives raised by Major Seton from among the island's slaves for service against the rebellious Caribs and French forces.*

VALUE:

Bronze	£600–700

77. CAPTURE OF CEYLON MEDAL

Date: 1796.
Campaign: Ceylon 1795.
Branch of Service: HEIC forces.
Ribbon: Yellow cord.
Metal: Gold or silver.
Size: 50mm.
Description: The plain design has an English inscription on the obverse, and the Farsi equivalent on the reverse.
Comments: *Awarded for service in the capture of Ceylon (Sri Lanka) from the Dutch during the French Revolutionary Wars. It is generally believed that the gold medals were awarded to Captains Barton and Clarke while the silver medals went to the native gunners of the Bengal Artillery.*

VALUE:

Gold (2)	—
Silver (121)	£550–650

78. DAVISON'S NILE MEDAL

Date: 1798.   **Campaign:** Battle of the Nile 1798.
Branch of Service: Royal Navy.
Ribbon: 32mm, deep navy blue.
Metal: Gold, silver, gilt-bronze and bronze.   **Size:** 47mm.
Description: (Obverse) Peace caressing a shield decorated with the portrait of Horatio Nelson; (reverse) the British fleet at Aboukir Bay.
Comments: *Nelson's victory at the mouth of the Nile on 1 August 1798 was celebrated in a novel manner by his prize agent, Alexander Davison, whose name and London address appear in the edge inscription of the medal designed by Kuchler. Originally issued without a suspender, many recipients added a ring to enable the medal to be worn.*

VALUE:

Gold (admirals and captains)	From £5000	Gilt-bronze (petty officers)	£120–160
Silver (junior officers)	£400–500	Bronze (ratings)	£80–100

79. SERINGAPATAM MEDAL

Date: 1808.   **Campaign:** Seringapatam, India, 1799.
Branch of Service: HEIC forces.
Ribbon: 38mm gold.
Metal: Gold, silver-gilt, silver, bronze and pewter.   **Size:** 48mm or 45mm.
Description: (Obverse) the British lion fighting a Bengal tiger with the date of the capture of the fortress IV MAY MDCCXCIX (1799) in the exergue; (reverse) the assault on Seringapatam.
Comments: *The British and native troops who took part in the renewed campaign against Tippoo Sultan were awarded this medal in 1808 in various metals without suspension (a number of different types of suspenders and rings were subsequently fitted by individual recipients). The medal was designed by Kuchler and struck in England and Calcutta, the latter version being slightly smaller. There are several different strikings of these medals.*

VALUE:

Gold 48mm (113)	From £3500	Silver 45mm	£220–260
Gold 45mm	From £3000	Bronze 48mm (5000)	£130–160
Silver-gilt 48mm (185)	£400–450	Pewter 48mm (45,000)	£80–120
Silver 48mm (3636)	£350–400		

80. EARL ST. VINCENT'S MEDAL

Date: 1800.   **Campaign:** Mediterranean.
Branch of Service: Royal Navy.
Ribbon: None.
Metal: Gold or silver.   **Size:** 48mm
Description: (Obverse) left-facing bust of the Earl in Admiral's uniform; (reverse) a sailor and marine.
Comments: *A private medal presented by Admiral Earl St Vincent to the petty officers and men of HMS* Ville de Paris *who remained loyal during the mutiny of the Mediterranean fleet. The gold medals are believed to have been presented by Earl St Vincent to friends and senior naval colleagues.*

VALUE:

Gold	From £3000
Silver	£350–450

81. EGYPT MEDAL

Date: 1801.   **Campaign:** Egypt 1801.
Branch of Service: HEIC forces.
Ribbon: Yellow cord.
Metal: Gold or silver.   **Size:** 48mm.
Description: (Obverse) a sepoy holding a Union Jack, with an encampment in the background. A four-line Farsi text occupies the exergue; (reverse) a warship and the Pyramids.
Comments: *Issued by the Honourable East India Company to British and Indian troops in the Company's service who took part in the conquest of Egypt under Generals Baird and Abercromby.*

VALUE:

Gold (16)	Rare
Silver (2200)	£400–500

82. SULTAN'S MEDAL FOR EGYPT

Date: 1801.
Campaign: Egypt 1801.
Branch of Service: British forces.
Ribbon: None. Originally suspended by gold hook and chain.
Metals: Gold or silver.
Size: Various (see below).
Description: The very thin discs have an elaborate arabesque border enclosing the *toughra* or sign manual of the Sultan.
Comments: *This medal was conferred by Sultan Selim III of Turkey on the British officers and NCOs who took part in the campaign against the French. It was produced in five gold versions for award to different ranks of commissioned officers, as well as one in silver for award to sergeants and corporals.*

VALUE:

Gold 54mm studded with jewels	Rare
Gold 54mm plain	£1800–2000
Gold 48mm	£1200–1500
Gold 43mm	£700–900
Gold 36mm	£500–550
Silver 36mm	£400–450

83. HIGHLAND SOCIETY'S MEDAL FOR EGYPT

Date: 1801.
Campaign: Egypt 1801.
Branch of Service: British forces.
Ribbon: None.
Metals: Gold, silver and bronze.
Size: 49mm.
Description: The medal was designed by Pidgeon. (Obverse) the right-facing bust of General Sir Ralph Abercromby, with a Latin inscription alluding to his death in Egypt; (reverse) a Highlander and the date 21 MAR. 1801 with the Gaelic inscription NA FIR A CHOISIN BUAIDH (These are the heroes who achieved victory in Egypt).
Comments: *The Highland and Agricultural Society (now Royal) was founded in 1784 to promote the development of agriculture in Scotland generally and the Highlands in particular. General Abercromby (born at Tullibody, 1734) commanded the British expedition to Egypt, and the landing at Aboukir Bay on 2 March 1801 in the face of strenuous French opposition, is justly regarded as one of the most brilliant and daring exploits of all time. The French made a surprise attack on the British camp on the night of 21 March and Abercromby was struck by a ricochet; he died aboard the flagship seven days later. Medals in gold were presented to the Prince Regent and Abercromby's sons, but silver and bronze medals were later struck and awarded to senior officers of the expedition as well as soldiers who had distinguished themselves in the campaign.*

VALUE:

Gold	—
Silver	£600–800
Bronze	£250–300

84. BOULTON'S TRAFALGAR MEDAL

Date: 1805.
Campaign: Battle of Trafalgar 1805.
Branch of Service: Royal Navy.
Ribbon: 32mm navy blue (originally issued without suspension).
Metals: Gold, silver, white metal, gilt-bronze or bronze.　　**Size:** 48mm.
Description: (Obverse) bust of Nelson; (reverse) a battle scene.
Comments: *Matthew Boulton of the Soho Mint, Birmingham, struck this medal on his own initiative for presentation to the survivors of the battle of Trafalgar. It was awarded in gold, silver and white metal, but bronze and gilt-bronze specimens also exist. The edge bears an incuse inscription "From M. Boulton to the Heroes of Trafalgar".*

VALUE:

Gold	£6000–10,000	Gilt-bronze	£400–600
Silver	£400–800	Bronze	£150–220
White metal	£120–300	*NB These prices are dependent on attribution.*	

85. DAVISON'S TRAFALGAR MEDAL

Date: 1805.
Campaign: Battle of Trafalgar 1805.
Branch of Service: Royal Navy.
Ribbon: 32mm navy blue.
Metal: Pewter with a copper rim.　　**Size:** 52mm.
Description: (Obverse) bust of Nelson; (reverse) a man-of-war with an appropriate biblical quotation from Exodus "The Lord is a Man-of-War".
Comments: *Alexander Davison, Nelson's prize agent, had this medal struck for award to the ratings who took part in the battle.*

VALUE:　　　£500–600

86. CAPTURE OF RODRIGUEZ, ISLE OF BOURBON AND ISLE OF FRANCE

Date: 1810.
Campaign: Indian Ocean 1809-10.
Branch of Service: HEIC forces.
Ribbon: Yellow cord.
Metal: Gold or silver.
Size: 49mm.
Description: (Obverse) a sepoy in front of a cannon with the Union Jack; (reverse) a wreath with inscriptions in English and Farsi.
Comments: *The East India Company awarded this medal to native troops of the Bengal and Bombay Armies for the capture of three French islands in the Indian Ocean (the latter two being better known today as Mauritius and Reunion) between July 1809 and December 1810.*

VALUE:

Gold (50)	£4000–6000
Silver (2200)	£350–450

87. BAGUR AND PALAMOS MEDAL

Date: 1811.
Campaign: Peninsular War 1810.
Branch of Service: Royal Navy.
Ribbon: Red with yellow edges.
Metal: Gold or silver.
Size: 45mm.
Description: (Obverse) the conjoined crowned shields of Britain and Spain in a wreath with ALIANZA ETERNA (eternal alliance) round the foot; (reverse) inscription in Spanish GRATITUDE OF SPAIN TO THE BRAVE BRITISH AT BAGUR 10 SEPT. 1810, PALAMOS 14 SEPT. 1810.
Comments: *Awarded by the Spanish government to the crews of the British warships* Ajax, Cambrian *and* Kent *who landed at Bagur and Palamos to seize French ships. The British force was, in fact, driven back with very heavy losses.*

VALUE:

Gold (8)	£3000–4000
Silver (600)	£500–600

88. JAVA MEDAL

Date: 1811.
Campaign: Java 1811.
Branch of Service: HEIC forces.
Ribbon: Yellow cord.
Metals: Gold or silver.
Size: 49mm.
Description: (Obverse) the assault on Fort Cornelis; (reverse) inscriptions in English and Farsi.
Comments: *Awarded by the HEIC for the seizure of Java from the Dutch. The 750 British officers and men who took part in the operation were not only awarded this medal but were eligible for the Military GSM with Java clasp, issued 38 years later. Senior officers of the Company were given the gold medal, while junior officers, NCOs and sepoys received the silver version.*

VALUE:

Gold (133)	£3000–4000
Silver (6519)	£350–450

89. NEPAUL MEDAL

Date: 1816.
Campaign: Nepal 1814-16.
Branch of Service: HEIC native troops.
Ribbon: Yellow cord.
Metal: Silver.
Size: 51mm.
Description: (Obverse) a fortified mountain-top with a cannon in the foreground; (reverse) Farsi inscription.
Comments: *This medal marked the campaign to pacify Nepal led by Generals Marley, Ochterlony and Gillespie (the last named being killed in action). At the conclusion of the war Ochterlony began recruiting Gurkha mercenaries, a policy which has continued in the British Army to this day. The clasp "Nepaul" was granted with the Army of India Medal to British forces in 1851.*

VALUE: £500–600

90. CEYLON MEDAL

Date: 1818.
Campaign: Ceylon (Sri Lanka) 1818.
Branch of Service: British and HEIC forces.
Ribbon: 38mm deep navy blue.
Metal: Gold or silver.
Size: 35mm.
Description: The very plain design has "Ceylon 1818" within a wreath (obverse) and REWARD OF MERIT at top and bottom of the reverse, the personal details being engraved in the centre.
Comments: *Awarded by the Ceylon government for gallant conduct during the Kandian rebellion. Only selected officers and men of the 19th, 73rd and 83rd Foot, the 1st and 2nd Ceylon Regiments and 7th, 15th and 18th Madras Native Infantry received this medal.*

VALUE:

Gold (2)	—
Silver (45)	£800–1200

91. BURMA MEDAL

Date: 1826.
Campaign: Burma 1824-26.
Branch of Service: HEIC native forces.
Ribbon: 38mm crimson edged with navy blue.
Metals: Gold or silver.
Size: 39mm.
Description: (Obverse) the Burmese elephant kneeling in submission before the British lion; (reverse) the epic assault on Rangoon by the Irrawaddy Flotilla.
Comments: *Granted to native officers and men who participated in the campaign for the subjugation of Burma. This was the first of the HEIC campaign medals in what was to become a standard 1.5 inch (38mm) diameter. The medal was fitted with a large steel ring for suspension and issued unnamed. British troops in this campaign were belatedly (1851) given the clasp "Ava" to the Army of India Medal.*

VALUE:

Gold (750)	£750–1500
Silver (24,000)	£300–400

92. COORG MEDAL

Date: 1837.
Campaign: Coorg rebellion 1837.
Branch of Service: HEIC loyal Coorg forces.
Ribbon: Yellow cord.
Metals: Gold, silver or bronze.
Size: 50mm.
Description: (Obverse) a Coorg holding a musket, with kukri upraised; (reverse) weapons in a wreath with the inscription FOR DISTINGUISHED CONDUCT AND LOYALTY TO THE BRITISH GOVERNMENT COORG APRIL 1837, the equivalent in Canarese appearing on the obverse.
Comments: *Native troops who remained loyal during the Canara rebellion of April-May 1837 were awarded this medal by the HEIC the following August. Bronze specimens were also struck but not officially issued and may have been restrikes or later copies. Bronzed and silvered electrotype copies are also known.*

VALUE:

Gold (44)	£4000–6000
Silver (300)	£400–600
Bronze	£80–100

93. NAVAL GOLD MEDAL

Date: 1795.
Campaign: Naval actions 1795-1815.
Branch of Service: Royal Navy.
Ribbon: 44mm white with broad dark blue edges.
Metal: Gold.
Size: 51mm and 38mm.
Description: The medals were glazed on both sides and individually engraved on the reverse with the name of the recipient and details of the engagement in a wreath of laurel and oak leaves. (Obverse) the winged figure of Victory bestowing a laurel wreath on the head of Britannia standing in the prow of a galley with a Union Jack shield behind her, her right foot on a helmet, her left hand holding a spear.
Comments: *Instituted in 1795, a year after Lord Howe's naval victory on "the glorious First of June", this medal was awarded continually till 1815 when the Order of the Bath was expanded into three classes. Large medals were awarded to admirals and small medals went to captains. As medals were awarded for separate actions it was possible for officers to wear more than one, and Lord Nelson himself had three.*

VALUE:

Large medal (23)	From £25,000
Small medal (116)	From £8,000

94. NAVAL GENERAL SERVICE MEDAL

Date: 1847.
Campaign: Naval battles and boat actions 1793-1840.
Branch of Service: Royal Navy.
Ribbon: 32mm white with dark blue edges.
Metal: Silver.
Size: 36mm.
Description: (Obverse) the Young Head profile of Queen Victoria by William Wyon; (reverse) Britannia with her trident seated on a sea horse.
Clasps: No fewer than 230 different clasps for major battles, minor engagements, cutting-out operations and boat service were authorised. These either have the name or date of the action, the name of a ship capturing or defeating an enemy vessel, or the words BOAT SERVICE followed by a date. No fewer than 20,933 medals were awarded but most of them had a single clasp. Multi-clasp medals are worth very considerably more. The greatest number of clasps to a single medal was seven (two awards made); four medals had six clasps and fourteen medals had five clasps. For reasons of space only those clasps which are met with fairly often in the salerooms are listed below. At the other end of the scale it should be noted that only one recipient claimed the clasps for *Hussar* (17 May 1795), *Dido* (24 June 1795), *Spider* (25 August 1795), *Espoir* (7 August 1798), *Viper* (26 December 1799), *Loire* (5 February 1800), *Louisa* (28 October 1807), *Carrier* (4 November 1807), *Superieure* (10 February 1809), *Growler* (22 May 1812) and the boat actions of 15 March 1793, 4 November 1803, 4 November 1810 and 3-6 September 1814. In several cases no claimants came forward at all. The numbers of clasps awarded are not an accurate guide to value, as some actions are rated more highly than others, and clasps associated with actions in the War of 1812 have a very strong following in the USA as well as Britain. Clasps for famous battles, such as Trafalgar, likewise command a high premium out of all proportion to the number of clasps awarded.
Comments: *Instituted in 1847 and issued to surviving claimants in 1848, this medal was originally intended to cover naval engagements of the French Revolutionary and Napoleonic Wars (1793-1815) but was almost immediately extended to cover all naval actions of a more recent date, down to the expedition to Syria in 1840. It was fitted with a straight suspender.*

VALUE:

Fleet Actions		Ship Actions	
1 June 1794 (540)	£500–600	Mars 21 April 1798 (26)	£1000–1200
14 March 1795 (95)	£550–650	Lion 15 July 1798 (23)	£1000–1200
23 June 1795 (177)	£500–600	Acre 30 May 1799 (41)	£800–1000
St Vincent (348)	£550–650	London 13 March 1806 (27)	£1000–1200
Camperdown (298)	£550–600	Curacao 1 Jany 1807 (65)	£700–800
Nile (326)	£600–700	Stately 22 March 1808 (31)	£900–1000
12 Octr 1798 (78)	£600–700	Lissa (124)	£600–700
Egypt (618)	£320–350	Shannon with Chesapeake (42)	£2500–3000
Copenhagen (555)	£700–800	Gluckstadt 5 Jany 1814 (44)	£900–1000
Gut of Gibraltar (142)	£550–650	Gaieta 24 July 1815 (88)	£600–700
Trafalgar (1710)	£800–900		
4 Novr 1805 (296)	£550–650	Boat Service	
St Domingo (396)	£350–400	16 July 1806 (51)	£600–650
Martinique (486)	£280–320	1 Novr 1809 (110)	£500–550
Basque Roads (529)	£350–400	28 June 1810 (25)	£700–800
Guadaloupe (483)	£280–320	29 Sepr 1812 (25)	£800–1000
Java (665)	£280–320	8 Ap and May 1813 (57)	£1500–1700
St Sebastian (293)	£300–350	2 May 1813 (48)	£650–750
Algiers (1328)	£250–280	8 April 1814 (24)	£1800–2000
Navarino (1142)	£300–350	24 May 1814 (12)	£1000–1200
Syria (6978)	£150–180	14 Decr 1814 (205)	£800–1000

95. ARMY GOLD CROSS

Date: 1813.
Campaigns: Peninsular War and War of 1812.
Branch of Service: British Army.
Ribbon: 38mm crimson edged with dark blue.
Metal: Gold. **Size:** 38mm.
Description: A cross pattée with a laurel border having a rose at the centre on each of the four flat ends. At the centre of the cross appears a British lion statant. The scrolled top of the cross is fitted with an elaborate ring decorated with laurel leaves looped through a plain swivel ring fitted to the suspender. The arms of the cross on both obverse and reverse bear the names of four battles in relief.
Clasps: Large borders of laurel leaves enclosing the name of a battle in raised relief within an elliptical frame, awarded for fifth and subsequent battles.
Comments: *Arguably the most prestigious award in the campaign series, the Army Gold Cross was approved by the Prince Regent in 1813. It was granted to generals and officers of field rank for service in four or more battles of the Peninsular War. Three crosses had six clasps, two had seven, while the Duke of Wellington himself had the unique cross with nine clasps, representing participation in thirteen battles.*
VALUE: Gold cross without clasp (61) From £10,000

96. MAIDA GOLD MEDAL

Date: 1806.
Campaign: Peninsular War, Battle of Maida 1806.
Branch of Service: British Army.
Ribbon: 38mm crimson edged with navy blue.
Metal: Gold. **Size:** 39mm.
Description: (Obverse) laureated profile of George III; (reverse) winged figure of Victory hovering with a laurel wreath over the head of Britannia, shield upraised, in the act of throwing a spear. The name and date of the battle appears on Britannia's left, with the *trinacria* or three-legged emblem on the right.
Clasps: None.
Comments: *This small gold medal was authorised in 1806 and awarded to the thirteen senior officers involved in the battle of Maida in Calabria when a small British force under General Sir John Stuart defeated a much larger French army with heavy loss. A small unknown number of gold and silver specimens are known to exist.*
VALUE: Rare

97. ARMY GOLD MEDAL

Date: 1810.
Campaigns: Peninsular War 1806-14 and War of 1812.
Branch of Service: British Army.
Ribbon: 38mm crimson edged with navy blue.
Metal: Gold.
Size: 54mm and 33mm.
Description: (Obverse) Britannia seated on a globe, holding a laurel wreath over the British lion and holding a palm branch in her left hand while resting on a shield embellished with the Union Jack. The name of the first action is generally engraved on the reverse.
Clasps: For second and third actions.
Comments: *The Maida medal (no. 96) established a precedent for the series of medals instituted in 1810. The name of the battle was inscribed on the reverse, usually engraved, though that for Barossa was die-struck. These medals were struck in two sizes, the larger being conferred on generals and the smaller on officers of field rank. Second or third battles were denoted by a clasp appropriately inscribed, while those who qualified for a fourth award exchanged their medal and bars for a gold cross. The award of these gold medals and crosses ceased in 1814 when the Companion of the Bath was instituted.*
VALUE:

Large medal	From £8000
Small medal	From £3000

98. MILITARY GENERAL SERVICE MEDAL

Date: 1847.

Campaigns: French Revolutionary and Napoleonic Wars 1793-1814.

Branch of Service: British Army.

Ribbon: 31mm crimson edged with dark blue.

Metal: Silver.

Size: 36mm.

Description: (Obverse) the Wyon profile of Queen Victoria; (reverse) a standing figure of the Queen bestowing victor's laurels on a kneeling Duke of Wellington. The simple inscription TO THE BRITISH ARMY appears round the circumference, while the dates 1793-1814 are placed in the exergue. Despite this, the earliest action for which a clasp was issued took place in 1801 (Abercromby's Egyptian campaign).

Clasps: Only 29 battle or campaign clasps were issued but multiple awards are much commoner than in the naval medal, the maximum being fifteen. While it is generally true to say that multi-clasp medals are worth more than single-clasp medals, there are many in the latter category (noted below) which command higher prices. The figures quoted below are based on the commonest regiments. Clasps awarded to specialists and small detached forces rate more highly than medals to the principal regiment in a battle or campaign. In particular, it should be noted that one naval officer, Lieut. Carroll, received the Military GSM and clasp for Maida, while a few other officers of the Royal Navy and Royal Marines received the medal with the clasps for Guadaloupe, Martinique or Java, and these, naturally, are now very much sought after. Paradoxically, the clasps for Sahagun and Benevente alone are very much scarcer than the clasp inscribed Sahagun and Benevente, awarded to surviving veterans who had participated in both battles. The clasps are listed below in chronological order.

Comments: *Like the Naval GSM, this medal was not sanctioned till 1847 and awarded the following year. Unlike the Naval medal, however, the Military GSM was confined to land actions up to the defeat of Napoleon in 1814 and the conclusion of the war with the United States.*

VALUE:

Egypt	£300–350	Chateauguay	£1400–1600
Maida	£320–350	Chrystler's Farm	£1500–1800
Roleia	£500–600	Vittoria	£200–220
Vimiera	£300–350	Pyrenees	£220–250
Sahagun	£500–600	St Sebastian	£250–280
Benevente	£4500–5500	Nivelle	£220–250
Sahagun and Benevente	£350–400	Nive	£220–250
Corunna	£250–300	Orthes	£220–250
Martinique	£250–280	Toulouse	£200–220
Talavera	£300–400	2 clasps	£250–300
Guadaloupe	£250–280	3 clasps	£300–350
Busaco	£280–320	4 clasps	£350–400
Barrosa	£280–300	5 clasps	£400–450
Fuentes D'Onor	£250–300	6 clasps	£450–500
Albuhera	£350–400	7 clasps	£500–550
Java	£280–320	8 clasps	£550–650
Ciudad Rodrigo	£250–300	9 clasps	£800–1000
Badajoz	£300–350	10 clasps	£900–1100
Salamanca	£220–250	11 clasps	£1100–1300
Fort Detroit	£1400–1800	12 or more clasps	From £1500

99. WATERLOO MEDAL

Date: 1815.
Campaign: Waterloo 1815.
Branch of Service: British Army.
Ribbon: 38mm, crimson edged in dark blue.
Metal: Silver.
Size: 37mm.
Description: (Obverse) the profile of the Prince Regent; (reverse) the seated figure of Victory above a tablet simply inscribed WATERLOO with the date of the battle in the exergue.
Comments: *This was the first medal awarded and officially named to all ranks who took part in a particular campaign. It was also issued, however, to those who had taken part in one or more of the other battles of the campaign, at Ligny and Quatre Bras two days earlier. The ribbon was intended to be worn with an iron clip and split suspension ring but many recipients subsequently replaced these with a more practical silver mount which would not rust and spoil the uniform. Some 39,000 medals were issued. The value of a Waterloo medal depends to a large extent on the regiment of the recipient. Medals awarded to those formations which saw the heaviest action and bore the brunt of the losses are in the greatest demand, whereas medals named to soldiers in General Colville's reserve division which did not take part in the fighting, are the least highly rated.*

VALUE:

Heavy Cavalry	£450–600
Scots Greys	£600–1000
Light Cavalry	£350–450
Royal Artillery	£250–400
Foot Guards	£400–500
1st, 27th, 28th, 30th, 42nd, 44th, 73rd, 79th, 92nd Foot	£500–900
Other Foot regiments	£350–450
Colville's division (35th, 54th, 59th, 91st Foot)	£250–350
King's German Legion	£300–600

100. BRUNSWICK MEDAL FOR WATERLOO

Date: 1815.
Campaign: Battle of Waterloo 1815.
Branch of Service: Brunswick troops.
Ribbon: Yellow with light blue stripes towards the edges.
Metal: Bronze.
Description: (Obverse) Duke Friedrich Wilhelm of Brunswick who was killed in the battle; (reverse) a wreath of laurel and oak leaves enclosing the German text "Braunschweig Seinen Kriegern" (Brunswick to its warriors) and the names of Quatre Bras and Waterloo.
Comments: *The Prince Regent authorised this medal for issue to the contingent from the Duchy of Brunswick.*

VALUE: £130–180

101. HANOVERIAN MEDAL FOR WATERLOO

Date: 1815.
Campaign: Battle of Waterloo 1815.
Branch of Service: Hanoverian troops.
Ribbon: Crimson edged with light blue.
Metal: Silver.
Description: (Obverse) the Prince Regent, his name and title being rendered in German. (Reverse) a trophy of arms below the legend HANNOVERSCHER TAPFERKEIT (Hanoverian bravery), with the name and date of the battle wreathed in the centre.
Comments: *The Prince Regent authorised this medal on behalf of his father George III in his capacity as Elector of Hanover and this was conferred on survivors of the battle. Suspension was by iron clip and ring similar to the British Waterloo Medal.*

VALUE: £140–200

102. NASSAU MEDAL FOR WATERLOO

Date: 1815.
Campaign: Battle of Waterloo 1815.
Branch of Service: Nassau forces.
Ribbon: Dark blue edged in yellow.
Metal: Silver.
Size: 25mm.
Description: (Obverse) Duke Friedrich of Nassau; (reverse) the winged figure of Victory crowning a soldier with laurels, the date of the action being in the exergue.
Comments: *Friedrich Duke of Nassau distributed this medal on 23 December 1815 to all of his own troops who had been present at the battle.*

VALUE: £120–140

103. SAXE-GOTHA-ALTENBURG MEDAL

Date: 1815.
Campaign: Germany and Waterloo 1814-15.
Branch of Service: Saxe-Gotha-Altenburg Foreign Legion.
Ribbon: Green with black edges and gold stripes.
Metal: Gilt bronze or bronze.
Size: 42mm.
Description: (Obverse) a crown with the legend IM KAMPFE FUER DAS RECHT (in the struggle for the right); (reverse) an ornate rose motif with the name of the duchy and the dates of the campaign in roman numerals.
Comments: *Gilded medals were issued to officers, but other ranks received a bronze version.*

VALUE:
Gilt-bronze   £220–260
Bronze   £150–180

104. ARMY OF INDIA MEDAL

Date: 1851.
Campaigns: India 1803–26.
Branch of Service: British and HEIC troops.
Ribbon: 32mm pale blue.
Metal: Silver.
Size: 35mm.
Description: (Obverse) the Wyon profile of Queen Victoria; (reverse) the seated figure of Victory beside a palm tree, with a wreath in one hand and a laurel crown in the other. The medal is suspended by a rococo mount fitted to a plain suspender.
Clasps: The medal was not awarded without a campaign clasp and, unusually, in multi-clasp medals, the last clasp awarded was mounted closest to the medal itself, so that the battle roll has to be read downwards. There were two dies of the reverse, leading to the long- or short-hyphen varieties, both of comparable value. In all, some 4500 medals were awarded, but there is a very wide divergence between the commonest and rarest bars. Multi-clasp medals are rare, and medals awarded to Europeans are much scarcer than those to Indian troops.
Comments: *The last of the medals authorised in connection with the Napoleonic Wars, it was instituted and paid for by the Honourable East India Company in March 1851 for award to surviving veterans of the battles and campaigns in India and Burma between 1803 and 1826. Despite the dates 1799–1826 in the exergue, the medal was in fact awarded for service in one or other of four wars: the Second Mahratta War (1803–4), the Nepal War (1814–16), the Pindaree or Third Mahratta War (1817–18) and the Burmese War (1824–26), together with the siege of Bhurtpoor (1825–26). The medal is scarce, and examples with the clasps for the Second Mahratta War are much sought after, partly because few veterans were still alive 48 years after the event to claim their medals, and partly because of the war's association with Arthur Wellesley, the Duke of Wellington, who died in the very year in which the medal was awarded.*

VALUE:
Prices for medals bearing the following clasps are for European recipients. Medals to Indians are generally less expensive.

Allighur (66)	£2000–2500
Battle of Delhi (40)	£2500–2800
Assye (87)	£2000–2500
Asseerghur (48)	£2000–2500
Laswarree (100)	£1000–1200
Argaum (126)	£2000–2500
Gawilghur (110)	£2000–2500
Defence of Delhi (5)	Rare
Battle of Deig (47)	£2000–2500
Capture of Deig (103)	£1800–2200
Nepaul (505)	£400–500
Kirkee (5)	Rare
Poona (75)	£900–1000
Kirkee and Poona (88)	£800–900
Seetabuldee (2)	Rare
Nagpore (155)	£650–700
Seetabuldee and Nagpore (21)	Rare
Maheidpoor (75)	£800–1000
Corygaum (4)	Rare
Ava (2325)	£250–300
Bhurtpoor (1059)	£350–400
2 clasps (300)	Rare
3 clasps (150)	Rare
4 clasps (23)	Rare
5 or more clasps (10 x 5, 2 x 6, 1 x 7)	Rare

105. GHUZNEE MEDAL

Date: 1839.
Campaign: Ghuznee 1839.
Branch of Service: British and HEIC forces.
Ribbon: 35mm half crimson, half dark green.
Metal: Silver.
Size: 37mm.
Description: (Obverse) the impressive gateway of the fortress of Ghuznee; (reverse) a mural crown enclosed in a laurel wreath with the date of capture.
Comments: *This was the second medal awarded for a particular campaign (after Waterloo) and was granted to both British and Indian troops who took part in the assault on Ghuznee in July 1839 which brought the first Afghan War to a close, overthrew the pro-Russian Dost Mohamed and restored Shah Soojah who instituted the Order of the Dooranie Empire (awarded to British generals and field officers) in appreciation. The Ghuznee medal was issued unnamed by the Honourable East India Company, but many recipients subsequently had their names impressed or engraved in various styles. No clasps were issued officially, but unauthorised clasps are occasionally encountered.*

VALUE:

British recipient	£200–400
Indian recipient	£150–200
Unnamed as issued	£140–180

106. ST JEAN D'ACRE MEDAL

Date: 1840.
Campaign: Syria 1840.
Branch of Service: Royal Navy, Royal Marines and British Army.
Ribbon: Red with white edges.
Metal: Gold, silver or copper (bronzed).
Size: 30mm.
Description: (Obverse) a fortress flying the Ottoman flag, with six five-pointed stars round the top. A commemorative inscription and date in Arabic appear at the foot. (Reverse) the Toughra of the Sultan in a laurel wreath.
Comments: *Awarded by the Sultan of Turkey to British, Austrian and Turkish forces under Sir Charles Napier, taking part in the liberation of this important city on the Syrian coast after eight years of Egyptian occupation. The medal has a plain ring suspension. The clasp "Syria" to the Naval GSM was awarded in 1848 in respect to this operation, and this medal generally accompanies the St Jean d'Acre medal.*

VALUE:

Gold (captains and field officers)	£400–500
Silver (junior officers)	£60–80
Copper (petty officers, NCOs and other ranks)	£30–50

107. CANDAHAR, GHUZNEE, CABUL MEDAL

Date: 1842.
Campaign: Afghanistan 1841–42.
Branch of Service: British and HEIC troops.
Ribbon: 40mm watered silk of red, white, yellow, white and blue.
Metal: Silver.
Size: 35mm.
Description: Although the medals have a uniform obverse, a profile of the Queen captioned VICTORIA VINDEX, reverses are inscribed with the names of individual battles, or combinations thereof, within wreaths surmounted by a crown.
Comments: *The Honourable East India Company instituted this series of medals in 1842 for award to both HEIC and British troops who took part in the First Afghan War. The issue of this medal to units of the British Army, to Europeans serving in the Company's forces, and to Indian troops is further complicated by the fact that unnamed medals are generally common. In addition, the medal for Cabul is known in two versions, with the inscription CABUL or CABVL, the latter being a major rarity as only fifteen were issued. Beware of modern copies of the Candahar and Cabul medals.*

VALUE:	Imperial Regiments	Indian Units	Unnamed
Candahar	£400–500	£200–250	£150–200
Cabul	£250–300	£140–180	£100–150
Cabvl (15)	Rare	Rare	Rare
Ghuznee/Cabul	£400–600	£250–300	£200–250
Candahar/Ghuznee/ Cabul	£300–350	£200–250	£150–200

108. JELLALABAD MEDALS

Date: 1842.
Campaign: Afghanistan 1841-42.
Branch of Service: British and HEIC forces.
Ribbon: 44mm watered silk red, white, yellow, white and blue.
Metal: Silver.
Size: 39mm and 35mm.
Description: There are two different types of this medal, awarded by the HEIC to surviving defenders of the fortress of Jellalabad between 12 November 1841 and 7 April 1842. The first, struck in Calcutta, has a mural crown and JELLALABAD on the obverse, with the date of the relief of the garrison on the reverse; the second type shows the Wyon profile of Victoria (obverse) and the winged Victory with mountain scenery in the background and JELLALABAD VII APRIL round the top and the year in roman numerals in the exergue (reverse).
Comment: *The first type, struck in Calcutta, was considered to be unsuitable and holders were invited to exchange their medals for the second, more attractive, issue which was produced in London, although very few recipients took up the offer. The latter type was also awarded to the next of kin of soldiers killed in action.*

VALUE:	Imperial Regiments	Indian Units	Unnamed
First type (Crown)	£360–450	£250–300	£200–250
Second type (Victory)	£500–700	—	£300–350

109. MEDAL FOR THE DEFENCE OF KELAT-I-GHILZIE

Date: 1842.
Campaign: Afghanistan 1842.
Branch of Service: European and native troops, HEIC.
Ribbon: 40mm watered silk red, white, yellow, white and blue.
Metal: Silver.
Size: 36mm.
Description: (Obverse) a shield bearing the name of the fort, surmounted by a mural crown and encircled by laurels; (reverse) a trophy of arms above a tablet inscribed INVICTA (unbeaten) and the date in roman numerals.
Comments: *Awarded to those who took part in the defence of the fort at Kelat-i-Ghilzie in May 1842, it is the rarest medal of the First Afghan War. No British imperial regiments took part, but 55 Europeans in the Company's service received the medal. It was also awarded to 877 native troops (including a contingent supplied by Shah Soojah) but few of their medals appear to have survived.*

VALUE:

European recipients	£3500–4500
Indian recipients	£1500–2000
Unnamed	£300–400

110. CHINA WAR MEDAL

Date: 1842.
Campaign: China 1841-42.
Branch of Service: British and HEIC forces.
Ribbon: 39mm crimson with yellow edges.
Metal: Silver.
Size: 36mm.
Description: The medal has the usual Wyon obverse, but the reverse was to have shown a British lion with its forepaws on a dragon. This was deemed to be offensive to the Chinese and was replaced by an oval shield bearing the royal arms, a palm tree and a trophy of weapons with the Latin motto ARMIS EXPOSCERE PACEM (to pray for peace by force of arms) round the top and CHINA 1842 at the foot.
Comments: *Originally intended for issue to all ranks of the Honourable East India Company, it was subsequently awarded by the British government in 1843 to all who had taken part in the campaign in China popularly known as the First Opium War which ended with the seizure of Nanking.*

VALUE:

Royal Navy	£180–220
Indian and Bengal marine units	£250–350
British imperial regiments	£180–220
Indian Army	£140–160
Specimens of the original reverse	From £500

111. SCINDE MEDAL

Date: 1843.
Campaign: Scinde 1843.
Branch of Service: HEIC forces and 22nd Foot.
Ribbon: 44mm watered silk red, white, yellow, white and blue.
Metal: Silver.
Size: 36mm.
Description: The usual Wyon profile obverse was married to three different reverse types showing a crowned laurel wreath inscribed with the name of one or two campaigns and the date.
Comments: *Authorised in September 1843, this silver medal marked Sir Charles Napier's conquest of Scinde. The two major battles in the campaign, at Meeanee and Hyderabad, accomplished the complete rout of the forces of the Amirs of Scinde. The medals were originally issued with steel suspenders but the commanding officer of the 22nd Foot had the medals awarded to his men fitted with silver suspenders, at his own expense. Medals to the Indus Flotilla are particularly sought after by collectors.*

VALUE:

	22nd Foot	Indian units
Meeanee	£600–800	£250–350
Hyderabad	£500–600	£200–250
Meeanee/Hyderabad	£400–500	£200–250

112. GWALIOR STAR

Date: 1843.
Campaign: Gwalior 1843.
Branch of Service: British and HEIC forces.
Ribbon: 44mm watered silk red, white, yellow, white and blue.
Metals: Bronze, with a silver centre.
Size: Max. width 45mm; max. height 52mm.
Description: Six-pointed bronze star with a silver centre star. The silver stars in the centre bear the name of one or other of the battles and the date 29 December 1843 on which both battles were fought. The plain reverse bears the name and regiment of the recipient.
Comments: *Bronze from guns captured at the battles of Maharajpoor and Punniar during the Gwalior campaign was used in the manufacture of these stars, thus anticipating the production of the Victoria Cross in the same manner. They were presented by the Indian government to all ranks who took part in these actions. When first issued, these stars were fitted with hooks to be worn like a breast decoration, but later ornate bar or ring suspensions were fitted to individual fancy and worn with the standard Indian ribbon of the period.*

VALUE:

Maharajpoor	£200–250
Punniar	£250–300

Awards to India recipients are usually somewhat less.

113. SUTLEJ MEDAL

Date: 1846.
Campaign: Sutlej 1845-46.
Branch of Service: British and HEIC forces.
Ribbon: Dark blue with crimson edges.
Metal: Silver.
Size: 36mm.
Description: (Obverse) Wyon profile of Queen Victoria; (reverse) standing figure of Victory holding aloft a laurel crown, with a pile of captured weapons at her feet. The legend ARMY OF THE SUTLEJ appears round the top. The medal was fitted with an ornamental scroll suspender.
Clasps: Mounted above the suspender with roses between: Ferozeshuhur, Aliwal or Sobraon.
Comments: *The practice of issuing medals inscribed with different battles now gave way to the style of medals with specific battle or campaign clasps which set the precedent for the Naval and Military GSMs and later awards. As a compromise, however, the exergue of the reverse bears the name and date of the action for which the medal was first granted, and thus several different types are known.*

VALUE:	British regiments	Europeans in HEIC units	Indian units
Moodkee	£140–180	£120–140	£80–100
Moodkee 1 clasp	£180–220	£140–160	£100–120
Moodkee 2 clasps	£250–300	£150–200	£140–160
Moodkee 3 clasps	£350–400	£250–300	£160–200
Ferozeshuhur	£140–150	£150–200	£80–120
Ferozeshuhur 1 clasp	£180–200	£150–200	£100–150
Ferozeshuhur 2 clasps	£250–300	£280–360	£150–200
Aliwal	£130–160	£140–160	£80–100
Aliwal 1 clasp	£180–200	£160–180	£120–140
Sobraon	£130–160	£120–140	£80–100
Glazed gilt specimen	£200–250		

114. PUNJAB MEDAL

Date: 1849.
Campaign: Punjab 1848-49.
Branch of Service: British and HEIC forces.
Ribbon: Dark blue with yellow stripes towards the edges.
Metal: Silver.
Size: 36mm.
Description: (Obverse) Wyon profile of Queen Victoria; (reverse) Sir Walter Gilbert receiving the Sikh surrender. TO THE ARMY OF THE PUNJAB appears round the top and the year in roman numerals in the exergue. The medal has a scroll suspender.
Clasps: Mooltan, Chilianwala, Goojerat. Unusually the clasps read downwards from top to bottom
Comments: *This medal was granted to troops taking part in the campaigns which ended in the annexation of the Punjab. Unlike the Sutlej medal, however, this silver medal had a standard design. Large numbers of this medal were awarded to native troops, however many were melted down and therefore surprisingly few remain on the market in comparison with medals to European recipients.*

VALUE:	British units	Europeans in HEIC units	Indian units
No clasp	£100–120	£80–100	£60–80
Mooltan	£170–190	£140–160	£100–120
Chilianwala	£180–220	£140–160	£100–120
Goojerat	£170–190	£160–180	£140–160
Mooltan/Goojerat	£180–200	£160–180	£140–160
Chilianwala/Goojerat	£180–200	£160–180	£140–160
24th Foot casualty at Chilianwala	£320–360	—	—
Glazed gilt specimen	£200–250		

115. SOUTH AFRICA MEDAL

Date: 1854.
Campaigns: Southern Africa 1834–53.
Branch of Service: Royal Navy and Army.
Ribbon: Gold with broad and narrow deep blue stripes towards each
  end.
Metal: Silver.
Size: 36mm.
Description: (Obverse) Wyon profile of Queen Victoria; (reverse) a
  British lion drinking at a waterhole beside a protea shrub, the date
  1853 being in the exergue.
Clasps: None.
Comments: *Authorised in November 1854, this medal was awarded in
  respect of three campaigns in southern Africa: 1834–35, 1846–47 and
  1850–53, but as the medal was issued with a standard reverse and no
  campaign clasps it is impossible to tell when and where the recipient served
  without reference to the medal rolls. The majority of recipients were British
  troops but several hundred sailors of the Royal Navy also received the
  medal and a much smaller number of local forces. Of particular interest are
  medals awarded to men who survived the sinking of the troopship
  Birkenhead on its way to the Cape.*

VALUE:

	1834–35	1846–47	1850–53
British Army	£250–300	£220–270	£170–190
Royal Navy	£280–320	£250–290	£180–220
HMS *Birkenhead*			£400–600
Local forces	£260–280	£230–250	£150–180

116. SIR HARRY SMITH'S MEDAL FOR GALLANTRY

Date: 1851.
Campaign: Eighth Kaffir War 1850-51.
Branch of Service: Cape Mounted Rifles.
Ribbon: Dark blue with crimson edges.
Metal: Silver.
Size: 34mm.
Description: (Obverse) British lion passant gardant with a laurel
  wreath over its head; date 1851 in the exergue. (Reverse) PRE-
  SENTED BY round top and FOR GALLANTRY IN THE FIELD
  round the foot. HIS EXCELLENCY SIR H. G. SMITH and the name
  of the recipient appear across the centre.
Comments: *Sir Harry Smith (1787–1860) served with distinction in the
  Kaffir War of 1834–35, gained his KCB in the Gwalior campaign and a
  baronetcy for his decisive victory at Aliwal in the Sikh War. In 1847 he
  returned to South Africa as governor of Cape Colony. Although short of
  troops he conducted the eighth Kaffir War (1850–53) with great resource-
  fulness but was recalled to England in 1852 before the Kaffirs had been
  subdued. Harrismith in the Orange Free State was named in his honour,
  while Ladysmith in Natal was named after his beautiful and spirited
  Spanish wife Juanita, the forces' sweetheart of her day. Sir Harry had this
  medal struck at his own expense and awarded to troopers of the Cape
  Mounted Rifles who took part in the epic ride through the Kaffir lines from
  Fort Cox to Kingwilliamstown in 1851. Only 31 medals were presented, of
  which 22 are believed to be still extant.*

VALUE:
Unnamed	£1200–1500
Named	2000–3000

117. INDIA GENERAL SERVICE MEDAL

Date: 1854.

Campaigns: Indian 1854-95.

Branch of Service: British and Indian forces.

Ribbon: Three crimson and two dark blue bars of equal width.

Metal: Silver or bronze.

Size: 36mm.

Description: (Obverse) Wyon profile of Queen Victoria; (reverse) Victory crowning a semi-nude seated warrior.

Clasps: 24 (see below).

Comments: *This medal was the first of five general service medals issued to cover minor campaigns in India. It was instituted in 1854 and continued for forty-one years, retaining the original Wyon profile of Queen Victoria throughout the entire period. Although the medal itself is quite common, some of its clasps are very rare, notably* Kachin Hills 1892–93 *awarded to the* Yorkshire Regiment *and* Chin Hills 1892–93 *awarded to the* Norfolk Regiment. *The maximum number of clasps to one medal recorded is seven. At first the medal was awarded in silver to all ranks regardless of race or branch of the services, but from 1885 onwards it was issued in bronze to native support personnel such as bearers, sweepers and drivers.*

VALUE:

	British Army	Indian Army	Bronze
Pegu	£70–80	—	—
Persia	£70–80	£55–65	—
North West Frontier	£70–80	£50–60	—
Umbeyla	£80–90	£55–65	—
Bhootan	£70–80	£50–60	—
Looshai	—	£80–100	—
Perak	£70–80	£70–80	—
Jowaki 1877–78	£70–80	£60–70	—
Naga 1879–80	—	£130–150	—
Burma 1885–87	£50–60	£55–65	£50–60
Sikkim 1888	£100–120	£60–70	£80–100
Hazara 1888	£60–70	£80–90	£75–90
Burma 1887–89	£50–60	£40–50	£50–60
Burma 1887–9	£70–80	—	—
Chin Lushai 1889–90	£100–120	£40–50	£110–130
Lushai 1889–92	£180–220	£120–150	£170–190
Samana 1891	£70–80	£50–60	£60–70
Hazara 1891	£60–70	£40–50	£50–60
NE Frontier 1891	£80–90	£40–50	£80–90
Hunza 1891	—	£180–200	£350–380
Burma 1889–92	£60–70	£55–65	£50–60
Chin Hills 1892–93	£280–300	£110–130	£320–350
Kachin Hills 1892-93	£380–420	£180-200	£700–750
Waziristan 1894–95	£80–90	£40–50	£40–50

118. BALTIC MEDAL

Date: 1856.
Campaign: Baltic Sea 1854–55.
Branch of Service: Royal Navy, Royal Marines and Royal Sappers and Miners.
Ribbon: Yellow with light blue edges.
Metal: Silver.
Size: 36mm.
Description: (Obverse) Wyon profile of Queen Victoria; (reverse) Britannia seated on a plinth decorated by a cannon, with a coastal scene in the background and BALTIC round the top.
Comments: *Authorised in 1856, this medal was granted to officers and men of the Royal Navy and Royal Marines for operations against Russia in the Baltic at the same time as the war in the Crimea. It was also awarded to about 100 members of the Royal Sappers and Miners engaged in the demolition of Russian fortifications of Bomarsund and Sveaborg. Medals were generally issued unnamed but often privately named afterwards, the exception being medals to the Sappers and Miners which were officially impressed.*

VALUE:

Unnamed	£50–70
Privately named	£60–80
Impressed to Sappers and Miners	£400–500

119. CRIMEA MEDAL

Date: 1854.
Campaign: Crimea 1854–56.
Branch of Service: British Army, Navy and Marines.
Ribbon: Pale blue with yellow edges.
Metal: Silver.
Size: 36mm.
Description: (Obverse) Wyon profile of Queen Victoria; (reverse) a Roman soldier, armed with circular shield and short sword, being crowned by a flying Victory.
Clasps: Unusually ornate, being shaped like oak leaves with acorn finials: Alma, Inkerman, Azoff, Balaklava, Sebastopol, but the maximum found on any medal is four. Unofficial clasps for Traktir, Mamelon Vert, Malakoff, Mer d'Azoff and Kinburn are sometimes found on medals awarded to French troops.
Comments: *Medals may be found unnamed, unofficially or regimentally named, or officially impressed. Medals awarded to participants in the most famous actions of the war—the Thin Red Line (93rd Foot) and the Charge of the Light and Heavy Brigades—rate a very high premium. The prices quoted are for medals officially impressed to the Army.*

VALUE:

No clasp	£80–120
Alma	£130–150
Inkerman	£150–170
Azoff	£100–120
Balaklava	£160–180
93rd Foot	£400–450
Heavy Bde	£500–700
Light Bde (Charger)	From £2000
Sebastopol	£80–100
2 clasps	£150–180
3 clasps	£200–250
4 clasps	£300–350

120. TURKISH CRIMEA MEDAL

Date: 1855.
Campaign: Crimea 1855-56.
Branch of Service: British, French and Sardinian forces.
Ribbon: Crimson with green edges.
Metal: Silver.
Size: 36mm.
Description: (Obverse) a cannon, weapons and the four Allied flags with the name and date in the exergue; (reverse) the Toughra and Arabic date according to the Moslem calendar.
Clasps: None.
Comments: *Instituted by the Sultan of Turkey, this silver medal was conferred on troops of the three Allies who fought in the Crimea. The obverse types differed in the arrangement of the flags, corrsponding with the inscription in English, French or Italian in the exergue. Although the medals were intended to be issued to British, French and Sardinian troops respectively, they were issued haphazardly. They were unnamed, but many were privately engraved or impressed later. There is a dangerous copy emanating from the West Country of the UK.*

VALUE:

CRIMEA (British Issue)	£40–50
LA CRIMEE (French Issue)	£100–150
LA CRIMEA (Sardinia Issue)	£35–45

121. INDIAN MUTINY MEDAL

Date: 1858.
Campaign: Sepoy mutiny, India 1857-58.
Branch of Service: British Army, Navy and Indian forces.
Ribbon: White with two red stripes.
Metal: Silver.
Size: 36mm.
Description: (Obverse) Wyon profile of Queen Victoria; (reverse) the standing figure of Britannia bestowing victor's laurels, with the British lion alongside. INDIA appears round the top with the dates 1857-1858 in the exergue.
Clasps: Delhi, Defence of Lucknow, Relief of Lucknow, Lucknow, Central India. The maximum recorded for a single medal is four (Bengal Artillery) or three (imperial troops, 9th Lancers).
Comments: *This medal was awarded to troops who took part in operations to quell the Sepoy mutiny which had been the immediate cause of the uprising, although it also served to focus attention on the Honourable East India Company's conduct of affairs and led directly to the transfer of the administration of India to the Crown. Medals with the clasp for the defence of Lucknow awarded to the original defenders rate a considerable premium, as do medals awarded to members of the Naval Brigade which witnessed most of the fighting in the mopping-up operations.*

VALUE:

	British Navy	British Army
No clasp	£250–350	£70–100
Delhi	—	£140–200
Defence of Lucknow		
original defender	—	£500–600
first relief force	—	£300–350
Relief of Lucknow	£400–500	£140–180
Lucknow	£400–500	£120–150
Central India	—	£120–150
2 clasps	£400–500	£1160–200
3 clasps (9th Lancers)	—	£450–500

*Medals to Indian recipients although scarcer on the market, generally bring a little less than their British counterparts. Four clasp medals to the Bengal Artillery bring from £800 if verified.

122. SECOND CHINA WAR MEDAL

Date: 1861.
Campaign: Second China War 1857-60.
Branch of Service: British Army and Navy.
Ribbon: 33mm crimson with yellow edges.
Metal: Silver.
Size: 36mm.
Description: As the First China War medal, but without the year 1842 at the foot.
Clasps: Fatshan 1857, Canton 1857, Taku Forts, Pekin 1860.
Comments: *This medal was awarded to British sevicemen who took part, alongside the French, in the campaign against China which had been provoked by hostile acts against European nationals. The Royal Navy, under Admiral Sir Michael Seymour, destroyed a Chinese flotilla at Fatshan Creek, preparing the way for the attack on Canton whose capture brought the first phase to an end in June 1858. Reinforcements were meanwhile diverted to help put down the Indian mutiny. Fighting broke out again and this time large numbers of troops were involved in the assault on the Taku forts and the sack of Pekin (Beijing). Examples of the China medal of 1842, with or without clasps for 1857-60, have been recorded to recipients who fought in the Second China War. Medals may be found unnamed or with names officially engraved (Indian Army) or impressed (British Army, India Marine). Although those to the Navy were all issued unnamed, they are occasionally encountered unofficially named. Awards to Army and Navy personnel are other factors governing values.*

VALUE:

No clasp	£40–50
China 1842	Rare
Fatshan 1857	£50–60
Canton 1857	£130–160
Taku Forts 1858	£60–70
Taku Forts 1860	£120–140
Pekin 1860	£120–140
2 clasps	£160–180
3 clasps	£80–100

123. NEW ZEALAND MEDALS

Date: 1869.
Campaigns: First and Second Maori Wars 1845–47 and 1860–66.
Branch of Service: Army, Navy and local volunteers.
Ribbon: Blue with a central orange stripe.
Metal: Silver.
Size: 36mm.
Description: (Obverse) Veiled head of Queen Victoria. (Reverse) Date of service in a wreath, with NEW ZEALAND round the top and VIRTUTIS HONOR (honour of valour) round the foot. Suspender ornamented with New Zealand wattle.
Comments: *These medals were unusual in having the recipient's dates of service die-struck on the centre of the reverse, though medals were also issued without dates. As the medal was only awarded to surviving veterans, the numbers issued in respect of the earlier conflict are understandably small. Many of the dates are very scarce, especially those issued to naval personnel in the first war.*

VALUE:

First war

Undated	£150–170
1845–46	£250–280
1845–47	£280–320
1846–47	£300–320
1846	£500–600
1847	£400–450
1848	Rare

Second war

Undated	£130–140
1860	£500–550
1860-61	£180–200
1860-63	From £1500
1860-64	£180–220
1860-65	£180–200
1860-66	£170–190
1861	Rare
1861-63	Rare
1861-64	£200–220
1861-65	Rare
1861-66	£130–150
1862-66	Rare
1863	£400–450
1863-64	£160–180
1863-65	£170–190
1863-66	£170–190
1864	£200–220
1864-65	£170–190
1864-66	£140–160
1865	£280–320
1865-66	£150–180
1866	£150–180

124. ABYSSINIAN WAR MEDAL

Date: 1869.
Campaign: Abyssinia (Ethiopia) 1867–68.
Branch of Service: Royal Navy, British and Indian Armies.
Ribbon: Red with broad white edges.
Metal: Silver.
Size: 33mm diameter.
Description: (Obverse) the veiled portrait of Victoria framed by a zigzag pattern with floral ornament alternating with the letters of the name ABYSSINIA. The recipient's name and unit were embossed in the centre of the reverse except most to Indian troops which were impressed. Suspension is by a ring via a large crown standing proud from the top of the medal.
Clasps: None.
Comments: *The imprisonment of British subjects by King Theodore of Abyssinia precipitated a punitive expedition under General Sir Robert Napier involving ships of the Royal Navy, a naval brigade and troops of the British and Indian armies. Because casualties were unusually light (only two killed and 27 wounded), medals from this campaign are not so highly rated as those from other nineteenth century wars.*

VALUE:

British troops	£140–180
Royal Navy	£120–150
RN Rocket Brigade	£250–300
Indian troops	£80–120

125. CANADA GENERAL SERVICE MEDAL

Date: 1899.
Campaign: Canada 1866–70.
Branch of Service: Royal Navy, British Army and Canadian units.
Ribbon: Red, white and red.
Metal: Silver.
Size: 36mm.
Description: (Obverse) crowned and veiled Old Head bust of Queen Victoria by Sir Thomas Brock (reflecting the very late issue of the medal). (Reverse) Canadian flag surrounded by maple leaves.
Clasps: Fenian Raid 1866, Fenian Raid 1870, Red River 1870.
Comments: *This medal was not authorised until January 1899, thirty years after the event, and was issued by the Canadian government to British and Canadian local forces who took part in operations to put down the Fenian raids of 1866 and 1870 and the Red River rebellion of the latter year. Of the 16,100 medals awarded, 15,000 went to local forces. Naval medals command a premium.*

VALUE:

	Canadian forces	British Army	Royal Navy
Fenian Raid 1866	£90–120	£120–150	£180–220
Fenian Raid 1870	£120–140	£140–180	—
Red River 1870	£350–400	£450–550	—
2 clasps	£150–200	—	—
3 clasps	Rare	—	—

126. ASHANTEE MEDAL

Date: 1874.
Campaign: Gold Coast 1873–74.
Branch of Service: Royal Navy, Army and native troops.
Ribbon: Orange with black bars at the sides and two narrow black stripes towards the centre.
Metal: Silver.
Size: 36mm.
Description: The obverse and reverse are similar to the East and West Africa Medal of 1887–1900, differing solely in thickness and the method of naming. The veiled profile of Victoria graces the obverse while the reverse, designed by Sir Edwin Poynter, shows a skirmish in the jungle between British soldiers and Ashantee warriors.
Clasps: Coomassie.
Comments: *All ranks who took part in operations against King Kalkali of Ashantee, Gold Coast, were awarded this medal, approved in June 1874. The campaign lasted only four weeks but was fought with great ferocity and resulted in the award of four VCs. There was also a very high incidence of sickness and disease among the troops, notably the naval contingent. Unusually the medals are named in engraved capitals filled in with black.*

VALUE:

	Navy	Army	Natives
No clasp	£80–100	£100–120	£70–90
Coomassie	£160–180	£140–180	£100–130

127. SOUTH AFRICA MEDAL

Date: 1879.
Campaign: South Africa 1877-79.
Branch of Service: Royal Navy, Army and colonial units.
Ribbon: Gold with thin dark blue stripes towards the edges and two thick dark blue stripes towards the centre.
Metal: Silver.
Size: 36mm.
Description: The same design as no. 115, except that the date 1853 in the exergue is replaced by a Zulu shield and four crossed assegais.
Clasps: 1877, 1877–8, 1877–8–9, 1878, 1878–9, 1879.
Comments: *The campaign began in 1877 with an attack on the Fingoes by the Galeka and Gaika tribes and culminated in the showdown between the Zulus and the British when Lord Chelmsford's column was annihilated at Isandhlwana. When the 3000 Zulus advanced on Rorke's Drift, however, they were checked with heavy losses by a tiny garrison of 139 men. During the defence no fewer than eleven VCs were won—the largest number for a single action. The campaign concluded with the defeat of Dinizulu and his warriors at Ulundi.*

VALUE:

	Navy	Army	Colonial
No clasp	£100–140	£100–120	£80–100
1877	—	—	£1100–1300
1877–8	£350–450	£170–190	£170–190
1877–8–9	£400–500	£180–220	£170–190
1878	—	£220–250	£180–200
1878–9	£250–300	£220–250	£180–200
1879	£160–180	£150–200	£120–140
Isandhlwana casualty	£1200–1500		
Rorke's Drift participant	£6000–10,000		

128. AFGHANISTAN MEDAL

Date: 1878.
Campaign: Afghanistan 1878–80.
Branch of Service: British and Indian Armies.
Ribbon: Dark green with broad crimson edges.
Metal: Silver or bronze.
Size: 36mm.
Description: (Obverse) veiled profile of Queen Victoria. (Reverse) a column on the march, with an elephant carrying cannon. The dates 1878–79–80 appear in the exergue.
Clasps: Ali Musjid, Peiwar Kotal, Charasia, Kabul, Ahmed Kel, Kandahar. Maximum number of clasps per medal is four.
Comments: *This medal was awarded to all who took part in the campaigns against Afghanistan known as the Second Afghan War. In 1877 the Amir refused to accept a British resident and the following year raised an army which began harrassing the Indian frontier. A treaty with Russia, however, granting it protective rights in Afghanistan, precipitated an armed response from Britain. In 1880 General Roberts led a column from Kabul to Kandahar to relieve General Burrows and the resulting battle led to the defeat of the Afghans and the conclusion of the war. Medals awarded to the 66th Foot (Berkshire regiment) and E Battery of B Brigade, Royal Artillery rate a high premium as these units sustained the heaviest casualties at the battle of Maiwand in July 1880.*

VALUE:	British units	Indian units
No clasp bronze	—	£140–180
No clasp silver	£50–60	—
Ali Musjid	£50–60	£40–60
Periwar Kotal	£50–60	£40–60
Charasia	£50–60	£40–60
Kabul	£50–60	£40–60
Ahmed Khel	£50–60	£40–60
Kandahar	£50–60	£40–60
2 clasps	£100–120	£60–80
3 clasps	£150–200	£100–120
4 clasps	£250–300	£140–180
Maiwand casualties:		
66th Foot	£450–550	—
E Bty, B Bde RA	£400–500	—

129. KABUL TO KANDAHAR STAR

Date: 1880.
Campaign: Afghanistan 1878–80.
Branch of Service: British and Indian Armies.
Ribbon: Watered silk red, white, yellow, white and blue.
Metal: Bronze from captured guns.
Size: Height 60mm, width 45mm.
Description: (Obverse) a rayed five-pointed star surmounted by a crown with a ring for suspension. The centre is inscribed KABUL TO KANDAHAR with 1880 at the foot and the VRI monogram of the Queen Empress in the centre. Stars were either issued unnamed, or had the recipient's name impressed (to British) or engraved (to Indian troops) on the reverse.
Clasps: None.
Comments: *This star, struck by Jenkins of Birmingham, was awarded to those who took part in the epic 300-mile march from the Afghan capital to Kandahar, led by General Roberts to relieve the beleaguered forces of General Burrows.*

VALUE:	
Unnamed	£50–60
Impressed (British troops)	£100–120
Engraved (Indian troops)	£70–90

130. CAPE OF GOOD HOPE GENERAL SERVICE MEDAL

Date: 1900.
Campaign: Uprisings in Transkei, Basutoland and Bechuanaland 1880-97.
Branch of Service: Local forces and volunteers.
Ribbon: Dark blue with a central yellow stripe.
Metal: Silver.
Size: 36mm.
Description: (Obverse) Jubilee bust of Queen Victoria by Sir Joseph Boehm; (reverse) arms of Cape Colony.
Clasps: Transkei, Basutoland, Bechuanaland.
Comments: *Instituted by the Cape government, this medal acknowledged service in putting down the Transkei (1880-1) and Bechuana (1896-7) rebellions and dealing with the unrest that erupted sporadically in Basutoland for much of this period. The medal was awarded, with one or more campaign clasps, to local forces and volunteer regiments.*

VALUE:

Transkei (1070)	£220–260
Basutoland (2150)	£120–140
Bechuanaland (2580)	£110–130
2 clasps	£180–220
3 clasps (23)	Rare

131. EGYPT MEDAL

Date: 1882.
Campaign: Egypt 1882–89.
Branch of Service: Royal Navy and Army.
Ribbon: Three blue and two white stripes.
Metal: Silver.
Size: 36mm.
Description: (Obverse) the veiled profile of Queen Victoria; (reverse) the Sphinx.
Clasps: 13, listed below. Maximum number for one medal is 7, but only one such award was made. Common two-clasp combinations are denoted below by /.
Comments: *British involvement in Egypt deepened after the opening of the Suez Canal in 1869, many British officers being seconded to the Khedive's Army. When the Army mutinied in 1882 and triggered off a general anti-European uprising, an Anglo-French expedition was mounted. Subsequently the French withdrew before a landing was effected. Trouble erupted in the Sudan (under Anglo-Egyptian administration) in 1884 where General Gordon was besieged at Khartoum. Further campaigns aimed at the overthrow of the Mahdi and the reconquest of the Sudan. These prolonged operations created immense logistical problems. Nile transportation in particular was a matter resolved only when Canadian voyageurs were recruited to handle the river-boats. In addition, a contingent of troops from New South Wales "answered the Empire's call" and medals awarded to them for the Suakin campaign of 1885 are much sought after. Except where noted, the prices quoted below are for medals awarded to British Army personnel. Medals awarded to Indian or Egyptian troops are generally worth about 25 per cent less than comparable awards to British Army units.*

VALUE:

No clasp (dated)	£30–40
No clasp (undated)	£40–50
Alexandria 11th July	£50–60
Tel-el-Kebir	£50–60
El-Teb	£100–120
Tamaai	£80–100
El-Teb-Tamaai	£60–70
Suakin 1884	£50–60
The Nile 1884-85	£60–80
The Nile 1884-85/Abu Klea	£150–180
The Nile 1884-85/Kirbekan	£130–150
Suakin 1885	£60–80
Suakin 1885/Tofrek	£120–150
Gemaizah 1888	£70–90
Toski 1889	£130–160
2 clasps	£60–80
3 clasps	£150–170
4 clasps	£200–220
5 clasps	£350–400
Canadian boatmen	£500–600
NSW units (Suakin 1885)	From £600

132. KHEDIVE'S STAR

Date: 1882.
Campaign: Egypt 1892-91.
Branch of Service: Royal Navy and Army.
Ribbon: 37mm deep blue.
Metal: Bronze.
Size: Height 60mm; width 45mm.
Description: A five-pointed star with a circular centre showing the Sphinx and Pyramids surrounded by a band inscribed EGYPT followed by a year round the top, with 'Khedive of Egypt' and the year in the Moslem calendar in Arabic at the foot. (Reverse) the Khedive's monogram surmounted by a crown. The star is suspended by a ring from an ornamental clasp in the centre of which is a star and crescent.
Clasps: Tokar.
Comments: *This star, struck by Jenkins of Birmingham, was conferred by Khedive Tewfik of Egypt on those who qualified for the Egypt medal and it was invariably worn alongside, to the detriment of the silver medal which suffered abrasion from the points of the star. There was also an undated version found with or without a campaign clasp for Tokar, awarded in 1891. These stars were issued unnamed.*

VALUE:

1882	£30–35
1884	£40–45
1884-86	£30–35
Undated	£40–45
Undated with Tokar bar	£30–35

133. GENERAL GORDON'S STAR FOR THE SIEGE OF KHARTOUM

Date: 1884.
Campaign: Mahdist uprising, Sudan 1884.
Branch of Service: British and Sudanese forces.
Ribbon: Deep blue.
Metal: Silver or pewter.
Size: Height 80mm; maximum width 54mm.
Description: Star with three concentric circles and seven groups of rays on which are superimposed seven crescents and stars. Suspension by a ring from a Crescent and Star ornament.
Clasps: None.
Comments: *To boost the morale of the defenders Charles Gordon, commanding the garrison at Khartoum, had this star cast locally in a sand mould, using his own breast star of the Order of Mejidieh as the model. Exceptionally, recipients had to purchase their medals, the proceeds going to a fund to feed the poor.*

VALUE:

Silver	£400–600
Pewter	£300–350
Silver gilt	£700–900

134. NORTH WEST CANADA MEDAL

Date: 1885.
Campaign: Riel's rebellion 1885.
Branch of Service: Mainly local forces.
Ribbon: Blue-grey with red stripes towards the edges.
Metal: Silver.
Size: 36mm.
Description: (Obverse) bust of Queen Victoria; (reverse) the inscription NORTH WEST CANADA 1885 within a frame of maple leaves.
Clasps: Saskatchewan,
Comments: *Paradoxically, while the medal for the Fenian Raids of 1866–70 was not sanctioned till 1899, this medal for service in the North West was authorised immediately after the conclusion of operations against the Metis led by Louis Riel. It was issued unnamed, with or without the clasp for Saskatchewan where the bulk of the action took place. Of particular interest are medals to officers and men aboard the steamship Northcote involved in a boat action; exceptionally, their medals were impressed. Other medals may be encountered with unofficial naming. The medal was awarded to sixteen British staff officers but the majority of medals (5600 in all) went to local forces.*

VALUE:
No clasp	£150–200
Saskatchewan	£280–320
Northcote recipient	£500–600

135. ROYAL NIGER COMPANY'S MEDAL

Date: 1899.
Campaign: Nigeria 1886–97.
Branch of Service: Officers and men of the Company's forces.
Ribbon: Three equal stripes of yellow, black and white.
Metal: Silver or bronze.
Size: 39.5mm.
Description: (Obverse) the Boehm bust of Queen Victoria; (reverse) the Company's arms in a laurel wreath.
Clasps: Nigeria 1886-97 (silver), Nigeria (bronze).
Comments: *This medal was issued in silver to Europeans and bronze to natives for service in the vast territories administered by the Royal Niger chartered company. Silver medals were impressed in capitals, but those in bronze were more usually stamped with the recipient's service (constabulary) number. Specimens of both versions were later struck from the original dies but these lack name or number.*

VALUE:
Silver named (85)	£1000–1200
Original Silver specimen	£80–100
Bronze named (250)	£350–400
Original Bronze specimen	£60–80

136. IMPERIAL BRITISH EAST AFRICA COMPANY'S MEDAL

Date: 1890.
Campaign: East Africa (Kenya and Uganda) 1888–95.
Branch of Service: Company forces.
Ribbon: Plain blue.
Metal: Silver.
Size: 39mm.
Description: (Obverse) the Company badge, a crowned and radiant sun, with a Suaheli inscription in Arabic round the foot signifying "the reward of bravery"; (reverse) plain except for a wreath. Suspension is by a plain ring or an ornamental scroll.
Comments: *The rarest of the medals awarded by the chartered companies, this medal was originally intended solely as a gallantry award; but after the BEA Company was wound up in 1895 further issues were authorised by the Foreign Office for service in Witu (1890) and the Ugandan civil war (1890-91). Less than thirty medals are known.*

VALUE: From £400

137. EAST AND WEST AFRICA MEDAL

Date: 1887.
Campaigns: East and West Africa 1887–1900.
Branch of Service: Royal Navy, Army and native forces.
Ribbon: Yellow with broad black bars at the edges and two thin black bars towards the centre (as for Ashantee Medal).
Metal: Silver or bronze.
Size: 36mm.
Description: As for the Ashantee Medal (q.v.), distinguished only by its clasps.
Clasps: 21 (see below). A 22nd operation (Mwele, 1895–96) was denoted by engraving on the rim of the medal.
Comments: *This medal was awarded for general service in a number of small campaigns and punitive expeditions. Though usually awarded in silver, it was sometimes struck in bronze for issue to native servants, bearers and drivers. British regiments as such were not involved in any of the actions, but individual officers and NCOs were seconded as staff officers and instructors and their medals bear the names of their regiments. Units of the Royal Navy were also involved in many of the coastal or river actions. Especially sought after are naval medals with the bar for Lake Nyassa 1893 in which the ships* Pioneer *and* Adventure *were hauled in sections overland through 200 miles of jungle.*

VALUE:

	Royal Navy	Europeans	Natives
1887–8	£180–220	£130–140	£100–120
Witu 1890	£100–120	£130–160	£80–100
1891–2	£140–160	£140–160	£100–120
1892	£130–150	£120–150	£100–120
Witu August 1893	£130–150	—	£11—130
Liwondi 1893	£1300–1500	—	—
Juba River 1893	£1300–1500	—	—
Lake Nyassa 1893	£1300–1500	—	—
1893–94	£140–160	£140–160	£90–110
Gambia 1894	£120–140	—	£100–120
Benin River 1894	£120–140	£120–140	£90–110
Brass River	£140–160	—	—
M'wele 1895–6	£100–120	£100–120	£80–100
1896–98	—	£300–350	£150–200
Niger 1897	—	£250–300	£150–200
Benin 1897	£80–100	£100–120	£150–200
Dawkita 1897	—	Rare	Rare
1897–98	—	£130–150	£100–120
1898	£600–800	£140–170	£120–140
Sierra Leone 1898–99	£120–140	£100–120	£80–100
1899	—	£220–250	£150–170
1900	—	£200–220	£130–150

138. BRITISH SOUTH AFRICA COMPANY'S MEDAL

Date: 1896.

Campaign: South Africa 1890-97.

Branch of Service: British Army and colonial units.

Ribbon: Seven equal stripes, four yellow and three dark blue.

Metal: Silver.

Size: 36mm.

Description: (Obverse) the Old Head bust of Queen Victoria; (reverse) a charging lion impaled by a spear, with a mimosa bush in the background and a litter of spears and a shield on the ground.

Clasps: Mashonaland 1890, Matabeleland 1893, Rhodesia 1896, Mashonaland 1897.

Comments: *Originally instituted in 1896 for award to troops taking part in the suppression of the Matabele rebellion, it was later extended to cover operations in Rhodesia (1896) and Mashonaland (1897). The medal, as originally issued, had the inscription MATABELELAND 1893 at the top of the reverse. The medal was re-issued with RHODESIA 1896 or MASHONALAND 1897 inscribed on the reverse, but holders of medals for their first campaign only added clasps for subsequent campaigns. Rather belatedly, it was decided in 1927 to issue medals retrospectively for the Mashonaland campaign of 1890; in this instance the name and date of the campaign were not inscribed on the reverse though the details appeared on the clasp. An unusually ornate suspender has roses, thistles, shamrocks and leeks entwined. Only one medal is known with all four clasps, while only fifteen medals had three clasps.*

VALUE:

	British regiments
Mashonaland 1890	£400–500
Matabeleland 1893	£100–120
with 1 clasp	£140–180
with 2 clasps	£300–350
Rhodesia 1896	£80–100
with 1 clasp	£140–180
Mashonaland 1897	£120–140

139. HUNZA NAGAR BADGE

Date: 1891.

Campaign: Hunza and Nagar 1891.

Branch of Service: Jammu and Kashmir forces.

Ribbon: Large (46mm x 32mm) with a broad red diagonal band and white centre stripe and green upper left and lower right corners.

Metal: Bronze.

Size: 55mm x 27mm.

Description: A uniface rectangular plaque featuring three soldiers advancing on the crenellated hill fort of Nilt, with mountains in the background. The inscription HUNZA NAGAR 1891 appears lower right. It was intended to be worn as a brooch at the neck but subsequently many were fitted with a suspender for wear with a red and green ribbon.

Clasps: None.

Comments: *Gurney of London manufactured this badge which was awarded by the Maharajah of Jammu and Kashmir to his own troops who served in the operation against the border states of Hunza and Nagar and qualified for the Indian general service medal with clasp for Hunza 1891. The punitive expedition was led by Colonel A. Durand in response to the defiant attitude of the Hunza and Nagar chiefs towards the British agency at Gilgit.*

VALUE: £300–350

140. CENTRAL AFRICA MEDAL

Date: 1895.

Campaigns: Central Africa 1891–98.

Branch of Service: Mainly local forces.

Ribbon: Three equal stripes of black, white and terracotta representing the Africans, Europeans and Indians.

Metal: Silver or bronze.

Size: 36mm.

Description: Obverse and reverse as the East and West Africa (Ashantee) medal, distinguished only by its ribbon.

Clasps: Originally issued without a clasp but one for Central Africa 1894–98 was subsequently authorised.

Comment: *Though generally issued in silver, a bronze version was awarded to native servants. The first issue of this medal had a simple ring suspension and no clasp. For the second issue a clasp, Central Africa 1894–98 was authorised and the medal was issued with a straight bar suspender, which is very rare.*

VALUE:

Without clasp (ring)	£180–220
Clasp and ring suspension	£240–280
Clasp and bar suspension	£250–400
Bronze	From £1000

141. HONG KONG PLAGUE MEDAL

Date: 1894.

Campaign: Hong Kong, May-September 1894.

Branch of Service: Royal Navy, Royal Engineers, KSLI and local personnel.

Ribbon: Red with yellow edges and two narrow yellow stripes in the centre.

Metal: Silver.

Size: 36mm.

Description: (Obverse) a Chinese lying on a trestle table being supported by a man warding off the winged figure of Death while a woman tends to the sick man. The year 1894 appears on a scroll in the exergue, while the name of the colony in Chinese pictograms is inscribed on the left of the field. (Reverse) inscribed PRESENTED BY THE HONG KONG COMMUNITY round the circumference, and FOR SERVICES RENDERED DURING THE PLAGUE OF 1894 in seven lines across the centre. It was fitted with a plain ring for suspension.

Clasps: None.

Comments: *The colonial authorities in Hong Kong awarded this medal to nurses, civil servants, police, British Army and Royal Navy personnel who rendered assistance when the crown colony was stricken by a severe epidemic of bubonic plague in May 1894. Despite stringent measures, over 2500 people died in the ensuing three months. About 400 medals were issued in silver and awarded to 300 men of the King's Shropshire Light Infantry, 50 petty officers and ratings of the Royal Navy and NCOs and other ranks of the Royal Engineers, as well as about the same number of police and junior officials, while 45 were struck in gold for award to officers, nursing sisters and senior officials.*

VALUE:

Gold (45)	From £3000
Silver (400)	£400–500

142. INDIA MEDAL

Date: 1895.
Campaign: India 1895–1902.
Branch of Service: British and Indian forces.
Ribbon: Crimson with two dark green stripes.
Metal: Silver or bronze.
Size: 36mm.
Description: Issued with two different obverses, portraying Queen Victoria (1895–1901) and King Edward VII in field marshal's uniform (1901–02). (Reverse) British and Indian soldiers supporting a standard.
Clasps: Seven, mainly for actions on the North West Frontier (see below).
Comments: *This medal replaced the India GSM which had been awarded for various minor campaigns over a period of four decades from 1854. Combatant troops were given the medal in silver but native bearers and servants received a bronze version.*

VALUE:

	British regiments	Indian	Bronze
Defence of Chitral 1895	—	£600–700	Rare
Relief of Chitral 1895	£60–70	£40–50	£50–60
Punjab Frontier 1897-98	£45–55	£35–45	£40–50
pair with Malakand 1897	£80–90	£50–60	£60–70
pair with Samana 1897	£80–90	£50–60	£70–80
pair with Tirah 1897-98	£70–80	£40–50	£50–60
Waziristan 1901-02	—	£80–90	£60–70

143. JUMMOO AND KASHMIR MEDAL

Date: 1895.
Campaign: Defence of Chitral 1895.
Branch of Service: Native levies.
Ribbon: White with red stripes at the edges and a broad central green stripe.
Metal: Bronze, silver.
Size: 35mm high; 38mm wide.
Description: This medal, by Gurney of London, has a unique kidney shape showing the arms of Jummoo (Jammu) and Kashmir on the obverse. (Reverse) a view of Chitral fort with troops in the foreground.
Clasps: Chitral 1895.
Comments: *Awarded by the Maharajah of Jummoo (Jammu) and Kashmir to the Indian troops who participated in the defence of Chitral (a dependency of Kashmir) during the siege of 4 March to 20 April by Chitralis and Afghans led by Umra Khan and Sher Afzul.*

VALUE:

Named	£250–300
Unnamed	£180–220
Silver	Rare

144. ASHANTI STAR

Date: 1896.
Campaign: Gold Coast 1896.
Branch of Service: British forces.
Ribbon: Yellow with two black stripes.
Metal: Bronze.
Size: 44mm.
Description: A saltire cross with a four-pointed star in the angles, surmounted by a circular belt inscribed ASHANTI 1896 around a British crown. The plain reverse is simply inscribed FROM THE QUEEN.
Clasps: None.
Comments: *Issued ed unnamed, but the colonel of the West Yorkshire Regiment had the medals of the second battalion engraved at his own expense. Some 2000 stars were awarded to officers and men serving in the expedition led by Major-General F.C. Scott against the tyrannical King Prempeh. It is believed that the star was designed by Princess Henry of Battenberg whose husband died of fever during the campaign.*

VALUE:

Unnamed	£80–100
Named to West Yorkshire Regiment	£150–200

145. QUEEN'S SUDAN MEDAL

Date: 1899.
Campaign: Reconquest of the Sudan 1896–97.
Branch of Service: Royal Navy, Army and local forces.
Ribbon: Half-yellow and half-black representing the desert and the Sudanese nation, divided by a thin crimson stripe representing the British forces.
Metal: Silver or bronze.
Size: 36mm.
Description: (Obverse) the Jubilee bust of Queen Victoria. (Reverse) a seated figure of Victory holding palms and laurels with flags in the background, the word SUDAN appearing on a tablet at her feet.
Clasps: None.
Comments: *Unusually, no clasps were granted for individual actions which included the celebrated battle of Omdurman in which young Winston Churchill charged with the cavalry. Medals named to the 21st Lancers are especially desirable on that account.*

VALUE:

Bronze named	£120–180
Silver named	£60-80
21st Lancers (confirmed charger)	£600–1000

146. KHEDIVE'S SUDAN MEDAL

Date: 1897.
Campaign: Sudan 1896-1908.
Branch of Service: Royal Navy and British and Egyptian Armies.
Ribbon: 38mm yellow with a broad central deep blue stripe, symbolising the desert and the River Nile.
Metal: Silver or bronze.
Size: 39mm.
Description: (Obverse) an oval shield surrounded by flags and a trophy of arms; (reverse) an elaborate Arabic inscription. Bar suspender.
Clasps: Fifteen (see below) but medals with more than the two clasps 'The Atbara' and 'Khartoum' are unusual. Inscribed in English and Arabic.
Comments: *Instituted by the Khedive of Egypt in February 1897 and granted to those who served in the reconquest of Dongola province in the Sudan (1896-8) as well as in subsequent operations for the pacification of the southern provinces. It was awarded to officers and men of the British and Egyptian Armies and Royal Navy personnel who served on the Nile steamboats.*

VALUE:

No clasp silver	£50–70	Jerok	£70–90
No clasp bronze	£70–80	Nyam-Nyam	£70–90
Firket	£50–70	Talodi	£80–100
Hafir	£50–70	Katfia	£80–100
Abu Hamed	£50–70	Nyima	£70–90
Sudan 1897	£50–70	2 clasps	£50–70
The Atbara	£50–60	3 clasps	£60–80
Khartoum	£50–60	4 clasps	£60–80
Gedaref	£50–70	5 clasps	£80–100
Gedid	£50–70	6 clasps	£80–120
Sudan 1899	£50–70	7 clasps	£160–180
Bahr-el-Ghazal 1900–2	£120–150	8 clasps	£180–200

147. EAST AND CENTRAL AFRICA

Date: 1897.
Campaigns: East and Central Africa 1897–99.
Branch of Service: British, Indian and local forces.
Ribbon: Half yellow, half red.
Metal: Silver or bronze.
Size: 36mm.
Description: (Obverse) the Jubilee bust of Queen Victoria; (reverse) a standing figure of Britannia with the British lion alongside.
Clasps: Five (see below).
Comments: *Instituted for service in operations in Uganda and the southern Sudan, it was awarded in silver to combatants and in bronze to camp followers. Most of the medals were awarded to troops of the Uganda Rifles and various Indian regiments. The few British officers and NCOs were troop commanders and instructors seconded from their regiments and their medals are worth very much more than the prices quoted, which are for native awards.*

VALUE:

No clasp silver	£180–200
Lubwa's (with clasp Uganda 1897-98)	£250–280
Uganda 1897-98	£180–220
1898 (silver)	£210–230
1898 (bronze)	£350–400
Uganda 1899	£210–230

148. BRITISH NORTH BORNEO COMPANY'S MEDALS

Date: 1897.

Campaign: North Borneo 1897–1915.

Branch of Service: Company forces.

Ribbon: Originally 36mm gold watered silk, 32mm yellow with maroon edges and a central blue stripe (Punitive Expeditions and Rundum) or 32mm yellow with a central green stripe (Tambunan).

Metal: Silver or bronze.

Size: 39mm.

Description: (Obverse) the Company arms; (reverse) the British lion standing in front of a bush adorned by the Company flag, with a small wreath in the exergue.

Clasps: Four (see below).

Comments: *This series of medals was made by the British North Borneo Company for service in what is now Brunei, Sabah and Sarawak. The medals, struck by Spink and Son of London, were issued in silver and bronze (except for Rundum) to British and Bornean officials, Sikh troops and a small number of servants. The first obverse showed the Company arms with supporters, crest and motto. This medal was issued unnamed and unnumbered. Specimens from the original dies are known with the S of Spink or Son erased and the word "Copy" on the rim. The medal was re-issued for a second expedition in 1898 and on this occasion it was named and numbered to the recipient. For a third expedition, in 1899–1900, the second obverse was used, showing the Company shield without supporters, motto or crest, but inscribed BRITISH NORTH BORNEO and with the date 1900 round the foot. This was used in conjunction with a new reverse showing the Company crest, two arms supporting a flag. This medal had a yellow ribbon with a central green stripe. In 1915 an expedition to raise the siege of Rundum was marked by the issue of a silver medal, similar to the 1897 medal but only struck in silver and fitted with a Rundum clasp.*

VALUE:

	Silver	Bronze
Punitive Expedition (1897)	£60–80	£40–60
Punitive Expeditions (1898)	£70–80	£40–60
Tambunan	£70–80	£50–60
Rundum	£80–100	—

149. SULTAN OF ZANZIBAR'S MEDAL

Date: 1896.

Campaign: East Africa 1896.

Branch of Service: Sultan's forces.

Ribbon: Plain bright scarlet.

Metal: Silver.

Size: 36mm.

Description: (Obverse) a facing bust of Sultan Hamid bin Thwain surrounded by a Suaheli inscription in Arabic; (reverse) same inscription set in four lines.

Clasps: Pumwani, Jongeni, Takaungu, Mwele (inscribed only in Arabic).

Comments: *Awarded to the Zanzibari contingent who served under Lieut. Lloyd-Matthews RN in East Africa alongside British and imperial forces.*

VALUE: £200

150. QUEEN'S SOUTH AFRICA MEDAL

Date: 1899.

Campaign: Anglo-Boer War 1899-1902.

Branch of Service: British and Imperial forces.

Ribbon: Red with two narrow blue stripes and a broad central orange stripe.

Metal: Silver or bronze.

Size: 36mm.

Description: (Obverse) the Jubilee bust of Queen Victoria; (reverse) Britannia holding the flag and a laurel crown towards a large group of soldiers, with warships offshore. The words SOUTH AFRICA are inscribed round the top.

Clasps: 26 authorised but the maximum recorded for a single medal is nine to the Army and eight to the Navy.

Comments: *Because of the large number of British and imperial forces which took part and the numerous campaign and battle clasps awarded, this is one of the most popular and closely studied of all medals, offering immense scope to the collector. A total of 178,000 medals were awarded. Numerous specialist units were involved for the first time, as well as locally raised units and contingents from India, Canada, Australia and New Zealand. Of particular interest are the medals awarded to war correspondents and nurses which set precedents for later wars. Although nurses received the medal they were not issued with clasps to which they were entitled. A small number of bronze medals without a clasp were issued to bearers and servants in Indian units. The original issue of the QSA depicts Britannia's outstretched hand pointing towards the R of AFRICA and bears the dates 1899–1900 on the reverse field. Less than 70 of these were issued to Lord Strathcona's Horse who had returned to Canada before the war ended, but as the war dragged on the date was removed before any other medals were issued, although some medals can be found with a "ghost" of this date still to be seen. On the third type reverse there is again no date but Britannia's hand points towards the F. The prices for clasps given below are for clasps issued in combination with others. Some clasps are much scarcer when issued singly than combined with other clasps and conversely some clasps are not recorded on their own.*

150. QUEEN'S SOUTH AFRICA MEDAL *continued*

VALUE:

	RN	British	SA/Indian	Aus/NZ	Canadian
No clasp bronze	—	—	£50–60	—	—
No clasp silver	£40–50	£30–40	£70–80	£75–85	£110–120
Cape Colony	£45–55	£35–45	£35–45	£45–50	£110–120
Rhodesia	—	—	£90–100	£90–100	£260–280
Relief of Mafeking	—	—	£70–80	£150–160	£350–370
Defence of Kimberley	—	£120–130	£70–80	—	—
Talana	—	£125–135	£80–90	—	—
Elandslaagte	—	£80–90	—	—	—
Defence of Ladysmith	£100–120	£60–80	£70–80	—	—
Belmont	£70–80	£40–50	—	£185–200	—
Modder River	£75–85	£40–50	—	£185–200	—
Tugela Heights	—	£40–50	—	—	—
Natal	£200–220	£45–55	£50–60	—	£180–200
Relief of Kimberley	£120–140	£40–50	£40–50	£100–110	—
Paardeberg	£50–60	£40–50	£55–60	£90–100	£130–140
Orange Free State	£120–130	£30–40	£30–40	£50–60	£125–135
Relief of Ladysmith	£75–80	£45–55	£60–70	—	—
Driefontein	£70–80	£40–50	—	£40–50	£180–200
Wepener	—	£230–240	£150–160	—	—
Defence of Mafeking	—	—	£900–1200	—	—
Transvaal	£60–70	£25–35	£35–45	£50–60	£180–200
Johannesburg	£75–85	£45–55	£50–60	£50–60	£120–130
Laing's Nek	£80–90	£60–75	—	—	—
Diamond Hill	£80–90	£45–55	£55–65	£60–70	£180–200
Wittebergen	—	£40–50	£90–100	£65–75	—
Belfast	£75–85	£60–70	£50–60	£60–70	£120–140
South Africa 1901	£60–70	£40–50	£40–50	£60–70	£140–150
South Africa 1902	£120–130	£40–50	£40–50	£60–70	£120–130
2 clasps	£50–60	£40–50	£40–50	£80–90	£120–130
3 clasps	£70–80	£45–55	£50–60	£100–110	£120–130
4 clasps	£80–90	£45–55	£50–60	£120–130	£140–150
5 clasps	£90–100	£50–60	£55–65	£150–160	£200–220
6 clasps	£100–120	£60–70	£90–100	£220–230	£260–275
7 clasps	£160–170	£100–120	£150–160	£360–375	—
8 clasps	£260–275	£220–250	£380–400	—	—
Relief dates on reverse	—	—	—	—	£1500–1750
Nurses	—	£80–100	—	—	—
War Correspondents	—	£350–400	—	—	—

151. QUEEN'S MEDITERRANEAN MEDAL

Date: 1899.

Campaign: Mediterranean garrisons 1899-1902.

Branch of Service: British militia forces.

Ribbon: Red with two narrow dark blue stripes and a central broad orange stripe (as for Queen's South Africa Medal).

Metal: Silver.

Size: 36mm.

Description: Similar to the Queen's South Africa Medal but inscribed MEDITERRANEAN at the top of the reverse.

Clasps: None.

Comments: *Awarded to officers and men of the militia battalions which were sent to Malta and Gibraltar to take over garrison duty from the regular forces who were drafted to the Cape.*

VALUE:
Silver (5000)   £90–100

152. KING'S SOUTH AFRICA MEDAL

Date: 1902.
Campaign: South Africa 1901–02.
Branch of Service: British and imperial forces.
Ribbon: Three equal stripes of green, white and orange.
Metal: Silver.
Size: 36mm.
Description: (Obverse) bust of King Edward VII in field marshal's uniform; (reverse) as for Queen's medal.
Clasps: Two: South Africa 1901, South Africa 1902.
Comments: *This medal was never issued without the Queen's medal and was awarded to all personnel engaged in operations in South Africa in 1901–02 when fighting was actually confined to numerous skirmishes with isolated guerrilla bands. Very few medals were awarded to RN personnel as the naval brigades had been disbanded in 1901. Apart from about 600 nurses and a few odd men who received the medal without a clasp, this medal was awarded with campaign clasps—most men were entitled to both clasps, single clasp medals being very rare*

VALUE:

No clasp (nurses)	£70–90
1901 / 1902 (RN)	£80–100
1901 / 1902 (Army)	£20–30
1901 / 1902 (Canada)	£40–50
1901 / 1902 (Aus, NZ)	£40–40
1902 alone	From £100

153. ST JOHN AMBULANCE BRIGADE MEDAL FOR SOUTH AFRICA

Date: 1902.
Campaign: South Africa 1899–1902.
Branch of Service: St John Ambulance Brigade.
Ribbon: Black with narrow white edges.
Metal: Bronze.
Size: 37mm.
Description: (Obverse) King Edward VII; (reverse) the arms of the Order with a legend in Latin, SOUTH AFRICA and the dates 1899 and 1902.
Clasps: None.
Comments: *Issued by the Order of St John of Jerusalem to the members of its ambulance brigade who served during the Boer War or who played an active part in the organisation, mobilisation and supply roles. Medals were engraved on the edge with the recipient's name and unit. It is most often associated with the two South Africa medals, but fourteen members who went on from South Africa to serve during the Boxer Rebellion were also awarded the China Medal.*

VALUE:

Bronze (1871)	£70–90

154. KIMBERLEY STAR

Date: 1900.
Campaign: Defence of Kimberley 1899–1902.
Branch of Service: British and local forces.
Ribbon: Half yellow, half black, separated by narrow stripes of red, white and blue.
Metal: Silver.
Size: Height 43mm; max. width 41mm.
Description: A six-pointed star with ball finials and a circular centre inscribed KIMBERLEY 1899–1900 with the civic arms in the middle. (Reverse) plain, but for the inscription MAYOR'S SIEGE MEDAL 1900. Suspended by a plain ring from a scrolled bar.
Clasps: None
Comments: *The Mayor and council of Kimberley awarded this and the following star to the defenders of the mining town against the Boer forces. Two medals were struck in gold but about 5000 were produced in silver. Those with the "a" Birmingham hallmark for 1900 rate a premium over stars with later date letters.*

VALUE:

hallmark "a"	£80–100
later date letters	£60–80

155. KIMBERLEY MEDAL

Date: 1900.
Campaign: Defence of Kimberley 1899–1900.
Branch of Service: Local forces.
Ribbon: As above.
Metal: Silver
Size: 38mm.
Description: (Obverse) the figure of Victory above the Kimberley Town Hall, with the dates 1899–1900 in the exergue. (Reverse) two shields inscribed INVESTED 15 OCT. 1899 and RELIEVED 15 FEB. 1900. The imperial crown appears above and the royal cypher underneath, with the legend TO THE GALLANT DEFENDERS OF KIMBERLEY round the circumference.
Clasps: None.
Comments: *Although awarded for the same purpose as the above, this silver medal is a much scarcer award.*

VALUE:

Silver	£350–400

156. YORKSHIRE IMPERIAL YEOMANRY MEDAL

Date: 1900.
Campaign: South Africa 1900–02.
Branch of Service: Yorkshire Imperial Yeomanry.
Ribbon: Yellow.
Metal: Silver.
Size: 38mm.
Description: Three versions were produced. The first two had the numeral 3 below the Prince of Wales's feathers and may be found with the dates 1900–1901 or 1901–1902, while the third type has the figures 66, denoting the two battalions involved. The uniform reverse has the white rose of Yorkshire surmounted by an imperial crown and enclosed in a laurel wreath with the legend A TRIBUTE FROM YORKSHIRE.
Clasps: None.
Comments: *Many medals wre produced locally and awarded to officers and men of county regiments. The medals struck by Spink and Son for the Yorkshire Imperial Yeomanry, however, are generally more highly regarded as they were much more extensively issued, and therefore more commonly met with, than the others.*

VALUE:

3rd Battalion 1900–1901	£60–70
3rd Battalion 1901–1902	£70–80
66th Battalion 1900–1901	£100–120

157. MEDAL FOR THE DEFENCE OF OOKIEP

Date: 1902.
Campaign: Defence of Ookiep 1902.
Branch of Service: British and colonial forces.
Ribbon: Dark brown with a central green stripe.
Metal: Silver or bronze.
Size: 36mm.
Description: (Obverse) a miner and copper-waggon, with the Company name and date of foundation (1888) round the circumference; (reverse) a thirteen-line text. Fitted with a scroll suspender.
Clasps: None.
Comments: *This medal was awarded by the Cape Copper Company to those who defended the mining town of Ookiep in Namaqualand when it was besieged from 4 April to 4 May 1902 by a Boer commando led by Jan Christian Smuts, later Field Marshal, Prime Minister of South Africa and a member of the Imperial War Cabinet. The defence was conducted by Lieut. Colonel Sheldon, DSO and Major Dean, the Company's manager. The garrison consisted of 206 European miners, 660 Cape Coloureds, 44 men of the 5th Warwickshire militia and twelve men of the Cape Garrison Artillery.*

VALUE:

Silver (officers)	Rare
Bronze (other ranks)	£500–600

158. CHINA WAR MEDAL

Date: 1901.
Campaign: Boxer Rebellion 1900.
Branch of Service: British and imperial forces.
Ribbon: Crimson with yellow edges.
Metal: Silver or bronze.
Size: 36mm.
Description: (Obverse) bust of Queen Victoria; (reverse) trophy of arms , similar to the 1857-60 China Medal but inscribed CHINA 1900 at the foot.
Clasps: Taku Forts, Defence of Legations, Relief of Pekin.
Comments: *Instituted for service during the Boxer Rebellion and the subsequent punitive expeditions, this medal was similar to that of 1857-60 with the date in the exergue altered to 1900. There are three types of naming: in small, impressed capitals for European troops, in large impressed capitals for naval recipients, and in engraved cursive script for Indian forces. The medal was issued in silver to combatants and in bronze to native bearers, drivers and servants. The international community was besieged by the Boxers, members of a secret society, aided and abetted by the Dowager Empress. The relieving force, consisting of contingents from Britain, France, Italy, Russia, Germany and Japan, was under the command of the German field marshal, Count von Waldersee. The British Legation Guard, comprising 80 Royal Marines and a number of 'odd men', won the clasp for Defence of Legations, the most desirable of the campaign bars in this conflict.*

VALUE:

	Royal Navy	Army	Indian units
Silver no clasp	£70–80	£70–80	£40–50
Bronze no clasp	—	—	£60–70
Taku Forts	£180–200	—	—
Defence of Legations	£2000–3000	—	—
Relief of Pekin (silver)	£140–150	£140–180	£80–100
Relief of Pekin (bronze)	—	—	£120–150
2 clasps	£280–320	—	—

159. TRANSPORT MEDAL

Date: 1903.
Campaigns: Boer War 1899-1902 and Boxer Rebellion 1900.
Branch of Service: Mercantile Marine.
Ribbon: Red with two blue stripes.
Metal: Silver.
Size: 36mm.
Description: (Obverse) bust of King Edward VII in the uniform of an Admiral of the Fleet; (reverse) HMS *Ophir* below a map of the world.
Clasps: S. Africa 1899-1902, China 1900.
Comments: *The last of the medals associated with the major conflicts at the turn of the century, it was instituted for award to the officers and men of the merchant vessels used to carry troops and supplies to the wars in South Africa and China.*

VALUE:

South Africa 1899-1902 (1219)	£200–220
China 1900 (322)	£300–350
Both clasps (178)	£400–450

160. ASHANTI MEDAL

Date: 1901.
Campaign: Gold Coast 1900.
Branch of Service: British and local forces.
Ribbon: Black with two broad green stripes.
Metal: Silver or bronze.
Size: 36mm.
Description: (Obverse) bust of King Edward VII in field marshal's uniform. (Reverse) a lion on the edge of an escarpment looking towards the sunrise, with a native shield and spears in the foreground. The name ASHANTI appeared on a scroll at the foot.
Clasps: Kumassi.
Comments: *A high-handed action by the colonial governor provoked a native uprising and the siege of the garrison at Kumassi. The medal was awarded to the defenders as well as personnel of the two relieving columns. Very few Europeans were involved as most were in South Africa fighting the Boers. The medal was awarded in silver to combatants and bronze to native tansport personnel and servants.*

VALUE:

	Silver	Bronze
No clasp	£150–170	£250–300
Kumassi	£180–200	Rare

161. AFRICA GENERAL SERVICE MEDAL

Date: 1902.
Campaigns: Minor campaigns in Africa 1902 to 1956.
Branch of Service: British and colonial forces.
Ribbon: Yellow with black edges and two thin central green stripes.
Metal: Silver or bronze.
Size: 36mm.
Description: (Obverse) effigies of Edward VII, George V and Elizabeth II; (reverse) similar to that of the East and Central Africa medal of 1897–99, with AFRICA in the exergue.
Clasps: 34 awarded in the reign of Edward VII, ten George V and only one Elizabeth II (see below).
Comments: *This medal replaced the East and West Africa Medal 1887–1900, to which 21 clasps had already been issued. In turn, it remained in use for 54 years, the longest-running British service medal. Medals to combatants were in silver, but a few bronze medals were issued during the 1903–04 operations in Northern Nigeria and the Somaliland campaigns of 1902 and 1908 to transport personnel and these are now much sought after, as are any medals with the effigy of George V on the obverse. With the exception of the 1902–04 Somali campaign and the campaign against the Mau Mau of Kenya (1952–56) European troops were not involved in any numbers, such personnel consisting mostly of detached officers and specialists.*

161. AFRICA GENERAL SERVICE MEDAL *continued*

VALUE:

	RN	British units	African/Indian regiments
N. Nigeria	—	—	£110–130
N. Nigeria 1902	—	—	£110–130
N. Nigeria 1903	—	—	£100–120
N. Nigeria 1903-04	—	—	£150–170
N. Nigeria 1903-04 (bronze)	—	—	£130–150
N. Nigeria 1904	—	—	£130–150
N. Nigeria 1906	—	—	£130–150
S. Nigeria	—	—	£180–200
S. Nigeria 1902	—	—	£130–150
S. Nigeria 1902-03	—	—	£130–150
S. Nigeria 1903	—	—	£120–140
S. Nigeria 1903-04	—	—	£150–170
S. Nigeria 1904	—	—	£120–140
S. Nigeria 1904-05	—	—	£150–170
S. Nigeria 1905	—	—	£250–300
S. Nigeria 1905-06	—	—	£140–160
Nigeria 1918	—	—	£110–130
East Africa 1902	—	—	£300-350
East Africa 1904	—	—	£170–190
East Africa 1905	—	—	£170–190
East Africa 1906	—	—	£170–190
East Africa 1913	—	—	£180–220
East Africa 1913-14	—	—	£170–190
East Africa 1914	—	—	£180–220
East Africa 1915	—	—	£170–190
East Africa 1918	—	—	£170–190
West Africa 1906	—	—	£170–190
West Africa 1908	—	—	£180–220
West Africa 1909-10	—	—	£180–200
Somaliland 1901	—	—	£250–300
Somaliland 1901 (bronze)	—	—	£200–250
Somaliland 1902-04	£60–70	£60–70	£50–60
Somaliland 1902-04 (bronze)	—	—	£70–80
Somaliland 1908-10	£70–80	—	£65–75
Somaliland 1908-10 (bronze)	—	—	£80–90
Somaliland 1920	£100–120	—	£80–90
as above but RAF	—	£180–200	—
Jidballi (with Somaliland 1902–04)	—	£150–160	£110–130
Uganda 1900	—	—	£170–190
B.C.A. 1899-1900	—	—	£120–150
Jubaland	£180–200	—	£90–100
Jubaland (bronze)	—	—	£250–300
Jubaland 1917-18	—	—	£160–180
Jubaland 1917-18 (bronze)	—	—	£125–150
Gambia	£240–260	—	£100–120
Aro 1901-1902	£200–250	—	£170–190
Lango 1901	—	—	£200–250
Kissi 1905	—	—	£220–250
Nandi 1905-06	—	—	£120–140
Shimber Berris 1914-15	—	—	£200–220
Nyashaland 1915	—	—	£120–150
Kenya	£75–85	£45–65	£30–40
Kenya (to RAF)	—	£55–60	—
2 clasps	£80–120	£100–140	£100–250
3 clasps	—	—	£300–400
4 clasps	—	—	£325–450
5 clasps	—	—	£350–475
6 clasps	—	—	£375–500

162. TIBET MEDAL

Date: 1904.
Campaign: Tibet 1903–04.
Branch of Service: British and Indian regiments.
Ribbon: Green with two white stripes and a broad maroon central stripe.
Metal: Silver or bronze.
Size: 36mm.
Description: (Obverse) bust of King Edward VII; (reverse) the fortified hill city of Lhasa with TIBET 1903–04 at the foot.
Clasps: Gyantse.
Comments: *The trade mission led by Colonel Sir Francis Younghusband to Tibet was held up by hostile forces, against whom a punitive expedition was mounted in 1903. This medal was awarded mainly to Indian troops who took part in the expedition, camp followers being awarded the medal in bronze. A clasp was awarded to those who took part in the operations near Gyantse beteen 3 May and 6 July 1904.*

VALUE:

	British	Indian	Bronze
Without clasp	£160–180	£80–100	£50–60
Gyantse	£300–350	£150–170	£150–170

163. NATAL REBELLION

Date: 1908.
Campaign: Natal 1906.
Branch of Service: Local forces.
Ribbon: Crimson with black edges.
Metal: Silver.
Size: 36mm.
Description: (Obverse) right-facing profile of King Edward VII. (Reverse) an erect female figure representing Natal with the sword of justice in her right hand and a palm branch in the left. She treads on a heap of Zulu weapons and is supported by Britannia who holds the orb of empire in her hand. In the background, the sun emerges from behind storm clouds.
Clasp: 1906.
Comments: *The Natal government instituted this medal for services in the operations following the Zulu rebellion. Local volunteer units bore the brunt of the action and it is interesting to note that one of the recipients was Sergeant-Major M.K. Gandhi who later led India to independence.*

VALUE:

without clasp (2000)	£90–110
clasp 1906 (8000)	£100–120
Natal Naval Corps (200)	£200–250

164. INDIA GENERAL SERVICE MEDAL

Date: 1908.
Campaigns: India 1908 to 1935.
Branch of Service: British and Indian forces.
Ribbon: Green with a broad blue central band.
Metal: Silver.
Size: 36mm.
Description: Three obverse types were used: Edward VII (1908–10), George V Kaisar-i-Hind (1910–30) and George V Indiae Imp (1930–35). (Reverse) the fortress at Jamrud in the Khyber Pass, with the name INDIA in a wreath at the foot.
Clasps: Fourteen, some in bronze (see below).
Comments: *This medal was awarded for a number of minor campaigns and operations in India before and after the First World War. The medals were struck at the Royal Mint in London and by the Indian government in Calcutta, the only difference being in the claw suspenders, the former being ornate and the latter plain. Medals with the bars North West Frontier 1908 and Abor 1911–12 were also issued in bronze to native bearers.*

VALUE:

	British Army	RAF	Indian regiments
NW Frontier 1908	£40–50	—	£20–30
bronze	—	—	£60–70
Abor 1911–12	—	—	£140–180
bronze	—	—	£250–300
Afghanistan NWF 1919	£25–35	£100–120	£15–20
*Mahsud 1919–20			
& Waziristan 1919–21	£60–70	£120–150	£30–40
Malabar 1921–22	£70–80	—	£25–35
Waziristan 1921–24	£30–40	£70–90	£20–30
Waziristan 1925	—	£300–350	—
NW Frontier 1930–31	£30–40	£60–70	£15–20
Burma 1930–32	£40–50	Rare	£25–30
Mohmand 1933	—	£180–200	£25–30
NW Frontier 1935	£35–45	£60–70	£20–25

*Not awarded singly; only found in combination with Waziristan 1919-21.

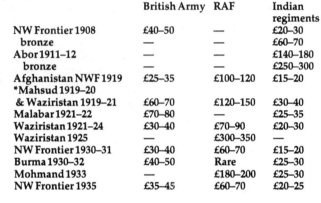

165. KHEDIVE'S SUDAN MEDAL

Date: 1911.
Campaign: Sudan 1910 to 1922
Branch of Service: British and Egyptian forces.
Ribbon: Black with thin red and green stripes on either side.
Metal: Silver or bronze.
Size: 36mm.
Description: (Obverse) an Arabic inscription signifying the name of Khedive Abbas Hilmi and the date 1328 in the Moslem calendar (1910 AD). He was deposed in December 1914 when Egypt was declared a British protectorate, and succeeded by his nephew who was proclaimed Sultan. Sultan Hussein Kamil changed the Arabic inscription and date to AH 1335 (1916–17) on later issues of the medal. (Reverse) a lion poised on a plinth with the sunrise in the background.
Clasps: 16, inscribed in English and Arabic.
Comments: *Introduced in June 1911 as a replacement for the previous Khedive's Sudan medal of 1896–1908, it was awarded for minor operations in the southern Sudan between 1910 and 1922. The silver medal was issued with clasps to combatants, and without a clasp to non-combatants, while the bronze version was granted to camp followers.*

VALUE:

Silver without clasp type I	£90–110	Darfur 1916	£180–200
Silver without clasp type II	£90–110	Fasher	£220–240
Bronze without clasp type I	£160–180	Lau Nuer	£240–260
Bronze without clasp type II	£160–180	Nyima 1917-18	£180–200
Atwot	£220–240	Atwot 1918	£220–240
S. Kordofan 1910	£180–200	Garjak Nuer	£240–260
Sudan 1912	£220–240	Aliab Dinka	£260–280
Zeraf 1913-14	£260–280	Nyala	£260–280
Mandal	£260–280	Darfur 1921	£280–320
Miri	£260–280	2 clasps	£260–280
Mongalla 1915-16	£260–280		

166. 1914 STAR

Date: 1917.
Campaign: France and Belgium 1914.
Branch of Service: British forces.
Ribbon: Watered silk red, white and blue.
Metal: Bronze.
Size: Height 50mm; max. width 45mm.
Description: A crowned four-pointed star with crossed swords and a wreath of oak leaves, having the royal cypher at the foot and a central scroll inscribed AUG NOV 1914. Uniface, the naming being inscribed incuse on the plain reverse.
Clasps: 5th Aug. - 22nd Nov. 1914. The clasp was sewn on to the ribbon, the first of this type.
Comments: *Awarded to all those who had served in France and Belgium between 5 August and 22 November 1914. In 1919 King George V authorised a clasp bearing these dates for those who had actually been under fire during that period. The majority of the 400,000 recipients of the star were officers and men of the prewar British Army, the "Old Contemptibles" who landed in France soon after the outbreak of the First World War and who took part in the retreat from Mons, hence the popular nickname of Mons Star by which this medal is often known.*

VALUE:

1914 Star	£14–16
With "Mons" clasp	£20–25

167. 1914-15 STAR

Date: 1917.
Campaign: First World War 1914–15.
Branch of Service: British and imperial forces.
Ribbon: Watered silk red, white and blue (as above).
Metal: Bronze.
Size: Height 50mm; max. width 45mm.
Description: As above, but AUG and NOV omitted and scroll across the centre inscribed 1914–15.
Clasps: None.
Comments: *Awarded to those who saw service in any theatre of war between 5 August 1914 and 31 December 1915, other than those who had already qualified for the 1914 Star. No fewer than 2,350,000 were awarded, making it the commonest British campaign medal up to that time.*

VALUE:

1914–15 Star	£4–6

168. BRITISH WAR MEDAL

Date: 1919.
Campaign: First World War, 1914–20.
Branch of Service: British and imperial forces.
Ribbon: Orange watered centre with stripes of white and black at each side and borders of royal blue.
Metal: Silver or bronze.
Size: 36mm.
Description: (Obverse) the uncrowned left-facing profile of King George V by Sir Bertram Mackennal. (Reverse) St George on horseback trampling underfoot the eagle shield of the Central Powers and a skull and cross-bones, the emblems of death. Above, the sun has risen in victory. The figure is mounted on horseback to symbolise man's mind controlling a force of greater strength than his own, and thus alludes to the scientific and mechanical appliances which helped to win the war.
Clasps: None.
Comments: *This medal was instituted to record the successful conclusion of the First World War, but it was later extended to cover the period 1919–20 and service in mine-clearing at sea as well as participation in operations in North and South Russia, the eastern Baltic, Siberia, the Black Sea and Caspian. Some 6,500,000 medals were awarded in silver, but about 110,000 in bronze were issued mainly to Chinese, Indian and Maltese personnel in labour battalions. It was originally intended to award campaign clasps, but 79 were recommended by the Army and 68 by the Navy, so the scheme was abandoned as impractical. The naval clasps were actually authorised (7 July 1920) and miniatures are known with them, though the actual clasps were never issued.*

VALUE:

Silver (6,500,000)	£6–8
Bronze (110,000)	£30–40

169. MERCANTILE MARINE WAR MEDAL

Date: 1919.
Campaign: First World War 1914–18.
Branch of Service: Mercantile Marine.
Ribbon: Red and green with a central white stripe, symbolising port and starboard navigation lights.
Metal: Bronze.
Size: 36mm.
Description: (Obverse) Mackennal profile of King George V; (reverse) a steamship ploughing through an angry sea, with a sinking submarine and a sailing vessel in the background, the whole enclosed in a laurel wreath.
Clasps: None.
Comments: *Awarded by the Board of Trade to members of the Merchant Navy who had undertaken one or more voyages through a war or danger zone.*

VALUE:
      Bronze (133,000)   £10–12

170. VICTORY MEDAL

Date: 1919.
Campaign: First World War 1914–19.
Branch of Service: British forces.
Ribbon: 38mm double rainbow (indigo at edges and red in centre).
Metal: Yellow bronze.
Size: 36mm.
Description: (Obverse) the standing figure of Victory holding a palm branch in her right hand and stretching out her left hand. (Reverse) a laurel wreath containing a four-line inscription THE GREAT WAR FOR CIVILISATION 1914–1919.
Clasps: None.
Comments: *Issued to all who had already got the 1914 or 1914–15 Stars and most of those who had the British War Medal, some six million are believed to have been produced. It is often known as the Allied War Medal because the same basic design and double rainbow ribbon were adopted by thirteen other Allied nations (though the USA alone issued it with campaign clasps). The Union of South Africa produced a version with a reverse text in English and Dutch (not Afrikaans as is often stated).*

VALUE:
      British pattern   £2–3
      South African pattern   £8–12

171. TERRITORIAL FORCE WAR MEDAL

Date: 1919.
Campaign: First World War 1914–19.
Branch of Service: Territorial forces.
Ribbon: Watered gold silk with two dark green stripes towards the edges.
Metal: Bronze.
Size: 36mm.
Description: (Obverse) effigy of King George V; (reverse) a wreath enclosing the text FOR VOLUNTARY SERVICE OVERSEAS 1914–19.
Clasps: None.
Comments: *Granted to all members of the Territorial Force embodied before 30 September 1914, who had completed four years service by that date, and who had served outside the United Kingdom between 4 August 1914 and 11 November 1918. Those who had already qualified for the 1914 or 1914–15 Stars, however, were excluded. Only 34,000 medals were awarded, making it by far the scarcest of the First World War medals. The value of individual medals depends on the regiment or formation of the recipient.*

VALUE:
Infantry	£40–50
RA, RE or support arms	£30–40
Yeomanry	£80–100
RFC or RAF	Rare
Nursing sisters	£70–90

172. MEMORIAL PLAQUE

Date: 1919.
Campaign: First World War.
Branch of Service: British forces.
Ribbon: None.
Metal: Bronze.
Size: 120mm.
Description: The plaque shows Britannia bestowing a laurel crown on a rectangular tablet bearing the full name of the dead in raised lettering. In front stands the British lion, with dolphins in the upper field, an oak branch lower right, and a lion cub clutching a fallen eagle in the exergue. The inscription round the circumference reads HE (or SHE) DIED FOR FREEDOM AND HONOVR. A parchment scroll was issued with each plaque giving the deceased's name and unit.
Comments: *Awarded to the next of kin of those who lost their lives on active service during the War.*

VALUE:
He died (1,355,000)	£10–12
She died (600)	£700–900
Parchment scroll	£10–12

173. NAVAL GENERAL SERVICE MEDAL

Date: 1915.

Campaigns: Naval actions 1915 to 1962.

Branch of Service: Royal Navy.

Ribbon: White with broad crimson edges and two narrow crimson stripes towards the centre.

Metal: Silver.

Size: 36mm.

Description: (Obverse) effigy of the reigning monarch (see below). (Reverse) Britannia and two seahorses travelling through the sea.

Clasps: Seventeen (see below).

Comments: *Instituted for service in minor operations for which no separate medal might be issued, it remained in use for almost half a century. In that period five different obverses were employed: George V (1915-36), George VI Ind Imp (1936-49), George VI Fid Def (1949-52), Elizabeth II Br Omn (1952-53) and Elizabeth II Dei Gratia (1953-62). Medals issued with the first three clasps include the name of the recipient's ship but this lapsed in later awards.*

VALUE:

Persian Gulf 1909-1914	£40–50
Iraq 1919-1920	£800–1000
NW Persia 1920	Rare
NW Persia 1919-20	Rare
Palestine 1936-39	£45–55
SE Asia 1945-46	£70–80
Minesweeping 1945-51	£80–100
Palestine 1945-48	£50–60
Malaya (George VI)	£45–55
Malaya (Elizabeth II)	£50–60
Yangtze 1949	£250–300
to HMS *Amethyst*	£400–450
Bomb and Mine Clearance 1945-53	£350–450
Bomb and Mine Clearance Mediterranean	£700–900
Cyprus	£50–60
Near East	£50–60
Arabian Peninsula	£140–180
Brunei	£120–140

174. GENERAL SERVICE MEDAL

Date: 1918.
Campaigns: Minor campaigns 1918 to 1962.
Branch of Service: Army and RAF.
Ribbon: Purple with a central green band.
Metal: Silver.
Size: 36mm
Description: (Obverse) five different effigies of the reigning monarch (see preceding entry). (Reverse) a standing figure of Victory in a Greek helmet and carrying a trident, bestowing palms on a winged sword.
Clasps: Sixteen (see below).
Comments: *Awarded to military and RAF personnel for numerous campaigns and operations that fell short of full-scale war. It did not cover areas already catered for in the Africa and India general service medals.*

VALUE:

	British units	RAF	Indian and local units
S. Persia	—	Rare	£30–40
Kurdistan	£40–50	£80–100	£20–30
Iraq	£35–45	£80–100	£20–25
N.W. Persia	£40–50	£180–220	£25–35
Southern Desert Iraq	—	£180–220	£80–100
Northern Kurdistan	—	£300–350	£100–120
Palestine	£30–40	£30–40	£20–30
S.E. Asia 1945-46	£60–70	£50–60	£25–35
Bomb and Mine Clearance 1945-49	£250–300	£250–300	—
Bomb and Mine Clearance 1945-56	350–400	£350–400	—
Palestine 1945-48	£25–35	£20–30	£15–20
Malaya (George VI)	£25–30	£25–30	£20–25
Malaya (Elizabeth II)	£25–30	£25–30	£20–25
Cyprus	£25–30	£25–30	£20–25
Near East	£40–50	£40–50	—
Arabian Peninsular	£30–40	£30–40	£20–25
Brunei	£110–130	£100–120	£60–80

175. INDIA GENERAL SERVICE MEDAL

Date: 1937.

Campaign: India 1936–39.

Branch of Service: British and Indian Armies and RAF.

Ribbon: Grey flanked by narrow red stripes, with broad green stripes at the edges.

Metal: Silver.

Size: 36mm.

Description: (Obverse) crowned effigy of King George VI; (reverse) a tiger with the word INDIA across the top.

Clasps: North-West Frontier 1936–37, North-West Frontier 1937–39.

Comments: *The fifth and last of the IGS series, it was introduced when the change of effigy from George V to George VI became necessary, anticipating a similarly long life. It was not awarded after the outbreak of the Second World War, while the partition and independence of the Indian sub-continent afterwards rendered it obsolete. The medal was struck at the Royal Mint, London for award to British Army troops and RAF personnel, but the Calcutta Mint struck the medals awarded to the Indian Army.*

VALUE:

	British Army	RAF	Indian Army
North West Frontier 1936-37	£40–50	£60–70	£20–25
North West Frontier 1937-39	£50–60	£60–80	£20–25
2 clasps	£60–70	£100–120	£30–40

176. NORTH BORNEO GENERAL SERVICE MEDAL

Date: 1937.

Campaign: North Borneo 1937-41.

Branch of Service: British North Borneo Company forces.

Ribbon: Half green, half yellow.

Metal: Silver.

Size: 36mm.

Description: (Obverse) the arms of the Company; (reverse) the seated figure of Britannia with shield and trident, and a palm leaf in the exergue.

Clasps: None.

Comments: *Although it could be granted for meritorious service or individual acts of gallantry, as a rule it was granted for at least eighteen years service. The medal terminated with the Japanese occupation of Borneo in 1942 and only 42 medals are believed to have been awarded.*

VALUE:

    Silver   **Rare**

SECOND WORLD WAR STARS

Eight different campaign stars were issued for the Second World War. Apart from some Commonwealth issues, these were issued unnamed. It was decided that the maximum number of stars that could be earned by any one person was five, while those who qualified for more received a clasp to be sewn on the ribbon of the appropriate star. Only one clasp per ribbon was permitted. Thus the stars could bear the following clasps:

1 1939-45 (Battle of Britain)
2 Atlantic (Air Crew Europe or France and Germany)
3 Air Crew Europe (Atlantic or France and Germany)
4 Africa (North Africa 1942-43, 8th Army or 1st Army)
5 Pacific (Burma)
6 Burma (Pacific)
7 Italy
8 France and Germany (Atlantic)

The ribbons are believed to have been designed by King George VI personally and have symbolic significance in each case.

When ribbons alone are worn, the clasp is denoted by a silver rosette, the Battle of Britain being represented by a gilt rosette. As the clasps were sewn on to the ribbon and the stars issued unnamed, it is pointless to put valuations on examples with campaign clasps. The sole exception is the Battle of Britain, on account of its rarity and historic interest; but in this case it is advisable that the medal be supported by documentary provenance and form part of a group in which at least one of which medals is named to the recipient.

177. 1939-45 STAR

Date: 1943.
Campaign: Second World War 1939-45.
Branch of Service: British forces.
Ribbon: Equal stripes of dark blue, red and light blue symbolising the Royal Navy, Army and RAF respectively.
Metal: Bronze.
Size: Height 44mm; max. width 38mm.
Description: The six-pointed star has a circular centre with the GRI/VI monogram, surmounted by a crown and inscribed THE 1939-1945 STAR round the foot.
Clasps: Battle of Britain, sewn directly on to the ribbon.
Comments: *The first in a series of eight bronze stars issued for service in the Second World War, it was awarded to personnel who had completed six months' service between 3 September 1939 and 15 August 1945, though in certain cases the minimum period was shortened. Any service curtailed by death, injury or capture also qualified, as did the award of a decoration or a mention in despatches. The clasp awarded to RAF aircrew for action during the Battle of Britain was denoted by a gilt rosette when the ribbon was worn alone.*

VALUE:

1939-45 Star	£4–6
Battle of Britain clasp	£100–120

178. ATLANTIC STAR

Date: 1945.
Campaign: Atlantic 1939-45.
Branch of Service: Mainly Royal Navy.
Ribbon: Watered silk dark blue, white and green representing the ocean.
Metal: Bronze.
Size: Height 44mm; max. width 38mm.
Description: As above, but inscribed THE ATLANTIC STAR.
Clasps: Air Crew Europe, France and Germany.
Comments: *This star was awarded in the Royal Navy for six months' service afloat between 3 September 1939 and 8 May 1945 in the Atlantic or home waters, and to personnel employed in the convoys to North Russia and the South Atlantic. Merchant Navy personnel also qualified, as did RAF and Army (air crews and maritime gunners) who served afloat. Entitlement to the France and Germany or Air Crew Europe stars was denoted by clasps to that effect, if the Atlantic Star was previously awarded.*

VALUE: £14–16

179. AIR CREW EUROPE STAR

Date: 1945.
Campaign: Air operations over Europe 1939-44.
Branch of Service: RAF aircrew.
Ribbon: Pale blue (the sky) with black edges (night flying) and a narrow yellow stripe on either side (enemy searchlights).
Metal: Bronze.
Size: Height 44mm; max. width 38mm.
Description: As above, but inscribed THE AIR CREW EUROPE STAR.
Clasps: Atlantic or France and Germany.
Comments: *Awarded for operational flying from UK bases over Europe, for a period of two months between 3 September 1939 and 4 June 1944. Entitlement to either the Atlantic Star or France and Germany Star was denoted by the appropriate bar. This star is by far the most coveted of all the Second World War stars.*

VALUE: £100–120

180. AFRICA STAR

Date: 1945.
Campaign: Africa 1940-43.
Branch of Service: British and Commonwealth forces.
Ribbon: Pale buff symbolising the sand of the desert, with a broad red central stripe, a dark blue stripe on the left and a light blue stripe on the right symbolising the three services.
Metal: Bronze.
Size: Height 44mm; max. width 38mm.
Description: As above, but inscribed THE AFRICA STAR.
Clasps: North Africa 1942-43, 8th Army, 1st Army.
Comments: *Awarded for entry into an operational area in North Africa between 10 June 1940 (the date of Italy's declaration of war) and 12 May 1943 (the end of operations in North Africa), but service in Abyssinia (Ethiopia), Somaliland, Eritrea and Malta also qualified for the award. A silver numeral 1 or 8 worn on the ribbon denoted service with the First or Eighth Army between 23 October 1942 and 23 May 1943. A clasp inscribed North Africa 1942-43 was awarded to personnel of the Royal Navy Inshore Squadrons and Merchant Navy vessels which worked inshore between these dates. RAF personnel also qualified for this clasp, denoted by a silver rosette on the ribbon alone.*

VALUE: £4–5

181. PACIFIC STAR

Date: 1945.
Campaign: Pacific area 1941-45.
Branch of Service: British and Commonwealth forces.
Ribbon: Dark green (the jungle) with a central yellow stripe (the beaches), narrow stripes of dark and light blue (Royal Navy and RAF) and wider stripes of red (Army) at the edges.
Metal: Bronze.
Size: Height 44mm; max. width 38mm.
Description: As above, but inscribed THE PACIFIC STAR.
Clasps: Burma.
Comments: *Awarded for operational service in the Pacific theatre of war from 8 December 1941 to 15 August 1945. Service with the Royal and Merchant navies in the Pacific Ocean, Indian Ocean and South China Sea and land service in these areas also qualified. Personnel qualifying for both Pacific and Burma Stars got the first star and a clasp in respect of the second.*

VALUE: £22–28

182. BURMA STAR

Date: 1945.
Campaign: Burma 1941-45.
Branch of Service: British and Commonwealth forces.
Ribbon: Three equal bands of dark blue (British forces), red (Commonwealth forces) and dark blue. The dark blue bands each have at their centres a stripe of bright orange (the sun).
Metal: Bronze.
Size: Height 44mm; max. width 38mm.
Description: As above, but inscribed THE BURMA STAR.
Clasps: Pacific
Comments: *Qualifying service in the Burma campaign counted from 11 December 1941 and included service in Bengal or Assam from 1 May 1942 to 31 December 1943, and from 1 January 1944 onwards in these parts of Bengal or Assam east of the Brahmaputra. Naval service in the eastern Bay of Bengal, off the coasts of Sumatra, Sunda and Malacca also counted.*

VALUE: £10–12

183. ITALY STAR

Date: 1945.
Campaign: Italy 1943-45.
Branch of Service: British and Commonwealth forces.
Ribbon: Five equal stripes of red, white, green, white and red (the Italian national colours).
Metal: Bronze.
Size: Height 44mm; max. width 38mm.
Description: As above, but inscribed THE ITALY STAR.
Clasps: None.
Comments: *Awarded for operational service on land in Italy, Sicily, Greece, Yugoslavia, the Aegean area and Dodecanese islands, Corsica, Sardinia and Elba at any time between 11 June 1943 and 8 May 1945.*

VALUE: £5–7

184. FRANCE AND GERMANY STAR

Date: 1945.

Campaign: France and Germany 1944-45.

Branch of Service: British and Commonwealth forces.

Ribbon: Five equal stripes of blue, white, red, white and blue (the national colours of the United Kingdom, France and the Netherlands).

Metal: Bronze.

Size: Height 44mm; max. width 38mm.

Description: As above, but inscribed THE FRANCE AND GERMANY STAR.

Clasps: Atlantic.

Comments: *Awarded for operational service in France, Belgium, the Netherlands or Germany from 6 June 1944 to 8 May 1945. Service in the North Sea, English Channel and Bay of Biscay in connection with the campaign in northern Europe also qualified. Prior eligibility for the Atlantic or Air Crew Europe Stars entitled personnel only to a bar for France and Germany. Conversely a first award of the France and Germany Star could earn an Atlantic bar.*

VALUE: £14–16

185. DEFENCE MEDAL

Date: 1945.

Campaign: Second World War 1939-45.

Branch of Service: British and Commonwealth forces.

Ribbon: Two broad bars of green (this green and pleasant land) superimposed by narrow stripes of black (the black-out), with a wide band of orange (fire-bombing) in the centre.

Metal: Cupro-nickel or silver.

Size: 36mm.

Description: (Obverse) the uncrowned effigy of King George VI; (reverse) two lions flanking an oak sapling crowned with the dates at the sides and wavy lines representing the sea below. The words THE DEFENCE MEDAL appear in the exergue.

Clasps: None.

Comments: *Awarded to service personnel for three years' service at home or six months' service overseas in territories subjected to air attack or otherwise closely threatened. Personnel of Anti-Aircraft Command, RAF ground crews, Dominion forces stationed in the UK, the Home Guard, Civil Defence, National Fire Service and many other civilian units qualified for the medal. The medal was generally issued unnamed in cupro-nickel, but a Canadian version was struck in silver.*

VALUE:

Cupro-nickel	£8–10
Silver	£12–15

186. WAR MEDAL 1939–45

Date: 1945.
Campaign: Second World War 1939-45.
Branch of Service: British and Commonwealth forces.
Ribbon: Narrow red stripe in the centre, with a narrow white stripe on either side, broad red stripes at either edge and two intervening stripes of blue.
Metal: Cupro-nickel or silver.
Size: 36mm.
Description: (Obverse) effigy of King George VI; (reverse) a triumphant lion trampling on a dragon symbolising the Axis powers.
Clasps: None.
Comments: *All fulltime personnel of the armed forces wherever they were serving, so long as they had served for at least 28 days between 3 September 1939 and 2 September 1945 were eligible for this medal. It was granted in addition to the campaign stars and the Defence Medal. A few categories of civilians, such as war correspondents and ferry pilots who had flown in operational theatres, also qualified. No clasps were issued with this medal but a bronze oak leaf denoted a mention in despatches. The medal was struck in cupro-nickel and issued unnamed, but those issued to Australian and South African personnel were officially named. The Canadian version of the medal was struck in silver.*

VALUE:

Cupro-nickel	£4–5
Named (Australian or South African)	£15–20
Silver (Canadian)	£10–12

187. INDIA SERVICE MEDAL

Date: 1945.
Campaign: India 1939-45.
Branch of Service: Indian forces.
Ribbon: Grey-blue with black edges and a narrow central black stripe.
Metal: Cupro-nickel.
Size: 36mm.
Description: (Obverse) the effigy of the King Emperor; (reverse) a map of the Indian sub-continent with INDIA at the top and 1939-45 round the foot.
Clasps: None.
Comments: *Awarded to officers and men of the Indian forces for three years' non-operational service in India. In effect, it took the place of the Defence Medal in respect of Indian forces.*

VALUE: £8–12

188. CANADIAN VOLUNTEER SERVICE MEDAL

Date: 1943.
Campaign: Second World War 1939-45.
Branch of Service: Canadian forces.
Ribbon: Narrow stripes of green and red flanking a broad central stipe of dark blue.
Metal: Silver.
Size: 36mm.
Description: (Obverse) seven men and women in the uniforms of the various services, marching in step; (reverse) the Canadian national arms.
Clasps: Maple leaf
Comments: *Awarded for eighteen months' voluntary service in the Canadian forces. The clasp denoted overseas service.*

VALUE:
Silver medal	£14–16
With Maple leaf clasp	£18–22

189. AFRICA SERVICE MEDAL

Date: 1943.
Campaign: Second World War 1939-45.
Branch of Service: South African forces.
Ribbon: A central orange stripe, with green and gold stripes on either side.
Metal: Silver.
Size: 36mm.
Description: (Obverse) depicts a map of the African Continent; (reverse) bears a leaping Springbok. Inscribed AFRICA SERVICE MEDAL on the left and AFRIKADIENS-MEDALJE on the right.
Clasps: None.
Comments: *Awarded to Union service personnel who served at home and abroad during the War for at least thirty days. Medals were fully named and gave the service serial number of the recipient, prefixed by the letters N (Negro or Native), C (Cape Coloured) or M (Malay recruited in the Capetown area), a curious example of Apartheid at work.*

VALUE:
Silver medal (190,000)	£8–12

190. AUSTRALIA SERVICE MEDAL

Date: 1949.
Campaign: Second World War 1939-45.
Branch of Service: Australian forces.
Ribbon: A broad central band of khaki bordered in red, with a dark blue and a light blue bar at either edge.
Metal: Cupro-nickel.
Size: 36mm.
Description: (Obverse) the effigy of King George VI; (reverse) the Australian arms supported by a kangaroo and an emu.
Clasps: None.
Comments: *Awarded to all Australian personnel who had seen eighteen months' overseas or three years' home service. The medals were named to the recipients and their service numbers were prefixed by the initial of their state: N (New South Wales), Q (Queensland), S (South Australia), T (Tasmania), V (Victoria) and W (Western Australia).*

VALUE:
Cupro-nickel medal (180,000)	£15–18

191. NEW ZEALAND WAR SERVICE MEDAL

Date: 1946.
Campaign: Second World War 1939-45.
Branch of Service: New Zealand forces.
Ribbon: Black with white edges.
Metal: Cupro-nickel.
Size: 36mm.
Description: (Obverse) effigy of King George VI; (reverse) the text FOR SERVICE TO NEW ZEALAND 1939-45 with a fern leaf below. Suspension was by a pair of fern leaves attached to a straight bar.
Clasps: None.
Comments: *Issued unnamed, to all members of the New Zealand forces who completed one month full-time or six months part-time service between September 1939 and September 1945.*

VALUE:

Cupro-nickel medal (240,000)	£15–18

192. SOUTH AFRICAN MEDAL FOR WAR SERVICE

Date: 1946.
Campaign: Second World War 1939-46.
Branch of Service: South African forces.
Ribbon: Three equal stripes of orange, white and blue, the South African national colours.
Metal: Silver.
Size: 36mm.
Description: (Obverse) effigy of King George VI; (reverse) a wreath of protea flowers enclosing the dates 1939 and 1945. Inscribed in English and Afrikaans: SOUTH AFRICA FOR WAR SERVICES on the left and SUID AFRIKA VIR OORLOGDIENSTE on the right.
Clasps: None.
Comments: *Men and women who served for at least two years in any official voluntary organisation in South Africa or overseas qualified for this medal so long as the service was both voluntary and unpaid. Those who already had the South African War Service Medal were ineligible.*

VALUE:

Silver (17,500)	£25–35

193. SOUTHERN RHODESIA WAR SERVICE MEDAL

Date: 1946.
Campaign: Second World War 1939-45.
Branch of Service: Southern Rhodesian forces.
Ribbon: Dark green with black and red stripes at each edge.
Metal: Cupro-nickel.
Size: 36mm.
Description: (Obverse) King George VI; (reverse) the Rhodesian national arms. FOR SERVICE IN SOUTHERN RHODESIA round the top and the dates 1939-1945 at the foot.
Clasps: None.
Comments: *This very scarce medal was awarded only to those who served in Southern Rhodesia during the period of the War but who were ineligible for one of the campaign stars or war medals.*

VALUE:

Cupro-nickel (1700)	£130–150

194. NEWFOUNDLAND VOLUNTEER WAR SERVICE MEDAL

Date: 1981.
Campaign: Second World War 1939-45.
Branch of Service: Newfoundland forces.
Ribbon: Deep claret with edges of red, white and blue.
Metal: Bronze.
Size: 37mm.
Description: (Obverse) the royal cypher of George VI surmounted by a crown topped by a caribou, the Newfoundland national emblem. (Reverse) Britannia on a scallop shell background guarded by two lions.
Clasps:
Comments: *While the Second World War was being fought, Newfoundland was still a separate British colony which did not enter the Canadian Confederation till 1947. Consequently Newfoundland servicemen did not qualify for the Canadian Volunteer Service medal, and this deficiency was not remedied until July 1981 when the Newfoundland provincial government instituted tis medal. Those who had served with the Canadian forces, on the other hand, and already held the Canadian medal, were not eligible for this award. The medal could be claimed by next-of-kin of those who died in or since the war.*

VALUE: Rare

195. KOREA MEDAL

Date: July 1951.
Campaign: Korean War 1950-53.
Branch of Service: British and Commonwealth forces.
Ribbon: Yellow, with two blue stripes .
Metal: Cupro-nickel or silver.
Size: 36mm.
Description: (Obverse) Right-facing bust of Queen Elizabeth II by Mary Gillick; there are two obverse types, with or without BR: OMN. (Reverse) Hercules wrestling with the Hydra, KOREA in the exergue.
Clasps: None.
Comments: *Awarded to all British and Commonwealth forces who took part in the Korean War between July 1950 and June 1953. British medals were issued in cupro-nickel impressed in small capitals, medals to Australian and New Zealand forces were impressed in large capitals and the Canadian version was struck in silver and has CANADA below the Queen's bust. Particularly prized are medals issued to the 'Glorious Gloucesters' who played a gallant part in the battle of the Imjin River.*

VALUE:

British, first obverse	£50–70
British, second obverse	£100–150
To Gloucester Regiment	£250–300
Australian or New Zealand naming	£70–90
Canadian, silver (27,000)	£60–70

196. SOUTH AFRICAN MEDAL FOR KOREA

Date: 1952.
Campaign: Korea 1950-53.
Branch of Service: South African forces.
Ribbon: Sky blue central band flanked by dark blue stripes and edges of orange.
Metal: Silver.
Size: 38mm.
Description: (Obverse) maps of South Africa and Korea with an arrow linking them and the words VRYWILLIGERS and VOLUNTEERS in the field. (Reverse) the then South African arms surmounted by the crowned EIIR.
Clasps: None.
Comments: *Awarded to the 800 personnel in the contingent sent to Korea by the Union of South Africa. Suspension is by a ring and claw.*

VALUE:
>
> Silver (800)   £280–300

197. UNITED NATIONS KOREA MEDAL

Date: December 1950.
Campaign: Korea 1950-53.
Branch of Service: All UN forces.
Ribbon: Seventeen narrow stripes alternating pale blue and white.
Metal: Bronze.
Size: 35mm.
Description: (Obverse) the wreathed globe emblem of the UN; (reverse) inscribed FOR SERVICE IN DEFENCE OF THE PRINCIPLES OF THE CHARTER OF THE UNITED NATIONS.
Clasps: Korea.
Comments: *National variants were produced, but the British type was granted to all personnel of the British and Commonwealth forces who had served at least one full day in Korea. Moreover, as those who served in Korea after the armistice in June 1953 were also entitled to the UN medal it is sometimes found in groups without the corresponding British medal.*

VALUE: £18–22

198. CAMPAIGN SERVICE MEDAL

Date: 1964.
Campaign: Minor campaigns and operations since 1962.
Branch of Service: British forces.
Ribbon: Deep purple edged with green.
Metal: Silver.
Size: 36mm.
Description: (Obverse) a crowned bust of Queen Elizabeth II; (reverse) an oak wreath enclosing a crown and the words FOR CAMPAIGN SERVICE. It has a beaded and curved suspension above which are mounted campaign clasps.
Clasps: Twelve to date (see below); the maximum clasps awarded so far seems to be six.
Comments: *This medal was instituted for award to personnel of all services, and thus did away with the need for separate Army and Navy general service medals. Awards range from a mere 70 for South Vietnam to over 130,000 for service in Northern Ireland.*

VALUE:

Borneo	£20–30
Radfan	£40–50
South Arabia	£25–35
Malaya Peninsula	£20–30
South Vietnam	Rare
Northern Ireland	£25–35
Dhofar	£80–100
Lebanon	£400–450
Mine Clearance	£400–450
Gulf	£350–450
Kuwait	£600–800
N. Iraq & S. Turkey	£450–650
2 clasps	£40–60
3 clasps	£70–90
4 clasps	From £100

199. UNITED NATIONS EMERGENCY FORCE MEDAL

Date: 1957.
Campaign: Israel and Egypt 1956–57.
Branch of Service: All UN forces.
Ribbon: Sand-coloured with a central light blue stripe and narrow dark blue and green stripes towards each edge.
Metal: Bronze.
Size: 35mm.
Description: (Obverse) the UN wreathed globe emblem with UNEF at the top; (reverse) inscribed IN THE SERVICE OF PEACE. Ring suspension.
Clasps: None.
Comments: *Awarded to all personnel who served with the UN peace-keeping forces on the border between Israel and Egypt following the Six Day War of 1956. These medals were awarded to troops from Brazil, Canada, Colombia, Denmark, Finland, Indonesia, Norway, Sweden and Yugoslavia.*

VALUE:

Bronze	£10–15

200. VIETNAM MEDAL

Date: July 1968.
Campaign: Vietnam 1964-68.
Branch of Service: Australian and New Zealand forces.
Ribbon: A broad central band of bright yellow surmounted by three thin red stripes (the Vietnamese national colours) and bordered by broader red stripes, with dark and light blue stripes at the edges, representing the three services.
Metal: Silver.
Size: 36mm.
Description: (Obverse) the crowned bust of Queen Elizabeth II; (reverse) a nude male figure pushing apart two spheres representing different ideologies.
Clasps: None.
Comments: *Awarded to personnel who served in Vietnam a minimum of one day on land or 28 days at sea after 28 May 1964. The medal was impressed in large capitals (Australian) or small capitals (New Zealand).*

VALUE:

Australian recipient (18,000)	£140–160
New Zealand recipient (4000)	£140–160

201. SOUTH VIETNAM CAMPAIGN MEDAL

Date: 1964.
Campaign: Vietnam 1960-68.
Branch of Service: Allied forces in Vietnam.
Ribbon: White with two broad green stripes towards the centre and narrow green edges.
Metal: Bronze.
Size: Height 42mm; max. width 36mm.
Description: A six-pointed star, with gold rays in the angles. The gilt enamelled centre shows a map of Vietnam engulfed in flames; (reverse) a Vietnamese inscription in the centre.
Comments: *Awarded by the government of South Vietnam to Australian and New Zealand forces who served at least six months in Vietnam. The original issue, of Vietnamese manufacture, was relatively crude and issued unnamed. Subsequently medals were produced in Australia and these are not only of a better quality but bear the name of the recipient.*

VALUE:

Unnamed	£10–15
Named	£20–30

202. RHODESIA MEDAL

Date: 1980.
Campaign: Rhodesia 1979–80.
Branch of Service: British and Rhodesian forces.
Ribbon: Sky blue, with a narrow band of red, white and dark blue in the centre.
Metal: Rhodium-plated cupro-nickel.
Size: 36mm.
Description: (Obverse) the crowned bust of Queen Elizabeth II; (reverse) a sable antelope with the name of the medal and the year of issue.
Clasps: None.
Comments: *This medal was awarded to personnel serving in Rhodesia for fourteen days between 1 December 1979 and 20 March 1980, pending the elections and the emergence of the independent republic of Zimbabwe. Medals are named in impressed capitals.*

VALUE:

Cupro-nickel (2500)	£300–350

203. SOUTH ATLANTIC MEDAL

Date: 1982.
Campaign: Falkland Islands and South Georgia 1982.
Branch of Service: British forces.
Ribbon: Watered silk blue, white, green, white and blue.
Metal: Cupro-nickel.
Size: 36mm.
Description: (Obverse) crowned profile of Queen Elizabeth II; (reverse) laurel wreath below the arms of the Falkland Islands with SOUTH ATLANTIC MEDAL inscribed round the top.
Clasps: None, but a rosette denoting service in the combat zone.
Comments: *Awarded to all personnel who took part in operations in the South Atlantic for the liberation of South Georgia and the Falkland Islands following the Argentinian invasion. To qualify, the recipient had to have at least one full day's service in the Falklands or South Georgia, or 30 days in the operational zone including Ascension Island. Those who qualified under the first condition were additionally awarded a large rosette for wear on the ribbon.*

VALUE:

Army (7000)	£180–200
Royal Navy (13,000)	£140–160
Royal Marines (3700)	£150–180
Royal Fleet Auxiliary (2000)	£120–150
RAF (2000)	£180–220
Merchant Navy and civilians (2000)	£80–100

204. GULF MEDAL

Date: 1992.
Campaign: Kuwait and Saudi Arabia 1990-91.
Branch of Service: British forces.
Ribbon: Sand-coloured broad central band flanked by narrow stripes of dark blue, red and light blue (left) or light blue, red and dark blue (right) representing the sands of the desert and the three armed services.
Metal: Cupro-nickel.
Size: 36mm.
Description: (Obverse) crowned profile of Queen Elizbeth II; (reverse) an eagle and automatic rifle superimposed on an anchor, symbolising the three armed services. The dates of the Gulf War appear at the foot.
Clasps: 2 Aug 1990, 16 Jan - 28 Feb 1991.
Comments: *Awarded to personnel who had thirty days continuous service in the Middle East (including Cyprus) between 2 August 1990 and 7 March 1991, or seven days between 16 January 1991 and 28 February 1991, or service with the Kuwait Liaison Team on 2 August 1990, the date of the Iraqi invasion. Two clasps were sanctioned and awarded to personnel who qualified for active service with the Liaison Team or in the operations to liberate Kuwait. A rosette is worn on the ribbon alone to denote the campaign clasps. Naming is in impressed capitals. More than 45,000 medals were awarded. See also the Kuwait and Iraq-Turkey clasps awarded to the Campaign Service Medal.*

VALUE:

No clasp	£125–175
16 Jan to 28 Feb 1991	£150–200
2 Aug 1990	Rare

205. SAUDI ARABIAN MEDAL FOR THE LIBERATION OF KUWAIT

Date: 1991.
Campaign: Gulf War 1991.
Branch of Service: British and Allied forces.
Ribbon: Green with edges of red, black and white (the Saudi national colours).
Metal: White metal.
Size: approx. 45mm across
Description: The white metal medal has a star of fifteen long and fifteen short round-tipped rays, surmounted by a bronze circle bearing a crowned and enwreathed globe on which appears a map of Arabia. Above the circle is a palm tree with crossed scimitars, the state emblem of Saudi Arabia. A scroll inscribed in Arabic and English LIBERATION OF KUWAIT appears round the foot of the circle.
Clasps: None.
Comments: *Awarded by the government of Saudi Arabia to all Allied personnel who took part in the campaign for the liberation of Kuwait, although only a few of the 45,000 British servicemen were subsequently given permission by the Foreign and Commonwealth Office to wear it. The contract for production was shared between Spink and a Swiss company, but subsequently a flatter version, more practicable for wear with other medals, was manufactured in the United States.*

VALUE: —

206. KUWAITI LIBERATION MEDALS

Date: 1991.
Campaign: Liberation of Kuwait 1991.
Branch of Service: Allied forces.
Ribbon: Equal stripes of green, white and red (the Kuwaiti national colours).
Metal
Size:
Description: The circular medals have different decorative treatments of the Kuwaiti state emblem on the obverse, enshrined in a five-petalled flower (Second Grade), a five-pointed star with radiate background (Third Grade) and a plain medallic treatment (Fourth Grade). All grades, however, have a straight bar suspender of different designs.
Clasps: None.
Comments: *This medal was issued in five grades and awarded according to the rank of the recipient. The Excellent Grade was only conferred on the most senior Allied commanders, the First Grade went to brigadiers and major-generals, the Second Grade to officers of field rank (colonels and majors), the Third Grade to junior officers (captains, lieutenants and equivalent ranks in the other services), and the Fourth Grade to all other ranks.*

HM Government has decreed that British personnel may accept their medals as a keepsake but permission to wear them in uniform has so far been refused. The Canadian Government has followed the same policy, but the personnel of other Allied nations are permitted to wear their medals.

VALUE: —

207. UNITED NATIONS MEDAL

Date: 1951.
Campaigns: Various supervisory or observation roles since 1948.
Branch of Service: UN forces.
Ribbons: Various (see below).
Metal: Bronze.
Size: 35mm.
Description: (Obverse) the wreathed globe emblem surmounted by the letters UN; (reverse) plain.
Clasps: None.
Comments: *Apart from the UN Korea and UNEF medals, there have been numerous awards to personnel who served in one or other of the UN peace-keeping actions around the world since the end of the Second World War. The all-purpose medal has been awarded with various distinctive ribbons for service in many of the world's trouble spots.*

UNTSO   United Nations Truce Supervision Organization (Israel, Egypt, Syria since 1948).
Blue ribbon with two narrow white stripes towards the edges.
UNOGIL   United Nations Observation Group in Lebanon (1958).
Same ribbon as UNTSO.
ONUC   Organisation des Nations Unies au Congo (1960–64).
Originally the same ribbon as UNTSO with clasp CONGO, but a green ribbon, with white and blue edges was substituted in 1963.
UNTEA   United Nations Temporary Executive Authority (Netherlands New Guinea, 1962).
Blue ribbon with a white central stripe bordered green.
UNMOGIP   United Nations Military Observer Group in India and Pakistan since 1949.
Dark green ribbon shading to light green with white and blue edges.
UNIPOM   United Nations India Pakistan Observation Mission (1965–66).
Ribbon as UNMOGIP.
UNYOM   United Nations Yemen Observation Mission (1963–64).
Ribbon with brown centre, yellow stripes and light blue edges.
UNFICYP   United Nations Force in Cyprus (1964 -).
Pale blue ribbon with central white stripe bordered in dark blue.
UNEF 2   United Nations Emergency Force 2 patrolling Israeli-Egyptian cease-fire (1973–).
Pale blue ribbon with sand centre and two dark blue stripes.
UNDOF   United Nations Disengagement Observer Force, Golan Heights (1974–).
Ribbon of red, white, black and pale blue.
UNIFIL   United Nations Interim Force in Lebanon (1978–).
Pale blue ribbon with green centre bordered white and red.
UNIIMOG   United Nations Iran-Iraq Monitoring Observation Group.
Pale blue with red, white and green edges.
UNAVEM   United Nations Angola Verification Mission.
Pale blue ribbon with yellow edges separated by narrow stripes of red, white and black.
ONUCA   Observadores de las Naciones Unidas en Centro America (Nicaragua and Guatemala).
Pale blue ribbon with dark blue edges and nine thin central green or white stripes.
UNTAG   United Nations Transitional Assistance Group (Namibia, 1990).
Sand ribbon with pale blue edges and thin central stripes of blue, green, red, sand and deep blue.
ONUSAL   Observadores de las Naciones Unidas en El Salvador.
Pale blue ribbon with a white central stripe bordered dark blue.
UNIKOM   United Nations Iraq Kuwait Observation Mission.
Sand ribbon with a narrow central stripe of pale blue.
MINURSO   Mission des Nations Unies pour la Referendum dans le Sahara Occidental (UN Mission for the Referendum in Western Sahara).
Ribbon has a broad sandy centre flanked by stripes of UN blue.
UNAMIC   United Nations Advanced Mission in Cambodia.
UNTAC   United Nations Transitional Authority in Cambodia.
UNPROFOR   United Nations Protection Force (1992–) operating in the former Yugoslavia, especially Bosnia.
Blue ribbon with central red stripe edged in white and green or brown edges.
UNHQ   General service at UN headquarters, New York.
Plain ribbon of pale blue, the UN colour.

VALUE:
      Any medal regardless of ribbon   £10–15

LONG AND MERITORIOUS SERVICE MEDALS

A large, varied but until recently relatively neglected category comprises the medals awarded for long service and good conduct or meritorious service. Their common denominator is that the grant of such awards is made in respect of a minimum number of years of unblemished service—"undetected crime" is how it is often described in the armed forces. As their title implies, long service and good conduct medals combine the elements of lengthy service with no transgressions of the rules and regulations. Meritorious service, on the other hand, implies rather more. Apart from a brief period (1916-28) when awards were made for single acts of gallantry, MSMs have generally been granted to warrant officers and senior NCOs as a rather superior form of long service medal.

Long service and good conduct medals do not appear to excite the same interest among collectors as campaign medals. Perhaps this may be accounted for by their image of stolid devotion to duty rather than the romantic connotations of a medal with an unusual clasp awarded for service in some remote and all but forgotten outpost of the Empire. Nevertheless their importance should not be overlooked. Especially in regard to groups consisting primarily of the Second World War medals, they serve a useful purpose in establishing the provenance of the group, on account of the fact that they are invariably named to the recipient.

Service medals include not only such well known types as the Army LSGC (known affectionately as "the mark of the beast" on account of its high incidence on the chests of sergeant-majors), but also awards to the Territorial and Reserve forces, the auxiliary forces, the nursing services, and organisations such as the Royal Observer Corps and the Cadet Force, the Police, the Red Cross and St John's Ambulance Brigade. The Special Constabulary and Fire Brigades also have their own medals bestowed according to length of service and distinguished conduct. These medals may lack the glamour of naval and military awards but in recent years they have become increasingly fashionable with collectors and will certainly repay further study in their own right.

As many of these medals have been in use for eighty years or more with a standard reverse, variation usually lies in the obverse, changed for each successive sovereign. In addition, considerable variety has been imparted by the use of crowned or uncrowned profiles and busts, and changes in titles.

The following is a summary of the principal obverse types which may be encountered, referred to in the text by their type letters in brackets:

Queen Victoria (A) Young Head by William Wyon 1838-60

Queen Victoria (B) Veiled Head by Leonard C. Wyon 1860-87

Queen Victoria (C) Jubilee Head by Sir Joseph E. Boehm 1887-93

Queen Victoria (D) Old Head by Sir Thomas Brock 1893-1901

Edward VII (A) Bareheaded bust in Field Marshal's uniform

Edward VII (B) Bareheaded bust in Admiral's uniform

Edward VII (C) Coinage profile by George W. de Saulles

George V (A) Bareheaded bust in Field Marshal's uniform

George V (B) Bareheaded bust in Admiral's uniform

George V (C) Crowned bust in Coronation robes

George V (D) Crowned bust in Delhi Durbar robes

George V (E) Coinage profile by Bertram Mackennal 1931-36

George VI (A) Crowned bust in Coronation robes

George VI (B) Crowned profile IND: IMP 1937-48

George VI (C) Crowned profile FID: DEF 1949-52

George VI (D) Coinage profile IND: IMP 1937-48

George VI (E) Coinage profile FID: DEF 1949-52

Elizabeth II (A) Tudor crown 1953-80

Elizabeth II (B) Imperial crown 1980-

Elizabeth II (C) Coinage bust BR: OMN 1953-54

Elizabeth II (D) Coinage bust without BR: OMN 1955-

Queen Victoria (A) Young Head   *Queen Victoria (D) Old Head*

Edward VII (A) Bareheaded bust in Field Marshal's uniform

George V (A) Bareheaded bust in Field Marshal's uniform

George V (B) Bareheaded bust in Admiral's uniform

George V (C) Crowned bust in Coronation robes

George V (E) Coinage profile by Bertram Mackennal

George VI (B) Crowned profile IND: IMP 1937-48

George VI (C) Crowned profile FID: DEF 1949-52

George VI (D) Coinage profile IND: IMP 1937-48

George VI (E) Coinage profile FID: DEF 1949-52

Elizabeth II (A) Tudor crown 1953-80

Elizabeth II (C) Coinage bust BR: OMN 1953-54

Elizabeth II (D) Coinage bust without BR: OMN.

208. ROYAL NAVAL MERITORIOUS SERVICE MEDAL

Instituted: 14 January 1919, by Order in Council.
Branch of Service: Royal Navy.
Ribbon: Crimson edged in white, with a central white stripe.
Metal: Silver
Size: 36mm.
Description: (Obverse) effigy of the reigning monarch; (reverse) imperial crown surmounting a wreath containing the words FOR MERITORIOUS SERVICE. The medal was named in large seriffed capitals round the rim.
Comments: *Awarded without annuity or pension to petty officers and ratings of the Royal Navy. Originally it was awarded either for specific acts of gallantry not in the presence of the enemy or for arduous and specially meritorious service afloat or ashore in action with the enemy. Bars were granted for second awards. It was superseded in 1928 by the British Empire Medal for Gallantry or Meritorious Service, but re-instated on 1 December 1977. In this guise it has been awarded to senior petty officers of the Royal Navy, warrant officers and senior NCOs of the Royal Marines, and equivalent ranks in the WRNS and QARNNS, who have at least 27 years service and are already holders of the LSGC medal and three good conduct badges. The medal is not awarded automatically when these criteria are satisfied, as no more than 59 medals may be awarded annually. The revived medal is identical to the Army MSM and can only be distinguished by the naming giving rank and name of ship.*

VALUE:

George V (B) (1020)	£180–220
Elizabeth II (D)	£240–280

209. ROYAL MARINES MERITORIOUS SERVICE MEDAL

Instituted: 15 January 1849, by Order in Council.
Branch of Service: Royal Marines.
Ribbon: Plain dark blue.
Metal: Silver.
Size: 36mm.
Description: (Obverse) effigy of the monarch; (reverse) a crowned laurel wreath enclosing the words FOR MERITORIOUS SERVICE.
Comments: *Annuities not exceeding £20 a year might be granted in addition to the medal for distinguished service. Sergeants with a minimum of 24 years service (the last fourteen as a sergeant), 'with an irreproachable and meritorious character' were considered eligible for the award which was extended to discharged sergeants in 1872 when the service qualification was reduced to 21 years. The award of the MSM for gallantry was discontinued in 1874 when the Conspicuous Gallantry Medal was reconstituted. Only six MSMs for gallantry were ever awarded. The medal was identical with the Army MSM, distinguished solely by its ribbon and the naming to the recipient. Under the royal warrants of 1916-19 Marine NCOs became eligible for immediate awards of the MSM for arduous or specially meritorious service. The medals in this case were worn with crimson ribbons with three white stripes and had the obverse showing the King in the uniform of an Admiral or a Field Marshal, depending on whether the award was for services afloat, or with the naval brigades on the Western Front. The use of this medal ceased in 1928 when the BEM for Gallantry was instituted. The Royal Marines MSM was revived in 1977 solely as a long service award and is the same as the naval MSM already noted, differing only in the details of the recipient.*

VALUE: **Rare**

210. ARMY MERITORIOUS SERVICE MEDAL

Instituted: 19 December 1845.
Branch of Service: Army.
Ribbon: Plain crimson (till 1916), white edges added (1916-17), three white stripes (since August 1917).
Metal: Silver.
Size: 36mm.
Description: (Obverse) effigy of the monarch; (reverse) a crowned laurel wreath inscribed FOR MERITORIOUS SERVICE.
Comments: *A sum of £2000 a year was set aside for distribution to recipients in the form of annuities not exceeding £20, paid for life to NCOs of the rank of sergeant and above for distinguished or meritorious service. The number of medals awarded was thus limited by the amount of money available in the annuity fund, so that medals and annuities were only granted on the death of previous recipients or when the fund was increased. Until November 1902 holders were not allowed to wear the LSGC as well as the MSM, but thereafter both medals could be worn, the LSGC taking precedence. In 1979, however, the order of precedence was reversed. Until 1951 the MSM could only be awarded when an annuity became available, but since then it has often been awarded without the annuity, the latter becoming payable as funds permit. Since 1956 recipients must have at least 27 years service to become eligible. What was, in effect, a second type of MSM was introduced in October 1916 when immediate awards for exceptionally valuable and meritorious service were introduced. In January 1917 this was extended to include individual acts of gallantry not in the presence of the enemy. No annuities were paid with the immediate awards which terminated in 1928 with the institution of the Gallantry BEM. Bars for subsequent acts of gallantry or life-saving were introduced in 1916, seven being awarded up to 1928. The standard crown and wreath reverse was used but in addition to the wide range of obverse types swivelling suspension was used until 1926, and immediate and non-immediate awards may be distinguished by the presence or absence respectively of the recipient's regimental number. Recent awards of the Elizabethan second bust medals have reverted to swivelling suspension.*

VALUE:

Victoria (A) 1847 on edge (110)	£300–400
Victoria (A) 1848 below bust (10)	Rare
Victoria (A) (990)	£175–200
Edward VII (725)	£100–150
George V (A) swivel (1050)	£50–75
George V (A) non-swivel (400)	£65–85
George V (E) (550)	£120–150
George VI (D) (1090)	£60–80
George VI (E) (5600)	£50–75
George VI (B) (55)	£750–800
Elizabeth II (C) (125)	£150–175
Elizabeth II (D) (2750)	£120–150

211. ROYAL AIR FORCE MERITORIOUS SERVICE MEDAL

Instituted: June 1918

Branch of Service: Royal Air Force.

Ribbon: Half crimson, half light blue, with white stripes at the centre and edges.

Metal: Silver.

Size: 36mm.

Description: (Obverse) effigy of the monarch; (reverse) a crowned laurel wreath enclosing the words FOR MERITORIOUS SERVICE. Originally medals were named in large seriffed capitals and were issued in respect of the First World War and service in Russia (1918-20), but later medals were impressed in thin block capitals. The RAF version had a swivelling suspension, unlike its military counterpart.

Comments: *Awarded for valuable services in the field, as opposed to actual flying service. This medal was replaced by the BEM in 1928, but revived in December 1977 under the same conditions as the military MSM. No more than 70 medals are awarded annually. The current issue is similar to the naval and military MSMs, differing only in the naming which includes RAF after the service number.*

VALUE:

George V (E) (854)	£200–250
Elizabeth II (D)	£180–220

212. COLONIAL MERITORIOUS SERVICE MEDALS

Instituted: 31 May 1895.

Branch of Service: Colonial forces.

Ribbon: According to issuing territory (see below).

Metal: Silver.

Size: 36mm.

Description: (Obverse) as British counterparts; (reverse) as British type, but with the name of the dominion or colony round the top.

Comments: *Awarded for service in the British dominions, colonies and protectorates.*

Canada: Ribbon as for British Army MSM. CANADA on reverse till 1936; imperial version used from then until 1958. No medals with the Victorian obverse were awarded, but specimens exist.

Cape of Good Hope: Crimson ribbon with central orange stripe. Only one or two Edward VII medals issued.

Natal: Crimson ribbon with a central yellow stripe. Exceptionally, it was awarded to volunteers in the Natal Militia. Fifteen Edward VII medals awarded.

Commonwealth of Australia: Crimson ribbon with two dark green central stripes. Issued between 1903 and 1975.

New South Wales: Crimson ribbon with a dark blue central stripe. Issued till 1903.

Queensland: Crimson ribbon with light blue central stripe. Issued till 1903.

South Australia: Plain crimson ribbon. Issued till 1903.

Tasmania: Crimson ribbon with a pink central stripe. Issued till 1903.

New Zealand: Crimson ribbon with a light green central stripe. Issued since 1898.

VALUE   Rare

213. INDIAN ARMY MERITORIOUS SERVICE MEDAL 1848

Instituted: 20 May 1848, by General Order of the Indian government.
Branch of Service: Forces of the Honourable East India Company and later the Indian armed services.
Ribbon: Plain crimson.
Metal: Silver.
Size: 36mm.
Description: (Obverse) the Wyon profile of Queen Victoria; (reverse) the arms and motto of the Honourable East India Company.
Comments: *Awarded with an annuity up to £20 to European sergeants, serving or discharged, for meritorious service. It was discontinued in 1873.*

VALUE:
    Victoria   £200–250

214. INDIAN ARMY MERITORIOUS SERVICE MEDAL 1888

Instituted: 1888.
Branch of Service: Indian Army.
Ribbon: Plain crimson (till 1917); three white stripes added (1917).
Metal: Silver.
Size: 36mm.
Description: (Obverse) the sovereign's effigy; (reverse) a central wreath enclosing the word INDIA surrounded by the legend FOR MERITORIOUS SERVICE with a continuous border of lotus flowers and leaves round the circumference.
Comments: *For award to Indian warrant officers and senior NCOs (havildars, dafadars and equivalent band ranks). Eighteen years of exceptionally meritorious service was the minimum requirement, subject to the availability of funds in the annuity. At first only one medal was set aside for each regiment and thereafter awards were only made on the death, promotion or reduction of existing recipients. On promotion the medal was retained but the annuity ceased. It became obsolete in 1947.*

VALUE:
Victoria (B)	£80–100
Edward VII (A)	£40–50
George V (D)	£30–40
George V (C)	£30–50
George VI (B)	£30–40

215. AFRICAN POLICE MEDAL FOR MERITORIOUS SERVICE

Instituted: 14 July 1915.

Branch of Service Non-European NCOs and men of the colonial police forces in East and West Africa.

Ribbon: Sand-coloured with red edges.

Metal: Silver.

Size: 36mm

Description: (Obverse) effigy of the sovereign; (reverse) a crown surmounted by a lion passant gardant within a palm wreath and having the legend FOR MERITORIOUS SERVICE IN THE POLICE and AFRICA at the foot.

Comments: *Awarded for both individual acts of gallantry and distinguished, meritorious or long service. In respect of the lastnamed, a minimum of 15 years exemply service was required. It wss superseded by the Colonial Police Medal in 1938.*

VALUE:

George V (A) IND: IMP 1915-31	£300–400
George V (A) INDIAE IMP 1931-7	£250–350
George VI (B) 1938	Rare

216. UNION OF SOUTH AFRICA MERITORIOUS SERVICE MEDAL

Instituted: 24 October 1914, by Government gazette.

Branch of Service: Service personnel of South Africa, Southern Rhodesia and Swaziland.

Ribbon: Crimson with blue edges and a central white, blue and white band.

Metal: Silver.

Size: 36mm.

Description: As British military MSM.

Comments: *A total of 46 gallantry and 300 meritorious service awards were made up to 1952 when the medal was discontinued.*

VALUE: Rare

217. ROYAL HOUSEHOLD FAITHFUL SERVICE MEDALS

Instituted: 1872 by Queen Victoria.

Branch of Service: Royal Household.

Ribbon: Originally Royal Stuart tartan; later, a different ribbon for each monarch: dark blue and red diagonal stripes descending from left to right (George V), the same but descending from right to left (George VI) or dark blue with three red stripes (Elizabeth II).

Metal: Silver.

Size: 27mm (Victoria); 29mm (later awards).

Description: (Obverse) the sovereign's effigy; (reverse) the personal details of the recipient engraved on it. The Victorian medal has a very elaborate suspension ornamented with the crowned royal monogram, with a laurel bar brooch fitting at the top. This medal was not originally intended to be worn with a ribbon, although it had a strip of Royal Stuart tartan behind it. The same medal, but struck in 22 carat gold, was presented to John Brown, the Queen's personal servant. The concept was revived by George V, a silver medal of more conventional appearance being struck with the text FOR LONG AND FAITHFUL SERVICE on the reverse. Thirty, forty and fifty year service bars were also awarded.

Comments: *Intended as a reward to servants of the Royal Household for long and faithful service of at least 25 years. A further 10 years merited a bar. Different ribbons were used for each monarch, corresponding to the crowned cypher joining the medal to the suspension bar on either side of which the recipient's years of service were inscribed. Only two medals have been recorded with the profile of Edward VIII (1936).*

VALUE:

Victoria	From £500
George V (E)	£200–250
Edward VIII	Rare
George VI (D)	£240–280
Elizabeth II (C)	£250–300

218. ROYAL NAVAL LONG SERVICE AND GOOD CONDUCT MEDAL

Instituted: 24 August 1831, by Order in Council.
Branch of Service: Royal Navy.
Ribbon: Plain dark blue (1831); dark blue with white edges (1848).
Metal: Silver.
Size: 34mm (1831); 36mm (1848).
Description: First type: (Obverse) an anchor surmounted by a crown and enclosed in an oak wreath; (reverse) the recipient's details. Plain ring for suspension.

Second type, adopted in 1848: (Obverse) the sovereign's effigy; (reverse) a three-masted man-of-war surrounded by a rope tied at the foot with a reef knot and having the legend FOR LONG SERVICE AND GOOD CONDUCT round the circumference. This medal originally had a wide suspender bar 38mm, but a narrow suspender was substituted in 1874. Normally the obverse was undated, but about 100 medals were issued in 1849-50 with the obverse of the Naval GSM, with the date 1848 below the Queen's bust. Engraved naming was used from 1875 to 1877, but from then until 1901 impressed naming was adopted. Later medals used the various obverse effigies noted below.
Comments: *Originally awarded for 21 years exemplary conduct, but the period was reduced to 10 years in 1874, then later increased to 15 years. Bars for additional periods of 15 years were instituted by George V. In March 1981 commissioned officers of the naval services became eligible after 15 years service, provided at least 12 years were served in the ranks.*

VALUE:

Anchor 1831-47 (644)	£350–450
Victoria (A) wide suspender (3572)	£120–160
1848 type (100)	Rare
Victoria (A) narrow suspender (4400)	£50–70
impressed naming (18,200)	£45–55
Edward VII (B)	£20–30
George V (B) 1910-30 swivel	£15–20
non-swivelling bar	£20–25
George V (E) 1931-36	£20–25
George VI (D) 1937-48	£20–25
George VI (E) 1949-52	£20–30
Elizabeth II (C) 1953-54	£25–35
Elizabeth II (D) 1954-	£20–30

219. ROYAL NAVAL RESERVE DECORATION

Instituted: 1908.

Branch of Service: Royal Naval Reserve.

Ribbon: Plain green ribbon, white edges being added from 1941 onwards.

Metal: Silver and silver-gilt.

Size: Height 54mm; max. width 33mm.

Description: A skeletal badge with the royal cypher in silver surrounded by an oval cable and reef knot in silver-gilt, surmounted by a crown and suspension ring.

Comments: *Granted for 15 years commissioned service (sub-lieutenant and above) in the Royal Naval Reserve, active service in wartime counting double. Bars are awarded for additional periods of 15 years. Recipients were entitled to the letters RD after their name, altered to VRD since 1966.*

VALUE:

Edward VII	£100–120
George V	£80–100
George VI (GRI)	£80–100
George VI (GVIR)	£80–100
Elizabeth II	£110–130

220. ROYAL NAVAL RESERVE LONG SERVICE AND GOOD CONDUCT MEDAL

Instituted: 1908.

Branch of Service: Royal Naval Reserve.

Ribbon: Plain green, white edges and a central white stripe being added in 1941. On the amalgamation of the RNR and RNVR in 1958 the ribbon was changed to five equal stripes of blue, white, green, white and blue.

Metal: Silver.

Size: 36mm.

Description: (Obverse) effigy of the monarch; (reverse) a battleship with the motto DIUTERNE FIDELIS (faithful for ever) at the foot.

Comments: *Awarded to petty officers and ratings of the RNR for 15 years service, war service counting double, with bars for additional 15 year periods.*

VALUE:

Edward VII (B)	£20–25
George V (B)	£15–20
George V (E)	£20–25
George VI (D)	£20–25
George VI (E)	£20–25
Elizabeth II (C)	£40–50
Elizabeth II (D)	£30–40

221. ROYAL NAVAL VOLUNTEER RESERVE DECORATION

Instituted: 1908.
Branch of Service: Royal Naval Volunteer Reserve.
Ribbon: 38mm originally plain dark green; dark blue with a central green stripe flanked by narrow red stripes (since 1919).
Metal: Silver and silver-gilt.
Size: Height 54mm; max. width 33mm.
Description: Similar to RNR decoration.
Comments: *Awarded to commissioned officers of the RNVR. The qualifying period was 20 years, service in the ranks counting half and war service counting double. In 1966 the decoration was replaced by the RD following the merger of the RNR and RNVR.*

VALUE:

Edward VII	£100–120
George V	£70–90
George VI GRI	£80–100
George VI GVIR	£90–100
Elizabeth II	£110–130

222. ROYAL NAVAL VOLUNTEER RESERVE LONG SERVICE AND GOOD CONDUCT MEDAL

Instituted: 1908.
Branch of Service: Royal Naval Volunteer Reserve.
Ribbon: Originally plain green, but subsequently a broad central green bar edged in red with blue stripes at the ends was adopted.
Metal: Silver.
Size: 36mm.
Description: Identical to the RNR medal, but distinguished by the ribbon and the naming which includes the letters RNVR.
Comments: *Awarded to petty officers and ratings for 12 years service with the necessary training, character assessed as 'very good' or better throughout the period. War service counted double.*

VALUE:

Edward VII (B)	Rare
George V (B)	£30–40
George V (E)	£40–50
George VI (D)	£30–40
George VI (E)	£30–40
Elizabeth II (D)	£50–70

223. ROYAL FLEET RESERVE LONG SERVICE AND GOOD CONDUCT MEDAL

Instituted: 1919.
Branch of Service: Royal Fleet Reserve.
Ribbon: Blue bordered with thin red stripes and white edges.
Metal: Silver.
Size: 36mm.
Description: Similar to the RNR LSGC but with ring suspension instead of a bar suspender.
Comments: *Awarded for 15 years service in the Fleet Reserve.*

VALUE:

George V (B)	£15–20
George V (E)	£15–20
George VI (D)	£20–25
George VI (E)	£20–25
Elizabeth II (C)	£40–50
Elizabeth II (D)	£30–40

224. ROYAL NAVAL AUXILIARY SICK BERTH RESERVE LONG SERVICE AND GOOD CONDUCT MEDAL

Instituted: 1919.
Branch of Service: Royal Naval Auxiliary Sick Berth Reserve.
Ribbon: Green with a white central stripe and white edges.
Metal: Silver.
Size: 36mm.
Description: Very similar to the RNR equivalent, but the letters RNASBR appear after the recipient's name.
Comments: *Arguably the longest title of any British medal, it continued until the RNASBR was disbanded in 1949. The Auxiliary Sick Berth Reserve was created in 1903, members being recruited from the St John organisation. About 780 medals were granted prior to the Second World War and a further 715 between 1939 and 1949.*

VALUE:

George V (B)	£70–90
George V (E)	£80–100
George VI (D)	£70–90

225. ROYAL NAVAL WIRELESS AUXILIARY RESERVE LONG SERVICE AND GOOD CONDUCT MEDAL

Instituted: 1939.
Branch of Service: Royal Naval Wireless Auxiliary Reserve.
Ribbon: Broad green stripe with narrow red stripes on either side and blue edges.
Metal: Silver.
Size: 36mm.
Description: Similar to the RNR equivalent, but the letters RNWAR after the recipient's name. The last of the service medals with a battleship reverse.
Comments: *Issued till 1957 when the RNWAR was disbanded. It was awarded for 12 years service, only about 200 having been issued.*

VALUE:

George VI (D)	£140–160
Elizabeth II (C)	£140–160

226. ROYAL NAVAL AUXILIARY LONG SERVICE MEDAL

Instituted: July 1965.
Branch of Service: Royal Naval Auxiliary Service (RNXS), formerly the Royal Naval Minewatching Service.
Ribbon: Dark blue with a narrow green central stripe and broad white bars at the edges bisected by thin dark green stripes.
Metal: Cupro-nickel.
Size: 36mm.
Description: (Obverse) the Queen's effigy; (reverse) a fouled anchor in an oak wreath surmounted by a naval crown.
Comments: *Awarded for 12 years service.*

VALUE:	Elizabeth II (D)	£80–100

227. ROCKET APPARATUS VOLUNTEER LONG SERVICE MEDAL

Instituted: 1911 by the Board of Trade.
Branch of Service: Rocket Life Saving Apparatus Volunteers,
Ribbon: Watered blue silk with broad scarlet edges.
Metal: Silver.
Size: 36mm.
Description: (Obverse) the effigy of the reigning monarch with the date 1911 below the truncation. (Reverse) exists in four types. The first refers to the Board of Trade but when that department handed over responsibility to the Ministry of Transport in 1942 the wording was amended to read ROCKET APPARATUS VOLUNTEER MEDAL round the circumference. In 1953 the inscription was changed to COAST LIFE SAVING CORPS and then in 1968 to COASTGUARD AUXILIARY SERVICE.
Comments: *Awarded for 20 years service with the Rocket Life Saving Apparatus Volunteers. The RLSAV became the Coast Life Saving Corps in 1953 and the Coastguard Auxiliary Service in 1968, these titles being reflected in the wording on the reverse.*

VALUE:

George V (E)	£30–40
George VI (D) BoT	£40–50
George VI (D) Rocket Apparatus	£40–50
Elizabeth II (E) Coast Life Saving	£60–80
Elizabeth II (E) Coastguard Auxiliary	£60–70

228. ROYAL NAVAL DOCKYARD POLICE MEDAL

Instituted: 1921.
Branch of Service: Hong Kong Dockyard Police.
Ribbon: Bright yellow with two central stripes of dark blue.
Metal: Silver.
Size: 36mm.
Description: (Obverse) the reigning sovereign; (reverse) a laurel wreath enclosing the words ROYAL NAVAL DOCKYARD POLICE HONG KONG. Fitted with ring suspension.
Comments: *Awarded on completion of 15 years exemplary service. Although the Dockyard closed in 1961 men who transferred to other police divisions continued to be awarded the medal up to 1973. About 280 medals in all were issued.*

VALUE:

George V (E)	£200–250
George VI (D)	£160–180
George VI (E)	£200–250
Elizabeth II (C)	£200–250

229. ARMY LONG SERVICE AND GOOD CONDUCT MEDAL

Instituted: 1830.

Branch of Service: Army.

Ribbon: Plain crimson was used till 1917 when white stripes were added to the edges.

Metal: Silver.

Size: 36mm.

Description: Over the long period in which this medal has been in use it has undergone a number of changes. Until 1901 the obverse bore a trophy of arms with the royal arms in an oval shield in the centre while the reverse bore the inscription FOR LONG SERVICE AND GOOD CONDUCT. The first issue had the royal arms with the badge of Hanover on the obverse and small suspension ring with a plain crimson ribbon. A large ring was substituted in 1831. On the accession of Queen Victoria in 1837 the Hanoverian emblem was dropped from the arms. In 1855 a swivelling scroll suspension was substituted and in 1874 small lettering replaced the original large lettering on the reverse. From 1901, however, the effigy of the reigning sovereign was placed on the obverse and the trophy of arms and heraldic shield moved to the reverse. In 1920 the swivelling scroll suspension gave way to a fixed suspender. In 1930 the title of the medal was changed to the Long Service and Good Conduct (Military) Medal; at the same time the design was modified. A fixed suspension bar was added, bearing the words REGULAR ARMY or the name of a dominion (India, Canada, Australia, New Zealand or South Africa). This replaced the Permanent Forces of the Empire LSGC Medal (see below).

Comments: *Originally awarded to soldiers of exemplary conduct for 21 years service in the infantry or 24 years in the cavalry, but in 1870 the qualifying period was reduced to 18 years. During the Second World War commissioned officers were permitted to acquire this medal so long as they had completed at least 12 of their 18 years service in the ranks. Canada discontinued the LSGC medal in 1950 when the Canadian Forces Decoration was instituted, while South Africa replaced it with the John Chard Medal later the same year. From 1930 onwards the lettering of the reverse inscription was in tall, thin letters. In 1940 bars for further periods of service were authorised. The LSGC is invariably named to the recipient. The William IV and early Victorian issues (to 1854) were impressed in the style of the Waterloo Medal and also bore the date of discharge and award.*

229. ARMY LONG SERVICE & GOOD CONDUCT MEDAL *continued*

The 1855 issue was not dated, while lettering was impressed in the style of the Military General Service Medal. Later Victorian issues, however, were engraved in various styles, while medals from 1901 onwards are impressed in small capitals of various types. Medals to Europeans in the Indian Army are engraved in cursive script.

VALUE:

William IV small ring 1830–31	£420–450
William IV large ring 1831–37	£380–420
Victoria without Hanoverian arms 1837–55	£100–120
Victoria swivelling scroll suspension 1855–74	£80–100
Victoria small reverse lettering 1874–1901	£40–50
Edward VII (A) 1902–10	£30–40
George V (A) 1911–20	£20–30
George V (A) fixed suspender 1920–30	£20–30
George V (C) 1930–36	£25–35
Commonwealth bar	From £75
George VI (D) 1937–48	£20–30
Commonwealth bar	From £75
George VI (E) 1949–52	£25–35
Elizabeth II (C) 1953–54	£40–50
Elizabeth II (D) 1954–	£20–30
Commonwealth bar	From £100

230. ULSTER DEFENCE REGIMENT MEDAL FOR LONG SERVICE AND GOOD CONDUCT

Instituted: 1982.
Branch of Service: Ulster Defence Regiment.
Ribbon: Similar to the Military LSGC medal but with a central green stripe in addition.
Metal: Silver.
Size: 36mm.
Description: (Obverse) the imperial crowned bust of Queen Elizabeth II; (reverse) similar to the Military LSGC medal. Fitted with a fixed suspension bar inscribed UDR.
Comments: *Granted to personnel for 15 years exemplary service after 1 April 1970, with bars for additional 15-year periods. It is also awarded to officers provided that at least 12 of their 15 years service was in the ranks.*

VALUE:
    Elizabeth II (B)   £80–100

231. VOLUNTEER DECORATION

Instituted: 25 July 1892.
Branch of Service: Volunteer Force.
Ribbon: Plain green.
Metal: Silver and silver-gilt.
Size: Height 42mm; max. width 35mm.
Description: An oval skeletal badge in silver and silver-gilt, with the royal cypher and crown in the centre, within a wreath of oak leaves. It is suspended by a plain ring with a laurel bar brooch fitted to the top of the ribbon. Although issued unnamed, many examples were subsequently engraved or impressed privately. Two versions of the Victorian decoration were produced, differing in the monogram—VR for United Kingdom recipients and VRI for recipients in the dominions and colonies.
Comments: *The basic qualification was 20 years commissioned service in the Volunteer Force, a precursor of the Territorial Army, non-commissioned service counting half. By Royal Warrant of 24 May 1894 the decoration was extended to comparable forces overseas, the qualifying period for service in India being reduced to 18 years. The colonial VD was superseded in 1899 by the Colonial Auxiliary Forces Officers Decoration and the Indian Volunteer Forces Officers Decoration. In the United Kingdom it was superseded by the Territorial Decoration, on the formation of the TA in 1908.*

VALUE:

Victoria VR	£50–60
Victoria VRI	£150–200
Edward VII	£60–80

232. VOLUNTEER FORCE LONG SERVICE AND GOOD CONDUCT MEDAL

Instituted: 1894.
Branch of Service: Volunteer Force.
Ribbon: Plain green, but members of the Honourable Artillery Company were granted a distinctive ribbon in 1906, half scarlet, half dark blue with yellow edges—King Edward's racing colours.
Metal: Silver.
Size: 36mm.
Description: (Obverse) effigy of the reigning monarch; (reverse) a laurel wreath on which is superimposed ribbons inscribed FOR LONG SERVICE IN THE VOLUNTEER FORCE.
Comments: *Awarded for 20 years service in the ranks, officers who failed to qualify for the VD being eligible on account of their previous non-commissioned service. It was extended to colonial forces in June 1896, the titles of the sovereign being appropriately expanded for this version, and superseded in Britain by the Territorial Force Efficiency Medal in 1908, although it continued to be awarded in India until 1930.*

VALUE:

Victoria Regina (C) (UK)	£30–40
Victoria Regina et Imperatrix (C) (overseas)	£50–80
Edwardus Rex (A)	£30–40
Edwardus Rex et Imperator (A) (colonial)	£35–45
Edwardus Kaisar-i-Hind (A) (India)	£60–80
George V (A) (India)	£40–50

233. TERRITORIAL DECORATION

Instituted: 29 September 1908.
Branch of Service: Territorial Army.
Ribbon: 38mm plain dark green with a central yellow stripe.
Metal: Silver and silver-gilt.
Size: Height 46mm; max. width 35mm.
Description: A skeletal badge with the crowned monogram of the sovereign surrounded by an oval oak wreath, fitted with a ring for suspension.
Comments: *Awarded for 20 years commissioned service, service in the ranks counting half and war service double. It was superseded by the Efficiency Decoration in 1930.*

VALUE:
Edward VII	£60–70
George V	£50–60

234. TERRITORIAL FORCE EFFICIENCY MEDAL

Instituted: 1908.
Branch of Service: Territorial Force.
Ribbon: 32mm plain dark green with a central yellow stripe.
Metal: Silver.
Size: Height 38mm; max. width 31mm.
Description: An oval medal fitted with claw and ring suspension. (Obverse) the sovereign's effigy; (reverse) inscribed with the name of the medal in four lines.
Comments: *Granted for a minimum of 12 years service in the Territorial Force. It was superseded in 1921 by the Territorial Efficiency Medal when the service was renamed.*

VALUE:
Edward VII (A)	£50–60
George V (A)	£25–35

235. TERRITORIAL EFFICIENCY MEDAL

Instituted: 1921.
Branch of Service: Territorial Army.
Ribbon: 32mm plain dark green with yellow edges.
Metal: Silver.
Size: Height 38mm; max. width 31mm.
Description: As above, but with the name amended and inscribed in three lines.
Comments: *Introduced following the elevation of the Territorial Force to become the Territorial Army. It was superseded by the Efficiency Medal in 1930.*

VALUE:
George V (A)	£20–30

236. EFFICIENCY DECORATION

Instituted: 17 October 1930.

Branch of Service: Territorial Army (UK), the Indian Volunteer Forces and the Colonial Auxiliary Forces.

Ribbon: 38mm plain dark green with a central yellow stripe.

Metal: Silver and silver-gilt.

Size: Height 54mm; max. width 37mm.

Description: An oval skeletal badge in silver and silver-gilt with the crowned monogram in an oak wreath, the ring for suspension being fitted to the top of the crown. It differs also from the previous decorations in having a bar denoting the area of service: Territorial (UK), India, Canada, Fiji or other overseas country being inscribed as appropriate, but the previous ribbon was retained.

Comments: *Recipients in Britain were allowed to continue using the letters TD after their names, but in the Commonwealth the letters ED were used instead. The 20-year qualification was reduced to 12 years in 1949, bars for each additional 6 years being added. In 1969 the British bar was changed to T & AVR, on the establishment of the Territorial and Army Volunteer Reserve, the ribbon being then altered to half green, half blue, with a central yellow stripe. In 1982 the title of Territorial Army was resumed, so the inscription on the bar reverted to TERRITORIAL but the blue, yellow and green ribbon was retained.*

VALUE:

	Territorial	T&AVR	Commonwealth
George V	£50–70	—	£70–80
George VI (GRI)	£50–60	—	£60–70
George VI (GVIR)	£60–70	—	—
Elizabeth II	£60–70	£100–120	—

237. EFFICIENCY MEDAL

Instituted: 17 October 1930.

Branch of Service: Territorial Army (UK), Indian Volunteer Forces and Colonial Auxiliary Forces.

Ribbon: 32mm green with yellow edges. Members of the HAC wear the medal with the scarlet and blue ribbon edged in yellow.

Metal: Silver.

Size: Height 39mm; max. width 32mm.

Description: An oval silver medal. (Obverse) the monarch's effigy; (reverse) inscribed FOR EFFICIENT

237. EFFICIENCY MEDAL *continued*

SERVICE. In place of the simple ring suspension, however, there was now a fixed suspender bar decorated with a pair of palm leaves surmounted by a scroll inscribed TERRITORIAL or MILITIA (for UK volunteer forces), while overseas forces had the name of the country.

Comments: *This medal consolidated the awards to other ranks throughout the volunteer forces of Britain and the Commonwealth. The basic qualification was 12 years service, but war service and peacetime service in West Africa counted double. The Militia bar was granted to certain categories of the Supplementary Reserve until the formation of the Army Emergency Reserve in 1951. In 1969 the bar inscribed T & AVR was introduced, along with a ribbon half blue, half green, with yellow edges. The bar TERRITORIAL was resumed in 1982 but the ribbon remained the same. For the distinctive medal awarded in the Union of South Africa see number 252.*

VALUE:

	Territorial	Militia	T&AVR	Commonwealth
George V (C)	£25–35	£40–50	—	£30–40
George VI (A)	£15–20	£40–50	—	£70–90
George VI (C)	£15–20	£40–50	—	—
Elizabeth II (A)	£30–40	—	—	—
Elizabeth II (B)	£30–40	—	£60–80	—

238. ARMY EMERGENCY RESERVE DECORATION

Instituted: 17 November 1952.

Branch of Service Army Emergency Reserve.

Ribbon: 38mm dark blue with a central yellow stripe.

Metal: Silver and silver-gilt.

Size: Height 55mm; max. width 37mm.

Description: An oval skeletal badge, with the monarch's cypher surmounted by a crown in an oak wreath. Suspension is by a ring through the top of the crown and it is worn with a brooch bar inscribed ARMY EMERGENCY RESERVE.

Comments: *Awarded for 12 years commissioned service. Officers commissioned in the Army Supplementary Reserve or Army Emergency Reserve of Offices between 8 August 1942 and 15 May 1948 who transferred to the Regular Army Reserve of Offices after 10 years service were also eligible. War service counts double and previous service in the ranks counts half. The ERD was abolished in 1967 on the formation of the Territorial and Army Volunteer Reserve.*

VALUE:

Elizabeth II	£110–130

239. ARMY EMERGENCY RESERVE EFFICIENCY MEDAL

Instituted: 1 September 1953.
Branch of Service: Army Emergency Reserve.
Ribbon: 32mm dark blue with three central yellow stripes.
Metal: Silver.
Size: Height 39mm; max. width 31mm.
Description: This oval medal is similar to the Efficiency Medal previously noted, but has a scroll bar inscribed ARMY EMERGENCY RESERVE.
Comments: *Awarded for 12 years service in the ranks or for service in the Supplementary Reserve between 1924 and 1948 prior to transferring to the Army Emergency Reserve. War service counted double. It was abolished in 1967, following the formation of the Territorial and Army Volunteer Reserve.*

VALUE:
    Elizabeth II   £140–160

240. IMPERIAL YEOMANRY LONG SERVICE AND GOOD CONDUCT MEDAL

Instituted: December 1904, by Army Order.
Branch of Service: Imperial Yeomanry.
Ribbon: 32mm plain yellow.
Metal: Silver.
Size: Height 38mm; max. width 31mm.
Description: Upright oval. (Obverse) the sovereign's effigy; (reverse) inscribed IMPERIAL YEOMANRY round the top and the usual long service and good conduct inscription in four lines across the middle.
Comments: *Awarded to NCOs and troopers of the Imperial Yeomanry for 10 years exemplary service. It became obsolete in 1908 when the Territorial Force was created.*

VALUE:
    Edward VII (A) (1674)   £170–190

241. MILITIA LONG SERVICE AND GOOD CONDUCT MEDAL

Instituted: December 1904, by Army Order.
Branch of Service: Militia.
Ribbon: 32mm plain light blue.
Metal: Silver.
Size: Height 38mm; max. width 31mm.
Description: An upright oval medal. (Obverse) the effigy of the monarch; (reverse) similar to the preceding but inscribed MILITIA at the top of the reverse.
Comments: *Qualifying service was 18 years and 15 annual camps. It was superseded by the Efficiency Medal with the Militia bar in 1930.*

VALUE:
    Edward VII (A) (1446)   £100–120
    George V (C) (141)   £140–160

242. SPECIAL RESERVE LONG SERVICE AND GOOD CONDUCT MEDAL

Instituted: June 1908, by Army Order.
Branch of Service: Special Reserve.
Ribbon: Dark blue with a central light blue stripe.
Metal: Silver.
Size: Height 38mm; max. width 31mm.
Description: As the foregoing but inscribed SPECIAL RESERVE round the top of the reverse.
Comments: *Awarded to NCOs and men of the Special Reserve who completed 15 years service and attended 15 camps. A total of 1078 medals were awarded between 1908 and 1936, with solitary awards in 1947 and 1953.*

VALUE:

Edward VII (A)	£110–130
George V (C)	£120–140

243. INDIAN ARMY LONG SERVICE AND GOOD CONDUCT MEDAL (EUROPEAN)

Instituted: 20 May 1848, by General Order of the Indian government.
Branch of Service: Indian Army.
Ribbon: Plain crimson.
Metal: Silver.
Size: 36mm.
Description: (Obverse) a trophy of arms, not unlike its British counterpart, but a shield bearing the arms of the Honourable East India Company was placed in the centre. (Reverse) engraved with the recipient's name and service details. In 1859 some 100 medals were sent to India by mistake, with the Wyon profile of Queen Victoria on the obverse and a reverse inscribed FOR LONG SERVICE AND GOOD CONDUCT within an oak wreath with a crown at the top and a fouled anchor at the foot.
Comments: *Awarded to European NCOs and other ranks of the Indian Army on discharge after 21 years meritorious service. It was discontinued in 1873 after which the standard Army LSGC medal was granted.*

VALUE:

HEIC arms	£300–400
Victoria (A) (100)	£250–300

244. INDIAN ARMY LONG SERVICE AND GOOD CONDUCT MEDAL (INDIAN)

Instituted: 1888.
Branch of Service: Indian Army.
Ribbon: Originally plain crimson but white edges were added in 1917.
Metal: Silver.
Size: 36mm.
Description: (Obverse) the sovereign's effigy; (reverse) the word INDIA set within a palm wreath surrounded by a border of lotus flowers and leaves. The inscription FOR LONG SERVICE AND GOOD CONDUCT appears between the wreath and the lotus flowers.
Comments: *Awarded to native Indian NCOs and other ranks for 20 years meritorious service. The medal became obsolete in 1947 when India achieved independence.*

VALUE:

Victoria (B) Kaisar-i-Hind	£70–90
Edward VII (A) Kaisar-i-Hind	£40–50
George V (D) Kaisar-i-Hind	£20–30
George V (C) Rex Et Indiae Imp	£30–40
George VI (B)	£20–30

245. INDIAN VOLUNTEER FORCES OFFICERS'DECORATION

Instituted: May 1899, but not issued until 1903.
Branch of Service: Indian Volunteer Forces.
Ribbon: Plain green.
Metal: Silver and silver-gilt.
Size: Height 65mm; max. width 35mm.
Description: *An oval skeletal badge with the royal monogram within an oval band inscribed INDIAN VOLUNTEER FORCE surmounted by a crown fitted with a suspension bar*
Comments: *Awarded for 18 years commissioned service, with any service in the ranks counting half. It was superseded by the Efficiency Decoration with India bar in 1930.*

VALUE:

Edward VII	£140–160
George V	£130–150

246. COLONIAL AUXILIARY FORCES OFFICERS' DECORATION

Instituted: 18 May 1899.
Branch of Service: Colonial Auxiliary Forces.
Ribbon: Plain green.
Metal: Silver and silver-gilt.
Size: Height 66mm; max. width 35mm.
Description: Similar to the previous decoration, with an oval band inscribed COLONIAL AUXILIARY FORCES.
Comments: *Awarded to officers of auxiliary forces everywhere except in India, service in West Africa counting double. Although issued unnamed, it was usually impressed or engraved privately. Examples to officers in the smaller colonies command a considerable premium. It became obsolete in 1930.*

VALUE:

Victoria	£200–220
Edward VII	£180–200
George V	£120–140

247. COLONIAL AUXILIARY FORCES LONG SERVICE MEDAL

Instituted: 18 May 1899.
Branch of Service: Colonial Auxiliary Forces.
Ribbon: Plain green.
Metal: Silver.
Size: 36mm.
Description: (Obverse) the effigy of the reigning monarch; (reverse) an elaborate rococo frame surmounted by a crown and enclosing the five-line text FOR LONG SERVICE IN THE COLONIAL AUXILIARY FORCES.
Comments: *Awarded for 20 years service in the ranks, West African service counting double. It was superseded in 1930 by the Efficiency Medal with the appropriate colonial or dominion bar.*

VALUE:

Victoria (D)	£100–120
Edward VII (A)	£80–90
George V (A)	£70–80

248. COLONIAL LONG SERVICE AND GOOD CONDUCT MEDALS

Instituted: May 1895.
Branch of Service: Indian and Colonial forces.
Ribbon: Crimson with a central stripe denoting the country of service (see below).
Metal: Silver.
Size: 36mm.
Description: Similar to its British counterpart except that the name of the country appeared on the reverse.
Comments: *Awarded to warrant officers, NCOs and other ranks for distinguished conduct in the field, meritorious service and long service and good conduct. Medals of the individual Australian colonies were superseded in 1902 by those inscribed COMMONWEALTH OF AUSTRALIA. The Colonial LSGC medal was replaced in 1909 by the Permanent Forces of the Empire Beyond the Seas LSGC award.*

VALUE: Rare

249. PERMANENT FORCES OF THE EMPIRE BEYOND THE SEAS LONG SERVICE AND GOOD CONDUCT MEDAL

Instituted: 1909.
Branch of Service: Colonial and Dominion forces.
Ribbon: Maroon bearing a broad white central stripe with a narrow black stripe at its centre.
Metal: Silver.
Size: 36mm.
Description: (Obverse) the effigy of the reigning sovereign; (reverse) the legend PERMANENT FORCES OF THE EMPIRE BEYOND THE SEAS round the circumference, with FOR LONG SERVICE AND GOOD CONDUCT in four lines across the centre.
Comments: *This award replaced the various colonial LSGC medals, being itself superseded in 1930 by the LSGC (Military) Medal with appropriate dominion or colonial bar. It was awarded for 18 years exemplary service.*

VALUE:

Edward VII (A)	Rare
George V (C)	£60–80

250. ROYAL WEST AFRICA FRONTIER FORCE LONG SERVICE AND GOOD CONDUCT MEDAL

Instituted: September 1903.
Branch of Service: Royal West Africa Frontier Force.
Ribbon: Crimson with a relatively broad green central stripe.
Metal: Silver.
Size: 36mm.
Description: (Obverse) the effigy of the reigning monarch. Two reverse types were used, the word ROYAL being added to the regimental title in June 1928.
Comments: *Awarded to native NCOs and other ranks for 18 years exemplary service.*

VALUE: **Rare**

251. KING'S AFRICAN RIFLES LONG SERVICE & GOOD CONDUCT MEDAL

Instituted: March 1907.
Branch of Service: King's African Rifles.
Ribbon: Crimson with a broad green central stripe.
Metal: Silver.
Size: 36mm.
Description: Very similar to the foregoing, apart from the regimental name round the top of the reverse.
Comments: *Awarded to native NCO's and other ranks for 18 years exemplary service.*

VALUE: **Rare**

252. TRANS-JORDAN FRONTIER FORCE LONG SERVICE & GOOD CONDUCT MEDAL

Instituted: 20 May 1938.
Branch of Service: Trans-Jordan Frontier Force.
Ribbon: Crimson with a green central stripe.
Metal: Silver.
Size: 36mm.
Description: Similar to the previous medals, with the name of the Force round the circumference.
Comments: *This rare silver medal was awarded for 16 years service in the ranks of the Trans-Jordan Frontier Force. Service in the Palestine Gendarmerie or Arab Legion counted, so long as the recipient transferred to the Frontier Force without a break in service. Only 112 medals were awarded before it was abolished in 1948.*

VALUE: **Rare**

253. SOUTH AFRICA PERMANENT FORCE LONG SERVICE AND GOOD CONDUCT MEDAL

Instituted: 29 December 1939.
Branch of Service: South African forces.
Ribbon:
Metal: Silver.
Size: 36mm.
Description: (Obverse) Crowned effigy of King George VI; (reverse) FOR LONG SERVICE AND GOOD CONDUCT in four lines across the upper half and VIR LANGDURIGE DIENS EN GOEIE GEDRAG in four lines across the lower half. It also differs from its British counterpart in having a bilingual suspension bar.
Comments: *Awarded to NCOs and other ranks with a minimum of 18 years service.*

VALUE:

George VI (B)	£120–140
George VI (C)	£150–170

254. SOUTH AFRICAN EFFICIENCY MEDAL

Instituted: December 1939.
Branch of Service: Coast Garrison and Active Citizen Forces of South Africa.
Ribbon:
Metal: Silver.
Size: Height 38mm; max. width 30mm.
Description: An oval silver medal rather similar to the Efficiency Medal (number 235) but having a scroll bar inscribed UNION OF SOUTH AFRICA with its Afrikaans equivalent below. The reverse likewise bears a bilingual inscription.
Comments: *Awarded for 12 years non-commissioned service in the Coast Garrison and Active Citizen Forces. It was replaced in 1952 by the John Chard Medal.*

VALUE: **Rare**

255. CANADIAN FORCES DECORATION

Instituted: 15 December 1949.

Branch of Service: Canadian Forces.

Ribbon: 38mm red divided into four equal parts by three thin white stripes.

Metal: Silver-gilt (George VI) or gilded tombac brass (Elizabeth II).

Size: Height 35mm; max. width 37mm.

Description: A decagonal (ten-sided) medal. The George VI issue has a suspension bar inscribed CANADA and the recipient's details engraved on the reverse, whereas the Elizabethan issue has no bar, the recipient's details being impressed on the rim. The reverse has a naval crown at the top, three maple leaves across the middle and an eagle in flight across the foot. In the George VI version the royal cypher is superimposed on the maple leaves.

Comments: *Awarded to both officers and men of the Canadian regular and reserve forces for 12 years exemplary service, with a bar for each additional 10 years.*

VALUE:

George VI (E)	£50–60
Elizabeth II (D)	£40–50

256. VICTORIA VOLUNTEER LONG AND EFFICIENT SERVICE MEDAL

Instituted: 26 January 1881 but not given royal sanction until 21 April 1882.

Branch of Service: Volunteer Forces, Victoria.

Ribbon: White, with broad crimson bars at the sides.

Metal: Silver.

Size: 39mm.

Description: (Obverse) the crowned badge of Victoria with LOCAL FORCES VICTORIA round the circumference; (reverse) inscribed FOR LONG AND EFFICIENT SERVICE. Two types of obverse exist, differing in the motto surrounding the colonial emblem. The first version has AUT PACE AUT BELLO (both in peace and war) while the second version is inscribed PRO DEO ET PATRIA (for God and country).

Comments: *Awarded to officers and men of the Volunteers in the colony of Victoria for 15 years service. Awards to officers ended in 1894 with the introduction of the Volunteer Officers Decoration. This medal was replaced by the Commonwealth of Australia LSGC medal in 1902.*

VALUE: Rare

257. NEW ZEALAND LONG AND EFFICIENT SERVICE MEDAL

Instituted: 1 January 1887.
Branch of Service: Volunteer and Permanent Militia Forces of New Zealand.
Ribbon: Originally plain crimson, but two white central stripes were added in 1917.
Metal: Silver.
Size: 36mm.
Description: (Obverse) an imperial crown on a cushion with crossed sword and sceptre and NZ below, within a wreath of oak-leaves (left) and wattle (right) and having four five-pointed stars, representing the constellation Southern Cross, spaced in the field; (reverse) inscribed FOR LONG AND EFFICIENT SERVICE. Plain ring suspension.
Comments: *Awarded for 16 years continuous or 20 years non-continuous service in the Volunteer and Permanent Militia Forces of New Zealand. It became obsolete in 1931 following the introduction of the LSGC (Military) medal with bar for New Zealand.*

VALUE:
1887-1931	£75–100

258. NEW ZEALAND VOLUNTEER SERVICE MEDAL

Instituted: 1902.
Branch of Service: Volunteer Forces, New Zealand.
Ribbon: Plain drab khaki.
Metal: Silver.
Size: 36mm
Description: (Obverse) a right-facing profile of King Edward VII with NEW ZEALAND VOLUNTEER round the top and 12 YEARS SERVICE MEDAL round the foot; (reverse) a kiwii surrounded by a wreath. Plain ring suspension.
Comments: *This rare silver medal (obsolete by 1912) was awarded for 12 years service.*

VALUE: Rare

259. NEW ZEALAND TERRITORIAL SERVICE MEDAL

Instituted: 1912.
Branch of Service: Territorial Force, New Zealand.
Ribbon: Originally as above, but replaced in 1917 by a ribbon of dark khaki edged with crimson.
Metal: Silver.
Size: 36mm.
Description: (Obverse) left-facing bust of King George V in field marshal's uniform; (reverse) similar to the above.
Comments: *It replaced the foregoing but became obsolete itself in 1931 when the Efficiency Medal with New Zealand bar was adopted.*

VALUE:
George V	£75–100

260. ULSTER DEFENCE REGIMENT MEDAL FOR LONG SERVICE AND GOOD CONDUCT

Instituted: 1982.
Branch of Service: Ulster Defence Regiment.
Ribbon: Crimson with white edges and a narrow black central stripe.
Metal: Silver.
Size: 36mm.
Description: (Obverse) the imperial crowned profile of the Queen; (reverse) crowned harp with ULSTER DEFENCE REGIMENT round the circumference. Fitted with a scroll suspender surmounted by a fixed bar inscribed U.D.R.
Comments: *Awarded to NCOs and men of the Permanent Cadre of the Ulster Defence Regiment for 15 years irreproachable service since 1 April 1970, with bars for each additional 15-year period.*

VALUE:
    Elizabeth II (B)   —

261. ULSTER DEFENCE REGIMENT MEDAL

Instituted: 1982.
Branch of Service: Ulster Defence Regiment.
Ribbon: Dark green with a khaki central stripe edged in red.
Metal: Silver.
Size: 36mm.
Description: The medal is very similar to the foregoing but has a suspender of laurel leaves surmounted by a scroll bar bearing the regiment's initials.
Comments: *Awarded to part-time officers and men of the Ulster Defence Regiment with 12 years continuous service since 1 April 1970. A bar for each additional five-year period is awarded. Officers are permitted to add the letters UD after their names.*

VALUE:
    Elizabeth II (B)   £60–80

262. CADET FORCES MEDAL

Instituted: February 1950.
Branch of Service: Cadet Forces.
Ribbon: A broad green central band bordered by thin red stripes flanked by a dark blue stripe (left) and light blue stripe (right, with yellow edges.
Metal: Cupro-nickel.
Size: 36mm.
Description: (Obverse) the effigy of the reigning monarch; (reverse) a hand holding aloft the torch of learning. Medals are named to recipients on the rim, in impressed capitals (Army and Navy) or engraved lettering (RAF).
Comments: *Awarded to commissioned officers and adult NCOs for 12 years service in the Cadet Forces. A bar is awarded for each additional 8 years.*

VALUE:
    George VI (C)   £50–60
    Elizabeth II   £50–70

263. ROYAL OBSERVER CORPS MEDAL

Instituted: 31 January 1950.
Branch of Service: Royal Observer Corps.
Ribbon: Pale blue with a broad central silver-grey stripe edged in dark blue.
Metal: Cupro-nickel.
Size: 36mm.
Description: (Obverse) effigy of the reigning monarch; (reverse) an artist's impression of a coast-watcher of Elizabethan times, holding a torch aloft alongside a signal fire, with other signal fires on hilltops in the background. The medal hangs from a suspender of two wings.
Comments: *Awarded to officers and observers who have completed 12 years satisfactory service. A bar is awarded for each additional 12-year period.*

VALUE:

George VI (E)	£60–70
Elizabeth II (C)	£40–50
Elizabeth II (D)	£30–40

264. CIVIL DEFENCE LONG SERVICE MEDAL

Instituted: March 1961.
Branch of Service: Civil Defence and other auxiliary forces.
Ribbon: Blue bearing three narrow stripes of yellow, red and green.
Metal: Cupro-nickel.
Size: 36mm.
Description: (Obverse) the effigy of the reigning monarch. (Reverse) two types. Both featured three shields flanked by sprigs of acorns and oak leaves. The upper shield in both cases is inscribed CD but the initials on the lower shields differ, according to the organisations in Britain and Northern Ireland respectively - AFS and NHSR (British) or AERS and HSR (Northern Ireland).
Comments: *Issued unnamed to those who had completed 15 years service in a wide range of Civil Defence organisations. It was extended to Civil Defence personnel in Gibraltar, Hong Kong and Malta in 1965. The medal became obsolescent after the Civil Defence Corps and Auxiliary Fire Service were disbanded in 1968.*

VALUE:

British version	£15–20
Northern Ireland version	£70–90

265. WOMEN'S VOLUNTARY SERVICE LONG SERVICE MEDAL

Instituted: 1961.
Branch of Service: Women's Royal Voluntary Service.
Ribbon: Black with twin white stripes towards the end and broad red edges.
Metal: Cupro-nickel.
Size: 36mm.
Description: (Obverse) three flowers, inscribed SERVICE BEYOND SELF round the circumference. Although the WVS acquired the Royal title in 1966 only one reverse has so far been used, with the interlocking initials WVS in an ivy wreath.
Comments: *Issued unnamed and awarded for 15 years service. Bars for additional 15 year periods are awarded. To date some 20,000 medals and 3000 bars have been awarded to women, but ten male recipients have been granted the medal for service in the headquarters administration.*

VALUE: WVS medal   £15–20

266. VOLUNTARY MEDICAL SERVICE MEDAL

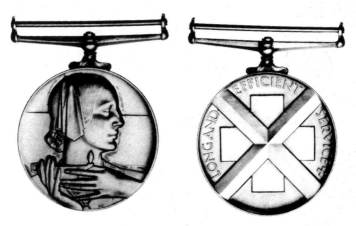

Instituted: 1932.
Branch of Service: British Red Cross Society and the St Andrews Ambulance Brigade (Scotland).
Ribbon: Red with yellow and white stripes.
Metal: Originally struck in silver but since the 1960s it has been produced in cupro-nickel.
Size: 36mm.
Description: (Obverse) the veiled bust of a female holding an oil lamp, symbolic of Florence Nightingale; (reverse) the crosses of Geneva and St Andrew, with the inscription FOR LONG AND EFFICIENT SERVICE.
Comments: *Awarded for 15 years service, with a bar for each additional period of five years. The service bars are embellished with a Geneva cross or saltire (St Andrew) cross, whichever is the more appropriate.*

VALUE: Silver   £14–18   **Cupro-nickel**   £8–12

267. SERVICE MEDAL OF THE ORDER OF ST JOHN OF JERUSALEM

Instituted: 1898.
Branch of Service: Order of St John of Jerusalem.
Ribbon: Three black and two white stripes of equal width.
Metal: Silver (1898-1947), silvered base metal (1947-60), silvered cupro-nickel (1960-66) and rhodium-plated cupro-nickel (since 1966).
Size: 38mm.
Description: (Obverse) an unusual veiled bust of Queen Victoria with her name and abbreviated Latin titles round the circumference. A new obverse was adopted in 1960 with a slightly reduced effigy of Queen Victoria and less ornate lettering. (Reverse) the royal arms within a garter surrounded by four circles containing the imperial crown, the Prince of Wales's feathers and the badges of the Order. Between the circles are sprigs of St John's Wort. Round the circumference is the Latin inscription MAGNUS PRIORATUS ORDINIS HOSPITALIS SANCTI JOHANNIS JERUSALEM IN ANGLIA in Old English lettering.
Comments: *Awarded for 15 years service to the Order in the United Kingdom (12 in the Dominions and 10 in the colonies). A silver bar was introduced in 1911 for additional periods of five years. From then till 1924 the bar was inscribed 5 YEARS SERVICE but then a design showing a Maltese cross flanked by spray's of St John's Wort was substituted. Bars for 20 years service were subsequently instituted in silver-gilt. Suspension by a ring was changed in 1913 to a straight bar suspender. The medal is worn on the left breast.*

VALUE:

Silver, ring suspension	£15–20
Silver, straight bar suspension	£12–16
Base metal, first obverse	£8–12
Base metal, second obverse	£8–12

268. ROYAL AIR FORCE LONG SERVICE AND GOOD CONDUCT MEDAL

Instituted: 1 July 1919.
Branch of Service: Royal Air Force.
Ribbon: Dark blue and maroon with white edges.
Metal: Silver.
Size: 36mm.
Description: (Obverse) the effigy of the reigning monarch; (reverse) the RAF eagle and crown insignia.
Comments: *Awarded to NCOs and other ranks of the RAF for 18 years exemplary service, reduced in 1977 to 15 years. Provision for bars for further periods of service was made from 1944 onwards. Before 1945 conduct below the required standard was permitted to count if the airman had displayed higher exemplary conduct against the enemy, gallantry or some special service in times of emergency. From 1944 prior service in the Navy and Army up to a maximum of four years could be counted. In 1947 officers became eligible for the medal provided they had had at least 12 years service in the ranks.*

VALUE:

George V (E)	£60–70
George VI (D)	£25–35
George VI (E)	£30–40
Elizabeth II (C)	£30–40
Elizabeth II (D)	£25–35

269. ROYAL AIR FORCE LEVIES LONG SERVICE AND GOOD CONDUCT MEDAL

Instituted: 1948.
Branch of Service: RAF Levies, Iraq.
Ribbon: As the preceding.
Metal: Silver.
Size: 36mm.
Description: Similar to the previous type but was fitted with a clasp inscribed ROYAL AIR FORCE LEVIES IRAQ.
Comments: *Awarded to the locally commissioned officers and men of the RAF Levies in Iraq, for 18 years service (the last 12 to be of an exemplary nature). The Iraq Levies were raised in 1919 and became the responsibility of the RAF in 1922, maintaining law and order by means of light aircraft and armoured cars. The force was disbanded in 1955 when the RAF withdrew from Iraq. Only about 300 medals were issued.*

VALUE:

George VI (D)	£1000–1200

270. AIR EFFICIENCY AWARD

Instituted: September 1942
Branch of Service: Royal Air Force.
Ribbon: Green with two light blue stripes towards the centre.
Metal: Silver.
Size: Height 38mm; max. width 32mm.
Description: An oval medal with a suspender in the form of an eagle with wings outspread. (Obverse) the effigy of the reigning monarch; (reverse) inscribed AIR EFFICIENCY AWARD in three lines.
Comments: *Granted for 10 years efficient service in the Auxiliary and Volunteer Air Forces of the United Kingdom and Commonwealth. A bar is awarded for a further ten-year period.*

VALUE:

George VI (D)	£60–70
George VI (E)	£70–80
Elizabeth II (C)	£80–90
Elizabeth II (D)	£70–80

271. POLICE LONG SERVICE AND GOOD CONDUCT MEDAL

Instituted: 14 June 1951.
Branch of Service: Police Forces.
Ribbon: Dark blue with twin white stripes towards each end.
Metal: Cupro-nickel
Size: 36mm.
Description: (Obverse) the effigy of the reigning monarch; (reverse) a standing female allegorical figure of Justice, with scales in one hand and a wreath in the other.
Comments: *awarded for 22 years full-time service in any UK constabulary. By a Royal Warrant of 1 May 1956 it was extended to police forces in Australia, Papua New Guinea and Nauru. The Australian award was replaced in 1976 by the National Medal.*

VALUE:

George VI (E)	£20–30
Elizabeth II (D)	£40–50
Elizabeth II (E)	£25–35

272. SPECIAL CONSTABULARY LONG SERVICE MEDAL

Instituted: 30 August 1919.
Branch of Service: Special Constabulary.
Ribbon: A broad red stripe in the centre flanked by black and white stripes.
Metal: Bronze.
Size: 36mm.
Description: (Obverse) the effigy of the reigning monarch; (reverse) a partial laurel wreath with a six-line text inscribed FOR FAITHFUL SERVICE IN THE SPECIAL CONSTABULARY. A second reverse was introduced in 1970 for 15 years service in the Ulster Special Constabulary, the text being modified to permit the inclusion of the word ULSTER. A third type was introduced in 1982 for 15 years service in the RUC Reserve and is thus inscribed.
Comments: *Awarded to all ranks in the Special Constabulary for 9 years unpaid service, with more than 50 duties per annum. War service with at least 50 duties counted triple. A clasp inscribed THE GREAT WAR 1914-18 was awarded to those who qualified for the medal during that conflict. Clasps inscribed LONG SERVICE, with the date, were awarded for additional periods.*

VALUE:

George V (C)	£4–6
George V (E)	£4–8
George VI (D)	£4–6
George VI (E)	£15–20
Elizabeth II (C)	£14–16
Elizabeth II (D)	£12–14
Elizabeth II (D) Ulster	£100–120
Elizabeth II (D) RUC Reserve	£120–140

273. ROYAL ULSTER CONSTABULARY SERVICE MEDAL

Instituted: 1982.
Branch of Service: RUC and its Reserve.
Ribbon: Green, with narrow central stripes of red, black and dark blue.
Metal: Cupro-nickel.
Size: 36mm.
Description: (Obverse) the effigy of Queen Elizabeth II; (reverse) the crowned harp insignia of the RUC with the words FOR SERVICE round the foot.
Comments: *Awarded for 18 months continuous service since 1 January 1971, but the award was made immediate on the recipient also being awarded a gallantry decoration or a Queen's commendation.*

VALUE:

Elizabeth II (D)	£80–100

274. COLONIAL POLICE LONG SERVICE MEDAL

Instituted: 1934.
Branch of Service: Colonial police forces.
Ribbon: Grey centre bordered with white and broad black bars towards the edges.
Metal: Silver.
Size: 36mm.
Description: (Obverse) the effigy of the reigning monarch; (reverse) a police truncheon superimposed on a laurel wreath.
Comments: *Awarded to junior officer for 18 years full-time and exemplary service. Bars have been awarded for subsequent periods.*

VALUE:

George V (C)	£80–100
George VI (B)	£50–60
George VI (C)	£50–60
Elizabeth II (A)	£60–70
Elizabeth II (B)	£60–70

275. COLONIAL SPECIAL CONSTABULARY LONG SERVICE MEDAL

Instituted: 1957.
Branch of Service: Colonial Special Constabulary.
Ribbon: Two thin white stripes on a broad grey centre, with broad black edges.
Metal: Silver.
Size: 36mm.
Description: (Obverse) the effigy of the reigning monarch; (reverse) the crowned royal cypher above the words FOR FAITHFUL SERVICE in a laurel wreath.
Comments: *Awarded for nine years unpaid or 15 years paid service in a colonial special constabulary. A bar is awarded for further ten-year periods.*

VALUE:

Elizabeth II (B)	£180–220

276. ROYAL CANADIAN MOUNTED POLICE LONG SERVICE MEDAL

Instituted: 14 January 1933, by Order in Council.
Branch of Service: Royal Canadian Mounted Police.
Ribbon: Dark blue with two gold stripes towards the edges.
Metal: Silver.
Size: 36mm.
Description: (Obverse) the effigy of the reigning monarch; (reverse)
the RCMP insignia with the legend FOR LONG SERVICE AND
GOOD CONDUCT.
Comments: *Awarded to all ranks of the RCMP who had served 20 years.
Bronze, silver or gold bars were awarded for 25, 30 or 35 years further
service.*

VALUE:

George V (C)	£500–600
George V (E)	£500–600
George VI (B)	£450–500
George VI (C)	£450–500
Elizabeth II (A)	£250–300

277. CEYLON POLICE LONG SERVICE AND GOOD CONDUCT MEDAL (I)

Instituted: 1925.
Branch of Service: Ceylon Police.
Ribbon: Very similar to that of the Special Constabulary Long Service
Medal.
Metal: Silver.
Size: 36mm.
Description: (Obverse) coinage profile of King George V by Sir
Bertram Mackennal; (reverse) an elephant surmounted by a crown.
Ring suspension.
Comments: *Awarded for 15 years active service. It was superseded in 1934
by the Colonial Police Long Service Medal.*

VALUE:

George V (E)	£300–350

278. CEYLON POLICE LONG SERVICE AND GOOD CONDUCT MEDAL (II)

Instituted: 1950.
Branch of Service: Ceylon Police.
Ribbon: Dark blue edged with khaki, white and pale blue.
Metal: Cupro-nickel.
Size: 36mm.
Description: (Obverse) the effigy of the reigning monarch; (reverse)
similar to the foregoing, but without the crown above the elephant,
to permit the longer inscription CEYLON POLICE SERVICE.
Straight bar suspender.
Comments: *Awarded for 18 years exemplary service. Bars for 25 and 30
years service were also awarded. It became obsolete when Ceylon (now Sri
Lanka) became a republic in 1972.*

VALUE:

George VI (C)	£280–320
Elizabeth II (A)	£250–300

279. CYPRUS MILITARY POLICE LONG SERVICE AND GOOD CONDUCT MEDAL

Instituted: October 1929.
Branch of Service: Cyprus Military Police.
Ribbon: Yellow, dark green and yellow in equal bands.
Metal: Silver.
Size: 36mm.
Description: (Obverse) King George V; (reverse) the title of the police round the circumference and the words LONG AND GOOD SERVICE in four lines across the middle.
Comments: *Awarded to those who had three good conduct badges, plus six years exemplary service since the award of the third badge, no more than four entries in the defaulters' book and a minimum of 15 years service. Officers who had been promoted from the ranks were also eligible. No more than 7 officers and 54 other ranks were awarded this medal during its brief life before it was superseded in 1934 by the Colonial Police Long Service Medal.*

VALUE:
George V   Rare

280. HONG KONG POLICE MEDAL FOR MERIT

Instituted: 1845.
Branch of Service: Hong Kong Police.
Ribbon: Various, according to class (see below).
Metal: Gold, silver or bronze.
Size: 36mm.
Description: (Obverse) the effigy of the reigning monarch; (reverse) inscribed in three lines HONG KONG POLICE FORCE FOR MERIT within a laurel wreath and beaded circle.
Comment: *Exceptionally awarded in five different classes according to the length and type of service. The 1st Class medal was struck in gold and worn with a watered yellow ribbon, the 2nd Class in silver with a plain yellow ribbon, the 3rd Class in bronze with a central black stripe on the yellow ribbon, the 4th Class in bronze with two central black stripes in the yellow ribbon, and the 5th Class (confined to the Police Reserve) in bronze had a green ribbon with two black central stripes. The 4th Class was engraved on the reverse above the wreath. These medals were superseded in April 1937 by the Hong Kong Police Silver Medal, only one of which was awarded before it was replaced by the Colonial Police Long Service Medal.*

VALUE: **From £50 according to class of award.**

281. HONG KONG ROYAL NAVAL DOCKYARD POLICE LONG SERVICE MEDAL

Instituted: 1920.
Branch of Service: Hong Kong Royal Naval Dockyard Police.
Ribbon: Yellow with two royal blue stripes towards the centre.
Metal: Gilt bronze.
Size: 31mm.
Description: (Obverse) the effigy of the reigning monarch; (reverse) the title of the Police within a laurel wreath. Swivel ring suspension.
Comments: *Awarded for 15 years service.*

VALUE:

George V (E)	£200–250
George VI (C)	£160–180
George VI (D)	£200–250

282. MALTA POLICE LONG SERVICE AND GOOD CONDUCT MEDAL

Instituted: 1921.
Branch of Service: Malta Police.
Ribbon: Dark blue with a narrow central silver stripe.
Metal: Silver.
Size: 36mm.
Description: (Obverse) the effigy of King George V; (reverse) an eight-pointed Maltese cross in a laurel wreath with the title of the service and FOR LONG SERVICE AND GOOD CONDUCT round the circumference.
Comments: *Awarded to sergeants and constables with 18 years exemplary service. Officers who had had 18 years in the ranks were also eligible for the award. It was superseded by the Colonial Police Long Service Medal in 1934. No more than 99 medals were awarded.*

VALUE:

George V (E)	£300–350
George V (C)	£350–400

283. NEW ZEALAND POLICE LONG SERVICE & GOOD CONDUCT MEDAL

Instituted: 1886.
Branch of Service: New Zealand Police.
Ribbon: Originally plain crimson but in 1917 it was changed to a pattern very similar to that of the Permanent Forces of the Empire Beyond the Seas LSGC medal.
Metal: Silver.
Size: 36mm.
Description: The original obverse was very similar to that of the NZ Long and Efficient Service Medal, with the crown, crossed sword and sceptre motif within a wreath of oak and fern leaves. By Royal Warrant of 8 September 1976 an obverse portraying Queen Elizabeth was introduced. The reverse was plain with the words FOR LONG SERVICE AND GOOD CONDUCT across the field.
Comments: *Awarded for 14 years service. Bars for further eight-year periods were added in 1959, reduced to seven years in 1963, the total length of service being indicated on the bar.*

VALUE:

Regalia obverse	£100–120
Elizabeth II	£90–110

284. SOUTH AFRICA POLICE GOOD SERVICE MEDAL

Instituted: 1923.
Branch of Service: South Africa Police.
Ribbon: Broad black centre, flanked by white stripes and green borders.
Metal: Silver.
Size: 36mm.
Description: (Obverse) South African coat of arms; (reverse) bilingual inscriptions separated by a horizontal line. Three versions of the medal have been recorded. In the first version inscriptions were in English and Dutch, the latter reading POLITIE DIENST with VOOR TROUWE DIENST (for faithful service) on the reverse. In the second, introduced in 1932, Afrikaans replaced Dutch and read POLISIE DIENS and VIR GETROUE DIENS respectively. In the third version, current from 1951 to 1963, the Afrikaans was modified to read POLISIEDIENS and VIR TROUE DIENS respectively.
Comments: *Awarded to other ranks for 18 years exemplary service or for service of a gallant or particularly distinguished character. In the latter instance a bar inscribed MERIT-VERDIENSTE was awarded. The medal was replaced by the South African Medal for Faithful Service.*

VALUE:

1st type	£20–30
2nd type	£15–25
3rd type	£15–25

285. SOUTH AFRICAN RAILWAYS AND HARBOUR POLICE LONG SERVICE AND GOOD CONDUCT MEDAL

Instituted: 1934.
Branch of Service: South African Railways and Harbour Police.
Ribbon: Similar to the Police Good Service Medal but with the colours reversed—a green central stripe flanked by white stripes and blue edges.
Metal: Silver.
Size: 36mm.
Description: (Obverse) the Union arms with S.A.R. & H. POLICE at the top and S.A.S.- EN HAWE POLISIE round the foot, but this was changed in 1953 to S.A.S. POLISIE at the top and S.A.R. POLICE at the foot. (Reverse) six line bilingual inscription.
Comments: *Awarded for 18 years unblemished service. Immediate awards for gallant or especially meritorious service earned a bar inscribed MERIT - VERDIENSTE (later with the words transposed). The medal was superseded in 1960 by the Railways Police Good Service Medal.*

VALUE:

1st type	£30–40
2nd type	£20–30

286. FIRE BRIGADE LONG SERVICE MEDAL

Instituted: 1 June 1954.
Branch of Service: Fire Services.
Ribbon: Red with narrow yellow stripes towards the end and yellow borders.
Metal: Cupro-nickel.
Size: 36mm.
Description: (Obverse) the Queen's effigy; (reverse) two firemen manning a hose. Ring suspension.
Comments: *Awarded to all ranks of local authority fire brigades, whether full- or part-time for 20 years exemplary service.*

VALUE:

Elizabeth II	£25–35

287. COLONIAL FIRE BRIGADE LONG SERVICE MEDAL

Instituted: 1934.
Branch of Service: Colonial Fire Services.
Ribbon: Blue with twin grey central stripes separated and bordered by thin white stripes.
Metal: Silver.
Size: 36mm.
Description: (Obverse) the effigy of the reigning monarch; (reverse) a fireman's helmet and axe. Ring suspension.
Comments: *Awarded to junior officers for 18 years full-time exemplary service. Bars are awarded for further periods of service.*

VALUE:

George V (E)	£300–350
George VI (D)	£250–300
George VI (E)	£250–300
Elizabeth II (C)	£250–300
Elizabeth II (D)	£250–300

288. CEYLON FIRE BRIGADE LONG SERVICE AND GOOD CONDUCT MEDAL

Instituted: 1950.
Branch of Service: Ceylon Fire Service.
Ribbon: Similar to the Police Medal, but with a thin central white stripe through the dark blue band.
Metal: Silver.
Size: 36mm.
Description: As the Police Medal, but with a reverse inscribed CEYLON FIRE SERVICES.

VALUE:

George VI	£300–400
Elizabeth II	£300–400

289. COLONIAL PRISON SERVICE LONG SERVICE MEDAL

Instituted: October 1955.
Branch of Service: Colonial Prison Services.
Ribbon: Green with dark blue edges and a thin silver stripe in the centre.
Metal: Silver.
Size: 36mm.
Description: (Obverse) Queen Elizabeth II; (reverse) a phoenix rising from the flames and striving towards the sun.
Comments: *Awarded to ranks of Assistant Superintendent and below for 18 years exemplary service. Bars are awarded for further periods of 25 or 30 years service.*

VALUE:
Elizabeth II   £30–40

290. SOUTH AFRICAN PRISON SERVICE FAITHFUL SERVICE MEDAL

Instituted: September 1922.
Branch of Service: South African Prison Service.
Ribbon: ??
Metal: Silver.
Size: 36mm.
Description: (Obverse) arms of the Union of South Africa, with GEVANGENIS DIENST round the top and PRISONS SERVICE round the foot. (Reverse) inscribed FOR FAITHFUL SERVICE across the upper half and in Dutch VOOR TROUWE DIENST across the lower half.
Comments: *Awarded to prison officers with 18 years exemplary service. Immediate awards for gallantry or exceptionally meritorious service received the Merit bar. In 1959 this medal was superseded by a version inscribed in Afrikaans.*

VALUE: £30–40

291. SOUTH AFRICA PRISONS DEPARTMENT FAITHFUL SERVICE MEDAL

Instituted: 1959.
Branch of Service: South African Prisons Department.
Ribbon: As above.
Metal: Silver.
Size: 36mm.
Description: (Obverse) arms of the Union of South Africa, with DEPARTEMENT VAN GEVANGENISS round the top and PRISONS DEPARTMENT round the foot. (Reverse) VIR TROUE DIENS across the upper half and FOR FAITHFUL SERVICE across the lower half.
Comments: *The conditions of the award were similar to the previous medal, the main difference being the change of title and the substitution of Afrikaans inscriptions for Dutch. This medal was superseded by the Prisons Department Faithful Service Medal of the Republic of South Africa, instituted in 1966.*

VALUE: £30–40

CORONATION AND JUBILEE MEDALS

The first official royal medal was that cast by Henry Basse in 1547 for the accession of the young King Edward VI. It is known cast in gold or silver and is a curious example of bad design and poor workmanship for such an august occasion. No coronation medals were produced in honour of either Mary or Elizabeth I, but under James VI and I there was a small silver medal struck at the Royal Mint to mark the king's accession in 1603. These early medals celebrated the accession of the new sovereign, rather than the act of crowning itself.

To mark the coronation of James I, however, a small silver medalet was struck for distribution among the people who attended the ceremony, and this may be regarded as the forerunner of the modern series. This bore a Latin title signifying that James was Caesar Augustus of Britain and Heir to the Caesars. Thereafter medals in gold, silver or base metals were regularly struck in connection with the coronations of British monarchs. These were purely commemorative and not intended for wear, so they lack rings or bars for suspension.

By the early 19th century medals were being struck by many medallists for sale as souvenirs to the general public. At least fifteen different medals greeted the coronation of William IV in 1830 and more than twice that number appeared seven years later for the coronation of Queen Victoria. That paled into insignificance compared with the number produced for the coronation of Edward VII in 1902. On that occasion numerous civic authorities, organizations, industrial concerns and business firms issued medals in celebration—well over a hundred different medals and medalets were produced.

Sir George Frampton designed two silver medals, and one of these was mounted with a suspender and a blue ribbon with a thin white stripe and scarlet edges. This medal was distributed to notable personages attending the ceremony and established the precedent for subsequent coronation medals which came to be regarded as an award in recognition of services rendered in connection with the coronation, from the Earl Marshal of England to the private soldiers taking part in the ceremonial parades. In more recent times the coronation medal has even been given to people who were not present at the ceremony but who performed notable public service in the coronation year.

Many other royal events have been commemorated by medals over the centuries. Royal weddings and the birth of the heir to the throne were regularly celebrated in this manner. Important anniversaries in long reigns have been the subject of numerous commemorative medals. The Golden Jubilee of George III in 1809-10, for example, resulted in over 30 different medals. Five times that number greeted the Golden Jubilee of Queen Victoria in 1887, but among them was an official medal intended for wear by those on whom it was conferred.

Even this, however, was not the first of the royal medals intended to be worn. This honour goes to a very large medal celebrating the proclamation of Victoria as Empress of India in 1877. Although fitted with a suspender bar and worn from a ribbon round the neck, it was not permitted for officers and men to wear this medal while in uniform. Later medals, however, were permitted to be worn when in uniform, but after other orders, decorations and campaign medals.

292. EMPRESS OF INDIA MEDAL

Date: 1877.
Ribbon: 42mm crimson edged in gold.
Metal: Gold or silver.
Size: 58mm.
Description: (Obverse) a left-facing bust of Queen
    Victoria wearing a veil and a coronet, her name and
    the date of her elevation being inscribed round the
    circumference. (Reverse) a broad zigzag border
    enclosing the words EMPRESS OF INDIA and its
    equivalent in Punjabi and Hindi across the field.
Comments: *Issued to celebrate the proclamation of
    Victoria as Empress of India on 1 January 1877. It was
    awarded in gold to Indian princes and high-ranking
    British officials. Indian civilians and selected officers
    and men of the various British and Indian regiments
    serving in India at the time were awarded the silver
    medal. It was issued unnamed but many examples were
    subsequently engraved or impressed privately.*

VALUE:

Gold	£1,800–2,200
Silver	£250–300

293. JUBILEE MEDAL

Date: 1887.
Ribbon: Broad central blue band with wide white stripes at the edges.
Metal: Gold, silver or bronze.
Size: 30mm.
Description: (Obverse) the bust of Queen Victoria by Sir Joseph Edgar
    Boehm; (reverse) an elaborate wreath in which are entwined the
    heraldic flowers of the United Kingdom. This encloses an eight-line
    inscription surmounted by a crown: IN COMMEMORATION OF
    THE 50th YEAR OF THE REIGN OF QUEEN VICTORIA 21 JUNE
    1887.
Comments: *Struck to celebrate the 50th anniversary of Victoria's accession
    to the throne. The medal in gold was given to members of the Royal Family
    and their personal guests. The silver medal was given to members of the
    Royal Household, government ministers, senior officials, distinguished
    foreign visitors, naval and military officers involved in the Jubilee parade
    on 21 June 1887 and the captains of vessels taking part in the great Naval
    Review at Spithead. The bronze medal was given to selected NCOs and
    men who took part in the parade or the Spithead Review. All medals were
    issued unnamed with a ring for suspension. When the Diamond Jubilee
    was celebrated ten years later holders of the 1887 medal were given a clasp
    in the form of a cable entwined around the date 1897 and surmounted by an
    imperial crown. Twin loops at the ends enabled the clasp to be sewn on to
    the ribbon.*

VALUE:

	without clasp	with clasp
Gold	£1,100–1,300	Rare
Silver	£70–80	£80–90
Bronze	£60–70	£70–80

294. JUBILEE (POLICE) MEDAL

Date: 1887.
Ribbon: Plain dark blue.
Metal: Bronze.
Size: 36mm.
Description: (Obverse) the veiled profile of Queen Victoria; (reverse) a wreath surmounted by a crown and enclosing the inscription: JUBILEE OF HER MAJESTY QUEEN VICTORIA. The year appears at the foot and the name of the force round the top.
Comments: *Issued to all ranks of the Metropolitan and City of London Police involved in the parades and celebrations on 21 June 1887. Medals are believed to have been issued with the inscription POLICE AMBULANCE round the top but confirmation of this is required. Clasps for 1897 were likewise issued ten years later.*

VALUE:

	without clasp	with clasp
Metropolitan Police	£15–20	£14–16
City of London Police	£40–50	£30–40

295. JUBILEE MEDAL

Date: 1897.
Ribbon: Dark blue with two broad white bands and dark blue edges.
Metal: Gold, silver or bronze.
Size: 30mm.
Description: This medal is very similar to the 1887 issue, differing solely in the date and anniversary on the reverse.

VALUE:

Gold (73)	£1,100–1,300
Silver (3040)	£70–80
Bronze (890)	£40–50

296. JUBILEE MEDAL (MAYORS AND PROVOSTS)

Date: 1897.
Ribbon: White with two broad dark blue bands and white edges.
Metal: Gold or silver.
Size: Height 48mm; max. width 40mm.
Description: A diamond-shaped medal with ring suspension, reminiscent of the *Klippe* coinage of central Europe. Both sides had circular centres with trefoil ornaments occupying the angles. (Obverse) the Wyon profile of the young Victoria at the time of her accession; (reverse) Sir Thomas Brock's Old Head veiled bust of the Queen.
Comments: *The gold version was presented to Lord Mayors and Lord Provosts while the silver medal was granted to Mayors and Provosts. Small silver medals of more conventional circular format were produced with these motifs and sold as souvenirs of the occasion.*

VALUE:

Gold (14)	Rare
Silver (512)	£110–130

297. JUBILEE (POLICE) MEDAL

Date: 1897.
Ribbon: Plain dark blue.
Metal: Bronze.
Size: 36mm.
Description: Very similar to the 1887 issue with the dates suitably amended and the name of the service round the top of the reverse.
Comments: *Separate issues were made in respect of the Police Ambulance service, St John Ambulance Brigade and the Metropolitan Fire Brigade. Holders of the previous medal merely received the 1897 clasp.*

VALUE:

Metropolitan Police (7500)	£12–16
City of London Police (535)	£40–50
Police Ambulance (210)	£180–200
St John Ambulance Brigade (910)	£60–70
Metropolitan Fire Brigade (950)	£60–70

298. CEYLON DIAMOND JUBILEE MEDAL

Date: 1897.
Ribbon: Plain red.
Metal: Gold.
Size: 35mm.
Description: (Obverse) the Boehm bust of Queen Victoria with the dates 1837-1897 at the foot. (Reverse) an elephant and a stupa (dome-shaped Buddhist shrine), with two lines of concentric inscriptions: TO COMMEMORATE SIXTY YEARS OF HER MAJESTY'S REIGN and, unusually, THE RT. HON. SIR J. WEST RIDGEWAY K.C.B., K.C.M.G., GOVERNOR. A crown above the rim was fixed to a ring for suspension.
Comments: *Awarded to local dignitaries and leading officials in the Ceylon government.*

VALUE:

Gold	Rare

299. HONG KONG DIAMOND JUBILEE MEDAL

Date: 1897.
Ribbon: Three equal bands of dark blue, maroon and dark blue.
Metal Silver, possibly also bronze.
Size: 36mm.
Description: (Obverse) the Boehm bust of Queen Victoria with the date 1897 at the foot; (reverse) a seascape with a British three-masted sailing ship and a Chinese junk in the background and two figures shaking hands in the foreground. The name of the colony appears at the top, while two concentric inscriptions read SIR WILLIAM ROBINSON G.C.M.G. GOVERNOR and TO COMMEMORATE SIXTY YEARS OF HER MAJESTY'S REIGN 1837-1897.
Comments: *Very little is known for certainty about this medal, on account of the fact that the colonial records were destroyed during the Japanese occupation.*

VALUE:

Silver	—
Bronze (?)	—

300. VISIT TO IRELAND MEDAL

Date: 1900.
Ribbon: Plain dark blue.
Metal: Bronze.
Size: 36mm.
Description: (Obverse) a half-length version of the Boehm bust of Queen Victoria; (reverse) the female allegorical figure of Hibernia looking out over Kingstown (Dun Laoghaire) harbour in which the Royal Yacht can be seen (far left). Unusually, the medal was mounted with a suspension bar decorated with shamrocks.
Comments: *Commemorating Queen Victoria's visit to Ireland in 1900, this medal was awarded to officers of the Royal Irish Constabulary and Dublin Metropolitan Police who were involved in security and policing the various events connected with the visit. The medal was worn with the same ribbon as the Jubilee Police medals.*

VALUE:

Bronze (2285)	£50–60	

301. CORONATION MEDAL

Date: 1902.
Ribbon: Dark blue with a central red stripe and white edges.
Metal: Silver or bronze.
Size: Height 42mm; max. width 30mm.
Description: (Obverse) the left-facing conjoined busts of King Edward VII and Queen Alexandra, both crowned and wearing coronation robes. (Reverse) the crowned royal cypher above the date of the actual ceremony. The medal has an elaborate raised rim decorated with a wreath culminating in a crown through which the ring for suspension was looped.
Comments: *This medal celebrated the coronation of King Edward VII on 9 August 1902. It was presented in silver to members of the Royal Family, foreign dignitaries, high officials of the government, senior officials and service officers involved in the celebrations. Selected NCOs and other ranks of the Army and Navy taking part in the parades were awarded the medal in bronze. Both versions were issued unnamed.*

VALUE:

Silver (3493)	£50–60
Bronze (6054)	£35–40

302. CORONATION MEDAL (MAYORS AND PROVOSTS)

Date: 1902.
Ribbon: Dark blue with a narrow white central stripe and crimson borders.
Metal: Silver.
Size: 32mm.
Description: (Obverse) conjoined right-facing busts of the King and Queen; (reverse) the crowned cypher and date. It differed from the ordinary medal by having flat, broad borders decorated with the heraldic flowers of the United Kingdom culminating at the top in a simple suspension ring.
Comment

VALUE:

Silver	£90–110

303. CORONATION (POLICE) MEDAL

Date: 1902.
Ribbon: Red, with a narrow dark blue central stripe.
Metal: Silver or bronze.
Size: 36mm.
Description: (Obverse) the conjoined busts of King Edward VII and Queen Alexandra; (reverse) a crown above a nosegay of heraldic flowers with the words CORONATION OF HIS MAJESTY KING EDWARD VII 1902 in the upper field. The name or initials of the service appeared round the top, LCC MFB signifying London County Council Metropolitan Fire Brigade.
Comments: *Issued to all ranks of the police and associated services involved in the coronation celebrations, and awarded in silver or bronze to officers and other ranks respectively.*

VALUE:

	Silver	Bronze
Metropolitan Police	£250–300 (51)	£8–12 (16,700)
City of London Police	£500–600 (5)	£25–30 (1060)
LCC MFB	£350–400 (9)	£40–50 (1000)
St John Ambulance Brigade	—	£40–50 (912)
Police Ambulance Service	—	£180–120 (204)

304. CEYLON CORONATION MEDAL

Date: 1902.
Ribbon: Plain blue.
Metal: Gold.
Size: 35mm.
Description: (Obverse) a crowned left-facing bust of King Edward VII; (reverse) the elephant and stupa motif previously used. The concentric inscription on the reverse now tactfully omitted any reference to the governor: IN COMMEMORATION OF THE CORONATION OF H.M. KING EDWARD VII 1902. The medal was fitted with a ring for suspension.
Comments: *Like its predecessor, this rare medal was struck for presentation to local dignitaries and government officials.*

VALUE:
Gold   Rare

305. HONG KONG CORONATION MEDAL

Date: 1902.
Ribbon: None officially designated.
Metal: Bronze.
Size: 36mm.
Description: (Obverse) conjoined right-facing busts of King Edward VII and Queen Alexandra with their names round the circumference; (reverse) the maritime motif of the Diamond Jubilee medal with new inscriptions in two concentric curves: SIR HENRY A. BLAKE G.C.M.G. GOVERNOR (inner) and TO COMMEMORATE THE CORONATION OF THEIR MAJESTIES THE KING & QUEEN (outer). Fitted with a suspension ring.
Comments: *Issued to all British and Indian officers and other ranks serving in the colony as well as local police.*

VALUE:

Bronze	£30–50

306. DELHI DURBAR MEDAL

Date: 1903.
Ribbon: Pale blue with three dark blue stripes.
Metal: Gold or silver.
Size: 38.5mm.
Description: (Obverse) a right-facing crowned bust of the King Emperor with DELHI DARBAR 1903 on the right side; (reverse) a three-line inscription in Farsi across the field, with an elaborate border of roses, thistles, shamrocks and Indian flowers. Ring suspension.
Comments: *Struck to celebrate the Durbar of the King Emperor at Delhi on 1 January 1903. It was awarded in gold to the rulers of the Indian princely states and in silver to lesser dignitaries, government officials, and officers and other ranks of the armed services actually involved in the celebrations.*

VALUE:

Gold (140)	£800–1000
Silver (2570)	£80–100

307. VISIT TO SCOTLAND MEDAL

Date: 1903.
Ribbon: Plain red.
Metal: Bronze.
Size: 36mm.
Description: Very similar to the Police Coronation medal but the year was changed to 1903 and the inscription SCOTTISH POLICE appeared round the top of the reverse. The medal was named to the recipient on the rim. An ornate clasp decorated with a thistle was worn above the suspension bar.
Comments: *Struck to commemorate Their Majesties' post-coronation tour of Scotland in May 1903. It was awarded to the police and troops involved in parades and escort duties.*

VALUE:

Bronze (2950)	£40–50

308. VISIT TO IRELAND MEDAL

Date: 1903.
Ribbon: Pale blue.
Metal: Bronze.
Size: 36mm.
Description: (Obverse) bust of King Edward VII; (reverse) as 1900 medal with the date altered at the foot. The suspension brooch is ornamented with shamrocks.
Comments: *Struck to mark the King's visit to Ireland in July 1903 and granted on the same terms as the medal of 1900.*

VALUE:

Bronze (7750)	£50–60

309. CORONATION MEDAL

Date: 1911.
Ribbon: Dark blue with two thin red stripes in the centre.
Metal: Silver.
Size: 32mm.
Description: (Obverse) conjoined left-facing busts of King George V and Queen Mary in their coronation robes within a floral wreath; (reverse) the crowned royal cypher above the date of the coronation itself. Plain ring suspension.
Comments: *Medals were issued unnamed but may sometimes be found with unofficial engraving. Those who were also entitled to the Delhi Darbar Medal received a crowned clasp inscribed DELHI if they had previously been awarded the coronation medal. This was the first occasion that the medal might be awarded to those not actually present at the ceremony itself.*

VALUE:

Silver (16,000)	£20–25

310. CORONATION (POLICE) MEDAL

Date: 1911.
Ribbon: Red with three narrow blue stripes.
Metal: Silver.
Size: 32mm.
Description: (Obverse) a crowned left-facing bust of King George V; (reverse) an imperial crown with an ornate surround. The inscription CORONATION 1911 appears at the foot and the name of the service at the top. Ring suspension.
Comments: *By now the number of police and ancillary services had grown considerably, as witness the various reverse types which may be encountered in this medal.*

VALUE:

Metropolitan Police (19,783)	£10–15
City of London Police (1400)	£40–50
County and Borough Police (2565)	£40–50
Police Ambulance Service*	£280–320
London Fire Brigade (1374)	£40–50
Royal Irish Constabulary (585)	£10–80
Scottish Police (280)	£90–100
St John Ambulance Brigade*	£40–50
St Andrew's Ambulance Corps*	£120–150
Royal Parks (119)	£240–280

* *A total of 2623 medals was awarded to these three services, the Police Ambulance medal being the scarcest and St John Ambulance medal the commonest.*

311. VISIT TO IRELAND MEDAL

Date: 1911.
Ribbon: Dark green with thin red stripes towards either end.
Metal: Silver.
Size: 36mm.
Description: Very similar to the foregoing, distinguished only by the reverse which is inscribed CORONATION 1911 round the top, with the actual date of the visit round the foot.
Comments: *Granted to prominent civic dignitaries and members of the Irish police forces involved in the royal visit to Ireland which took place on 7-12 July 1911.*

VALUE:
  Silver (2500)   £45–50

312. DELHI DURBAR MEDAL

Date: 1911.
Ribbon: Dark blue with two narrow red stripes in the middle.
Metal: Gold or silver.
Size: 38.5mm.
Description: (Obverse) the conjoined crowned busts of King George V and Queen Mary in a floral wreath; (reverse) an elaborate Farsi text.
Comments: *This medal marked the Delhi Durbar held in the King Emperor's honour in December 1911. Most of the gold medals went to the Indian princely rulers and top government officials, while a good proportion of the 30,000 silver medals was awarded to officers and other ranks of the British and Indian Armies for exemplary service, without their necessarily being present at the Durbar itself.*

VALUE:
  Gold (200)   £800–850
  Silver (30,000)   £25–30

313. JUBILEE MEDAL

Date: 1935.
Ribbon: Red with two dark blue and one white stripes at the edges.
Metal: Silver.
Size: 32mm.
Description: (Obverse) left-facing conjoined half-length busts of King George V and Queen Mary in crowns and robes of state; (reverse) a crowned GRI monogram flanked by the dates of the accession and the jubilee.
Comments: *Issued to celebrate the Silver Jubilee of King George V and widely distributed to the great and good throughout the Empire.*

VALUE:
  Silver (85,000)   £14–18

314. CORONATION MEDAL

Date: 1937.
Ribbon: Blue edged with one red and two white stripes.
Metal: Silver.
Size: 32mm.
Description: (Obverse) conjoined busts of King George VI and Queen Elizabeth in their robes of state without any inscription. The stark simplicity of this motif was matched by a reverse showing the crowned GRI over the inscription CROWNED 12 MAY 1937, with the names of the King and Queen in block capitals round the circumference.
Comments: *Issued to celebrate the coronation of King George VI on 12 May 1937.*

VALUE:

Silver (90,000)	£14–18

315. CORONATION MEDAL

Date: 1953.
Ribbon: Dark red with two narrow blue stripes in the centre and narrow white edges.
Metal: Silver.
Size: 32mm.
Description: (Obverse) a right-facing bust of Queen Elizabeth II in a Tudor crown and robes of state, the field being otherwise plain. (Reverse) a similar crown over the royal monogram EIIR with the legend QUEEN ELIZABETH II CROWNED 2ND JUNE 1953 round the circumference. Ring suspension.
Comments: *This medal celebrated the coronation of Queen Elizabeth II on 2 June 1953. News that Edmund Hillary and Sherpa Tenzing had successfully attained the summit of Everest reached London on the morning of the Coronation. Subsequently the members of the Hunt Expedition were invited to Buckingham Palace on 16 July 1953 where, on Her Majesty's own initiative, they were presented with coronation medals engraved MOUNT EVEREST EXPEDITION on the rim, following the precedent of the Mwele medals of 1895-6.*

VALUE:

Silver (129,000)	£25–30
Mount Everest Expedition (37)	£600

316. JUBILEE MEDAL

Date: 1977.
Ribbon: White with thin red stripes at the edges, a broad blue stripe in the centre and a thin red stripe down the middle of it.
Metal: Silver.
Size: 32mm.
Description: (Obverse) Right-facing profile of Queen Elizabeth II wearing the imperial state crown—the first time this design was employed. (Reverse) a crown and wreath enclosing the words THE 25TH YEAR OF THE REIGN OF QUEEN ELIZABETH II 6 FEBRUARY 1977. A distinctive reverse was used in Canada, showing the dates of the reign flanking the royal monogram round the foot, CANADA round the top and a large stylised maple leaf in the centre.
Comments: *The 25th anniversary of the Queen's accession was marked by the release of this unnamed medal.*

VALUE:

General issue (30,000)	£130–150
Canadian issue (30,000)	£70–90

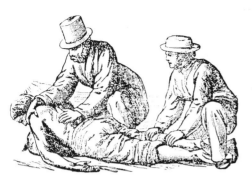

MEDALS FOR SAVING LIFE

Until the establishment of the government's own gallantry awards for the saving of life (the Sea Gallantry Medal of 1854 and the Albert Medal of 1866), it was left entirely to private individuals and organizations to reward those who risked their own lives to save the lives of others. Although the medals granted from the late eighteenth century onwards are unofficial, they are of considerable human interest and are now very much sought after, preferably with the citations, diplomas, printed testimonials and other collateral material. These medals are listed in broadly chronological order of their institution.

317. ROYAL HUMANE SOCIETY MEDALS

Date: 1774.

Ribbon: None (1774-1869); plain navy blue (1869); thin central yellow stripe and white edges added (silver medal, 1921).

Metal: Gold, silver or bronze.

Size: 51mm (1774-1869); 38mm (1869-).

Description: (Obverse) a cherub, nude but for a flowing cloak, blowing on a burnt-out torch explained by the Latin legend LATEAT SCINTILLVLA FORSAN (perhaps a tiny spark may be concealed). A three-line Latin text across the exergue reads SOC. LOND. IN RESUSCITAT INTERMORTUORUM INSTIT. with the date in roman numerals. (Reverse) an oak wreath containing the engraved details of the recipient and the date of the life-saving act. Round the circumference is a Latin motto HOC PRETIVM CIVE SERVATO TVLIT (He has obtained this reward for saving the life of a citizen). When the rescue attempt was unsuccessful, however, the medal was granted without this inscription. Later medals of similar design were struck also in bronze.

Comments: *The society was formed in 1774 for the specific purpose of diffusing knowledge about the techniques of resuscitation and saving life from drowning. From the society's inception large medals were struck in gold or silver. Monetary rewards, medals, clasps and testimonials were granted to those who saved life, or attempted to save life from drowning, but later the society's remit was broadened to include "all cases of exceptional bravery in rescuing or attempting to rescue persons from asphyxia in mines, wells, blasting furnaces or in sewers where foul air may endanger life".*

Although not intended for wear, the large medals were often pierced or fitted with a ring or bar for suspension from a ribbon. In 1869 permission was given for the medals to be worn. As a result the diameter was reduced to 38mm and a scroll suspension was fitted for wear with a navy blue ribbon. At the same time the Latin text of the "unsuccessful" and "successful" medals was altered to read VIT. PERIC. EXPOS. D.D. SOC REG. HVM. (the Royal Humane Society presented this gift, his life having been exposed to danger) and VIT. OB. SERV. D.D. SOC, REG. HVM. (the

Royal Humane Society presented this gift for saving life) respectively. Details of the recipient and the act were engraved on the rim. In 1921 the ribbon of the silver medal was changed to navy blue with a central yellow stripe and white edges, but the plain navy blue ribbon was retained for the bronze medal. Scrolled clasps with the initials R.H.S. were awarded for subsequent acts of lifesaving.

In 1873 the Stanhope Gold Medal, in memory of Captain C.S.S. Stanhope, RN, was instituted for award to the person performing the bravest act of life-saving during the year. The first Stanhope medals were similar to the society's silver medal, differing only in the addition of a clasp inscribed STANHOPE MEDAL and the year, but since the 1930s the Stanhope Medal has been identical to the other medals, differing solely in the metal. In 1921, however, the ribbon for the Stanhope Gold Medal was changed to one of navy blue with yellow and black edges.

VALUE:

	Gold	Silver	Bronze
Large successful	—	£150–200	£70–80
Large unsuccessful	—	£250–300	£80–120
Small successful	—	£140–160	£40–50
Small unsuccessful	—	£150–180	£40–50
Stanhope Gold Medal	£1,500–2,000		

318. HUNDRED OF SALFORD HUMANE SOCIETY MEDALS

Date: 1824.

Ribbon: Plain dark blue.

Metal: Gold, silver or bronze.

Size: 32mm (circular type); height 49mm; max. width 41mm (cruciform type).

Description: Circular silver or bronze medals were awarded from 1824 onwards, with the recipient's name and details engraved on the reverse, and featuring the society's emblem, a man bearing the body of a drowning man, on the obverse. Around the time of the society's centenary in 1889, however, a more elaborate type of medal was devised, with the circular medal superimposed on a cross of distinctive shape, so that the society's name could be inscribed on the arms.

Comments: *This society was formed in 1789 to serve the needs of the Salford and Manchester area. After a few years it was dissolved, but was revived again in 1824. These awards ceased in 1922.*

VALUE:

	Gold	Silver	Bronze
Circular medal	—	£110–130	£90–120
Cruciform medal	Rare	£60–80	—

319. ROYAL NATIONAL LIFEBOAT INSTITUTION MEDALS

Date: 1825.
Ribbon: Plain blue.
Metal: Gold, silver or bronze.
Size: 36mm.
Description: The first medals bore the effigy of George IV on the obverse and it was not until 1862 that this was replaced by a garlanded profile of Victoria by Leonard C. Wyon. Medals portraying Edward VII and George V were introduced in 1902 and 1911 respectively, but when permission to portray George VI was refused in 1937 the RNLI adopted a profile of its founder, Sir William Hillary, instead. All but the Edwardian medals have a reverse showing a drowning seaman being rescued by three men in a boat with the motto LET NOT THE DEEP SWALLOW ME UP. The Edwardian medals have the seated figure of Hope adjusting the lifejacket on a lifeboatman. The twin-dolphin suspension is fitted with a plain blue ribbon and clasps inscribed SECOND SERVICE, THIRD SERVICE and so on are awarded for subsequent acts of gallantry.
Comments: *The RNLI was founded on 4 March 1824 and began awarding medals the following year to 'persons whose humane and intrepid exertions in saving life from shipwreck on our coasts are deemed sufficiently conspicuous to merit honourable distinction'.*

VALUE:	Gold	Silver	Bronze
George IV	£1,200–1,500	£180–200	—
Victoria	£1,200–1,500	£220–250	—
Edward VII	£1,500–1,800	£600–800	—
George V	£1,400–1,800	£300–400	£250–300
Hillary	£800–1,200	£200–250	£180–200

320. MEDALS OF THE SOCIETY OF THE PROTECTION OF LIFE FROM FIRE

Date: 1836.
Ribbon: Plain scarlet.
Metal: Silver or bronze.
Size: 52mm (I and II), 45mm (III), 42mm (IV &V) or 40mm (VI).
Description: The first medal (type I) had a radiate eye in garter obverse and a reverse giving the recipient's details in an oak-leaf wreath. They were often unofficially fitted with a bar suspender. The Society was granted the Royal title in 1843 and a new medal (type II) was adopted the following year, with the word ROYAL added and the date at the foot of the obverse changed to 1844. In the early 1850s type III was introduced, with an obverse of a man carrying a woman away from a fire. This and type IV (1892) were struck in silver or bronze. As royal patronage ended with the death of Queen Victoria, a new medal (type V) was required in 1902 without the Royal title. Types IV and V show a man rescuing a woman and two children from a fire. The reverse of this medal has the words DUTY AND HONOR within a wreath, the recipient's details being placed on the rim. Type VI, awarded from 1984, is a bronze medal without suspension with the recipient's details engraved on the reverse.

VALUE:		Silver	Bronze
I	Eye and garter (1836)	—	—
II	Eye and garter (1844)	£350–400	—
III	Man and woman (1850s)	£150–200	—
IV	Man, woman and children (1892)	Rare	—
V	As type IV but "Royal" removed (1902)	£100–150	£80–100
VI	Details on reverse	—	Rare

321. LLOYD'S MEDALS FOR SAVING LIFE AT SEA

Date: 1836.
Ribbon: Blue, striped white, red and white in the centre.
Metal: Gold, silver or bronze.
Size: 73mm or 36mm.
Description: Both large and small medals had similar motifs. (Obverse) the rescue of Ulysses by Leucothoe; (reverse) an ornate wreath.
Comments: *The first medals, introduced in 1836, had a diameter of 73mm and were not intended for wear, but in 1896 the diameter was reduced to 36mm and a ring fitted for suspension with a ribbon.*

VALUE:

Large silver	£400–500
Large bronze	£200–250
Small silver	£200–250
Small bronze	£150–180

322. LIVERPOOL SHIPWRECK AND HUMANE SOCIETY'S MARINE MEDALS

Date: 1839.
Ribbon: Plain dark blue.
Metal: Gold, silver or bronze.
Size: 54mm (type I), 45mm x 36mm (oval, type II) or 38mm (type III).
Description: (Obverse) a man on a spar of wreckage, taking an inert child from its drowning mother, with the stark legend LORD SAVE US, WE PERISH. This motif was retained for smaller, oval medals (type II) introduced around 1867 with the name of the Society round the edge, and a simple wreath reverse. The suspender was mounted with the Liver Bird emblem. A smaller circular version (type III) was adopted in 1874/75 and fitted with a scroll suspender. In this type the Liver Bird appeared in a wreath on the reverse. Bars engraved with the details were awarded for subsequent acts of life-saving. In addition to the general Marine medals there were distinctive awards in connection with specific marine rescues and funded separately. These had the type III obverse, but the reverse was inscribed CAMP & VILLAVERDE or BRAMLEY-MOORE. A glazed silver medal inscribed IN MEMORIAM was granted to the next of kin of those who lost their lives while attempting to save the lives of others.
Comments: *The Society was formed in 1839 to administer funds raised to help and reward those who distinguished themselves in saving life as a result of a hurricane which swept the Irish Sea in January of that year. The first medals were struck in 1844 and presented for rescues dating back to November 1839. They were large (54mm) in diameter, without suspension.*

VALUE:

	Gold	Silver	Bronze
Large (54mm) 1844	Rare	£250–300	—
Oval 1867	—	£400–450	—
Small (38mm) 1874/5	£800–1200	£60–150	£50–80
Camp & Villaverde	—	£400–600	£400–450
Bramley-Moore	—	£400–500	£350–400
In Memoriam	—	£350–400	—

323. SHIPWRECKED FISHERMEN AND MARINERS ROYAL BENEVOLENT SOCIETY MEDALS

Date: 1851.
Ribbon: Navy blue.
Metal: Gold or silver.
Size: 36mm.
Description: (Obverse) the Society's arms; (reverse) inscribed PRESENTED FOR HEROIC EXERTIONS IN SAVING LIFE FROM DROWNING with a quotation from Job 29: 13 at the foot. The circumference is inscribed ENGLAND EXPECTS EVERY MAN WILL DO HIS DUTY, a quotation from Lord Nelson's signal to the fleet at Trafalgar, 1805. The first medals had a straight suspender but by 1857 a double dolphin suspender had been adopted (five variations of this suspender can be identified). Details of the recipient's name and the date of the rescue are engraved on the edge.
Comments: *The Society was founded in 1839 to raise funds for shipwrecked fishermen and mariners and the families of those lost at sea.*

VALUE	Gold	Silver
Straight suspender	Rare	£150–200
Dolphin suspender	£800–1,200	£150–200

324. TAYLEUR FUND MEDAL

Date: 1854.
Ribbon: Dark blue.
Metal: Gold (2) or silver.
Size: 45mm.
Description: (Obverse) a sinking ship with the legend TAYLEUR FUND FOR THE SUCCOUR OF SHIPWRECKED STRANGERS; (reverse) details of the award engraved.
Comments: *In January 1854 the emigrant ship* Tayleur *foundered in Bantry Bay, Ireland. A fund was started for the relief of the survivors and the surplus used to issue silver life-saving medals. The first awards were made in 1861. The medals were awarded for a total of only six separate rescues, the last in 1875. In December 1913 the residue of the Tayleur Fund was transferred to the RNLI and the issue of medals terminated.*

VALUE:

Gold (2)	—
Silver (37)	£250–350

325. HARTLEY COLLIERY MEDAL

Date: 1862.
Ribbon: None.
Metal: Gold (1) or silver.
Size: 53mm
Description: (Obverse) an angel with mine rescuers and disaster victims. Details of the award were engraved on the reverse.
Comments: *Some 204 miners perished in the disaster which overtook the Hartley Colliery, Northumberland on 10 January 1862. This medal was awarded to those involved in the rescue operations.*

VALUE:

Gold (1)	—
Silver (37)	£250–350

326. LIFE SAVING MEDAL OF THE ORDER OF ST JOHN

Date: 1874.
Ribbon: Black, embroidered with the eight-point cross in white (1874), black watered silk (1888), white inner and red outer stripes added, separated by a black line(1950) which was subsequently removed in 1954.
Metal: Gold, silver or bronze.
Size: 36mm.
Description: The first medals had a plain eight-pointed cross of the Order on the obverse with the legend AWARDED BY THE ORDER OF ST JOHN OF JERUSALEM IN ENGLAND. A second type of medal was adopted in 1888 and showed four tiny lions in the interstices of the cross, the legend now reading FOR SERVICE IN THE CAUSE OF HUMANITY. Clasps for further awards were instituted in 1892.
Comments: *Instituted on 15 December 1874 and awarded for gallantry in saving life, these medals were originally granted in bronze or silver, but gold medals were also struck from 1907.*

VALUE:

	Gold	Silver	Bronze
1st type 1874	—	£500–600	£400–500
2nd type 1888	£1,000	£500–600	£400–500

327. LIVERPOOL SHIPWRECK AND HUMANE SOCIETY'S FIRE MEDAL

Date: 1883.
Ribbon: Plain scarlet.
Metal: Gold, silver or bronze.
Size: 38mm.
Description: (Obverse) a fireman descending the stairs of a burning house carrying three children to their kneeling mother, her arms outstretched to receive them. (Reverse) the wreathed Liver Bird previously noted for the third type of Marine medal. The medal is fitted with a scroll suspender. Clasps engraved with the details are awarded for subsquent acts.
Comments: *The first recipient was William Oversly in November 1883, for rescuing a child from a burning house. The first woman recipient was Miss Julia Keogh (12 February 1895) who saved two children in a house fire.*

VALUE:

	Gold	Silver	Bronze
Fire medal	Rare	£250–300	£150–180

328. LLOYD'S MEDALS FOR MERITORIOUS SERVICE

Date: 1893.

Ribbon: Red with blue stripes towards the edges (1893); blue with broad white stripes towards the edges (since 1900).

Metal: Silver or bronze.

Size: 36mm x 38mm (star), 39mm x 29mm (oval), 36mm (circular).

Description: The original medal was a nine-pointed rayed star in bronze with the arms of Lloyd's on the obverse, suspended by a ring from a red ribbon with blue stripes towards the edge. A silver oval medal was introduced in 1900 with Lloyd's arms on the obverse and details of the recipient engraved on the reverse. This medal was fitted with a twin dolphin suspender and a blue ribbon with broad white stripes towards the edge. A third type, introduced in 1913, was a circular medal, struck in silver or bronze, with Lloyd's shield on the obverse. The fourth type, still current, was introduced in 1936 and has the full arms, with crest, motto and supporters, on the obverse. The ribbon is suspended by a ring.

Comments: *These medals have been awarded to officers and men for extraordinary services in the preservation of vessels and cargoes from peril.*

VALUE:

	Silver	Bronze
Star 1893	—	£100–120
Oval 1900	£400–450	—
Circular 1913	£320–350	£280–320
Circular 1936	—	—

329. LIVERPOOL SHIPWRECK AND HUMANE SOCIETY'S GENERAL MEDAL

Date: 1894.

Ribbon: Five equal stripes, three red and two white.

Metal: Gold, silver or bronze.

Size: 38mm.

Description: (Obverse) a cross pattee with a wreathed crown at the centre and the legend FOR BRAVERY IN SAVING LIFE with the date 1894 at the foot; (reverse) the wreathed Liver Bird of the Marine medal, type III. Fitted with an ornate bar suspender. Bars for subsequent awards are granted.

Comments: *The first award was made on 9 June 1894 to Constables Twizell and Dean who were both injured whilst stopping runaway horses.*

VALUE:

	Gold	Silver	Bronze
General medal	—	£80–120	£50–80

330. DRUMMOND CASTLE MEDAL

Date: 1896.
Ribbon: Plain crimson.
Metal: Silver.
Size: 38mm.
Description: (Obverse) the veiled profile of Queen Victoria; (reverse) a wreath enclosing the name of the ship and the date of its sinking with the legend FROM QUEEN VICTORIA A TOKEN OF GRATITUDE. Fitted with a scrolled suspender.
Comments: *Presented on behalf of Queen Victoria by officials from the British Embassy in Paris to inhabitants of Brest, Ushant and Molene for their generosity and humanity in rescuing and succouring the survivors of the SS Drummond Castle which struck a reef off Ushant on 16 June 1896. Of the 143 passengers and 104 crew, all but three perished. 282 medals were struck and 271 of these were awarded to those who helped save the living and assisted in the recovery and burial of the victims.*

VALUE:

Silver (282)	£180–220

331. CARNEGIE HERO FUND MEDAL

Date: 1908.
Ribbon: None.
Metal: Bronze.
Size: 90mm.
Description: (Obverse) an angel and a nude male figure surrounded by an inscription "HE SERVES GOD BEST WHO MOST NOBLY SERVES HUMANITY"; (reverse) two wreaths surrounding a central tablet inscribed "FOR HEROIC ENDEAVOUR TO SAVE HUMAN LIFE 19..." surrounding a further inscription "PRESENTED BY THE TRUSTEES OF THE CARNEGIE HERO FUND". Details of the recipient are engraved on the rim.
Comments: *The Carnegie Hero Fund Trust was established in Scotland by Andrew Carnegie in 1908. The first medallion was awarded posthumously on 26 November 1909 to Thomas Wright for a life saving act on 23 September 1908. To date 171 medllions have been awarded.*

VALUE:

Bronze	£250–350

332. C.Q.D. MEDAL

Date: 1909.
Ribbon: Plain dark blue.
Metal: Silver.
Size: 45mm.
Description: (Obverse) the SS Republic with the initials C.Q.D. at the top; (reverse) the words FOR GALLANTRY across the middle, with a very verbose inscription round the circumference and continued in eight lines across the field. Ring suspension.
Comments: *This medal takes its curious name from the CQD signal (Come Quick Danger) sent out by the Italian steamer* Florida *when it collided in thick fog with the White Star liner* Republic *on 21 January 1909. The liner* Baltic *responded to the call. The* Republic *was the more severely damaged vessel, but all of her passengers and crew were transferred, first to the* Florida *and then to the* Baltic, *before she sank. The saloon passengers of the* Baltic *and* Republic *subscribed to a fund to provide medals to the crews of all three ships in saving more than 1700 lives.*

VALUE:
Silver	£100–120

333. RSPCA LIFE-SAVING MEDAL

Date: 1909.
Ribbon: Blue with three white stripes in the centre, the central stripe being narrower than the others (silver); blue with a central white stripe flanked by narrow red and white stripes (bronze).
Metal: Silver or bronze.
Size: 36mm.
Description: (Obverse) a seated female figure surrounded by a cow, sheep, cat, dog, goat and horse; (reverse) plain, with an inscription. The recipient's name usually appears on the rim. Both medals have a brooch bar inscribed FOR HUMANITY.
Comments: *Instituted in 1909 by the Royal Society for the Prevention of Cruelty to Animals, this medal is awarded in silver or bronze for acts of gallantry in saving the lives of animals.*

VALUE:
Silver	£80–120
Bronze	£50–60

334. BOY SCOUT GALLANTRY MEDALS

Date: 1909.
Ribbon: Red (bronze), blue (silver) or half red, half blue (silver-gilt).
Metal: Bronze, silver and silver-gilt.
Size: 33mm.
Description: A cross pattée with the Scout fleur-de-lis emblem at the centre with the motto "BE PREPARED" and the words "FOR GALLANTRY". The name and details of the recipient are engraved on the plain reverse.
Comments: *The Scout movement began informally in 1907 and the Boy Scouts Association was founded a year later. Gallantry awards were instituted in 1908 and 1909. The bronze cross is awarded for "moderate risk", the silver for "considerable risk" and the silver-gilt for "extraordinary risk".*

VALUE:
Silver-gilt	£250–350
Silver	£150–220
Bronze	£100–150

335. CARPATHIA AND TITANIC MEDAL

Date: 1912.
Ribbon: Dark blue.
Metal: Gold, silver or bronze.
Size: Height 40mm; max. width 35mm.
Description: The ornately shaped medal, in the best Art Nouveau style, has the suspension ring threaded through the head of Neptune whose long beard flows into two dolphins terminating in a fouled anchor and ship's spars. (Obverse) the Carpathia steaming between icebergs; (reverse) a twelve-line inscription, with the name of the manufacturer at the foot. It was worn from a straight bar suspender.
Comments: *This medal recalls one of the greatest tragedies at sea, when the White Star liner* Titanic *struck an iceberg on her maiden voyage and sank with the loss of 1490 lives. The 711 survivors were picked up by the* Carpathia *whose officers and men were subsequently awarded this medal in gold, silver or bronze according to the rank of the recipient.*

VALUE:

Gold (14)	Rare
Silver (110)	£400–600
Bronze (180)	£300–400

336. CORPORATION OF GLASGOW BRAVERY MEDAL

Date: 1924
Ribbon: Green with red edges.
Metal: Gold, silver or bronze.
Size: 38mm (type I) or 33mm (type II).
Description: Type I: (obverse) an angel blowing a trumpet and holding a laurel wreath in front of a circular scrolled cartouche inscribed FOR BRAVERY; (reverse) plain, engraved with the name and details of the recipient. Type II: (obverse) wreath enclosing the words "FOR BRAVERY"; (reverse) Arms of the Corporation of Glasgow and details of the recipient. Fitted with a ring suspension and an ornate thistle brooch inscribed GALLANTRY in a scroll.
Comments: *Following the reorganisation of local government in Scotland in 1975, the award ceased and was replaced by the Strathclyde Regional Council Medal for Bravery.*

VALUE:

	Type I	Type II
Gold	£200–250	£200–250
Silver	£100–150	£50–100
Bronze	£50–80	—

337. LLOYD'S MEDAL FOR SERVICES TO LLOYDS

Date: November 1913.
Ribbon: Blue with broad white stripes towards the edge.
Metal: Silver.
Size: 36mm.
Description: (Obverse) Neptune in a chariot drawn by four horses; (reverse) an oak-leaf wreath enclosing a scroll inscribed FOR SERVICES TO LLOYD'S. Fitted with ring suspension.
Comments: *Instituted by Lloyd's Committee, this medal was intended to reward services of a general nature.*

VALUE:

Gold (14)	£1500–2000
Silver (10)	£800–1000

338. LLOYD'S MEDAL FOR BRAVERY AT SEA

Date: December 1940.
Ribbon: White with broad blue stripes at the sides.
Metal: Silver.
Size: 36mm.
Description: (Obverse) a seated nude male figure holding a laurel
  wreath, extending his hand towards a ship on the horizon; (reverse)
  a trident surmounted by a scroll inscribed BRAVERY, enclosed in a
  wreath of oak leaves. It has a ring suspender.
Comments: *Instituted by Lloyd's Committee, it was awarded to officers and
  men of the Merchant Navy and fishing fleets for exceptional bravery at sea
  in time of war. A total of 523 medals was awarded up to December 1947
  when it was discontinued.*

VALUE:
       Silver   £500–700

339. LIVERPOOL SHIPWRECK AND HUMANE SOCIETY'S SWIMMING MEDAL

Date: 1885
Ribbon: Five equal bars, three blue and two white.
Metal: Silver or bronze.
Size: Height 44mm; max. width 30mm.
Description: This extremely ornate medal has a twin dolphin suspender and a free form. (Obverse) a wreath
  surmounted by crossed oars and a trident, with a lifebelt at the centre enclosing the Liver Bird emblem on a
  shield; (reverse) plain, engraved with the recipient's name and details.
Comments: *Not granted for life-saving as such, but for proficiency in swimming and life-saving techniques.*

VALUE:
       Silver   £30–50
       Bronze   £20–40

340. BINNEY MEMORIAL MEDAL

Date: 1947.
Ribbon: None.
Metal: Bronze.
Size: 48mm.
Description: (Obverse) a bust of Captain R.D. Binney, CBE,
  RN; (reverse) inscription FOR COURAGE IN SUPPORT OF
  LAW AND ORDER and AWARDED TO above the
  recipient's name on a raised tablet.
Comments: *Instituted in memory of Captain Binney who was killed
  on 8 December 1944 in the City of London while attempting to
  apprehend two armed robbers single-handedly. It is awarded
  annually to the British citizen who displays the greatest courage in
  support of law and order within the areas under the jurisdiction of
  the Metropolitan Police and the City of London Police. The medal
  is not intended for wear.*

VALUE:
       Bronze   £400–600

MISCELLANEOUS MEDALS

Under this heading are grouped a very disparate range of medals whose only common denominator is that they do not fit conveniently into one or other of the preceding categories. They are not without considerable interest, the polar medals in particular having a very keen following and a buoyant market.

341. KING'S AND QUEEN'S MESSENGER BADGE

Instituted: 1485.
Ribbon: Plain blue.
Metal: Silver.
Size: 45mm x 35mm.
Description: An upright oval fitted with a plain suspension ring and having a greyhound suspended by a ring from the foot of the rim. (Obverse) the Garter inscribed HONI SOIT QUI MAL Y PENSE enclosing the crowned royal cypher. (Reverse) plain, engraved with dates of service. Occasionally found with additional dates and monarchs' details, indicating re-issue to other messengers.
Comments: *John Norman was the first gentleman messenger formally appointed by King Richard III. Henry VIII expanded the service into a corps of 40 King's Messengers under the control of the Lord Chamberlain. Nowadays the corps is controlled by the Foreign and Commonwealth Office. Originally the badge was worn at all times by messengers on duty; today it is only worn on formal occasions.*

VALUE: Rare

342. ARCTIC MEDAL

Instituted: 30 January 1857.
Ribbon: 38mm plain white.
Metal: Silver.
Size: Height 46mm; max. width 32mm.
Description: An octagonal medal with a beaded rim, surmounted by a nine-pointed star (representing the Pole Star) through which the suspension ring is fitted. (Obverse) an unusual profile of Queen Victoria, her hair in a loose chignon secured with a ribbon. (Reverse) a three-masted sailing vessel amid icebergs with a sledge party in the foreground and the dates 1818-1855 in the exergue. The medal was issued unnamed, but is often found privately engraved.
Comments: *Awarded retrospectively to all officers and men engaged in expeditions to the polar regions from 1818 to 1855, including those involved in the on-going search for the ill-fated Franklin Expedition of 1845-8. Thus the medal was granted to civilians, scientists, personnel of the French and US Navies and employees of the Hudson's Bay Company who took part in a number of abortive search parties for Sir John Franklin and his crew. Some 1106 medals, out of 1486 in all, were awarded to officers and ratings of the Royal Navy.*

VALUE:

Silver	£270–300

343. ARCTIC MEDAL

Instituted: 28 November 1876.
Ribbon: 32mm plain white.
Metal: Silver.
Size: 36mm
Description: A circular medal with a raised beaded rim and a straight bar suspender. (Obverse) a veiled bust of Queen Victoria wearing a small crown, dated 1877 at the foot; (reverse) a three-masted ship icebound.
Comments: *Granted to officers and men of HM ships* Alert *and* Discovery *who served in the Arctic Expedition between 17 July 1875 and 2 November 1876. The medal was later extended to include the crew of the private yacht* Pandora *commanded by Allen Young which cruised in polar waters between 25 June and 19 October 1875 and from 3 June to 2 November 1876. Medals were impressed with the name and rank of the recipient. Only 170 medals were awarded.*

VALUE:

Silver	£700–1000

344. POLAR MEDAL

Instituted: 1904.

Ribbon: 32mm plain white.

Metal: Silver or bronze.

Size: 33mm octagonal.

Description: (Obverse) the effigy of the reigning sovereign; (reverse) a view of the Royal Research Ship <u>Discovery</u> with a man-handling sledge party in the foreground.

Comments: *Originally issued in silver to officers and in bronze to petty officers and ratings, but the bronze medals were discontinued in 1939 and since then only silver medals have been awarded. Apart from the 1904 issue of bronze medals, all Polar Medals have been fitted with a clasp giving details of the service for which they were awarded. Medals are named to the recipient, engraved on the earlier issues and impressed in small capitals (Elizabethan issue). Clasps for subsequent expeditions are awarded. Altogether some 641 silver and 245 medals for the Antarctic and 71 silver medals for the Arctic have been awarded to date.*

Value:

	Silver	Bronze
Edward VII	from £1,250	from £1,000
George V (B)	from £1,000	from £750
George V (C)	from £1,000	from £750
George V (E)	from £1,000	from £750
George VI	from £800	from £750
Elizabeth II	from £800	from £700

345. KING EDWARD VII MEDAL FOR SCIENCE, ART AND MUSIC

Instituted: 1904

Ribbon: 35mm scarlet with a broad central band of dark blue and thin white stripes towards the edges.

Metal: Silver.

Size: 32mm.

Description: The raised rim consisted of a laurel wreath and has a ring for suspension. (Obverse) the conjoined busts of King Edward VII and Queen Alexandra; (reverse) the Three Graces engaged in various cultural pursuits.

Comments: *This short-lived medal was discontinued only two years later. It was awarded in recognition of distinguished services in the arts, sciences and music.*

VALUE:

Silver	£700–800

346. ORDER OF THE LEAGUE OF MERCY

Date: 1906.

Ribbon: 38mm watered white silk with a central broad stripe of dark blue.

Metal: Silver.

Size: Height 51mm; max. width 39mm.

Description: An enamelled red cross surmounted by the Prince of Wales's plumes enfiladed by a coronet, with a central medallion depicting a group of figures representing Charity, set within a laurel wreath.

Comments: *Appointments to the Order are sanctioned and approved by the sovereign on the recommendation of the Grand President of the League of Mercy as a reward for distinguished personal service to the League in assisting the support of hospitals. Ladies and gentlemen who have rendered such aid for at least five years are eligible for the award. In 1917 King George V instituted a bar to be awarded to those who gave continuing service over a period of many years after receiving the Order itself.*

VALUE:

Badge of the Order	£30–50

347. INDIAN TITLE BADGE

Instituted: 12 December 1911.

Ribbon: Light blue edged with dark blue (1st class); red edged with dark red (2nd class); or dark blue edged with light blue (3rd class).

Metal: Silver or silver-gilt.

Size: Height 58mm; max. width 45mm.

Description: A radiate star topped by an imperial crown with a curved laurel wreath below the crown and cutting across the top of a central medallion surrounded by a collar inscribed with the appropriate title. The medallion bears the left-facing crowned profile of King George V or the right-facing crowned bust of King George VI. (Reverse) plain, but engraved with the name of the recipient.

Comments: *Introduced by King George V on the occasion of the Delhi Durbar of 1911 and awarded in three classes to civilians and Viceroy's commissioned officers of the Indian Army for faithful service or acts of public welfare. Recipients proceeded from the lowest grade to higher grades, each accompanied by a distinctive title. Each grade was issued in Hindu and Muslim versions, differing in title: Diwan Bahadur (Muslim) or Sardar Bahadur (Hindu), Khan Bahadur (Muslim) or Rai or Rao Bahadur (Hindu) and Khan Sahib (Muslim) or Rai or Rao Sahib (Hindu), in descending order of grade. These title badges took precedence after all British and Indian orders and decorations, and before campaign medals.*

VALUE:

Diwan Bahadur	£60–70
Sardar Bahadur	£60–70
Khan Bahadur	£50–60
Rao Bahadur	£50–60
Khan Sahib	£40–50
Rao Sahib	£40–50

348. BADGES OF THE CERTIFICATE OF HONOUR

Instiued: 1920.
Ribbon: Plain yellow 38mm (neck) or 32mm (breast).
Metal: Bronze (African) or silver-gilt (non-African).
Size: 65mm x 48mm (neck); 45mm x 33mm (breast).
Description: Oval badges with a raised rim of laurel leaves terminating at the top in an imperial crown flanked by two lions. (Obverse) a crowned effigy of the reigning monarch; (reverse) the crowned cypher of the monarch or some emblem symbolic of the particular territory (Africa), or the colonial coat of arms (non-African colonies and protectorates), with the name of the territory inscribed round the top.
Comments: *Certificates of Honour were awarded to chiefs and other non-European dignitaries of the Empire for loyal and valuable service. Since 1954 recipients have been given the option of taking their award as a neck or breast badge. Both African and non-African types when worn as a breast badge take precedence over coronation and jubilee medals. These awards were quite distinct from the decorations known as the Native Chiefs Medals (see number 70).*

VALUE:

George V	—
George VI	—
Elizabeth II (neck)	—
Elizabeth II (breast)	—

349. NAVAL ENGINEER'S GOOD CONDUCT MEDAL

Instituted: 1842.
Ribbon: Originally plain dark blue but later broad blue with white edges.
Metal: Silver.
Size: 35mm.
Description: (Obverse) a two-masted paddle steamer with a trident in the exergue; (reverse) a circular cable cartouche enclosing a crowned fouled anchor and the legend FOR ABILITY AND GOOD CONDUCT. Between the cable and the rim the details of the recipient were engraved round the circumference. Considering the rarity of the award, it is even more remarkable that the medals have several unique features. Shaw's medal, for example, had oak leaves in the exergue, flanking the trident, but this feature was omitted from later medals. Medals have been recorded with a straight bar suspender, a steel clip and ring suspender or fixed ring suspension with one or two intermediate rings.
Comments: *This medal was abolished five years after it was instituted, only seven medals being awarded in that period: to William Shaw (1842), William Dunkin (1842), William Johnstone (1843), John Langley (1843), J.P. Rundle (1845), George Roberts (1845) and Samuel B. Meredith (1846). Restrikes were produced in 1875 and at a later date. The original medals have a grooved rim, the 1875 restrikes a diagonal grained rim and the later restrikes a plain, flat rim.*

VALUE:

Original	Rare
1875 restrike	£120–140
Later restrike	£80–100

350. INDIAN RECRUITING BADGE (GEORGE V)

Instituted: 1917.
Ribbon: Plain dark green.
Metal: Bronze.
Size: Height 45mm; max. width 48mm.
Description: A five-pointed star with ball finials, surmounted by a wreathed gilt medallion bearing a left-facing crowned bust of King George V, inscribed FOR RECRUITING WORK DURING THE WAR.
Comments: *Awarded to Indian officers and NCOs engaged in recruitment of troops. It could only be worn in uniform when attending durbars or state functions, but at any time in plain clothes.*

VALUE:

George V	£50–60

351. INDIAN RECRUITING BADGE (GEORGE VI)

Instituted: 1940.
Ribbon: Emerald green divided into three sections interspersed by narrow stripes of red (left) and yellow (right).
Metal: Silver and bronze.
Size: Height 42mm; max. width 39mm.
Description: A multi-rayed silver breast badge surmounted by an imperial crown with a suspension ring fitted through the top of the crown. In the centre is superimposed a bronze medallion bearing the left-facing crowned profile of King George VI, within a collar inscribed FOR RECRUITING.
Comments: *Awarded to selected civilian and military pensioners, full-time members of the Indian Recruiting Organisation, fathers and mothers having at least three children in the armed services, and wives having a husband and at least two children serving in the defence forces.*

VALUE:

George VI	£40–50

352. NAVAL GOOD SHOOTING MEDAL

Instituted: August 1902.
Ribbon: Dark blue with a red central stripe edged in white.
Metal: Silver.
Size: 36mm.
Description: (Obverse) the effigy of the reigning monarch; (reverse) a nude figure of Neptune holding five thunderbolts in each hand. In the background can be seen the bows of a trireme and the heads of three horses, with a trident in the field. The Latin motto AMAT VICTORIA CURAM (Victory loves care) appears round the circumference. Fitted with a straight suspension bar. The recipient's name, number, rank, ship and calibre of gun are impressed round the rim.
Comments: *Instituted to promote excellent gunnery performances in the annual Fleet Competitions, it was first awarded in 1903 but was discontinued in 1914. Subsequent success was marked by the issue of a clasp bearing the name of the ship and the date. A total of 974 medals and 62 bars was awarded. 53 men received one bar, three men got two bars and only one achieved three bars.*

VALUE:

Edward VII	£180–200
George V	£200–220

353. ARMY BEST SHOT MEDAL

Instituted: 30 April 1869.

Ribbon: Watered crimson with black, white and black stripes at the edges.

Metal: Bronze or silver.

Size: 36mm.

Description: (Obverse) the veiled diademmed profile of Queen Victoria; (reverse) Victory bestowing a laurel crown on a naked warrior armed with a quiver of arrows and a bow and holding a target, impaled with arrows, in his other hand. Fitted with a straight suspension bar.

Comments: *This medal, sometimes referred to as the Queen's Medal, was awarded annually to the champion in the Army marksmanship contests held at Bisley. It was originally struck in bronze, but was upgraded to silver in 1872. The award ceased in 1882, but was revived in 1923 and thereafter known as the King's Medal. The original reverse was retained, with the appropriate effigy of the reigning sovereign on the obverse. Since 1953 it has been known as the Queen's Medal again. In the post-1923 medals a bar bears the year of the award, with additional year clasps for subsequent awards. Until 1934 a single medal was awarded each year, but in 1935 two medals were granted, for the champion shots of the Regular and Territorial Armies respectively. Subsequently additional medals have been sanctioned for award to the military forces of India, Canada, Australia, New Zealand, Ceylon, Rhodesia, the British South Africa Police, the Union of South Africa, Pakistan, Jamaica and Ghana.*

VALUE:

Victoria bronze	Rare
Victoria silver	Rare
George V	£700–800
George VI	£700–800
Elizabeth II	£700–800

354. QUEEN'S MEDAL FOR CHAMPION SHOTS OF THE ROYAL NAVY AND ROYAL MARINES

Instituted: 12 June 1953.

Ribbon: Dark blue with a red central stripe bordered white.

Metal: Silver.

Size: 36mm.

Description: (Obverse) the effigy of Queen Elizabeth II; (reverse) Neptune (as on the Naval Good Shooting Medal).

Comments: *Instituted as the naval counterpart of the Army best shot medal.*

VALUE:

Elizabeth II	£700–800

355. QUEEN'S MEDAL FOR CHAMPION SHOTS OF THE ROYAL AIR FORCE

Instituted: 12 June 1953.
Ribbon: Broad crimson centre flanked by dark blue stripes bisected by thin light blue stripes.
Metal: Silver.
Size: 36mm.
Description: (Obverse) the effigy of Queen Elizabeth II; (reverse) Hermes kneeling on a flying hawk and holding the caduceus in one hand and a javelin in the other. The recipient's details are engraved on the rim and the medal is fitted with a straight bar suspender.
Comments: *Competed for at the annual RAF Small Arms Meeting at Bisley.*

VALUE:
    Elizabeth II   —

356. QUEEN'S MEDAL FOR CHAMPION SHOTS OF THE NEW ZEALAND NAVAL FORCES

Instituted: 9 July 1958.
Ribbon: Crimson centre bordered with white and broad dark blue stripes at the edges.
Metal: Silver.
Size: 36mm.
Description: (Obverse) the effigy of Queen Elizabeth II; (reverse) similar to that of the Naval Good Shooting Medal of 1903-14. Fitted with a clasp bearing the year of the award and a straight suspension bar.
Comments: *Awards were made retrospective to 1 January 1955. This medal is awarded for marksmanship in an annual contest of the New Zealand Naval Forces. Additional clasps are granted for further success.*

VALUE:
    Elizabeth II   Rare

357. UNION OF SOUTH AFRICA COMMEMORATION MEDAL

Instituted: 1910.
Ribbon: 38mm orange-yellow with a broad central dark blue stripe.
Metal: Silver.
Size: 36mm.
Description: (Obverse) the effigy of King George V; (reverse) a blacksmith beating on an anvil the links of a chain, symbolising the unification of the four countries (Cape Colony, Natal, Orange Free State and the Transvaal), with the date in the exergue.
Comments: *Awarded to those who played a prominent part in the ceremonies connected with the Union, as well as to certain officers and men of HMS Balmoral Castle, a Union Castle liner specially commissioned as a man-of-war to convey HRH the Duke of Connaught as the King's representative to South Africa for the celebrations.*

VALUE:

	Named	Unnamed
George V	£250–300	£200–240

358. LOYAL SERVICE DECORATION

Instituted: 1920.

Ribbon: A broad dark blue central stripe flanked on one side by a gold bar with a thin red stripe superimposed towards the edge, and on the other side by a yellow bar with a thin white stripe towards the edge. Transvaal recipients wore the ribbon with the red to the centre of the chest; Orange Free State recipients wore the ribbon with the white stripe to the centre of the chest.

Metal: Silver.

Size: 36mm.

Description: (Obverse) the arms of the Transvaal; (reverse) the arms of the Orange Free State. Fitted with a swivel suspender. Recipients wore the medal with the appropriate state arms showing.

Comments: *Awarded by the Union of South Africa to officers of the two former Boer republics for distinguished service during the Second Boer War of 1899-1902.*

VALUE:

Silver (591)   £100–150

359. ANGLO-BOER WAR MEDAL

Instituted: 1920.

Ribbon: Broad green and yellow stripes with three narrow stripes of red, white and dark blue in the centre. Transvaal recipients wore the ribbon with the green to the centre of the chest, while Orange Free State recipients wore it with the yellow towards the centre.

Metal: Silver.

Size: 36mm.

Description: Both sides inscribed ANGLO-BOER OORLOG round the top, with the dates 1899-1902 round the foot. Medallions set in a border of a square and quatrefoil show the arms of the Orange Free State on one side and the Transvaal on the other. The medal was worn with the side showing the arms of the appropriate state uppermost. Fitted with a straight bar swivelling suspender.

Comments: *Awarded by the Union government to officers and men of the former Boer republics for loyal service in the war against the British.*

VALUE:

Silver   £60–70

360. COMMONWEALTH INDEPENDENCE MEDALS

Since the partition of the Indian sub-continent in 1947 and the emergence of the Dominions of India and Pakistan, it has been customary for medals to be issued to mark the attainment of independence. As these medals are invariably awarded to British service personnel taking part in the independence ceremonies, they are appended here, in chronological order of institution, the date of the actual award, where later, being given in parentheses. These medals invariably have symbolic motifs with the date of independence inscribed. The distinctive ribbons are noted alongside. All are 32mm wide unless otherwise stated.

India 1947 (1948) three equal stripes of orange, white and green
Pakistan 1947 (1950) dark green with a central thin white stripe
Nigeria 1960 (1964) three equal stripes of green, white and green
Sierra Leone 1961 three equal stripes of green, white and blue
Jamaica 1962 black centre flanked by yellow stripes and green edges
Uganda 1962 (1963) six stripes of black, yellow, red, black, yellow and red
Malawi 1964 three equal stripes of black, red and green
Guyana 1966 36mm red centre flanked by yellow stripes and broad green edges. The green and yellow separated (left) by a thin black stripe and (right) by a thin pale blue stripe
Fiji 1970 Grey-blue with bars half red, half white, towards each end
Papua New Guinea 1975 Red bordered by thin stripes of yellow and white, with black edges
Solomon Islands 1978 five equal stripes of blue, yellow, white, yellow and green
Gilbert Islands (Kiribati) 1980 half red, half black, separated by a thin white stripe, and edged in yellow
Ellice Islands (Tuvalu) 1980 equal stripes of red, white and red edged yellow. the white stripe bisected by a thin black stripe
Zimbabwe 1980 Silver or bronze 38mm black centre flanked by red and yellow stripes with edges of green or blue
Vanuatu 1980 (1981) 25mm four equal stripes of red, black, yellow and dark brown
St Christopher, Nevis and Anguilla 1983 bars of green (left) and red (right) with a black central bar having two thin white stripes, flanked by yellow stripes

VALUE: From £20

361. MALTA GEORGE CROSS FIFTIETH ANNIVERSARY COMMEMORATIVE MEDAL

Instituted: 1992.
Ribbon: Watered dark blue with central stripes of white and red (the Maltese national colours).
Metal: Cupro-nickel.
Size: 36mm.
Description: (Obverse) the crowned arms of the island, which include the George Cross in the upper left corner, with the date 1992 at the foot. (Reverse) a replica of the George Cross with the eight-pointed Maltese Cross at the top and the date 1942 at the foot, with a legend BHALA SHIEDA TA'EROIZMU U DEDIKAZZJONI on one side and TO BEAR WITNESS TO HEROISM AND DEVOTION on the other. Suspension is by a fixed bar decorated with laurels, attached to a ring.
Comments: *Sanctioned by the government of Malta to celebrate the fiftieth anniversary of the award of the George Cross by King George VI to the island for its heroic resistance to prolonged Axis attack during the Second World War. The medal has been awarded to surviving veterans who served in Malta in the armed forces and auxiliary services between 10 June 1940 and 8 September 1943. Permission for British citizens to wear this medal was subsequently granted by the Queen.*

VALUE:
    Cupro-nickel   —

362. SHANGHAI JUBILEE MEDAL

Instituted: 1893.
Ribbon: Watered silk half bright red, half white.
Metal: Silver or bronze.
Size: 36mm.
Description: (Obverse) triple-shield arms of the municipality surrounded by a band with thistles, shamrocks and roses round the foot and NOVEMBER 17 1843 round the top. (Reverse) a scrolled shield with the words SHANGHAI JUBILEE and NOVEMBER 17 1843 and inscribed diagonally across the centre with the recipient's name in block capitals. The shield is flanked by Chinese dragons and above is a steamship and the sun setting on the horizon. The rim is engraved 'Presented by the Shanghai Municipality'. Issued with a small suspension ring, but often replaced by a straight bar.
Comments: *The British settlement in Shanghai was founded in 1843 and formed the nucleus of the International Settlement established in 1854 under the control of an autonomous Municipal Council. In effect the International Settlement was a quasi-British colony (not unlike Hong Kong in fact) until overrun by Imperial Japanese troops in 1941.*

VALUE:
Silver (625)	—
Bronze (100)	—

363. SHANGHAI MUNICIPAL COUNCIL EMERGENCY MEDAL

Instituted: 1937.
Ribbon: 38mm bright red, having a broad white central stripe bordered black and yellow edges separated from the red by thin black stripes.
Metal: Bronze.
Size: 40mm.
Description: An eight-pointed star with ring suspension. (Obverse) a central medallion superimposed on the radiate star with the triple-shield arms of the Municipality surrounded by a collar inscribed SHANGHAI MUNICIPAL COUNCIL. (Reverse) a laurel wreath enclosing the words FOR SERVICES RENDERED - AUGUST 12 TO NOVEMBER 12 1937.
Comments: *Awarded to members of the Police, Volunteer Corps, Fire Brigade and civilians for services during the emergency of August-November 1937 when fighting between the Chinese and Japanese in and around Shanghai threatened to encroach on the International Settlement. Issued unnamed, but accompanied by a certificate bearing the name and unit of the recipient.*

VALUE:
Bronze star	—

364. SHANGHAI VOLUNTEER CORPS LONG SERVICE MEDAL

Instituted: 1921.
Ribbon: Equal bands of red, white and blue, the red bisected by a thin green stripe, the white by black and the blue by yellow.
Metal: Silver.
Size: 36mm.
Description: (Obverse) an eight-pointed radiate star bearing a scroll at the top inscribed 4th APRIL 1854. The arms of the Municipality superimposed on the star and surrounded by a collar inscribed SHANGHAI VOLUNTEER CORPS. Round the foot of the medal is a band inscribed FOR LONG SERVICE. (Reverse) plain, engraved with the name of the recipient and his period of service.
Comments: *The Volunteer Corps was raised in 1853 to protect the British and other foreign settlements. The date on the scroll alludes to the Corps' first engagement, the Battle of Muddy Flat. The Corps was cosmopolitan in structure, although the British element predominated. It was disbanded in September 1942 after the Japanese overran the International Settlement. The medal was awarded for 12 years good service.*

VALUE
Silver	—

365. SHANGHAI MUNICIPAL POLICE DISTINGUISHED CONDUCT MEDAL

Instituted: 1924.
Ribbon: Red with a central blue stripe (1st class); red with a blue stripe at each edge (2nd class).
Metal: Silver or bronze.
Size: 36mm.
Description: (Obverse) arms of the Municipality and the inscription SHANGHAI MUNICIPAL POLICE; (reverse) the words FOR DISTINGUISHED CONDUCT. The recipient's name and rank was engraved round the rim.
Comments: *Awarded to officers and men of the Municipal Police in two classes, distinguished solely by their ribbons and the metal used (silver or bronze). A sliding clasp was fitted to the ribbon to denote a second award; this featured the Municipal crest and was engraved on the reverse with the details of the award.*

VALUE:
    Silver   —
    Bronze   —

366. SHANGHAI MUNICIPAL POLICE LONG SERVICE MEDAL

Instituted: 1925.
Ribbon: Brown with a central yellow band edged in white.
Metal: Silver.
Size: 36mm.
Description: (Obverse) arms of the Municipality within a collar inscribed SHANGHAI MUNICIPAL POLICE; (reverse) plain apart from the inscription FOR LONG SERVICE in two lines across the centre. The recipient's name and rank were engraved round the rim in upper and lower case lettering. Fitted with a swivelling scroll suspender.
Comments: *Awarded for 12 years good service in the Shanghai Municipal Police, an international force composed largely of Sikhs, Chinese and White Russians as well as British ex-soldiers and policemen. Dated clasps for further five year periods of service were awarded. The medal was abolished in 1942.*

VALUE:
    Silver   £280–300

367. SHANGHAI MUNICIPAL SPECIAL CONSTABULARY LONG SERVICE MEDAL

Instituted: 1929.
Ribbon: Dark brown with three white bars, each bisected by a thin yellow stripe.
Metal: Silver.
Size: 36mm.
Description: (Obverse) the arms of the Municipality with the motto OMNIA JUNCTA IN UNO (all joined in one) round the circumference. (Reverse) inscribed SHANGHAI MUNICIPAL POLICE (SPECIALS) FOR LONG SERVICE in six lines. A unique award to A.L. Anderson (1930) was inscribed on the reverse FOR DISTINGUISHED AND VALUABLE SERVICES.
Comments: *Awarded for 12 years active and efficient service in the Special Constabulary. Some 52 medals and 8 clasps for additional service are recorded in the* Shanghai Gazette, *but the actual number awarded was probably greater. The medal was discontinued in 1942.*

VALUE:
    With clasp   —
    Without clasp   —

368. SHANGHAI VOLUNTEER FIRE BRIGADE LONG SERVICE MEDAL

Instituted: 1904.
Ribbon: Red with white edges.
Metal: Gold, silver or bronze.
Size: 36mm.
Description: (Obverse) the arms and motto of the Municipality surrounded by a collar inscribed SHANGHAI VOLUNTEER FIRE BRIGADE ESTABLISHED 1866. (Reverse) a pair of crossed axes surmounted by a fireman's helmet under which is a horizontal tablet on which are engraved the recipient's dates of service. Round the circumference is inscribed FOR LONG SERVICE (top) and WE FIGHT THE FLAMES (foot) with quatrefoil ornaments separating the two inscriptions. Fitted with a swivelling scroll suspender.
Comments: *The medal in silver was awarded to members of the Volunteer Fire Brigade for five years service, for eight years service a clasp was added to the ribbon and for 12 years service the medal was awarded in gold. Bronze medals exist but are believed to have been specimens only.*

VALUE: —

ABBREVIATIONS AND INITIALS

The medal collector is constantly coming across initials and abbreviations on medals and in documents—many of which are commonplace and easily decipherable. However, there are many more which can cause problems when trying to identify a medal recipient. The following list represents only a small selection of the inexhaustible number of abbreviations encountered, but hopefully it will be of some assistance to the collector.

1 E Ang 1st East Anglian Regiment
1 R Dgns 1st Royal Dragoons
1 QDG 1st Queen's Dragoon Guards
11H 11th Royal Hussars
12L 12th Royal Lancers
13/18H 13th/18th Royal Hussars
14/20H 14th/20th Royal Hussars
15/19H 15th/19th Royal Hussars
3 E Ang 3rd East Anglian Regiment
4 QOH 4th Queen's Own Hussars
4H 4th Royal Hussars
5 DGds 5th Royal Inniskilling Dragoon Guards
7QOH 7th Queen's Own Hussars
7GR 7th Gurkha Rifles
A/ Acting
A Avn Army Aviation
Abn Inf Airborne Infantry
A/CWEM Acting Chief Weapons Engineering Mechanic
A/LMEM Acting Leading Marine Engineering Mechanic
A/LRO(G) Acting Leading Radio Operator (General)
A/PO Acting Petty Officer
A&SH The Argyll and Sutherland Highlanders
AAC Army Air Corps
AAU Air Ambulance Unit
AB Able Seaman; Airborne
ABDS Army Bomb Disposal Squad
AC Aircrewman
ACC Army Catering Corps
ADALS Assistant Director, Army Legal Service
AE Army Education Officer
AER Army Emergency Reserve
AFM Air Force Medal
AGS Africa General Service Medal
AIY Ayrshire Imperial Yeomanry
ALO Air Liaison Officer
ALS Army Legal Services
AM Albert Medal
AMA Acting Master at Arms
AMS Assistant Military Secretary; Army Medical Staff

AOC Army Ordnance Corps
APC Army Pay Corps
APTC Army Physical Training Corps
AQ Assistant Quartermaster; Administrative Quartermaster
Armd Armoured
ASC Army Service Corps; Air Service Command
ATO Ammunition Technical Officer
B&H The Bedfordshire & Hertfordshire Regiment
B&R Blues & Royals
BAAT British Army Advisory Team
BATT British Army Training Team
BAO British Army of Occupation
Bdr Bombadier
BDU Bomb Disposal Unit
BEM British Empire Medal
BF British Forces
BGS Brigadier, General Staff
BIY Bedford Imperial Yeomanry
BM Brigade Major
BORD.R Border Regiment
BR British
Brig Brigadier
Br Coy Bearer Company
BSA Police British South Africa Police
Buffs The Buffs (Royal East Kent Regiment)
BW Black Watch (Royal Highland Regiment)
BWM British War Medal
C&TC Commissariat and Transport Corps
C/Sgt Colour Sergeant
C&S Command & Staff
CAC Canadian Armoured Corps
CADAC Canadian Army Dental Corps
CAEA Chief Air Engineering Artificer
CAHTC Cape Auxiliary Horse Transport Corps
CAMN HIGH Cameron Highlanders
Capt Captain
CAR Central African Rifles
CASC Canadian Army Service Corps
CATO Commander Ammunition Technical Officers
CB Commander of the Order of the Bath
CBE Commander of the Order of the British Empire
CBF Commander British Forces

CC   Cadet Corps; Coastal Command; Combat Command
CCAEA   Charge Chief Air Engineering Artificer
CCCC   Cape Colony Cyclist Corps
CCMEA   Charge Chief Marine Engineering Artificer
CCS   Casualty Clearing Station
CD   Clearance Diver
C de G   Croix de Guerre
Cdr   Commander
CE   Canadian Engineers
CEO   Chief Executive Officer; Chief Education Officer
CG   Coast Guard; Commanding General
CGM   Conspicuous Gallantry Medal
Cheshire   The Cheshire Regiment
CI   Crown of India, Imperial Order; Counter-Intelligence
CIV   City Imperial Volunteers
CIE   Companion of the Order of the Indian Empre
CLY   County of London Yeomanry
CMEM   Chief Marine Engineering Mechanic
CMFR   Commonwealth Monitoring Force Rhodesia
CMG   Companion of the Order of St Michael and St George
CMM   Commander of the Order of Military Merit
CMO   Chief Medical Officer
CMMP   Corps of Military Mounted Police
CMP   Corps of Military Police
CMSC   Cape Medical Staff Corps
CMR   Cape Mounted Riflemen
CO   Commanding Officer
Col   Colonel
Coldm Gds   Coldstream Guards
Comd   Commander
COS   Chief of Staff
CP   Cape Police
CPO   Chief Petty Officer
CPOAEA   Chief Petty Officer Air Engineering Artificer
CPOWEA   Chief Petty Officer Weapons Engineering Artificer
CSI   Companion of the Order of the Star of India
CSM   Company Sergeant Major; Campaign Service Medal
CVO   Commander of the Royal Victorian Order
D   Diver
D Comd   Deputy Commander
D&D   The Devon and Dorset Regiment
DAD   Deputy Assistant Director
DADOS   Deputy Assistant Director of Ordnance Services
DADVRS   Deputy Assistant Director Veterinary & Remount Section
DAMA   Department of the Army Material Annex
DANS   Director of Army Nursing Services
DAPM   Deputy Assistant Provost Marshall
DAT   Director of Army Training
DBE   Dame Commander, Order of the British Empire
DCLI   The Duke of Cornwall's Light Infantry
DCM   Distinguished Conduct Medal
DCMG   Dame Commander of the Order of St Michael and St George
DCO   Duke of Cambridge's Own; Duke of Connaught's Own
DCOS   Deputy Chief of Staff

DCVO   Dame Commander of the Royal Victorian Order
DDSD   Deputy Director Staff Duties
DEO   Duke of Edinburgh's Own
DERR   The Duke of Edinburgh's Royal Regiment (Berkshire & Wiltshire)
Det   Detached; Detachment
Devon   The Devonshire Regiment
DFC   Distinguished Flying Cross
DFM   Distinguished Flying Medal
DG   Dragoon Guards
DI   Defence Intelligence
DLI   The Durham Light Infantry
DMT   District Mounted Troops
Dorset   The Dorset Regiment
DOS   Director of Ordnance Services
DS   Defence Secretary; Deputy Secretary; Defensive Section
DSC   Distinguished Service Cross
DSM   Distinguished Service Medal
DSO   Distinguished Service Order
DWR   The Duke of Wellington's Regiment
EAR   East African Rifles
ED   Efficiency Decoration
EF   Expeditionary Force
EGM   Empire Gallantry Medal
EM   Edward Medal; Efficiency Medal
EOD   Explosive Ordnance Disposal
ERD   Emergency Reserve Decoration
ERE   Extra Regimentally Employed
FA   Field Ambulance
FANYC   First Aid Nursing Yeomanry Corps
FBRA   Field Battery Royal Artillery
FC   Fighter Command
Fd   Field
FELF   Far East Land Forces
FF   Field Force
FFL   French Foreign Legion
FFR   Frontier Force Rifles
FM   Field Marshal
FMR   Frontier Mounted Rifles
FO   Flying Officer
FS   Fighter Squadron; Field Security
Fus   Fusilier
G Howards   Green Howards (Alexandra, Princess of Wales's Own Yorkshire Regiment)
G Or   General Operational Requirements
GBE   Grand Cross, Order of the British Empire
GC   George Cross
GCB   Knight Grand Cross Order of the Bath
GCH   Knight Grand Cross Hanoverian Order
GCIE   Knight Grand Commander Order of the Indian Empire
GCLH   Grand Cross Legion of Honour
GCM   Good Conduct Medal
GCMG   Knight Grand Cross Order of St Michael and St George
GCSI   Knight Grand Commander Order of the Star of India
GCVO   Knight Grand Cross Royal Victorian Order
Gdsmn   Guardsman
GLI   Guernsey Light Infantry
Glosters   The Gloucestershire Regiment (28th/61st Foot)
GM   George Medal
GMB   Grand Master Order of the Bath

GMBE Grand Master Order of the British Empire
GMIE Grand Master Order of the Indian Empire
GMMG Grand Master Order of St Michael and St George
GMSI Grand Master Order of the Star of India
GOC General Officer Commanding
Gordons The Gordon Highlanders (75th/92nd Regiment)
GPR Glider Pilot Regiment
GR Gurkha Rifles
Gren Gds Grenadier Guards
GS General Service
GSC General Service Corps
GSM General Service Medal
GSO General Staff Officer
HA Horse Artillery
HAC Honourable Artillery Company
HBM Her Britannic Majesty
HCR Household Cavalry Regiment
HG Home Guard; Horse Guards
HLI The Highland Light Infantry
HQ Headquarters
IAOC Indian Army Ordnance Corps
IASC Indian Army Service Corps
IC In Charge
IDSM Indian Distinguished Service Medal
IE Order of the Indian Empire
IG Irish Guards
Int Intelligence
Int Corps Intelligence Corps
Int & Svy Coy Intelligence and Surveillance Company
IO Intelligence Officer
IOM Indian Order of Merit
ISM Imperial Service Medal
ISO Imperial Service Order
IY Imperial Yeomanry
JSSC Joint Services Staff College
KAR King's African Rifles
KB Knight Bachelor
KBE Knight of the Order of the British Empire
KC Knight Commander
KCB Knight Commander Order of the Bath
KCH Knight Commander of the Royal Hanoverian Guelphic Order
KCIE Knight Commander Order of the Indian Empire
KCIO King's Commissioned Indian Officer
KCMG Knight Commander Order of St Michael and St George
KCSI Knight Commander Order of the Star of India
KCVO Knight Commander Royal Victorian Order
KDG King's Dragoon Guards
KG Knight of the Order of the Garter
KGCB Knight Grand Cross Order of the Bath
KGL King's German Legion
Kings The King's Regiment (Liverpool)
KLH Knight of the Legion of Honour
KM King's Medal
KOM Knight of the Order of Malta
KORB The King's Own Royal Border Regiment
KOSB The King's Own Scottish Borderers
KOYLI The King's Own Yorkshire Light Infantry
KPM King's Police Medal
KRRC The King's Royal Rifle Corps
KSG Knight of the Order of St George

KSLI The King's Shropshire Light Infantry
KT Knight of the Order of the Thistle
L/Cpl Lance Corporal
L/Sgt Lance Sergeant
LAC Leading Aircrewman
Lanc Fusiliers The Lancashire Fusiliers
Lanc R The Queen's Lancashire Regiment
LC Labour Corps
Leic The Royal Leicestershire Regiment
LG Life Guards; London Gazette
LI Light Infantry
Linc The Royal Lincolnshire Regiment
LM Legion of Merit
LMA Leading Medical Assistant
LS Leading Seaman
Lt Lieutenant
Lt-Cdr Lieutenant Commander
Lt-Col Lieutenant-Colonel
MA Military Attache
Maint Maintenance
Maj Major
Maj-Gen Major-General
Mal.LBC Maltese Labour Corps
MBE Member of the Order of the British Empire
MC Military Cross
MEM Marine Engineering Mechanic
MFA Mercantile Fleet Auxiliary
MFS Medical Field Service
MGC Machine Gun Corps
MH Medal of Honour
MI Mounted Infantry
MID Mentioned in Despatches
MKW Military Knights of Windsor
MM Military Medal; Medal of Merit
MMGS Motor Machine Gun Service
Mne Marine
MMR Mercantile Marine Service
MR Middlesex Regiment
MRCVS Member Royal College of Veterinary Surgeons
MSC Medical Staff Corps
MSM Meritorious Service Medal
MTO Motor Transport Office
MVO Member of the Royal Victorian Order
N Lanc The North Lancashire Regiment
NACS Naval Air Commando Squadron
NAS Naval Air Squadron
NCO Non-Commissioned Officer
NFA Natal Field Artillery
NGS Naval General Service (Medal)
NZEF New Zealand Expeditionary Force
OBE Officer of the Order of the British Empire
OBI Order of British India
OBLI Ox and Bucks Light Infantry
OC Officer Commanding
OCS Officer Cadet School
OEO Ordnance Executive Officer
OHBMS On Her Britannic Majesty's Service
OM Order of Merit
OR Operational Requirements; Other Ranks; Organised Reserve
Ord Ordnance
OS Ordinary Seaman; Ordnance Survey
PAOCVA Prince Albert's Own Cape Volunteer Rifles
PAVG Prince Albert's Volunteer Guard

Para The Parachute Regiment
PO Petty Officer
PO/AC Petty Officer Aircrewman
POMA Petty Officer Medical Assistant
POMEM Petty Officer Marine Engineering Mechanic
PR Public Relations
PSO Personnel Selection Officer
Pte Private
PVCP Permanent Vehicle Check Point
PWO The Prince of Wales's Own Regiment of Yorkshire
Q Ops Quartermaster General Branch Operations
QARANC Queen Alexandra's Royal Army Nursing Corps
QC Queen's Commendation for Brave Conduct
QFSM Queen's Fire Service Medal
QDG The Queen's Dragoon Guards
QGM Queen's Gallantry Medal
QLR The Queen's Lancashire Regiment
QM Quartermaster
QMAAC Queen Mary's Auxiliary Ambulance Corps
QORGY Queen's Own Royal Gloucester Yeomanry
QPM Queen's Police Medal
QRIH Queen's Royal Irish Hussars
QSA Queen's South Africa (Medal)
Queens The Queen's Regiment—Queen's Division
R Anglian Royal Anglian Regiment
R Fus Royal Fusiliers (City of London Regiment)
R Hamps The Royal Hampshire Regiment (37th / 67th Foot)
R Innis Royal Inniskilling
R Middlesex The Middlesex Regiment
R Signals Royal Corps of Signals
R Sussex The Royal Sussex Regiment
R Warwickshire The Royal Warwickshire Regiment
RA Regiment of Artillery
RAC Royal Armoured Corps
RAChD Royal Army Chaplains Department
RAEC Royal Army Educational Corps
RAFVR Royal Airforce Volunteer Reserve
RAMC Royal Army Medical Corps
RAOC Royal Army Ordnance Corps
RAPC Royal Army Pay Corps
RARO Regular Army Reserve of Officers
RASC Royal Army Service Corps
RAVC Royal Army Veterinary Corps
RB The Rifle Brigade
RTC Royal Corps of Transport
RE Corps of Royal Engineers
RECC Reconnaissance Corps
REME Corps of Royal Electrical and Mechanical Engineers
RF Royal Fusiliers
RFA Royal Field Artillery
Rfmn Rifleman
RGJ Royal Greenjackets
RHA Royal Horse Artillery
RHF The Royal Highland Fusiliers
RHG Royal Horse Guards
RI Royal Irish Rangers (27th (Inniskilling), 83rd and 87th)
RI Regt Royal Irish Regiment
RIC Royal Irish Corps
RIF The Royal Irish Fusiliers

RM Royal Marines
RMC Royal Military College / Royal Military Academy
RMLI Royal Marine Light Infantry
RMP Corps of Royal Military Police
RNF The Royal Northumberland Fusiliers
RNR Royal Naval Reserve
RNVR Royal Naval Volunteer Reserve
RO Radio Operator
RPC Royal Pioneer Corps
RRC Royal Red Cross (Medal)
RRF Royal Regiment of Fusiliers
RRW Royal Regiment of Wales
RS The Royal Scots (The Royal Regiment)
RSDG Royal Scots Dragoon Guards
RSF Royal Scots Fusiliers
R Sig Royal Signals
RSM Regimental Sergeant Major
RSO Regimental Supply Officer
RTR Royal Tank Regiment, Royal Armoured Corps
RUR The Royal Ulster Rifles
RVM Royal Victorian Medal
RVO Royal Victorian Order
RWF The Royal Welsh Fusiliers
RWK The Queen's Own Royal West Kent Regiment
RW Kent R Royal West Kent Regiment
S/L Squadron Leader
S/Sgt Staff Sergeant
SAC Special Air Corps
SAS Special Air Service Regiment
SC Staff College; Staff Captain; Second in Command; Signal Corps
SF Special Forces
SG Scots Guards
SGM Sea Gallantry Medal
Sgmn Signalman
Sgt Sergeant
SI Star of India (Order)
SJAB St John Ambulance Brigade
SMIO Special Military Intelligence Officer
SMIU Special Military Intelligence Unit
Smn Seaman
SO1 Staff Officer, Grade 1
Som LI Somerset Light Infantry
SWB The South Wales Borderers
TA Territorial Army
T&AVR Territorial and Army Volunteer Reserve
TEM Territorial Efficiency Medal
TF Territorial Force
TG Town Guard
Trg Gp Training Group
UKLF United Kingdom Land Forces
UNM United Nations Medal
UNSM United Nations Service Medal
V&A Victoria and Albert (Order)
VC Victoria Cross
WAAF Women's Auxiliary Air Force
WAFF West Afican Frontier Force
W/Cdr Wing Commander
W&S Worcestershire & Sherwood Foresters
WEA Weapons Engineering Artificer
WG Welsh Guards
Wilts Wiltshire Regiment
WOI Warrant Officer Class I
WOII Warrant Officer Class II
WRAC Women's Royal Army Corps

RESEARCHING YOUR MEDALS

The fact that many British medals are named enables the serious collector to engage in researching both the life and service history of the recipient as well as being able to learn about the history of his regiment/ship/unit or whatever with which he served. There is no easy or definitive guide to the range of research materials that are available, nor to the type of information likely to be found.The sort of information available varies greatly depending on whether the recipient was an officer or other rank, the service and unit with which he served, and the period at which he served. The experience and perseverance of the researcher can also affect the outcome.

When researching a medal and its recipient, experienced collectors regularly refer to a mixture of manuscript and printed sources:

Manuscript Sources

The Public Record Office (PRO, Ruskin Avenue, Kew, Middx) and the India Office Library and Records (IOR, Blackfriars Bridge Road, London SE1) are the two major depositories of official records of interest to the medal collector. Generally speaking the collector of medals to the British Armed Services will find the PRO records essential to their enquiries, whilst anyone interest in the Indian Army and Navy (formerly the armed services of the Honourable East India Company), also the participation of British Forces in Indian campaigns, will find the IOR to be an essential source of information. County Record Offices, National Libraries and Museums, and also Regimental Museums can also have important holdings of manuscript records.

A first visit to the PRO and the IOR can be daunting. The range of records held by both Record Offices is also awe-inspiring once research has gone beyond consulting medal rolls and service papers.

Whilst there is no substitute for *experience* in learning successfully to branch out from the main stream of records, it is important to be well prepared. It is important to have some idea of where to start looking and to realise the scope and limitations of the documents—it should be noted that the PRO is subject to the standard 30 year closure rule for records, with many personal records being closed for longer periods. A great deal of time can be spent in simply locating the relevant references and to help you be more informed and to help eliminate time-wasting there are a number of important guides available that will help you to locate the most relevant documents you wish to consult:

Cox, J. and Padfield, T., *Tracing your Ancestors in the Public Record Office*(1983).

Farrington, A., *Guide to the Records of the India Office Military Department* (1981).

Hamilton-Edwards, Gerald, *In Search of Army Ancestry* (1977).

Holding, N., *The Location of British Army Records: A National Directory of World War I Sources* (1984).

Holding, N., *World War I Army Ancestry* (1982).

Rodger, N.A.M., *Naval Records for Genealogists* (1988).

In addition it is worth noting that
1. The Public Record Office produces a range of leaflets which provide useful information about particular classes of records—records relating to military, naval and air services are particularly well-covered. The leaflets are free to visitors to the PRO.
2. The Mormons have published a wide range of guides to genealogical research which cover subjects of interest to medal/military researchers.
3. The National Army Museum occasionally holds a study day on the subject military research
4. New information is becoming available all the time and in new forms: for example, the PRO has been producing a video on genealogical research in all its manifestations.

Medal Entitlement/Verification

Most collectors start their research by checking with the campaign medal roll (if available) that the recipient is indeed entitled to the medal and any clasps. This is a logical point at which to begin. This is often regarded as a simple, routine procedure, but for the unwary there are pitfalls and complications. The following points should always be borne in mind:

1. Printed medal rolls will always contain errors in transcription, thus any discrepancies between a medal and the roll should whenever possible be checked back with the original manuscript roll. The more complex the original roll, the more transcription

errors are likely to occur (for example, the claimaints' lists for Naval General Service Medal 1793-1840 and even the Military General Service Medal 1793-1814 are good examples of rolls where difficulties are likely to arise).

2. Some rolls have not survived—for example that for the Gwalior Campaign 1843. In such instances prize or bhatta rolls may exist at either the Public Record Office or the India Office. The inclusion of a recipient's name will at least indicate that he was most likely "entitled" to a medal and/or clasp (prize rolls indicate the share of money—realised from the loot captured in an action and then sold—allocated to each participant; bhatta is an extra allowance of pay made for field service).

3. Some medal rolls are incomplete, some of the regimental rolls for the Crimea Medal 1854–56.

4. For many campaigns and medals many supplementary and late claimants lists have not survived.

5. Some medal rolls are difficult to search and therefore one has to take time in understanding the background to the documents one is looking at - the various lists of recipients for the Military General Service Medal 1794–1840 is a case in point.

It is important to note that the establishment of a recipient's entitlement is not the same thing as verifying a medal. Verification also requires the numismatic knowledge to know that the medal and clasps appear genuine. Where entitlement cannot be confirmed from the medal rolls, some collectors may be happy to rely on their numismatic knowledge to assure themselves that a medal is "genuine".

Published Sources

The published literature on medals is far-reaching and diverse, ranging from simply-produced booklets to detailed studies published in several volumes. A full bibliography of medallic and related works would in itself fill several volumes, particularly if fully cross-referenced.

The references which follow seek to provide a useful list of publications which either relate to orders, decorations and medals in general or to specific items in particular; the list includes medal rolls and casualty lists. No attempt has been made to include journal articles, as this would be an immense task; however a list of useful periodicals, some of which publish regular indexes, appears at the end.

Suggestions for other works that might be considered for inclusion in the next Yearbook are welcomed.

Most collectors seek to build up a solid library which reflects their main interests, but inevitably there are always books that have to be consulted elsewhere. Major libraries and national museums, such as the British Museum Library, the National Army Museum, The Imperial War Museum, the Hendon Royal Air Force Museum, the Greenwich Maritime Museum, and the Portsmouth Naval Musuem have extensive holdings of relevant material which can be consulted on the premises. City and County Reference Libraries are important for collectors who rarely visit London. Some Regimental Museums have libraries attached. Most libraries of any size will have a subject index to their collection of books (and sometimes manuscripts and photographs).

ORDERS, DECORATIONS AND MEDALS: GENERAL WORKS
(listed in alphabetical order by author)

Alexander, E.G.M., Barron, G.K.B. and Bateman, A.J., *South African Orders, Decorations and Medals* (1986).

Blatherwick, Surg. Cmdr. F.J., *Canadian Orders, Decorations and Medals* (1983).

Burke, J.B., *The Book of Orders of Knighthood and Decorations of Honour of All Nations* (1858).

Downey, M., *The Standard Catalogue of Orders, Decorations and Medals Awarded to Australians* (1971).

Elvin, C.N., *A Handbook of the Orders of Chivalry, War Medals and Crosses with Their Clasps and Ribbons and Other Decorations* (1892).

Hastings Irwin, D., *War Medals and Decorations* (1910).

Hieronymussen, Paul, *Orders, Medals and Decorations of Britain and Europe* (1967).

Honours and Awards of the Army, Navy and Air Force 1914-20 (1979).

Irwin, Ross W., *War Medals and Decorations of Canada* (1969).

Jocelyn, A., *Awards of Honour* (1956).

Litherland, A.R. and Simpkin, B.T., *Spink's Standard Catalogue of British Orders, Decorations and Medals* (1990).

Mayo, J.H., *Medals and Decorations of the British Army and Navy* (1897).

Mericka, V., *Book of Orders and Decorations* (1975).

Monick, S., *South African Military Awards 1912-1987* (1988).

Monick, S., *Awards of the South African Uniformed Public Services 1922-1987* (1988).

Narbeth, Colin, *Collecting Military Medals* (1971).

Nicolas, N.H., *History of the Orders of Knighthood of the British Empire; of the Order of the Guelphs of Hanover, and of the Medals, Clasps and Crosses, Conferred for Naval and Military Services* (1842).

Payne, A.A., *A Handbook of British and Foreign Orders, War Medals and Decorations awarded to the Army and Navy* (1911).

Purves, A.A., *Collecting Medals and Decorations* (1968).

Purves, A.A., *The Medals, Decorations and Orders of the Great War 1914-18* (1975).

Purves, A.A., *The Medals, Decorations and Orders of World War II 1939-45* (1986).

Purves, Alec A., *Orders, Decorations and Medals, a Select Bibliography* (1958).

Steward, W.A., *War Medals and Their History* (1915).

Tancred, G., *Historical Record of Medals and Honorary Distinctions* (1891).

Taprell-Dorling, Captain H. (ed. Alec A. Purves), *Ribbons and Medals* (1983).

ORDERS OF KNIGHTHOOD
(listed by the Order of Precedence)
GENERAL
De la Bere, Sir I. *The Queen's Orders of Chivalry* (1961).

Risk, J.C., *British Orders and Decorations* (1973).

ORDER OF ST PATRICK
Galloway, Peter, *The Order of St Patrick* (1983).

Grierson, G.A. and Grierson, J.F., *Statutes and Ordinances of the Most Illustrious Order of St. Patrick* (1831).

ORDER OF THE BATH
Risk, J.C., *The History of the Order of the Bath and its Insignia* (1982).

ORDER OF ST MICHAEL AND ST GEORGE
Abela, A.E., *The Order of St Michael and St George in Malta* (1988).

ORDER OF THE BRITISH EMPIRE
Burke, *Handbook to the Order of the British Empire* (1921).

ORDER OF ST. JOHN
Tozer, C.W., *The Insignia and Medals of the Grand Priory of the Most Venerable Order of the Hospital of St John of Jerusalem* (1975).

DECORATIONS & LIFE SAVING AWARDS
(books listed in alphabetical order by name of medal)
GENERAL
Abbott, P.E. and Tamplin, J.M.A., *British Gallantry Awards* (1981).
Clarke, John D., *Gallantry Medals and Awards of the World* (1993).
Dickson, W.R., *Seedie's Roll of Naval Honours & Awards 1939-59* (1990).
Honours & Awards to the Indian Army 1914-21 (1992).
Honours & Awards of the Old Contemptibles (1992).
Hypher, P.P., *Deeds of Valour Performed by Indian Officers and Soldiers During the Period from 1860 to 1925* (1927).
Royal Flying Corps: Casualties and Honours During the War of 1914-17 (1987).
Sainsbury, Major J.D., *For Gallantry in the Performance of Military Duty* (1980).
South African Honours and Awards 1899-1902 (1971).
Tank Corps Honours & Awards 1916-1919 (1982).
Wilson, Sir Arnold and McEwen, Captain J.H.F., *Gallantry* (1939).

ALBERT MEDAL
Henderson, D.V., *For Heroic Endeavour* (1988).

CHIEFS' MEDALS
Jamieson, A.M., *Indian Chief Medals and Medals to African and Other Chiefs* (1936).

DISTINGUISHED CONDUCT MEDAL
Abbott, P.E., *The Distinguished Conduct Medal 1855-1909* (1987).
Mackinlay, Gordon, *True Courage: The Distinguished Conduct Medal to Australians 1939-1972* (1993).
McDermott, P., *For Distinguished Conduct in the Field: The Register of the DCM 1920-22* (1994).
Walker, R.W., *The Distinguished Conduct Medal 1914-20.*

DISTINGUISHED FLYING MEDAL
Tavender, Ian, *The Distinguished Flying Medal: A Record of Courage* (1990).

DISTINGUISHED SERVICE MEDAL
Fevyer, W.H., *The Distinguished Service Medal.*
Fevyer, W.H., *The Distinguished Service Medal.*

DISTINGUISHED SERVICE ORDER
Creagh, General Sir O'Moore and Humphris, H.M., *The D.S.O.: A Complete Record of Recipients* (1978).

EDWARD MEDAL
Henderson, D.V., *For Heroic Endeavour* (1988)

EMPIRE GALLANTRY MEDAL
Henderson, D.V., *For Heroic Endeavour* (1988).

GEORGE CROSS
Bisset, Lieut. Colonel Ian. *The George Cross (1961)*
The Register of the George Cross (1981).
Smyth, Sir J., *The Story of the George Cross* (1968).

GEORGE MEDAL
Fevyer, W.H., *The George Medal.*
Henderson, D.V., *Dragons Can Be Defeated.*

INDIAN ORDER OF MERIT
Hypher, P.P., *Deeds of Valour of the Indian Soldier Which Won the Indian Order of Merit During the Period From 1837 to 1859* (1925).

LLOYD'S MEDAL
Brown, George. *Lloyd's War Medal for Bravery at Sea* (1992).

MILITARY MEDAL
Bate, Chris and Smith, Martin. *For Bravery in the Field: Recipients of the Military Medal 1919-1939, 1939-1945* (1991).

VICTORIA CROSS
Creagh, General Sir O'Moore and Humphris, H.M., *The Victoria Cross 1856-1920* (1993).
Crook, M.J., *The Evolution of the Victoria Cross* (1975).
Pallinger, D. and Staunton, A. *Victoria Cross Locator* (1991).
Smyth, Brig. Sir John, *The Story of the Victoria Cross* (1964).
Wilkins, P.A., *The History of the Victoria Cross* (1904).

CAMPAIGN MEDALS
(listed in chronological order by date of campaign medal)
GENERAL
Carter, T. and Long, W.H., *War Medals of the British Army 1650-1891* (1972).
Douglas-Morris, Captain K.J., *Naval Medals 1793-1856* (1987).
Johnson, Derek E., *War Medals* (1971).
Joslin, E.C., Litherland, A.R. and Simpkin, B.T., *British Battles and Medals* (1988).
Laffin, J., *British Campaign Medals.*
Long, W.H., *Medals of the British Navy.* (1895).
Vernon S.B., *Collector's Guide to Orders, Medals and Decorations* (With Valuations) (1990).

MILITARY GENERAL SERVICE MEDAL 1793-1814
Foster, Col. Kingsley O.N., *The Military General Service Medal Roll 1793-1814* (1947).
Mullen, A.L.T., *The Military General Service Medal 1793-1814.*
Newnham, A.J., *The Peninsula Medal Roll 1793-1814* (privately produced).
Vigors, Lieutenant Colonel D.D. and Macfarlane, Lieutenant Colonel A.M., *The Three Great Retrospective Medals 1793-1840 Awarded to Artillerymen* (1986).

NAVAL GENERAL SERVICE MEDAL 1793-1840
Douglas-Morris, Captain K.J., *The Naval General Service Medal Roll, 1793-1840* (1982).
Hailes, Colonel D.A., *Naval General Service Medal Roll 1793-1840* (privately produced).
MacKenzie, Col R.H., *The Trafalgar Roll: The Ships and the Officers* (1989).
Newnham A.J., *Naval General Service Medal Roll 1793-1840* (privately produced).
O'Byrne, William, *Naval Biographical Dictionary* (2 vols, 1849).
Vigors, Lieutenant Colonel D.D. and Macfarlane, Lieutenant Colonel A.M., *The Three Great Retrospective Medals 1793-1840 Awarded to Artillerymen* (1986).

ARMY OF INDIA MEDAL 1799-1826
Gould, R.W. and Douglas-Morris, Captain K.J., *The Army of India Medal Roll 1799-1826* (1974).
Vigors, Lieutenant Colonel D.D. and Macfarlane, Lieutenant Colonel A.M., *The Three Great Retrospective Medals 1793-1840 Awarded to Artillerymen* (1986).

WATERLOO MEDAL
Dalton, C., *The Waterloo Roll Call* (1904).

INDIA CAMPAIGN MEDALS
Biddulph, Major H., *Early Indian Campaigns and the Decorations Awarded for Them* (1913).

SOUTH AFRICA MEDAL 1835-53
Everson, Gordon R., *The South Africa 1853 Medal Roll* (1978).

NEW ZEALAND MEDAL 1845-66
Cowan, J., *The New Zealand Wars* (2 volumes) (1969).
Gudgeon, T.W., *Heroes of New Zealand and Maori History of the War* (1887).

INDIA GENERAL SERVICE MEDAL 1854-95
Parritt, Colonel B.A.H., *Red With Two Blue Stripes* (1974).

CRIMEA MEDAL 1854-56
Cook, F. and Cook, A., *Casualty Roll for the Crimea 1854-55* (1976).
Lummis, Canon W.M., *Honour the Light Brigade* (1973).
Returns Relating to the Crimea (Reprint).

INDIA MUTINY MEDAL 1857-59
Tavender, I.T., *Casualty Roll for the India Mutiny 1857-59* (1983).

CANADA GENERAL SERVICE MEDAL 1866-70
The Medal Roll of the Red River Campaign in 1870 in Canada (1982)

SOUTH AFRICA MEDAL 1877-79
Forsyth, D.R., *South African War Medal 1877-8-9: The Medal Roll.*
Holme, N., *The Silver Wreath. The 24th Regiment at Isandhlwana and Rorke's Drift 1879* (1979).
Mackinnon, J.P. and Shadbolt, S.H., *The South Africa Campaign of 1879* (1882).
Tavender, I.T., *Casualty Roll for the Zulu and Basuto Wars, South Africa 1877-79* (1985).
Whybra, J., *The Roll Call for Isandhlwana and Rorke's Drift* (1990).

AFGHANISTAN MEDAL 1878-80
Farrington, A., *The Second Afghan War 1878-80 Casualty Roll* (1986).
Shadbolt, S.H., *The Afghanistan Campaigns of 1878-80* (1882).

CAPE OF GOOD HOPE GENERAL SERVICE MEDAL 1880-97
Forsyth, D.R., *Cape of Good Hope General Service Medal: The Medal Roll.*

EGYPT MEDAL 1882-89
Maurice, Colonel J.F., *The Campaign of 1882 in Egypt.*

BRITISH SOUTH AFRICA COMPANY MEDAL 1890-97
Roberts, *The British South Africa Company Medal Rolls 1890-1897* (1993).

INDIA GENERAL SERVICE MEDAL 1895
Farrington, A., *The India General Service Casualty Roll* (1987).

ASHANTI STAR 1896
McInnes, Ian and Fraser, Mark, *The Ashanti Campaign 1896.*

QUEEN'S & KING'S SOUTH AFRICA MEDAL 1899-1902
British Naval Brigades in the South Africa War 1899-1902 (Reprint).
Dooner, M.G., *The Last Post: A Roll of All Officers Who Gave Their Lives in the South African War 1899-1902* (1980).
Fevyer, W.H. and Wilson, J.W., *The Queen's South Africa Medal to the Royal Navy and Royal Marines* (1983).
List of Casualties of the South Africa Frontier Force (Reprint 1972).
South African War Casualty Roll: Natal Field Force (1980).
Stirling, J., *British Regiments in South Africa* (1994.)
Stirling, J., *The Colonials in South Africa* (1990).

CAPE COPPER COMPANY'S MEDAL 1902
Forsyth, D.R., *Medal Roll of the Cape Copper Company's Medal.*

CHINA MEDAL 1900
Fevyer, W.H. and Wilson, J.W., *The China War Medal 1900 to the Royal Navy and Royal Marines* (1985).
Narbeth, C., *Taku Forts* (1980).

AFRICA GENERAL SERVICE MEDAL 1902
Magor, R.B., *African General Service Medals.*

NATAL REBELLION MEDAL 1906
Forsyth, D.R., *Natal Native Rebellion 1906: The Medal Roll.*

FIRST WORLD WAR MEDALS 1914-19
Jarvis, S.D. and Jarvis, D.B., *The Cross of Sacrifice* (1990-1994).
New Zealand Expeditionary Force Roll of Honour (Reprint).
Officers Died in the Great War (1988).
Parks, Major Edwin, *The Royal Guernsey Militia* (1993).
Soldiers Died in the Great War (volumes).
Williams, R.D., *Guide to Collecting and Researching Campaign Medals of the Great War* (1993).

Williamson, H.J., *The Roll of Honour, Royal Flying Corps and Royal Air Force for the Great War 1914-18* (1992).

SECOND WORLD WAR MEDALS
Prisoners of War (British, Empire and Commonwealth Forces) (3 volumes, reprint)

KOREA MEDALS 1950-53
Dyke, P., *Korea 1950-53: Mentions-in-Despatches* (1989).

Harding, Colonel E.D., *The Imjin Roll* (1976).

Ingraham, Kevin R., *The Honors, Medals and Awards of the Korean War 1950-1953* (1993).

MERITORIOUS SERVICE MEDALS
(listed alphabetically by author)

McInnes, Ian, *The Meritorious Service Medal to Aerial Forces* (1984).

McInnes, Ian, *The Meritorious Service Medal to Naval Forces* (1983).

LONG SERVICE & GOOD CONDUCT MEDALS
(listed alphabetically by author)

Douglas-Morris, Captain K.J., *The Naval Long Service Medals* (1991).

Tamplin, J.M.A., *The Army Emergency Reserve Decoration and the Efficiency Medal (Army Emergency Reserve)* (1989).

Tamplin, J.M.A., *The Colonial Auxiliary Forces Long Service Medal* (1984.)

Tamplin, J.M.A., *The Colonial Auxiliary Forces Officers' Decoration: the Indian Volunteer Forces Officers' Decoration* (1981).

Tamplin, J.M.A., *The Efficiency Decoration Instituted 1930* (1987).

Tamplin, J.M.A., *The Imperial Yeomanry Long Service and Good Conduct Medal* (1978).

Tamplin, J.M.A., *The Militia Long Service and Good Conduct Medal* (1979).

Tamplin, J.M.A., *The Special Reserve Long Service and Good Conduct Medal* (1979).

Tamplin, J.M.A., *The Territorial Decoration 1908-1930* (1983).

Tamplin, J.M.A., *The Territorial Force Efficiency Medal 1908-1921 and the Territorial Efficiency Medal 1922-1930* (1980).

Tamplin, J.M.A., *The Volunteer Long Service Medal* (1980).

Tamplin, J.M.A., *The Volunteer Officers' Decoration* (1980).

Williams, R.D., *The Victoria Volunteer Long and Efficient Service Medal and the Volunteer Officers' Decoration* (1976).

OTHER MEDALS
(listed alphabetically by author)

Cole, H.N., *Coronation and Royal Commemorative Medals 1887-1977* (1977).

Hibbard, M.G., *Boer War Tribute Medals* (1982).

Poulsom, Major N.W., *The White Ribbon: a Medallic Record of British Polar Expeditions* (1968).

Scarlett, R.J., *The Naval Good Shooting Medal 1903-1914* (1990).

PERIODICALS
The Journal of the Orders and Medals Research Society (OMRS Journal, for address see Society list below)

The Life Saving Awards Research Society Journal (for address see Society list).

Military Collectors Club of Canada Journal (MCCofC Journal, for address see Society list).

The Medal Collector (OMSA Journal, for address see Society list).

Medal News (Token Publishing, 105 High Street, Honiton, Devon EX14 8PE).

Spink's Medal Quarterly (Medal Department, Spink & Son Ltd, King Street, St James's, London SW1).

SOCIETIES FOR MEDAL COLLECTORS
Association de Collectionneurs de Decorations et Médailles (MEDEC) (Paasbloemstraat 81, 2060 Merksem, Belgium).

Bund Deutscher Ordenssammler e.v. (Postfach 1260, Eisenbergstr 10, D-6497 Steinau a.d. Str., Germany).

Life Saving Awards Research Society (9 Kerria Way, West End, Woking, Surrey GU24 9XA)

Medal Society of Ireland (Market Square, Bunclody, Co Wexford, Ireland).

Mid-Western Orders & Medals Society (MIDOMS) (5847 Gilbert Avenue, La Grange, IL 60525, USA).

Military Collector's Club of Canada (MCCofC) (15 Abel Place, St Albert, Alta T8N 2Z5).

Orders & Medals Society of America (OMSA) (PO Box 484, Glassboro, NJ 08028, USA).

Orders & Medals Research Society (OMRS) (21 Colonels Lane, Chertsey, Surrey KT16 8RH).

Ordenshistorik Selskab (Falkoneralle 79, DK 2000 Frederiksberg, Denmark).

Societé Suisse de Phaleristique (Box 1, CH-1137 Yens, Switzerland).

We would appreciate information from other Medal Societies so that we can include their details in the next YEARBOOK.

MUSEUMS AND COLLECTIONS

The majority of the museums listed below are the regimental museums of the British Army, Militia, Yeomanry and Territorials, but we have included other museums pertaining to the Royal Navy, the Royal Marines and the Royal Air Force where medals form a significant part of the collections. So, too, the museums of the police forces, fire brigades, Red Cross, Royal National Lifeboat Institution and similar bodies have been included where relevant. Readers should also bear in mind that many general museums in our town and cities boast fine collections of military medals pertaining to their local regiments. We have included those of which we are aware. The date of foundation is shown in brackets after the name.

Some service museums have been undergoing refits, relocations and amalgamations. We would welcome further information from readers about these changes and about other general museums in their areas with a good coverage of local regimental medals.

Space prevents us from going into details regarding the scope of individual museum holdings. We give the postal address and telephone number, with the name of the curator wherever possible. Hours of opening and admission charges (where applicable) are shown. Where two charges are listed, the first denotes the full adult price and the second the concessionary charge (OAPs, students and children). Where three charges are given the first is the full adult price, the second the OAP concession and the third the children's charge.

Some museums may have libraries holding archival material; this should be checked out and the conditions for use ascertained as such holdings will not have the resources to answer detailed research enquiries.

Where museums are devoted to one particular regimental/service/unit or whatever, they are listed by title in alphabetical order. This may not always accord with the exact official name of the museum which is given on the address line. The well-known national museums are listed alphabetically by name. More general museums which include medal collections are listed by the name of the town. If you cannot see the name of the museum you require at first glance, it may be worth searching through the full list, as some museums escape neat classification and would require extensive cross-referencing to do them full justice.

Aberdeen Maritime Museum (1984)
Provost Ross's House, Shiprow, Aberdeen. 0224 5857888. Monday - Saturday, 10am - 5pm. Admission free.

Airborne Forces Museum (1969)
Browning Barracks, Aldershot, Hants GU11 2BU. 0252 349619. £1.25 / 60p. Tuesday-Sunday, 10am - 4.30pm. Major D.M. Cuthbertson-Smith.

Aldershot Challenge (1989)
Wavell House, Cavans Road, Aldershot, Hants GU11 2LQ. 0252 21048. Only by appointment at present.

Aldershot Military Museum (1984)
Queen's Avenue, Aldershot, Hants GU11 2LG. 0252 314598. £1.50 / £1 / 50p. March-October, 10am - 5pm; November-February 10am - 4.30pm daily. Closed Christmas and New Year. E.H. Beck.

Argyll and Sutherland Highlanders Regimental Museum (1945)
Stirling Castle. 0786 75165. Free. Easter-September, Monday-Saturday, 10am - 5.30pm; Sunday, 11am - 5pm. October-Easter, Monday-Saturday, 10am - 4.30pm; Sunday, 11am - 4pm.

Army Physical Training Corps Museum (1949)
Army School of Physical Training, Queen's Avenue, Aldershot, Hants GU11 2LB. 0252 347131. Free. Monday-Friday, 8.30am - 12.30pm; 2pm - 4pm. Weekends by appointment. Closed in August, and two weeks each at Easter and Christmas. A.A. Forbes and J. Pearson.

Army Transport Museum (1983)
Flemingate, Beverley, Humberside HU17 0NG. 0482 860445. £2.50 / £1.50. Daily, 10am - 5pm. Closed 24-26 December. David Dawson.

Arundel Toy and Military Museum (1978)
Dolls House, 23 High Street, Arundel, West Sussex.
0903 507446 / 882908. £1.25 / 90p. June-August,
10.30am - 5pm daily. Otherwise open on Bank
Holidays and weekends in winter.

**Aylmer Military Collection and Isle of Wight Home
Guard Museum (1984)**
Nunwell House, Brading, Isle of Wight PO36 0JQ.
0983 407240. £2.30 / £1.80 / 60p (children
accompanied by adults). July-September, Sunday-
Thursday, 10am - 5pm. Otherwise by appointment.
J.A. Aylmer.

Ayrshire Yeomanry Museum
Rozelle House, Monument Road, Alloway by Ayr
KA7 4NQ. 0292 264091. Monday - Saturday 10am -
5pm, Sundays, April - October, 2 - 5pm.

Bangor, Museum of Welsh Antiquities (1898)
Ffordd Gwynedd, Bangor, Gwynedd, LL57 1DT.
0248 353368. 50p. Tuesday-Friday, 12.30pm - 4.30pm;
Saturday, 10.30am - 4.30pm. Includes medals and
militaria of the Welsh regiments. Patricia
Benneyworth.

**Barnsley, Towneley Hall Art Gallery and Museum
(1902)**
Barnsley, Lancs BB11 3RQ. 0282 424213. Free.
Monday-Friday, 10am - 5pm; Sunday, 12pm - 5pm.
Extensive collection of militaria and medals. Susan
Bourne.

Bath Police Museum (1985)
Manvers Street, Bath, Avon BA1 1JN. 0225 444343.
Free, by appointment only. Sergeant Mike Stanton.

Bedale, Badges and Battledress Museum (1990)
The Green, Crakehall, Bedale, North Yorkshire, DL8
1PH. 0677 424444. £1 / 80p / 50p. Easter-September,
Tuesday-Friday, 11am - 5pm; Saturday and Sunday,
1pm - 5pm. Barrie Morris.

**Bedfordshire and Hertfordshire Regimental
Museum**
Luton Museum, Wardown Park, Luton, Beds LU2
7HA. Monday - Friday 10am - 5pm, Sunday 1pm -
5pm.

Black Watch Museum (1924)
Balhousie Castle, Perth PH1 5HR. 0738 21281 ext
8530. Free. Easter-September, Monday-Friday, 10am -
4.30pm; Sundays and Bank Holidays, 2pm - 4.30pm.
Major A.R. McKinnell, MBE.

**Border Regiment and King's Own Royal Border
Regiment Museum (1973)**
Queen Mary's Tower, The Castle, Carlisle, Cumbria
CA3 8UR. 0228 32774. £2 / £1.50 / £1. April-
September, Monday-Saturday, 10am - 4pm; Sunday,
10am - 6pm. October-March, 10am - 4pm daily.
Stuart Eastwood.

British Red Cross Museum and Archives (1984)
Barnett Hill, Wonersh, Guildford, Surrey GU5 0RF.
0483 898595. Free, by appointment. Monday-Friday,
9.30am - 4.30pm. Margaret Poulter.

Caenarfon Air Museum
Caernarfon Airport, Dinas Dinlle, Caernarfon,
Gwynedd LL54 5TP. £2.50 / £1.50. March - November
9.30am - 5.30pm.

**Cambridge, Scott Polar Research Institute Museum
(1920)**
Lensfield Road, Cambridge CB2 1ER. 0223 336540.
Free. Monday-Saturday, 2.30pm - 4pm. Robert
Headland.

**Cameronians (Scottish Rifles) Regimental Museum
(1928)**
Mote Hill, off Muir Street, Hamilton, Lanarkshire
ML3 6BY. 0698 428688. Free. Monday-Wednesday,
Friday-Saturday, 10am - 1pm; 2pm - 5pm. John
McGourty.

Chester, Cheshire Military Museum (1972)
The Castle, Chester CH1 2DN. 0244 327617. 50p /
25p. Daily, 9am - 5pm. Lieut. Colonel R.C. Peel.

City of London Police Museum (1964)
37 Wood Street, London EC2P 2NQ. 071 601 2705.
Free, by appointment only. Roger Appleby.

Colchester, Military Miniatures Museum (1978)
13 Cheveling Road, Old Heath, Colchester, Essex CO2
8DL. 0206 794473. Free, by appointment only. Daily,
9am - 5pm. Anthony Debski.

Coldstream Museum
13 Market Square, Coldstream. 0361 82600. Easter -
end October, Monday - Saturday 10am - 5pm, Sunday
2 - 5pm.

Colne, British in India Museum (1972)
Newtown Street, Colne, Lancs BB8 0JJ. 0282 613129 /
870215. £1.20 / 50p. Monday-Saturday, 10am - 4pm.
Closed December, January and Bank Holidays.
Henry Nelson.

Devonshire Regiment Museum
Wyvern Barracks, Barrack Road, Exeter, Devon EX2
6AE. Monday-Friday, 10am-4.30pm. Closed Bank
Holidays. Lieutenant Colonel D.R. Roberts.

Dingwall Museum (1975)
Town Hall, High Street, Dingwall, Ross-shire IV15
9RY. 0349 65366. 50p / 25p. May-September,
Monday-Saturday, 10am - 5pm. Otherwise by
appointment only. Includes medals and militaria of
the Seaforth Highlanders, Duke of Ross-shire's Buffs.
Dr Anthony Woodham.

Diss, 100th Bomb Group Memorial Museum (1978)
Common Road, Dickleburgh, near Diss, Norfolk.
0379 740708. Medals and memorabilia of the Eighth
Air Force and 100th Bomb Group. Free. May-
September, Saturday, Sunday and Wednesday, 10am
- 5pm. October-April, weekends only, 10am - 4.30pm.
S.P. Hurry.

Dorchester, Dorset Military Museum (1927)
The Keep, Bridport Road, Dorchester, Dorset DT1
1RN. 0305 264066. £1 / 50p. Monday-Saturday,
9.30am - 5pm. Major J. Carroll.

**Duke of Cornwall's Light Infantry Regimental
Museum (1925)**
The Keep, Bodmin, Cornwall PL31 1EG. 0208 72810.
£1 / 50p. Monday-Friday, 8am - 4.45pm. Major W.H.
White.

**Duke of Edinburgh's Royal Regimental Museum
(1982)**
The Wardrobe, 58 The Close, Salisbury, Wilts SP1

2EX. 0722 414 536. £1.50 / £1 / 50p. Major J.H. Peters, MBE.

Duke of Wellington's Regiment Museum(1960)
Bankfield Museum, Boothtown Road, Halifax HX3 6HQ. 0422 352334 / 354823. Free. Tuesday-Saturday, 10am - 5pm; Sunday, 2.30pm - 5pm. John Spencer.

Durham Light Infantry Museum (1969)
Aykley Heads, Durham DH1 5TU. 091 384 2214. Free. Tuesday-Saturday, 10am - 5pm; Sunday, 2pm - 5pm. Stephen D. Shannon.

East Lancashire Regimental Museum (1934)
Blackburn Museum and Art Gallery, Museum Street, Blackburn, Lancs BB1 7AJ. 0254 667130. Free. Tuesday-Saturday, 10am - 5pm.

Essex Regimental Museum (1973)
Oaklands Park, Moulsham Street, Chelmsford, Essex CM2 9AQ. 0245 260614. Free. Monday-Saturday, 10am - 5pm; Saturday, 2pm - 5pm. Ian Hook.

Feltham, Army Museums Ogilby Trust (1954)
Falklands House, Elwood Avenue, Feltham, Middlesex TW13 7AA. 081 844 1613. Free, Daily, 9am - 4pm. Colonel P.S. Walton.

Fleet Air Arm Museum (1962)
RNAS Yeovilton, Somerset BA22 8HT. 0935 840505. £4.80 / £3.50 / £2.70. Daily, 10am - 5.30pm. Closed 4.30pm, November-February. Captain Jim Flindell RN.

Glasgow Art Gallery and Museum (1854)
Kelvingrove, Glasgow G3 8AG. 041 359 3929. Free. Monday-Saturday, 10am - 5pm; Sunday, 11am - 5pm. Includes medals of the Glasgow Yeomanry, Highland Light Infantry and other regiments associated with the city.

Gloucestershire Regiments Museum (1989)
Gloucester Docks, Gloucester GL1 2HE. 0452 522682. £2.50 / £1.50 / £1.25. Tuesday-Sunday and Bank Holidays, 10am - 5pm. Christine Beresford.

Gordon Highlanders' Regimental Museum (1961)
Regimental Headquarters, Viewfield Road, Aberdeen, AB1 7XH. 0224 318174. April-October, 2 days a week, 10am - 4pm, two weekends a month, 10am - 4pm. October-March by appointment only. Major David White.

Green Howards Regimental Museum
Trinity House Square, Richmond, Yorkshire DL10 4QN. 0748 822133. £1 / 75p / 50p. April - October, Weekdays 9.15am - 4.30pm, Sundays 2 - 4.30pm. Restricted hours the rest of the year

Guards Museum (1988)
Wellington Barracks, London SW1E 6HQ. 071 414 3271. £2 / £1. Monday-Thursday, weekends, 10am - 4pm. Captain David Horn.

Gurkha Museum (1974)
Peninsular Barracks, Romsey Road, Winchester, Hants SO23 8TS. 0962 842832. £1.50 / 75p. Tuesday-Saturday, 10am - 5pm. Major J. Lamond.

Hawkinge, Kent Battle of Britain Museum (1969)
Hawkinge, Kent CT18 7AG. 030 389 3140. £2.50 / £2 £1.50. Easter-end of May, October, 11am - 4pm. July-September, 10am - 5pm. Mike Llewellyn.

Hertford Regiment Museum
8 Bull Plain, Hertford SG14 1DJ. Tuesday-Saturday, 10am - 5pm.

Hertfordshire Yeomanry Museum
Paynes Park, Hitchin, Herts SG5 1EQ. 0462 434476. Free. Monday-Saturday, 10am - 5pm; Sunday, 2pm - 4pm. Closed Bank holidays.

Honourable Artillery Company Museum
Armoury House, City Road, London EC1 2BQ. Apply in writing for a visit.

Imperial War Museum (1917)
Lambeth Road, London SE1 6HZ. 071 416 5000. £3.70 / £2.70 / £1.85. Daily, 10am - 6pm.

Imperial War Museum (1976)
Duxford Airfield, Duxford, Cambridge CB2 4QR. 0223 835000. £5.50 / £3.80 / £2.75. March-October, 10am - 6pm daily; October-March, 10am - 4pm daily.

Inns of Court and City Yeomanry Museum (1947)
10 Stone Buildings, Lincoln's Inn, London WC2A 3TG. 071 405 8112. Free. Monday-Friday, 10am - 4pm. Major R.J.B. Gentry.

Intelligence Corps Museum
Templer Barracks, Ashford, Kent, TN23 3HH. 0233 657208. Free. Tuesdays and Thursdays, 9am - 12.30pm; 2pm - 4.30pm. Dick Shaw.

Kent and Sharpshooters Yeomanry Museum
Hever Castle, Tonbridge, Kent TN8 7NG. April - October 12 - 6pm

King's Own Royal Regiment (Lancaster) Museum (1929)
City Museum, Market Square, Lancaster LA1 1HT. 0524 64637. Free. Monday-Saturday, 10am - 5pm.

King's Own Scottish Borderers Regimental Museum (1954)
Berwick Barracks, The Parade, Berwick-upon-Tweed TD15 1DE. 0289 307426. £1.80 / 40p. Monday-Friday, 9.30am - 4.30pm; Saturday, 9.30am - 12pm. Lieut. Colonel C.G.O. Hogg.

King's Own Yorkshire Light Infantry Regimental Museum (1932)
Museum and Art Gallery, Chequer Road, Doncaster, South Yorkshire DN1 2AE. 0302 734293. Monday-Saturday, 10am - 5pm; Sunday, 2pm - 5pm. Colonel J.S. Cowley.

King's Regiment (Liverpool) Museum
William Brown Street, Liverpool L3 8EN. 051 2070001. Daily, 10am-5pm, Sunday 2pm-5pm. G.S. Boxer.

15th/19th King's Royal Hussars Regimental Museum (1959)
Fernham Barracks, Newcastle-upon-Tyne NE2 4NP. 091 261 1046 ext 3140-2. Free. Monday-Friday, 9am - 4pm.

Lamanva Military Vehicles
Lamanva, Nr Mabe, Falmouth, Cornwall TR10 9BJ 0326 72446. £2,75 / £1.50. Easter - October 10am -5pm, Rest of year 10am-4pm

Lancashire Fusiliers Regimental Museum (1933)
Wellington Barracks, Bury, Lanc BL8 2PL. 061 764

2208. 50p / 25p. Monday-Saturday (closed Thursday), 9am - 12.30pm; 1pm - 4.30pm.

Lancashire Regiment Museum and South Lancashire Regiment (Prince of Wales's Volunteers) (1934)
Peninsular Barracks, Warrington, Lancs WA2 7BP. 0925 33563. Free. Tuesday-Friday, 9am - 2pm. Otherwise by appointment. Lieut. Colonel E.G. Bostock.

17th/21st Lancers Regimental Museum (1964)
Belvoir Castle, Grantham, Lincs NG 31 6BR. 0476 870161. £3.20 / £2.20. April-October, Tuesday-Thursday, Saturday and Sunday, 11am - 5pm. Bank Holiday Mondays, 11am - 5pm. Major W.M. Walton, MBE.

Light Infantry Museum (1990)
Peninsular Barracks, Romsey Road, Winchester. 0962 864176. £1.50 / 75p. Tuesday-Saturday, 10am - 5pm; Sunday, 12pm - 4pm. Patrick Kirby.

Liverpool Scottish Regimental Museum
Forbes House, Score Lane, Childwell, Liverpool L16 6AN. 051 6474342. By appointment. D. Reeves.

London Fire Brigade Museum (1967)
94A Southwark Bridge Road, London SE1 0EG. 071 587 4273. Free. Monday-Friday, 9am - 4.30pm. John Rodwell.

London Scottish Regimental Museum (1935)
Regimental Headquarters, 95 Horseferry Road, London SW1P 2DX. 071 630 1639. Free, by appointment only.

Manchesters Museum (1987)
Town Hall, Ashton-under-Lyne, Lancs. 061 344 3078. Free. Monday-Friday, 10am - 4pm. J. Pollitt.

Metropolitan Police Historical Museum (1969)
New Scotland Yard, London SW1H 0BG. 081 305 2824. By appointment only. Richard Sharp.

Monmouth, The Castle and Regimental Museum (1989)
The Castle, Monmouth, Gwent NP5 3BS. 0600 772175 / 712935. Free. Summer daily, 2pm - 5pm; winter weekends 2pm - 5pm. Other times by appointment. Dr Eric Old.

National Army Museum (1960)
Royal Hospital Road, Chelsea, London SW3 4HT. 071 730 0717. Free. Daily, 10am - 5.30pm. Ian G. Robertson.

National Maritime Museum (1934)
Romney Road, Greenwich, London SE10 9NF. 081 858 4422. £7.45 / £5.45. Summer, Monday-Saturday, 10am - 6pm; Sunday, 12pm - 5pm. Winter, Monday-Saturday, 10am - 5pm; Sunday, 2pm - 5pm. Richard Ormond.

National Museum of Ireland (1877)
Kildare Street, Dublin 2, Republic of Ireland. 01 618811. Free. Tuesday-Saturday, 10am - 5pm; Sunday, 2pm - 5pm. Includes medals of the former Irish regiments.

Newark Air Museum (1968)
Winthrop Airfield, Newark-on-Trent NG24 2NY. 0636 707170. £2.50 / £1.50. April-October, Monday-

Friday, 10am - 5pm; weekends, 10am - 6pm. November-March, daily 101am - 4pm. Mike Smith.

Northamptonshire Regimental Museum
Abington Park Museum, Abington, Northampton. 0604 35412. Colonel J.P. Wetherall.

Order of St. John of Jerusalem Museum
St. John's Gate, St. John's Lane, Clerkenwell, London EC1M 4DA. 071 2536644. Tuesday-Friday 10am - 6pm, Saturday 10am - 4pm. Pamela Willis.

Oxfordshire & Buckinghamshire Light Infantry
TA Centre, Slade Park, Headington. Oxford OX3 7JL. 0865 716060. Free. Monday-Friday 10am - 4pm.

Polish Institute and Sikorski Museum
20 Princes Gate, London SW7 1QA. 071 589 9249. Monday - Friday 2pm -4pm.

Preston, County and Regimental Museum (1987)
Stanley Street, Preston, Lancs PR1 4YP. 0772 264075. £1 / children free. Monday-Saturday (closed Thursday), 10am - 5pm. Stephen Bull.

Prince of Wales's Own 9th /12th Lancers Regimental Museum (1972)
City Museum and Art Gallery, The Strand, Derby DE1 1BS. 0332 255581. Free. Monday, 11am - 5pm; Tuesday-Saturday, 10am - 5pm; Sunday and Bank Holidays, 2pm - 5pm. Nick Forder.

Prince of Wales Regiment of Yorkshire and Regimental Museum of the 4th/7th Royal Dragoon Guards (1925)
3A Tower Street York YO1 1SB. 0904 642 038. 50p / 25p. Monday-Friday, 9.30am - 4.30pm; Saturday, 10am - 4.30pm. Brigadier J.M. Cubiss.

Princess of Wales's Regimental Museum (1987)
Inner Bailey, Dover Castle, Kent CT16 1HU. 0304 240121. £5 / £3.70 / £2.50. Summer, 9.30am - 6pm daily; winter, 10am - 4pm. Lieut. Colonel L.M. Wilson, MBE.

Princess Patricia's Canadian Light Infantry Museum (1974)
Hatch Court, Hatch Beauchamp, Taunton, Somerset TA3 6AA. 0823 480120. £2.80 / £1. June-September, Tuesday and Bank Holiday Mondays, 2.30pm - 5pm. Otherwise by appointment. Dr and Mrs Odgers.

Queen Alexandra's Royal Army Nursing Corps Museum (1953)
Regimental Headquarters, Royal Pavilion, Farnborough Road, Aldershot, Hants GU11 1PZ. 0252 349301 / 349315. Free. Monday-Friday, 9.30am - 12 noon; otherwise by appointment. Major McCombe.

Queen's Dragoon Guards Regimental Museum (1967)
Cardiff Castle, Cardiff, South Glamorgan CF1 2RB. 0222 222253. £3 / £2 / £1.50. March, April and October, 10am - 5pm daily. May-September, 10am - 6pm. November-February, 10am - 4.30pm. Gareth Gill.

Queen's Lancashire Regiment (1929)
Fulwood Barracks, Preston, Lancs PR2 4AA. 0772 716 543 ext 2362. Free. Tuesdays and Thursdays only, 9am - 12pm; 2pm - 4pm. Major A.J. Maher, MBE.

Queen's Own Highlanders Regimental Museum
Fort George, Ardersier, Inverness-shire. 0463 224380. Free. April-September, Monday-Friday, 10am - 6pm; Sunday, 2pm - 6pm. October-March, Monday-Friday, 10am - 4pm.

Queen's Own Royal West Kent Regimental Museum (1966)
St Faith's Street, Maidstone, Kent ME14 1LH. 0622 754497. Free. Monday-Saturday, 10.30am - 5.30pm; Sunday, 2pm - 5pm. Colonel H.B.H. Waring, OBE.

16th/5th Queen's Royal Lancers and Staffordshire Yeomanry
Kitchener House, Lammascote Road, Stafford ST16 3TA. 0785 45840. Monday - Friday 9am - 4pm. Major D.J.H. Farquharson

Queen's Royal Surrey Regimental Museum (1979)
Clandon Park, Guildford, Surrey GU4 7RQ. 0483 223419. April-October, Sunday-Wednesday, 1.30pm - 5.30pm. Richard Ford.

Royal Air Force Museum (1963)
Grahame Park Way, Hendon, London NW9 5LL. 081 205 2266. £4.50 / £2.25. Daily, 10am - 6pm. Dr M.A. Fopp.

Royal Air Force Museum Reserve Collection (1965)
RAF Cardington, Beds MK42 0TH. 0234 742711. Free, by appointment only. Bruce James.

Royal Army Chaplains' Department Museum (1968)
Bagshot Park, Bagshot, Surrey GU19 5PL. 0276 471717, ext. 2845. Free. Monday-Friday, 10am - 4pm, by appointment. Closed in August. Major Margaret Anne Easey.

Royal Army Dental Corps Museum (1958)
Headquarters RADC, Evelyn Woods Road, Aldershot, Hants GU11 2LS. 0252 347782. Free. Monday-Friday, 10am - 12pm; 2pm - 4pm. Closed on bank holidays. Major Vincent Ward.

Royal Army Educational Corps Museum (1967)
Wilton Park, Beaconsfield, Bucks HP9 2RP. 0494 683290. Free, by appointment only. Simon Anglim.

Royal Army Medical Corps Museum (1952)
Keogh Barracks, Ash Vale, Aldershot, GU12 5RQ. 0252 340212. Free. Monday-Friday, 8.30am - 4pm; weekends and evenings by appointment. Lieut. Colonel Roy Eyeions, OBE.

Royal Army Ordnance Corps (Logistics) Museum (1993)
Blackdown Barracks, Deepcut, near Camberley Surrey GU16 6RW. 0252 340634. Free. Monday-Friday, 8.30am - 12.30pm; 1.30pm - 4.30pm. Lieut. Colonel W.P. Masterson.

Royal Artillery Regimental Museum (1946)
Old Royal Military Academy, Woolwich, London SE18 4DN. 081 781 5628. Free. Monday-Friday, 12.30pm - 4.30pm. Brigadier Ken Timbers.

Royal Corps of Signals Outstation Museum (1987)
Helles Barracks, Catterick Garrison, North Yorkshire DL9 4HH. 0748 873778. Free. Monday-Thursday, 10am - 4pm; Friday, 10am - 3pm. Liut. Colonel F.M. Orr, OBE.

Royal Corps of Transport Museum (1945)
Regimental Headquarters, Royal Corps of Transport,

Buller Barracks, Aldershot, Hants GU11 2BX. 0252 348834. Free. Monday-Friday, 9am - 12pm; 2pm - 4pm. Weekends by appointment. Closed on Bank Holidays. Lieut. Colonel M.H.G. Young.

Royal Devon Yeomanry (1845)
Museum of North Devon, The Square, Barnstaple, Devon EX32 8LN. 0271 46747. £1 / 50p .Tuesday-Saturday, 10am - 4.30pm. Jerry Lee.

Royal East Kent Regiment, Third Foot (The Buffs) Museum (1961)
Royal Museum and Art Gallery, High Street, Canterbury, Kent CT1 2JE. 0277 452747. Free. Monday-Saturday, 10am - 5pm. Kenneth Reedie.

Royal Electrical and Mechanical Engineers Museum (1958)
Isaac Newton Road, Arborfield Garrison, Reading, Berks, RG2 9LN. 0734 763567. Free. Monday-Friday, 9am - 12.30pm; 2pm - 4pm. Weekends by appointment. Closed on Bank Holidays. Lieut. Colonel Larry LeVar.

Royal Engineers Museum
Brompton Barracks, Chatham, Kent ME4 4UG. 0634 406397. £1/50p. Tuesday-Friday, 11.30am - 5pm, Spring/Summer Bank Holidays 10am - 5pm. Colonel G.W.A. Napier.

Royal Fusiliers Museum (1962)
HM Tower of London, EC3N 4AB. 071 488 5612. 25p. Daily, 9.30am - 4.30pm. Major B.C. Bowes-Crick.

Royal Hospital Chelsea
Hospital Road, Chelsea, London SW3 4SL. 071 730 0161. Free. Daily, 10am - 12pm; 2pm - 4pm. Major R.A.G. Courage, CVO, MBE.

Royal Green Jackets Museum
Peninsular Barracks, Romsey Road, Winchester. 0962 863846. £2 / £1. Monday-Saturday, 10am - 5pm; Sunday, 12pm - 4pm.

Royal Hampshire Regimental Museum (1933)
Serle's House, Southgate Street, Winchester, Hants SO23 9EG. 0962 863658. Free. Summer daily, 12pm - 4pm. Major James Kellie.

Royal Highland Fusiliers Regimental Museum (1960)
518 Sauchiehall Street, Glasgow G2 3LW. 041 332 0961. Free. Monday-Thursday, 9am - 4.30pm; Friday, 9am - 4pm. W. Shaw, MBE.

Royal Hussars Museum (1980)
Peninsular Barracks, Romsey Road, Winchester. 0962 863751. £1.50 / 75p. Tuesday - Friday, 10am - 4pm; weekends and Bank Holidays, 12pm - 4pm. Lieut. Colonel R.B. Merton

3th/18th Royal Hussars (Queen Mary's Own) Regiment (1957)
Cannon Hall Museum, Cawthorne, Barnsley, South Yorkshire S75 4AT. 0226 790270. Free. Tuesday-Saturday and Bank Holiday Mondays, 10.30am - 5pm; Saturday and Sunday, 2.30pm - 5pm. Brian Murray.

Royal Inniskilling Fusiliers Regimental Musuem (1938)
The Castle, Enniskillen, Co. Fermanagh, Northern Ireland BT74 7BB. 0365 323142. £1 / 75p. Summer,

Monday-Friday, 9.30am - 5pm; weekends, 2pm - 5pm. Winter, Monday-Friday, 930am - 12.30pm; 2pm - 5pm. Major George Stephens, MBE.

Royal Irish Fusiliers
Sovereign's House, The Mall, Armagh BT61 9AJ. 0861 522911. Weekdays 10am - 4.30pm. Major M. Wright.

Royal Irish Regiment Museum (1993)
Regimental Headquarters, Royal Irish Rangers, St Patrick's Barracks, Ballymena, BFPO 808, Northern Ireland. 0266 661388. Free. Monday-Friday, 10am - 4.30pm. Lieut. Carol Liles.

Royal Lancashire Regiment Museum (1969)
The Magazine, Oxford Street, Leicester. 0533 473220. Free. Monday-Thursday, Saturday, 10am - 5.30pm; Sunday, 2pm - 5.30pm. Y.C. Courtney.

Royal Lincolnshire Regimental Museum (1985)
Burton Road, Lincoln LN1 3LY. 0522 528468. £1 / 50p. May-September, daily, 10am - 5.30pm. October-April, Monday-Saturday, 10am - 5,30pm; Sunday, 2pm - 5.30pm.

Royal Marines Museum (1956)
Southsea, Hants PO4 9PX. 0705 819315. £2.50 / £1.50 / £1.25. Whitsun-September, daily, 9.30am - 5pm. Winter, 9.30am - 4.30pm. Colonel K.N. Wilkins, OBE.

Royal Military Police Museum (1979)
Rousillon Barracks, Broyle Road, Chichester, West Sussex PO19 4BN. 0243 786311 ext 4225. Free. April-September, Tuesday-Friday, 10.30am - 12.30pm; 1.30pm - 4.30pm; Saturday and Sunday, 2pm - 6pm. October-March, Tuesday-Friday, 10.30am - 12.30pm; 1.30pm - 4.30pm. Closed in January. Lieut. Colonel Maurice Squier.

Royal National Lifeboat Institution Museum(1937)
Grand Parade, Eastbourne, East Sussex BN21 4BY. 0323 730717. Free. April-December, 9.30am - 5pm daily. January-March, Monday-Friday, 9.30am - 5pm. J.M.Shearer.

Royal National Lifeboat Institution Museum (1969)
Pen-y-Cae, Barmouth, Gwynedd. Free. Easter-October, 10.30am - 6.30pm, daily.

Royal Naval Museum (1911)
HM Naval Base, Portsmouth PO1 3LR. 0705 733060. £2 / £1.75. Daily, 10.30am - 5pm. H. Campbell Murray.

Royal Norfolk Regimental Museum (1945)
Shirehall, Market Avenue, Norwich NR1 3JQ. 0603 223649. 80p / 40p. Monday-Saturday, 10am - 5pm; Sunday, 2pm - 5pm. Kate Thaxton.

Royal Northumberland Fusiliers Regimental Museum (1970)
The Abbot's Tower, Alnwick Castle, Alnwick, NE66 1NG. 0665 602152 / 510211. Easter-October, 11am - 5pm daily. Captain Peter H.D. Marr.

Royal Scots Regimental Museum (1951)
The Castle, Edinburgh EH1 2YT. 031 310 5016. Free. March-September, Monday-Saturday, 9.30am - 4.30pm; Sunday, 11am - 4.30pm. October-April, Monday-Friday, 9.30am - 4pm. Major Dick Mason.

Royal Signals Museum (1967)
Blandford Camp, Blandford, Dorset DT11 8RH. 0258

482248. Free. Monday-Friday, 10am - 5pm; Saturday and Sunday, 10am - 4pm.

Royal Sussex Regimental Museum (1930)
Redoubt Fortress, Royal Parade, Eastbourne, East Sussex BN21 4BP. 0323 410300. £1.50 / £1. April-October. Other times by appointment. B.R. Burns.

Royal Tank Regiment Museum (1923)
Bovington Camp, near Wareham, Dorset BH20 6JG. 0929 403463 / 403329 / 463953. £4 / £2. Daily, 10am - 5pm. Closed at Christmas. Lieut. Colonel G. Forty.

Royal Ulster Constabulary Museum (1983)
Brooklyn, Knock Road, Belfast BT5 6LE. 0232 650222. Free. Monday-Friday, 9am - 5pm. Robin Sinclair.

Royal Ulster Rifles Museum (1935)
Regimental Headquarters, The Royal Irish Rangers, 5 Waring Street, Belfast BT1 2EW. 0232 232086. Free. Monday-Friday, 10am -12pm; 2pm - 4pm. Major M.B.Murphy.

Royal Warwickshire Regimental Museum (1928)
St John's House, Warwick CV34 4NF. 0926 491653. Free. Tuesday-Saturday, 10am - 12.30pm; 1.30pm - 5.30pm; Sunday, 2.30pm - 5pm. Brigadier J.K. Chater.

Royal Welch Fusiliers Museum (1955)
Queen's Tower, Caernarfon Castle, Gwynedd LL55 2AY. 0286 673362. £3 / £2. March-October, 9.30am - 6.30pm daily; winter 9.30am - 4pm; Sunday, 2pm - 4pm. Captain Bryan H. Finchett-Maddock.

Royal Wiltshire Yeomanry Regimental Museum
Town Museum, Bath Road, Swindon SN1 4BA. Free. Monday-Friday, 10am - 5.30pm; Saturday, 10am - 4,30pm; Sunday, 2pm - 4.30pm.

St Helier, Elizabeth Castle and Militia Museum (1976)
St Helier, Jersey, Channel Islands. 0534 23971. £2 / £1. April-October, daily, 10am - 5pm.

Sandhurst Royal Military Academy (1960)
Royal Military Academy Sandhurst, Camberley GU15 4PQ. 0276 63344 ext 2457. Free, by appointment only.

School of Infantry and Small Arms School Corps Weapons Museum (1953)
School of Infantry, Warminster, BA12 0DJ. 0985 842487. Free. Daily, 9am - 4,30pm. Lieut. Colonel Tug Wilson, MBE.

Scottish Horse Museum
The Cross, Dunkeld, Perthshire. 50p Easter - September 10am - 5pm

Scottish National War Memorial
The Castle, Edinburgh. 031 220 4733. Free. Same hours as above. Thomas Barker.

Scottish United Services Museum (1930)
The Castle, Edinburgh. 031 225 7534. Free. Same hours as above. Stephen Wood.

Sherwood Foresters Regimental Museum (1923)
The Castle, Nottingham. 0602 483504. Free. Daily, 10am - 5.30pm. Major R.A. Creamer.

Shropshire Regimental Museum (1985)
Copthorne Barracks, Shrewsbury, Salop. 0743 262402. By appointment only. Geoffrey Archer Parfitt.

South Lancashire Regiment (Prince of Wales's Volunteers) and the Lancashire Regiment Museum (1934)

Peninsular Barracks, Warrington, Lancs WA2 7BP. 0925 33563. Free. Tuesday-Friday, 9am - 2pm. Otherwise by appointment. Lieut. Colonel E.G. Bostock.

South Nottinghamshire Hussars Museum (1974)
TA Centre, Hucknall Lane, Bulwell, Nottingham NG6 8AB. 0602 272251. Free, by appointment only.

South Wales Borderers and Monmouthshire Regimental Museum (1934)
The Barracks, Brecon, Powys LD3 7EB. 0874 623111 ext 2310. £1. October-March, Monday-Friday, 9am - 1pm; 2pm - 5pm. April-September, daily except Sunday, same hours. Major Bob Smith.

South Wales Police Museum (1950)
Police Headquarters, Cowbridge Road, Bridgend, Mid Glamorgan CF31 3SU. 0656 655555 ext 427. Free. Monday-Thursday, 10am - 1pm; 2pm - 4.30pm; Friday, 10am - 1pm; 2pm - 4pm. Jeremy Glenn.

Staff College Museum (1958)
Staff College, Camberley, Surrey GU15 4NP. 0276 412662 / 412647 / 412650. Free, by appointment only. Colonel Philip S. Newton, MBE.

Staffordshire Regimental Museum (1962)
Whittington Barracks, Lichfield, Staffs WS14 9PY. 021 311 3240 / 3229. Free. Monday-Friday, 9am - 4.30pm. Major R.D.W. McLean.

Suffolk Regimental Museum (1967)
The Keep, Gibraltar Barracks, Bury St Edmunds, Suffolk IP33 1HF. 0284 752394. Free. Weekdays, 10am - 12pm; 2pm - 4pm. Major A.G.B. Cobbold.

Tangmere, Military Aviation Museum (1992)
Tangmere, near Chichester, West Sussex PO20 6ES. 0243 775223. £3 / 50p. February-November, daily, 11am - 5.30pm. Andy Saunders.

Taunton, Somerset Military Museum (1974)
County Museum, The Castle, Taunton, Somerset TA1 1AA. 0823 255504. £1.20 / 80p / 30p. Monday-Saturday, 10am - 5pm. Brigadier A.I.H. Fyfe.

Welch Regiment Museum (1927)
The Black and Barbican Towers, Cardiff Castle, Cardiff, South Glamorgan CF1 2RB. 0222 229367. £2 / £1. Lieut. Bryn Owen, RN.

Wellington Museum
Apsley House, 149 Piccadilly, Hyde Park Corder, London W1V 9FA. 071 499 5676. £2/£1. Tuesday - Sunday 11am - 5pm. J. Voak.

West Midlands Police Museum (1991)
Sparkhill Police Station, 641 Stratford Road, Birmingham B11 6EA. Free, by apppointment only.

Woodbridge, 390th Bomb Group Memorial Air Museum (1981)
Parham Airfield, Parham, Woodbridge, Suffolk. 0359 51209. Free. Sundays and Bank Holidays, 11am - 6pm.

Worcestershire Regimental Museum (1973)
City Museum and Art Gallery, Foregate Street, Worcester. Free. Monday-Wednesday, Friday, 9.30am - 6pm; Saturday, 9.30am - 5pm. Brian Owen

York, Divisional Kohima Museum (1991)
Imphal Barracks, Fulford Road, York YO1 4AY. 0904 662381. Free, by appointment only.

York, Yorkshire Air Museum and Allied Air Forces Memorial (1984)
Halifax Way, Elvington, York YO4 5AU. 0904 605595. £2.50 / £1.50. Monday-Friday, 10.30am - 4pm; weekends, 10.30am - 5pm. Peter Douthwaithe.

Yorks and Lancs Regimental Museum (1947)
Brian O'Malley Central Library and Art Gallery, Walker Place, Rotherham, Yorkshire S65 1JH. 0709 382 121 ext 3625. Free. Tuesday-Saturday, 10am–5pm. Don Scott.

PROFESSIONAL DIRECTORY

On the following pages are the names and addresses of auctioneers, dealers, booksellers and fair organisers, all of whom will be of assistance to the medal collector. Most are full time and many have retail shops and the collector is usually welcome during normal business hours. Some have extensive stocks of medals whilst others include medals in a more diverse inventory. A number of dealers are part time or work from small premises or from home and appointments are necessary as many keep their stock in the bank for security. Telephone numbers have been included where known and it is always sensible to make contact before travelling any distance.

AUCTIONEERS

The following hold regular medal auctions or feature medals in general sales.

Bonham's
Montpelier Street, Knightsbridge, London SW7 1HH. 071 584 9161 (fax 071 589 4072). Auctioneers and valuers. 3–4 general numismatic sales (including medals) a year. Annual subscription to sale catalogues £10 (UK), £14 (Europe), £16/$US25 (rest of world).

Croydon Coin Auctions
272 Melfort Road, Thornton Heath, Surrey CR7 7RR. Tel/fax 081 684 6515 or 6565 4583. Regular coin sales which often feature interesting medals.

Floyd, Johnson & Paine
6427 W. Irving Park Road, Suite 160, Chicago, Illinois 60634, USA. (312) 777 0499 (fax 312 777 4017). New US auction. Write for further details.

Glendining's
101 New Bond Street, London W1Y 9LG. 071 493 2445 (fax 071 491 9181). Auctioneers and valuers. Approx 4 sales per year. Annual subscription to sale catalogues £30 (UK), £37 (overseas).

Jeffrey Hoare Auctions Inc.
345 Talbot Street, London, Ontario, Canada N6A 2R5. (519) 663 1087 (fax 519 473 1541). 3 sales a year devoted to Canadian, British and world medals, badges and militaria.

Sotheby's
Summers Place, Billingshurst, West Sussex RH14 9AD. 0403 783933. Auctioneers and valuers. Regular sales. Catalogues £10, annual subscription details available on request.

Spink & Son Ltd (Christie's International)
5-7 St James's, London SW1Y 6QS. 071 930 7888 (fax 071 839 4853). Telex 916711. Auctioneers, valuers and dealers. Usually three sales a year. Annual subscription to sale catalogues £20 (UK and Europe), £30 (rest of the world, £55 airmail).

Wallis & Wallis
West Street Auction Galleries, Lewes, Sussex BN7 2NJ. 0273 480208 (fax 0273 476562). Telex 896691 TLXIR G. Auctioneers and valuers of militaria, arms, armour and military medals. Monthly general sales and half-yearly connoisseurs' sales. Catalogues £4.50 (UK), £5.50 (overseas airmail).

DEALERS

Ackley Unlimited
PO Box 82144, Portland, Oregon, USA 97282-0144. (503) 659 4681. Orders, medals and decorations. Free quarterly lists on request.

Argyll Coins & Antiques
102 Bath Street, Glasgow G2. 041 332 0595. Monday-Friday, 10am–5pm. Coins, medals, gold and silverware.

Armoury of St. James's
17 Piccadilly Arcade, Piccadilly, London SW1Y 6NH. 071 493 5082 (fax 071 499 4422). Orders, decorations, medals, militaria.

Michael Autengruber
Schillstrasse 7B, D-63067 Offenbach, Germany. (69) 88 69 25 evenings. Orders, medals, literature. Catalogues $US3 (Europe), $US6 (elsewhere).

A.H. Baldwin & Sons Ltd
11 Adelphi Terrace, London WC2N 6BJ. 071 839
1310.

Paul Boulden
Antiques Market, 17 The Parade, The Barbican,
Plymouth, Devon. 0752 221443. Medals, militaria
and books. Lists £3 (UK), £6 (overseas) for 6 issues.

Bonus Eventus
Aartshertoginnestratt 27, 8400 Oostende, Belgium.
(059) 801696. Medals and miniature medals. Free
medal lists (specify full-size or miniatures).

Bostock Militaria
"Pinewood", 15 Waller Close, Leek Wootton, near
Warwick CV35 7QG. 0926 56381. British orders,
medals and decorations. Sae for free current lists.
Callers welcome by appointment.

Andrew Bottomley
The Coach House, Huddersfield Road, Thongs-
bridge, Holmfirth, West Yorkshire HD7 2TT.
Arms and armour, some medals. Catalogue £5.

Philip Burman
Blackborough End, Middleton, King's Lynn,
Norfolk PE32 1SE. 0553 840350. Large and varied
stock of orders, medals and decorations. Send
large sae for lists, issued 6 times a year.

John Burridge
91 Shenton Road, Swanbourne, Western Australia
6010. British and Commonwealth medals and
decorations.

Mark Carter
PO Box 470, Slough SL3 6RR, 0753 534777. British
and foreign orders, medals, decorations and
miniatures. Fairs organiser. Lists £5 (UK and
BFPO), £7.50 (overseas airmail).

Central Antique Arms & Militaria
Smith Street Antiques Centre, Warwick CV34 4JA.
0926 400554. British orders, decorations, medals
and militaria. Lists 50p.

Brian Clark
16 Lothian Road, Middlesborough, Cleveland TS4
2HR. 0642 240827. Orders, medals and
decorations. 9 lists a year, £3 (UK), £6 (overseas).

Coates
Little Arram Farm, Bewholme Lane, Seaton, Hull
HU11 5SX. 0964 533905. First World War medals,
groups and memorial plaques. Two 25p stamps
for lists.

Coldstream Military Antiques
55a High Street, Marlow, Bucks. Tel/fax 0628
822503. Medals, badges, insignia.

Collector's Lair
#205 - 15132 Stony Plain Road, Edmonton,
Alberta, Canada T5P 3X8. (403) 486 2907.
Medals, badges and unforms.

Norman W. Collett
PO Box 235, London SE23 1NS. 081 291 1435 (fax
081 291 3300). British medals and decorations, and
military books. Regular catalogues issued. Send
50p in stamps for the current 48 page medal list or
32 page book list.

Command Post of Militaria
578 Yates Street, Victoria, British Columbia,
Canada V8W 1K8. (604) 383 4421. Medals, badges
and uniforms.

Conglomerate Coins & Medals
206 Adelaide Street, Brisbane, Queensland 4000,
Australia. (07) 2211217 (fax 07 2299128). Medals
and medallions.

Peter R. Cotrel
7 Stanton Road, Bournemouth, Dorset BH10 5DS.
Mail order only—callers by appointment, 0202
516801. British, American and general foreign
medals and decorations. Medal albums and
accessories. Lists (sae for a sample).

C.J. & A.J. Dixon Ltd
23 Prospect Street, Bridlington, East Yorkshire
YO15 2AE. 0262 676877 (fax 0262 606600).
Publishers of *Dixon's Gazette*, 4 a year £6 (UK), £9
(overseas).

D.M.D. Services
6 Beehive Way, Reigate, Surrey RH2 8DY. 0737
240080. Victorian campaign medals and
decorations.

Downie's Militaria
7th Floor, 343 Little Collins Street, Melbourne, Vic
3000, Australia. (03) 670 0500 (fax 03 670 0311).
Emphasis on Australian and UK medals. Lists
available.

Frank Draskovic
PO Box 803, Monterey Park, CA 91754, USA.
Worldwide orders and medals, especially
European and Far Eastern.

M.J. & S.J. Dyas Coins and Medals
30 Shaftmoor Lane, Acocks Green, Birmingham
B27 7RS. 021 707 2808. All medals and First
World War memorial plaques a speciality. Lists £1
(UK), £2 (overseas).

Edinburgh Coin Shop (Hiram T. D. Brown)
2 Polwarth Crescent, Edinburgh EH11 1HW. 031
229 2915 / 3007. British medals and decorations.
4 lists and 10 auctions a year.

Gateway Militaria
Box 24049, 13 - 1853 Grant Avenue, Winnipeg,
Manitoba, Canada R3N 1ZO. (204) 489 3884 (fax
204 489 9118). Medals and badges.

Glasgow Coin Gallery
158 Bath Street, Glasgow G2 4TB. 041 333 1933.
Coins, medals, badges and banknotes. Monday-
Friday, 10.30am - 5pm.

Gordons Medals & Military Collectables
PO Box 4, Hornchurch, Essex RM11 2BQ. Tel/fax 0708 438987 (mobile 0831 104411). Stand G12-13, Grays in the Mews Antique Market, 1-7 Davies Street, London W1V 1AR. 071 629 2851. Monday-Friday, 10am–6pm. Specialist in campaign medals, British militaria, German and Third Reich documents and awards. Bimonthly catalogues £8 (UK and BFPO), £16 (overseas airmail).

Louis E. Grimshaw
612 Fay Street, R.R. #1 Kingston, Ontario, Canada K7L 4VI. (613) 549 2500. Military antiques and collectables, including medals. Catalogues of arms, medals and militaria . Single copies $C5 (Canada), $US4 (USA), $US6 (elsewhere).

Great War Medals
22 Selborne Road, Southgate, London N14 7DH. Mainly WW1 medals and books. 36 page catalogue of medals and decorations, £7.50 (UK), £11 (overseas).

W.D. Grissom
PO Box 12001, Suite 216, Chula Vista, California, USA 91912. American medals. Free lists.

H & B Medals Ltd
38 Chetwood Drive, Widnes, Cheshire WA8 9BL. 051 424 0630 / 051 228 6421. Callers by appointment only. British orders, decorations and medals. 4–6 lists a year, £3 (UK), £6 (overseas).

A.D. Hamilton & Co.
7 St Vincent Place, Glasgow G1 2DW. 041 221 5423 (fax 041 248 6019). British and foreign medals, groups and collections, badges and militaria. Monday-Saturday, 9am - 5.30pm.

Raymond D. Holdich
Trafalgar Square Collectors' Centre, 7 Whitcomb Street, London WC2. 071 930 1979. Monday–Friday, 11am–5.30pm. Saturday by appointment only. British gallantry awards and campaign medals, cap badges, world medals and decorations. Miniature and replacement medals supplied; medals mounted for wear.

Invicta International
740 Gladstone Avenue, Ottawa, Ontario, Canada K1R 6X5. (613) 232 2263. Worldwide medals, badges, insignia, wings, books and prints.

J & J Medals
26 Cathedral Street, Corn Exchange Buildings, Manchester M4 3EX. 061 832 3042 (mobile 0860 688167). Campaign medals, gallantry awards and decorations. Bi-monthly lists.

Steve Johnson
USA: PO Box 4706, Aurora, Illinois 60507, USA. (708) 851-0744 (fax (312) 777-4017). UK: PO Box 1SP, Newcastle upon Tyne NE99 1SP. 091 286 0257 (fax 091 286 1027). All world orders, medals, decorations and militaria.

Liverpool Medal Company Ltd
42 Bury Business Centre, Kay Street, Bury, Lancs BL9 6BU. 061 763 4610 / 4612 (fax 061 763 4963). British and world medals and decorations.

Manston Coins
Wednesday Antiques Market, The Paragon, Bath. 0761 416133 or 0272 663718. General medals.

March Medals
113 Gravelley Hill North, Erdington, Birmingham B23 6BJ. 021 384 4901. Orders of chivalry, decorations, campaign medals, military antiques, books, ribbons and accessories. Regular lists. Monday-Friday, 10am–5pm; Saturday, 10am - 2pm.

Michael's Medals & Miniatures
58a Stanfield Road, Talbot Park, Bournemouth BH9 2NP. 0202 512090. Victorian campaign medals and miniatures. Free lists.

Militaria House
238 Davenport Road, PO Box 99, Toronto, Ontario Canada M5R 1J6. Mail bid auctions of decorations, medals, insignia and militaria. 4 catalogues per year $25 (US and Canada), $30 (overseas).

The Military Shop
1350 Stratford Road, Hall Green, Birmingham B28 9EH. Medals and decorations, groups and medal literature. Lists available.

Miniature Medals
The Post Office, Moreton Morrell, Warwickshire CV35 9AL. Tel/fax 0926 651500. Lists.

Peter Morris
1 Station Concourse, Bromley North Railway Station, Kent. Postal: PO Box 223, Bromley, Kent BR1 4EQ. 081 313 3410 (shop hours), 081 466 1762 (other times). Monday-Friday, 10am–6pm; Saturday, 9am–2pm. Other times by appointment. Free quarterly lists on request.

Neate Militaria & Antiques
PO Box 26, Newmarket, Suffolk CB8 9JE. 0638 660288 (fax 0638 560207). Monday-Friday, 9am - 6pm. Lists available, £6 (UK, EC), £9 (overseas).

Detlev Niemann
Grosse Backerstr. 4, 20095 Hamburg 1, Germany. 01049-40-378171 (fax 01049-40-378172). Specialist in German orders, decorations, militaria, etc. Catalogue subscription £20 for 4 issues.

Pieces of History
PO Box 4470, Cave Creek, AZ 85331, USA. (602) 488 1377 (fax 602 488 1316). Worldwide medals badges, patches, accessories etc. Lists available.

Pobjoy Mint
Mint House, 92 Oldfields Road, Sutton, Surrey. 081 641 0370 (fax 081 644 1028). Manufacturers of orders, medals, decorations, commemorative medals, etc.

R & M International
PO Box 6278, Bellevue, Washington DC, USA
98008-0278. Well illustrated 64 page lists of
medals and decorations of the world, $US2.50.

George Rankin Coin Company Limited
325 Bethnal Green Road, London E2 6AH. 071 729
1280 (fax 071 729 5023). Coins, medals.

Roberts
PO Box 1, Brimpton, Reading, RG7 4RJ. 0734
819973 (fax 0734 811176). Campaign medals.
Medal and book lists £9 (UK), £15 (overseas).

Romsey Medals
5 Bell Street, Romsey, Hampshire SO51 8GY. 0794
512069 (fax 0794 830332). Orders, medals and
decorations.

Southern Medals
16 Broom Grove, Knebworth, Herts SG3 6BQ. 32
page lists of British and Commonwealth medals
and decorations. £6 (UK), £9 (overseas).

Spink & Son Ltd (Christie's International)
5-7 King Street, St James's, London SW1Y 6QS.
071 930 7888 (fax 071 839 4853). Telex 916711.
Dealers, auctioneers and valuers. The Medal
Gallery, Monday-Friday, 9am–5.30pm (Tuesday to
7.30pm). Publishers of *Spink Medal Quarterly*, £8
(UK), £15 or $US25 (overseas).

Sunset Militaria
Dinedor Cross, Herefordshire HR2 6PF. 0432
870420. Quarterly lists of medals, badges,
militaria and literature, sae for sample.

Jeremy Tenniswood
28 Gordon Road, Aldershot, Hants GU11 1ND.
0252 319791 (fax 0252 342339). Orders, medals
decorations, ribbons, uniforms. insignia, weapons.

Toad Hall Medals
Court Road, Newton Ferrers, near Plymouth,
South Devon PL8 1DH. 0752 872672 (fax 0752
872723). Lists available.

Eugene G. Ursual
PO Box 8096, Ottawa, Ontario, Canada K1G 3H6.
(613) 521 9691 (fax 613 523 3347). Medals, orders,
decorations, miniatures and militaria. 10 lists a
year $12 (Canada), $15 (USA), $20 (overseas).

Vernon
Box 1560MN, Wildomar, California, USA 92595.
Worldwide orders, medals and decorations. Lists
10 times a year, $3 (USA), $20 (oversea airmail).

Fred S. Walland
17 Gyllyngdune Gardens, Seven Kings, Essex IG3
9HH. 081 590 4389. Orders, medals and decorations. Lists £7.50 (UK and BFPO), £15 (overseas).

BOOKSELLERS/DEALERS

*In addition to the names listed below, it should be
noted that a number of the medal dealers listed above
regularly or occasionally include books on their
medal lists.*

Aviation Bookshop
656 Holloway Road, London N19 3PD. 071 272
3630. Aviation history - books, magazines, posters
and videos.

Michael Bartlett
Hillside, Lancarfen, Nr Barry, Glamorgan CF6
9AD. 0446 781442. British military history,
particularly the First World War. Regular lists
available.

Bufo Books
32 Tadfield Road, Romsey, Hants SO51 8AJ. 0794
517149. Mainly 20th century military history,
especially the Second World War.

D.L. Burke
9 Fishermans Walk, Shoreham-by-Sea, West
Sussex BN43 5LW. Specialist in military literature.
Regular lists available.

Andrew Burroughs
24 St. Martins, Stamford, Lincolnshire PE9 2LJ.
0780 51363. Military history. Lists available.

Buttercross Books
2 The Paddock, Bingham, Nottingham NG13 8HQ.
Tel/fax 0949 837147. Napoleonic era and First
World War. Lists available.

Califer Books
816/818 London Road, Leigh-on-Sea, Essex SS9
3NH. Tel/fax 0702 73986. Military history up to
1900.

Chelifer Books
Todd Close, Curthwaite, Wigton, Cumbria CA7
8BE. General military history, including unit
histories. Lists available.

The Collector
36 The Colonnade, Piece Hall, Halifax, West Yorks
HX1 1RS. Military, naval and aviation history, all
periods.

Q.M. Dabney & Company
PO Box 42026-MH, Washington, DC 20015, USA.
Military books of all periods. Lists $US1 each.

Peter de Lotz
20 Downside Crescent, Hampstead, London NW3
2AP. 071 794 5709. (fax 071 284 3058). Military,
naval and aviation history, with emphasis on
regimental and divisional histories.

Francis Edwards
13 Great Newport Street, Charing Cross Road,
London WC2H 4JA. 071 379 7669 (fax 071 836
5977). All aspects of military history. Lists
available.

Chris Evans Books
Unit 6, Jervoise Drive, Birmingham B31 2XU. Tel/
fax 021 477 6700. General military history. Lists
available.

Falconwood Transport and Military Bookshop.
5 Falconwood Parade, The Green, Welling, Kent
DA16 2PL. 081 303 8291. Military, naval and
aviation history.

Kenneth Fergusson
The Book Room, The Post Office, Twyning,
Tewkesbury, Glos GL20 6DF. 0684 295855.
Military and aviation history.

Ken Ford Military Books
93 Nutshalling Avenue, Rownhams, Southampton
SO1 8AY. 0703 739437. British colonial wars. Lists
available.

John Gaunt
21 Harvey Road, Bedford MK41 9LF. 0234 217686.
Numismatic books including medal reference
works.

G.M. Services
98 Junction Road, Andover, Hampshire SP10 3JA.
Tel/fax 0264 362048. Postal auctions of military
books.

Tony Gilbert Antique Books
101 Whipps Cross Road, Leytonstone, London E11
1NW. 081 530 7472. Military, naval and aviation
history.

Martin Gladman
235 Nether Street, Finchley, London N3 1NT. 081
343 3023. Military, naval and aviation history.

G.L. Green.
18 Aldenham Avenue, Radlett, Herts WD7 8HX.
01923 857077. Naval and maritime history.

George Harris
Heathview, Habberley Road, Bewdley, Worcs
DY12 1JH. 0299 402413. Napoleonic, Victorian
campaigns and the First World War.

David Hayles Military Books
35 St. Marks Road, Maidenhead, Berks SL6 6DJ.
0628 39535. Regular lists.

Hersant's Military Books
17 The Drive, High Barnet, Herts EN5 4JG. Tel/fax
081 440 6816. General military history. Lists
available by period.

Michael Hicks Beach
99 York Mansions, London SW11 4BN. 071 622
2270. British and Imperial military history.

Jerboa-Redcap Books
PO Box 1058, Highstown, N.J. 08520, USA. (609)
443 3817. British military books (all services),
including collectables. Catalogues $US2.

John Lewcock
6 Chewells Lane, Haddenham, Ely, Cambs CB6
3SS. 0353 741152. Naval history.

Roger Knowles
26 Church Road, Norton Canes, Cannock, Staffs
WS11 3PD. 0543 279313. Military history

Liverpool Medal Company Ltd
42 Bury Business Centre, Kay Street, Bury, Lancs
BL9 6BU. 061 763 4610/4612 (fax 061 763 4963).
Medal dealers, but publish an occasional separate
book catalogue four times a year.

Ian Lynn
258 Upper Fant Road, Maidstone Kent ME16 8BX.
0622 728525. Military history.

Marcet Books
4a Nelson Road, Greenwich, London SE10 9JB.
081 853 5408. Naval history.

G. & D.I. Marrin & Sons
149 Sandgate Road, Folkestone, Kent CT20 2DA.
0303 253016 (fax 0303 850956) Specialises in
material relating to the First World War.

McLaren Books
91 West Clyde Street, Helensburgh,
Dunbartonshire G84 8BB. 0436 76453. Naval
history.

Military Bookman
29 East 93rd Street, New York, NY 10128, USA.
(212) 348 1280. Large stock of military history
relating to all services worldwide and all periods.

Military Bookworm
PO Box 235, London SE23 1NS. 081 291 1435.
Decorations & medals, regimental & divisional
histories, and campaign histories. Subscription to
lists £9 (approx 9 per year).

Military History Bookshop
2 Broadway, London N11 3DU. Tel/fax 081 368
8568. Lists, subscription £2.50 (4 issues).

Military Parade Bookshop
The Parade, Marlborough, Wilts SN8 1NE. 0672
515470. Wide ranging new and secondhand
books. Lists available.

Motor Books
St Martins Court, London WC2N 4AL. 071 836
5376 (fax 071 497 2539). Comprehensive stock of
military books in print.

Military & Naval History
54 Regis Road, Tettenhall, Wolverhampton WV6
8RW. 0902 756402. British Military history. Lists
available.

Palladour Books
Cartref, Aberporth, Nr Cardigan, Dyfed SA43
2EN. 0239 811658. Mainly First and Second
World Wars.

Anthony J. Simmonds
23 Nelson Road, Greenwich, London SE10 9JB.
081 853 1727. Naval and maritime history.
Occasional catalogues.

Andrew Skinner
42 Earlspark Avenue, Newlands, Glasgow G43
2HW. 041 632 4903 (fax 041 632 8453). General
military history stock with special emphasis on
Scotland. Monthly lists.

Frank Smith Maritime Aviation Books
98/100 Heaton Road, Newcastle upon Tyne. 091
265 6333. Naval, maritime and aviation history.

Spink & Son Ltd (Christie's International)
5-7 St James's, London SW1Y 6QS. 071 930 7888
(fax 071 839 4853). Telex 916711. Auctioneers,
valuers, dealers, and publishers. The Medal
Department lists some books in the *Spink Medal
Quarterly*, £8 (UK), £15 or $US25 (overseas). Spink
have a separate Book Department.

Squirrel Publishing
6 & 7 Castle Gates, Shrewsbury SY1 2AE. 0743
272140 (fax 0743 366041). Numismatic books with
good stock of medal reference works.

Stephen Tilston
37 Bennett Park, Blackheath, London SE3 9RA.
Tel/fax 081 318 9181. General stock, but
specialising in the First World War. Lists available

THCL Books
185 Lammack Road, Blackburn, Lancs BB1 8LH.
Military book specialist aand publishers of
collectors' cards of medal heroes. Lists available.

Ken Trotman Ltd
Unit 11, 135 Ditton Walk, Cambridge CB5 8QD.
0223 211030 (fax 0223 212317). Large, wide-
ranging stock. Lists available: 3 per year.

Brian Turner Military Books
1132 London Road, Leigh-on-Sea, Essex SS9 2AJ.
Tel/fax 0702 78771. Printed works and
documentation relating to military, naval and
aviation history, specialising in the First World
War, India and Africa.

Robin Turner
30 Great Norwood Street, Cheltenham, Glos GL50
2BH. 0242 234303. Military, specialising in the
Napoleonic period.

Tom Donovan Military Books
52 Willow Road, Hampstead, London NW3 1TP.
071 431 2474 (fax 071 431 8314). Printed works,
documentation and manuscript material relating
to the British Military Services. Regular lists.

Mark Weber
35 Elvaston Place, London SW7 5NW. 071 225
2506 (fax 071 581 8233). Specialises in official war
histories and books by and about Sir Winston
Churchill.

Terence Wise
Pantiles, Garth Lane, Knighton, Powys LD7 1HH.
Military history especially regimental and
didvisional histories. Lists available.

Woodford Books
The Lodge, Well Street, Docking, King's Lynn,
Norfolk PE31 8LQ. 0485 518700. Medal and
military books, photograph albums, letters,
ephemera. Lists available.

Woolcott Books
Kingston House, Higher Kingston, Nr Dorchester,
Dorset DT2 8QE. 035 267773 (fax 0305 848218).
Military and colonial history, specialising in India,
Africa and nineteenth century campaigns.

World War Books
Oaklands, Camden Park, Tunbridge Wells, Kent
TN2 5AE. 0892 538465. Military, naval and
aviation books and documents, particularly First
World War, regimental histories, maps, diaries
and photographs. Lists available.

World War II Books
PO Box 55, Woking, Surrey GU22 8HP. 0483
722880 (fax 0483 721548). Second World War
military history. 12 lists per year.

R.J. Wyatt.
33 Sturges Road, Wokingham, Berks RG11 2HG.
0734 780325. All aspects of British military history,
with an emphasis on the First and Second World
Wars, Volunteers, and the Territorial Army.

Yesterday's Wars
190/4 South Gyle Mains, Edinburgh EH12 9ER.
031 334 4850. General military history. Updated
stocklist printouts continously available.

FAIRS

Many fairs are held regularly and organised by professionals, in addition a number of societies organise fairs for the public (Victorian Military Society, Aldershot Militaria Society, etc.). The dates are usually well advertised in MEDAL NEWS and other publications, however, times and venues are liable to change so it is advisable in every instance to telephone the organisers beforehand. Listed below are the major fair organisers and the events known to us.

Aldershot Militaria and Medal Fair
Princes Hall, Barrack Road, Aldershot, Surrey.
Mark Carter, 0753 534777.

Arms, Shooters, Militaria and Medal Fair
The Premier, Compton and Manx Suites, The National Motorcycle Museum, Birmingham. Up to 150 tables. Central Arms Fairs, 11 Berwick Close, Warwick CV34 5UF. 0926 400554 / 497340.

Bedford Arms Fair
The Corn Exchange, Bedford. Arms & Armour UK, 58 Harpur Street, Bedford MK40 2QT, 0234 344831.

Birmingham, Midlands Militaria Fair
St John's Hotel, Warwick Road, Solihull, Birmingham. Watergate Antiques, 56 Watergate Street, Chester, 0244 344516.

Bristol Militaria and Medal Fair
Merchant Suite, University of the West of England, Coldharbour Lane, Frenchay, Bristol.
Mark Carter, 0753 534777.

Britannia Medal Fair
Victory Services Club, 63-79 Seymour Street, Marble Arch, London W2. Six p.a. Britannia Enterprises, 28 Raglan Place, Burnopfield, Gateshead NE16 6NN. 0267 71869.

Centre of England Arms, Militaria and Medal Fair
Chesterfield Hotel, Chesterfield, Derbyshire.
Allan Vernon-Jones, Protea Fairs 0246 271307.

Cheltenham Arms Fair
Golden Valley Hotel, Gloucester Road, Cheltenham, Glos. Central Arms Fairs, 11 Berwick Close, Warwick CV34 5UF. 0926 400554 / 497340.

Cheshunt Militaria Fair
Wolsey Hall, Windmill Lane, Cheshunt, Herts.
Ron Sparks, 0705 839400 / 831804.

Collectors' Market
London Bridge Main Line Station, London SE1.
Every Saturday. Over 60 stands comprising medals, badges and militaria. 081 398 8065.

Didcot Militaria Fair
Civic Hall, Britwell Road, Didcot, Berks. Ron Sparks, 0705 839400 / 831804.

Dorking Militaria Fair
Dorking Halls, Reigate Road, Dorking, Surrey.
Ron Sparks, 0705 839400 / 831804.

Dunstable Arms & Armour Fair
The Queensway Hall, Dunstable. Arms & Armour UK, 58 Harpur Street, Bedford MK40 2QT, 0234 344831.

Farnham Militaria Fair
The Maltings, Farnham, Surrey. Aldershot Militaria Society. 0705 839400 / 831804.

Gloucester Militaria and Medal Fair
Gloucester Leisure Centre, Bruton Way, Inner Ring Road, Gloucester. Mark Carter (0753 534777).

London Arms Fairs
Earls Court Park Inn (formerly Ramada), Lillie Road, London SW6. 4 shows p.a. Douglas Fryer, 0273 475 959.

London Military Market
Angel Arcade, Camden Passage, Islington, London N1. Every Saturday, 8am–2pm. Over 35 stands. 062882 2503 or 0455 556971.

Midhurst Militaria Fair
The Grange, Bepton Road, off the A286, Midhurst, Surrey. Ron Sparks, 0705 839400 / 831804.

North Kent Military Collectors' Fair
The Inn on the Lake, Shorne, Gravesend, Kent.
Keith and Veronica Reeves, 0634 374098.

Park Lane Arms, Armour and Militaria Fair
The Marriott Hotel, Grosvenor Square, London W1. David A. Oliver, 0669 20618.

Reading Arms Fair
The Rivermead Leisure Centre, Richfield Avenue, Reading, Berks. Central Arms Fairs, 11 Berwick Close, Warwick CV34 5UF. 0926 400554 / 497340.

St Albans Aeronautica, Militaria and Medal Fair
The Mosquito Aircraft Museum, Salisbury Hall, London Colney, near St Albans. Sovereign Fairs, 0462 481122.

Surbiton Militaria Fair
Assembly Rooms, Maple Road, Surbiton Road, near Kingston-on-Thames. Ron Sparks, 0705 839400 / 831804.

Victorian Military Fair
New Connaught Rooms, Great Queen Street, London WC2. Victorian Military Society, 49 Belsize Park, London NW3 4EE. 071 722 5542.

Wakefield Medal and Militaria Fair
H & B Medals, 38 Chetwood Drive, Widnes, Cheshire WA8 9BL. 051 424 0630 / 051 228 6421.

Watford Arms, Militaria and Medal Fair
Bushey Hall School, London Road, Bushey, near Watford, Herts. Sovereign Fairs, 0462 481122.

Winchester Miltaria Exhibition & Fair
The Guildhall, Winchester. Winchester Miltaria Society. A. M. Tonge, 0243 377346.

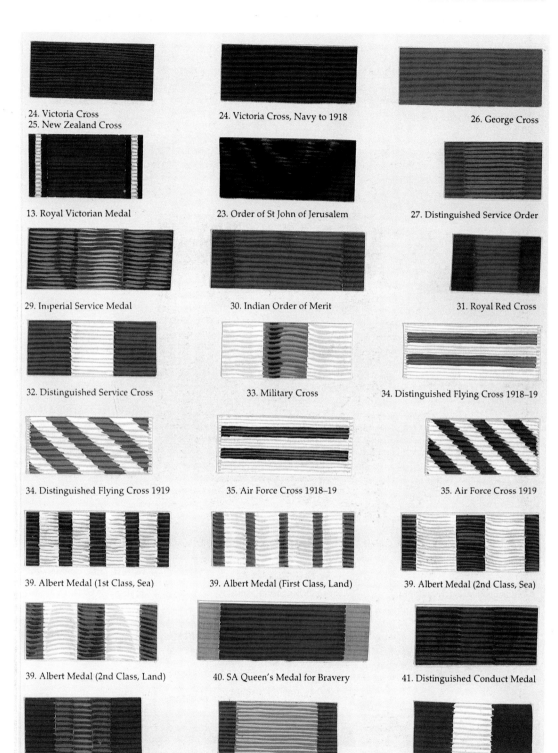

24. Victoria Cross
25. New Zealand Cross

24. Victoria Cross, Navy to 1918

26. George Cross

13. Royal Victorian Medal

23. Order of St John of Jerusalem

27. Distinguished Service Order

29. Imperial Service Medal

30. Indian Order of Merit

31. Royal Red Cross

32. Distinguished Service Cross

33. Military Cross

34. Distinguished Flying Cross 1918–19

34. Distinguished Flying Cross 1919

35. Air Force Cross 1918–19

35. Air Force Cross 1919

39. Albert Medal (1st Class, Sea)

39. Albert Medal (First Class, Land)

39. Albert Medal (2nd Class, Sea)

39. Albert Medal (2nd Class, Land)

40. SA Queen's Medal for Bravery

41. Distinguished Conduct Medal

43. DCM (KAR and WAFF)

44. Conspicuous Gallantry, RAF

44. Conspicuous Gallantry pre-1921

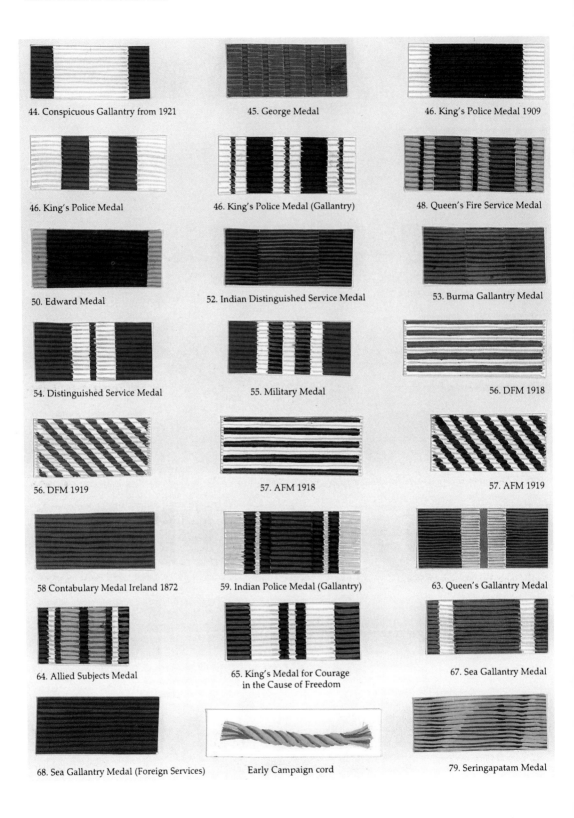

44. Conspicuous Gallantry from 1921

45. George Medal

46. King's Police Medal 1909

46. King's Police Medal

46. King's Police Medal (Gallantry)

48. Queen's Fire Service Medal

50. Edward Medal

52. Indian Distinguished Service Medal

53. Burma Gallantry Medal

54. Distinguished Service Medal

55. Military Medal

56. DFM 1918

56. DFM 1919

57. AFM 1918

57. AFM 1919

58 Contabulary Medal Ireland 1872

59. Indian Police Medal (Gallantry)

63. Queen's Gallantry Medal

64. Allied Subjects Medal

65. King's Medal for Courage
in the Cause of Freedom

67. Sea Gallantry Medal

68. Sea Gallantry Medal (Foreign Services)

Early Campaign cord

79. Seringapatam Medal

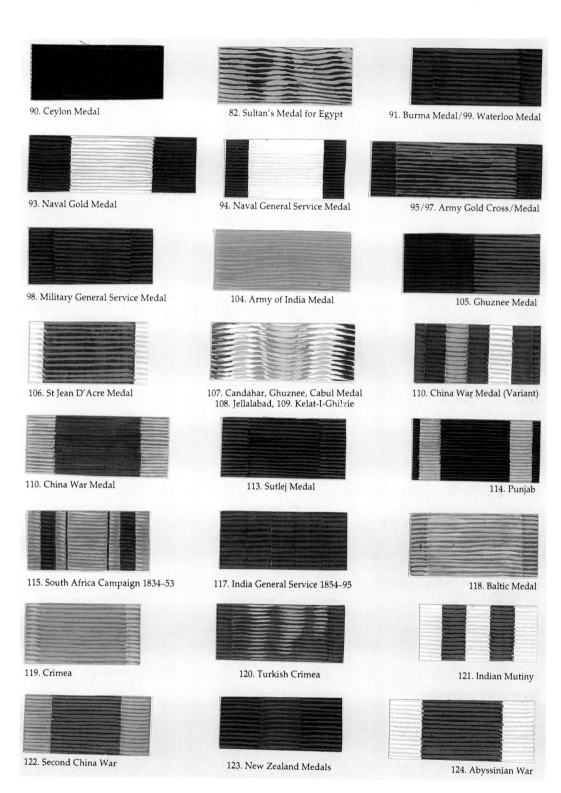

90. Ceylon Medal

82. Sultan's Medal for Egypt

91. Burma Medal/99. Waterloo Medal

93. Naval Gold Medal

94. Naval General Service Medal

95/97. Army Gold Cross/Medal

98. Military General Service Medal

104. Army of India Medal

105. Ghuznee Medal

106. St Jean D'Acre Medal

107. Candahar, Ghuznee, Cabul Medal
108. Jellalabad, 109. Kelat-I-Ghilzie

110. China War Medal (Variant)

110. China War Medal

113. Sutlej Medal

114. Punjab

115. South Africa Campaign 1834–53

117. India General Service 1854–95

118. Baltic Medal

119. Crimea

120. Turkish Crimea

121. Indian Mutiny

122. Second China War

123. New Zealand Medals

124. Abyssinian War

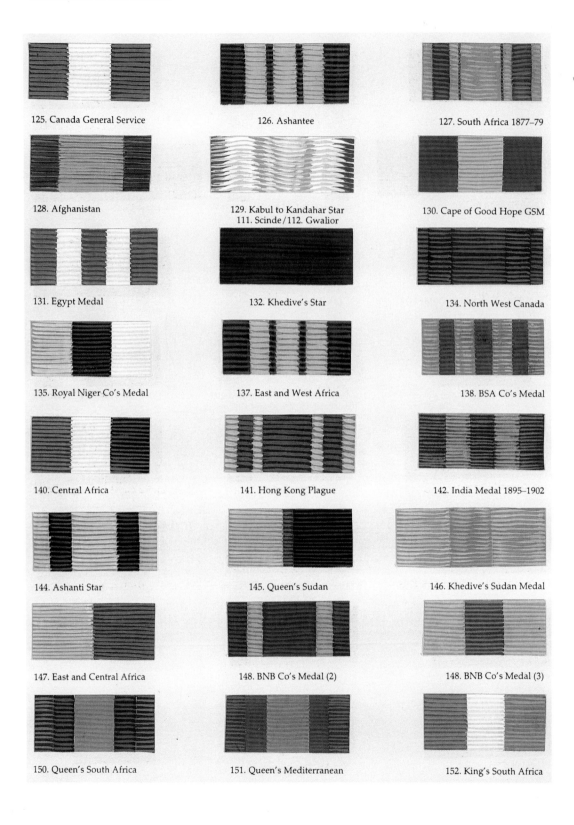

125. Canada General Service

126. Ashantee

127. South Africa 1877–79

128. Afghanistan

129. Kabul to Kandahar Star
111. Scinde/112. Gwalior

130. Cape of Good Hope GSM

131. Egypt Medal

132. Khedive's Star

134. North West Canada

135. Royal Niger Co's Medal

137. East and West Africa

138. BSA Co's Medal

140. Central Africa

141. Hong Kong Plague

142. India Medal 1895–1902

144. Ashanti Star

145. Queen's Sudan

146. Khedive's Sudan Medal

147. East and Central Africa

148. BNB Co's Medal (2)

148. BNB Co's Medal (3)

150. Queen's South Africa

151. Queen's Mediterranean

152. King's South Africa

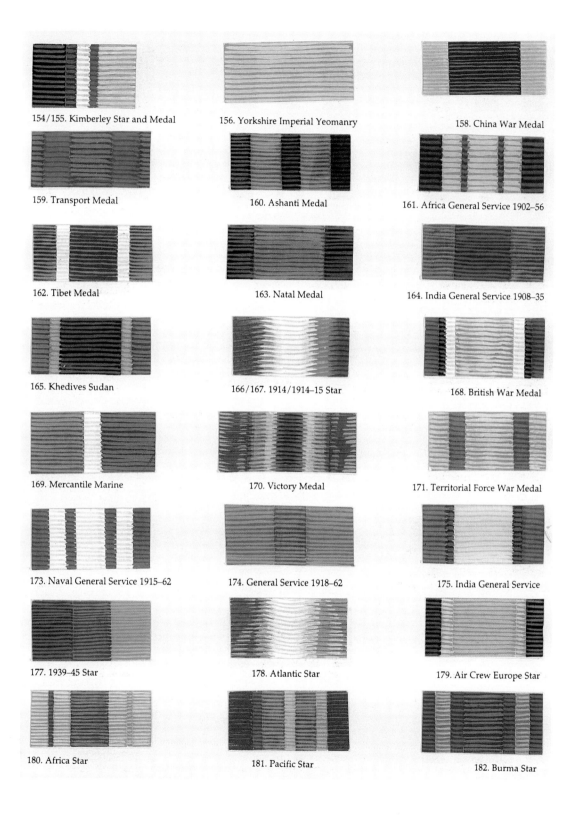

154/155. Kimberley Star and Medal

156. Yorkshire Imperial Yeomanry

158. China War Medal

159. Transport Medal

160. Ashanti Medal

161. Africa General Service 1902–56

162. Tibet Medal

163. Natal Medal

164. India General Service 1908–35

165. Khedives Sudan

166/167. 1914/1914–15 Star

168. British War Medal

169. Mercantile Marine

170. Victory Medal

171. Territorial Force War Medal

173. Naval General Service 1915–62

174. General Service 1918–62

175. India General Service

177. 1939–45 Star

178. Atlantic Star

179. Air Crew Europe Star

180. Africa Star

181. Pacific Star

182. Burma Star

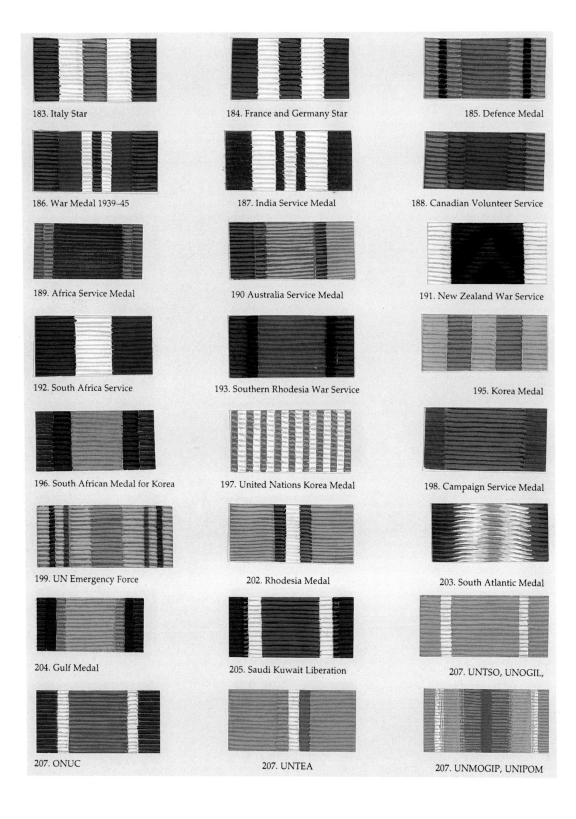

183. Italy Star

184. France and Germany Star

185. Defence Medal

186. War Medal 1939–45

187. India Service Medal

188. Canadian Volunteer Service

189. Africa Service Medal

190 Australia Service Medal

191. New Zealand War Service

192. South Africa Service

193. Southern Rhodesia War Service

195. Korea Medal

196. South African Medal for Korea

197. United Nations Korea Medal

198. Campaign Service Medal

199. UN Emergency Force

202. Rhodesia Medal

203. South Atlantic Medal

204. Gulf Medal

205. Saudi Kuwait Liberation

207. UNTSO, UNOGIL,

207. ONUC

207. UNTEA

207. UNMOGIP, UNIPOM

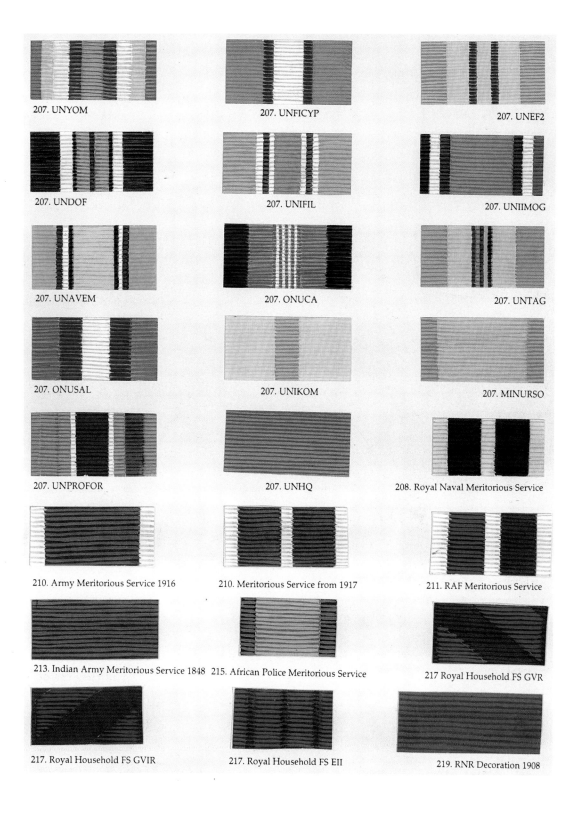

207. UNYOM

207. UNFICYP

207. UNEF2

207. UNDOF

207. UNIFIL

207. UNIIMOG

207. UNAVEM

207. ONUCA

207. UNTAG

207. ONUSAL

207. UNIKOM

207. MINURSO

207. UNPROFOR

207. UNHQ

208. Royal Naval Meritorious Service

210. Army Meritorious Service 1916

210. Meritorious Service from 1917

211. RAF Meritorious Service

213. Indian Army Meritorious Service 1848

215. African Police Meritorious Service

217 Royal Household FS GVR

217. Royal Household FS GVIR

217. Royal Household FS EII

219. RNR Decoration 1908

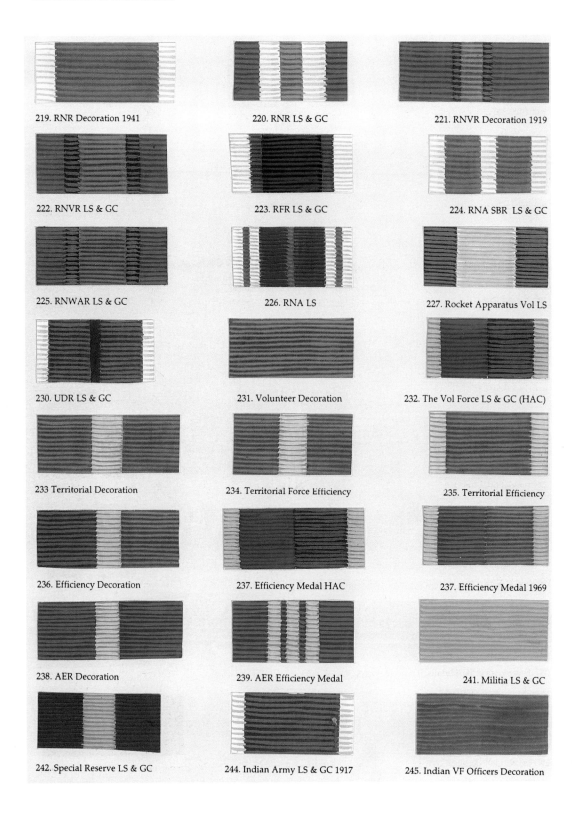

219. RNR Decoration 1941

220. RNR LS & GC

221. RNVR Decoration 1919

222. RNVR LS & GC

223. RFR LS & GC

224. RNA SBR LS & GC

225. RNWAR LS & GC

226. RNA LS

227. Rocket Apparatus Vol LS

230. UDR LS & GC

231. Volunteer Decoration

232. The Vol Force LS & GC (HAC)

233 Territorial Decoration

234. Territorial Force Efficiency

235. Territorial Efficiency

236. Efficiency Decoration

237. Efficiency Medal HAC

237. Efficiency Medal 1969

238. AER Decoration

239. AER Efficiency Medal

241. Militia LS & GC

242. Special Reserve LS & GC

244. Indian Army LS & GC 1917

245. Indian VF Officers Decoration

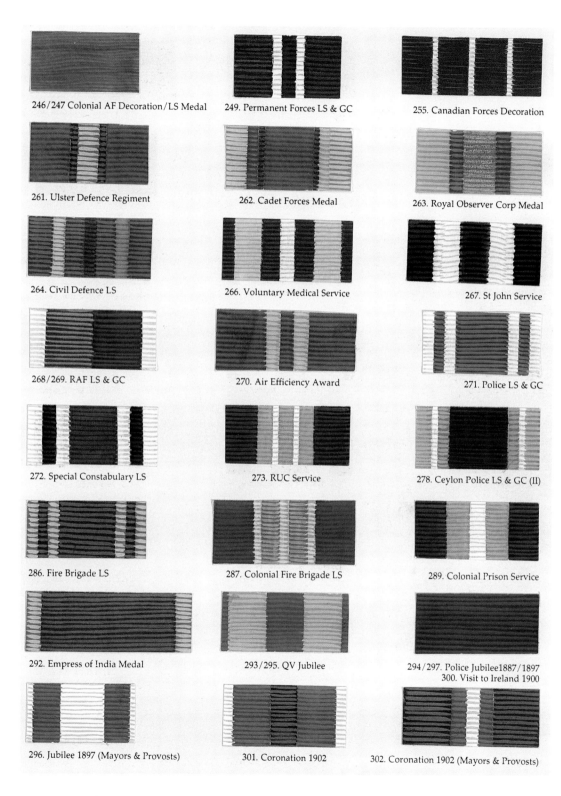

246/247 Colonial AF Decoration/LS Medal

249. Permanent Forces LS & GC

255. Canadian Forces Decoration

261. Ulster Defence Regiment

262. Cadet Forces Medal

263. Royal Observer Corp Medal

264. Civil Defence LS

266. Voluntary Medical Service

267. St John Service

268/269. RAF LS & GC

270. Air Efficiency Award

271. Police LS & GC

272. Special Constabulary LS

273. RUC Service

278. Ceylon Police LS & GC (II)

286. Fire Brigade LS

287. Colonial Fire Brigade LS

289. Colonial Prison Service

292. Empress of India Medal

293/295. QV Jubilee

294/297. Police Jubilee1887/1897
300. Visit to Ireland 1900

296. Jubilee 1897 (Mayors & Provosts)

301. Coronation 1902

302. Coronation 1902 (Mayors & Provosts)

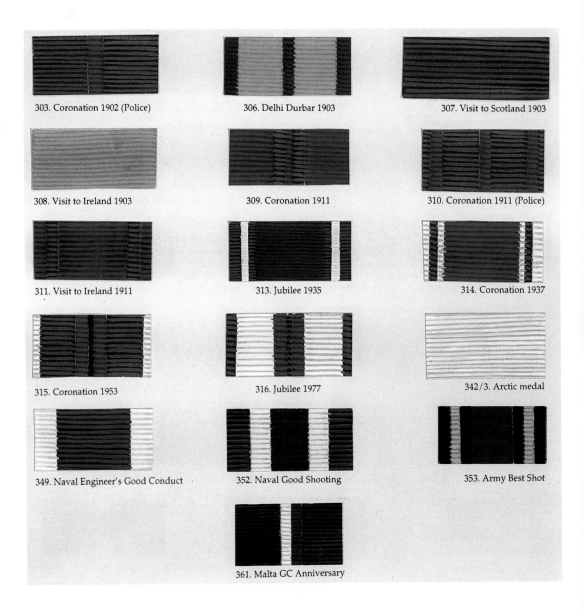

303. Coronation 1902 (Police)

306. Delhi Durbar 1903

307. Visit to Scotland 1903

308. Visit to Ireland 1903

309. Coronation 1911

310. Coronation 1911 (Police)

311. Visit to Ireland 1911

313. Jubilee 1935

314. Coronation 1937

315. Coronation 1953

316. Jubilee 1977

342/3. Arctic medal

349. Naval Engineer's Good Conduct

352. Naval Good Shooting

353. Army Best Shot

361. Malta GC Anniversary

INDEX TO MEDAL NEWS

In this the first issue of the MEDAL NEWS YEARBOOK we include the complete **Subject Index** to the parent magazine MEDAL NEWS, commencing with the March 1989 issue, when it became a separate publication.

MEDAL NEWS was born in 1981 from the amalgamation of *Medals International* and *Coins & Medals*, into the popular title *Coin & Medal News*. However, the success of this magazine and the continuing growth of both the coin and the medal collecting hobbies prompted the separation of the two sections in March 1989. Since then both *Coin News* and MEDAL NEWS have grown from strength to strength and today are the hobby's leading publications, not only in the UK but MEDAL NEWS is the *only* independent magazine in the world devoted to the collecting and study of medals.

NOTES

Each year index runs from February to December. For example the year 1990 includes the December 1990/January 1991 issue.

Names of ships are indicated in italics.

Names of people have been included where they appear to be the major subject of an article or where more than trivial information is included, however it was often a fairly arbitrary decision as to which names to include.

References are indicated **year/month: page** for example 90/10:18 means October 1990 page 18.

Abbreviations used:
(cr) Indicates the inclusion of a full or partial casualty list.
(mr) Indicates the inclusion of a medal roll.
(nr) Indicates nominal roll.
(i) Indicates that the reference gives information rather than the object itself. For example it tells you where to find a medal roll rather than reproducing the roll itself.
(p) Indicates that the reference is to a picture of a person or object where little or no other information is given.
(mp) Same as (p) except that the picture is of medals.
(br) Indicates Book Review.

INDEX TO MEDAL NEWS 1989

INDEX TO MEDAL NEWS 1990

INDEX TO MEDAL NEWS 1991

INDEX TO MEDAL NEWS 1992

INDEX TO MEDAL NEWS 1993

INDEX OF MEDALS

NOTES